VALUES, WORK, EDUCATION: THE MEANINGS OF WORK

VALUE INQUIRY BOOK SERIES

VIBS

Volume 22

VALUES, WORK, EDUCATION: THE MEANINGS OF WORK

Editors

Samuel M. Natale
Brian M. Rothschild

Assistant Editors

Joseph W. Sora
Tara M. Madden

Rodopi

Amsterdam - Atlanta, GA 1995

Cover design by Chris Kok based on a photograph, © 1984 by Robert Ginsberg, of statuary by Gustav Vigeland in the Frogner Park, Oslo, Norway.

∞ The paper on which this book is printed meets the requirements of "ISO 9706:1994, Information and documentation - Paper for documents - Requirements for permanence".

ISBN: 90-5183-852-2

Printed in The Netherlands

CONTENTS

FOREWORD

This volume is an examination of the world of work within the Value Inquiry Books Series (VIBS).

The central explorations include the varied aspects of the human preoccupation and need for "work" no matter how broadly construed. This volume explores the basic value bases which underscore this essentially social phenomenon ranging from a study of individual intelligence to corporate and social structures that impact on the meanings of work.

This study argues for a broadening of our understanding of the nature of what constitutes work and its varied components as well as a demand that we examine urgent concerns such as the re-negotiation of meaning within the domain of work, the interaction and interconnection between work and play as well as ethical aspects of varied individual and international conflicts.

Work is understood as the arena in which most individuals play out their sense of values individual, organizational, and social. This exciting volume aims to move the reader from "grey theory and green life" into the "multicolored poetry" of values as they apply to the study of work.

We have tried to explore the big problems here: meaning definition, verification, commitment, naming, interpretation, and understanding. Complex interrelationships are explored, and varied gender understandings articulated. Even the intriguing notion of work without workers is examined.

Cultural and social presuppositions are explored and some intriguing new roads chartered. This is a volume of excitement, courage and hope. We welcome the reader into this intriguing, informative and exciting new series.

Samuel M. Natale
Associate Editor
Value Inquiry Book Series

ACKNOWLEDGEMENTS

The editors of this book would like to express their appreciation to:

Joseph Ford
William O'Neill
Eduardo Paderon
Anthony Libertella
Hugh McCabe

for their proofreading efforts. We would also like to extend our gratitude to everyone at the Information Resource Technology Center at Iona College for all of their assistance.

INTRODUCTION

THE MEANINGS OF WORK

Samuel M. Natale
Joseph W. Sora
William O'Neill

Work has been defined as an "activity that produces something of value for other people" (Hall, p. 65). However, this definition does not include how the workers view the value of the activities that they perform. For some, work is a source of self-fulfillment and self-actualization; for others, a means to, or a necessity for, survival. While it is true that these meanings derive from both the nature of the work and the attitudes of the worker towards that work, no unified definition appears evident.

Work that contains a high level of autonomy is likely to be seen as an enjoyable activity providing an outlet of self-expression. Conversely, work that *controls* the worker is likely to be viewed as an unfortunate but necessary obligation of existence. Work can also fulfill certain social needs and provide the worker with a "social connection" to the larger community. "Within these parameters, 'meaning' and 'work' are in tension with each other in such a way that the experience of one anticipates the other." The meaning of work, then, is born from a highly individualized "network of direct and indirect influences or associations" (169). Historically, people have defined work in a wide variety of ways. In Greek and Roman times, work and slavery were inseparably associated. The Judaic traditions held work to be a curse from God. Christianity viewed it more positively as a "means by which original sin could be eliminated." The Protestant Work Ethic glorified work as being both "a way by which [man] humanity could prove himself [itself]" and as a "means to serve God." The Protestant Work Ethic (PWE) can rightly be called the first modern conception of work because it does not view work as an action performed only by certain classes, but rather an action in which the entire culture participates. Today we have long since witnessed the advent of a culture in which the "God of conventional western theism" no longer acts as the primary source of meaning and justification for the concept of work (Andersson, p. 96).

If we can no longer rely on the existence of God as the primary source by which all meanings of work (or of any other events of significance) have their genesis, and if work is not necessarily the primary focus of workers' lives, is it plausible to see work simply as a means of basic survival?

Generally speaking, researchers have designated four major reasons for which people work. Three of them directly concern the explorations of this book. Those are: work is intrinsically satisfying, i.e. fulfilling; work means survival; and work provides a level of social connectedness to the larger community. These reasons operate on a continuum and are not limiting. An individual may view work according to any one of these reasons, or a combination, at any given time.

Finally, work can also be perceived as intrinsically important, contributing to the worker's positive self-perception. Researchers argue the necessity of viewing work, at least in part, in these terms since work contributes "strongly to self-definition and self-evaluation" (Ronco, p. 10). Essentially, the worker's identity merges *with the work* and results in the work's becoming a central factor in one's self-understanding. In order for this positive self-perception to occur, certain characteristics must be present. One is that the work provide the worker with "autonomy control." *Autonomy control* refers to amount of personal control or independence that the worker has with regard to the pace of the work and the level of decision making involved with that work.

Others argue that safety and autonomy are the most important characteristics of a workplace, encouraging self-actualization (Inks, p. 8). If autonomy and safety are present, the worker has a better chance to express herself or himself positively within the work and therefore become involved with it.

Along with autonomy there must be intrinsic rewards as well. "Intrinsic rewards–the existence of challenge, meaning and variety–will have a strong positive impact on work commitment" (Cherrington, p. 65). Clifford E. Jargensen, who performed an exhaustive study which took place over thirty years with 57,000 people interviewed, echoes this understanding: "the variety of work had the highest correlation with job satisfaction" (p. 274). Similarly Loscocco points to various studies all of which have concluded that if work is performed for the intrinsic pleasures that spring from a variety of engaging tasks, then a degree of commitment and personal involvement with that work is generated. A work environment providing workers with *control, challenge, and variety* is more likely to promote personal involvement and self-expression and, thereby, a level of self-fulfillment. Work with intrinsic rewards such as challenge, variety, and autonomy enhances self-esteem.

Researchers also theorize that many workers view their work as a means of social connectedness, providing a social outlet or a means of social expression. The structure of the workplace encompasses more than the labor which occurs at that setting. Feelings of depersonalization and alienation indicate a real need for work to serve as a center of social growth. Work becomes the laboratory in which we work out our life project.

The social component of work is not consciously constructed, "but rather exist[s] as a result of human proclivities, of all the unwritten contracts that grow up between a company and its employees" (Zaleznik, 1989a, p. 58). This social dimension appears a natural and unavoidable offspring of the workplace viewed as a microcosm in which an inevitable amount of human socialization is going to occur.

The social dimension of work provides the worker with a reason for working that goes beyond pursuing economic rewards. One of the prime meanings of work is that it is a factor in "the forming of relationships" (Antony, p. 43) allowing the worker to "interact with others" and thereby offering a valuable "job reward" that may be a primary satisfaction for the worker. Based on his study of individuals working in the field of robotics, Duran points out that the most satisfying and important socialization occurs *within peer groups*. Individuals were more energized when approved by peers than when they achieved a significant task completion. Others believe that work acts as a means of connection to a larger community providing an inevitable sense of social connectedness to the environment that operates around the worker. It allows workers to understand "the way they fit into their immediate society" (Hollencamp, p. 182). Through work one can come to understand his or her position in and value to the surrounding community. It is, of course, possible to understand work as strictly a means by which individuals maintain their survival. Here, work is a means to the paycheck, which is a means to food, shelter and clothing. Today this attitude toward work as a wholly unfulfilling, yet necessary, action is an increasingly prevalent conception. Many believe that work is widely understood as "an activity done out of necessity, whether or not it is enjoyed" (Hollencamp, p. 45). The inevitable isolation which stems from a lack of social interaction at the workplace is reflected in "a reluctance to exert any more effort than the bare minimum needed to get by" (Zaleznik, 1989a, p. 59). Studs Terkel in his book, *Working*, argues that there is a direct correlation between the idea of anonymity and dissatisfaction with work: "Bob Cratchit may still be hanging on...but who knows Bob's name in this outfit–let alone his lame child's" (p. 15). In short, unless people feel a sense of being an important part of their organization, the work loses its enjoyment and is only for survival. Anonymity renders it impossible to extract any substantial meaning from work. Workers currently experience a severe lack of attachment in their workplace. Haughey proposes a nationwide *Universal Stock Ownership* plan in which those who do not own a substantial amount of stock (94% of the population) receive government loans to purchase such stock. Haughey feels that such a program will provide workers with a fundamental connection to the work environment, a connection largely absent from our culture.

Lack of autonomy renders work unfulfilling. When the workers position does not allow them to perform with autonomy, workers lack self-expression and are not likely to commit themselves to the work. Loscocco bases these conclusions on a study of *Plant 45* in which workers stated that their "desires to be committed to the job were often thwarted by any inability to exercise personal discretion or to provide input into the decision making process" (p. 156). Just as autonomy promotes a sense of self-actualization and self fulfillment, a lack of autonomy has the reverse effect and prevents the worker from being committed to or involved with the work.

Contemporary psychology, sociology and economics are instructive in our search as well. Just as greed defined the 1980s, some see downward mobility defining the 1990s. The Yankelovich Monitor, a survey of consumer values and behaviors, reports that Americans have become more willing than ever to change jobs or take a pay cut in exchange for meaningful work. Men and women alike are choosing to drop out rather than shoulder the burden of maintaining both a career and a home life. Not everyone is financially secure enough to afford downward mobility, but most people who have scaled back their lives agree that it is worth the effort (Kaylin, p. 221).

The role of work may well have changed drastically. It is said that if the world is to break out of its economic sluggishness and achieve greater long term growth, we must change our living habits and re-examine our values. A modern technological society requires well-trained, educated, and disciplined citizens. Since the 1960s, however, there has been an expansion of rights, an extension of freedom from constraints, an elimination of social taboos. All this tolerance has led to a decline in educational attainment, labor productivity, and family stability culminating in social disorder. The key, some argue, to changing all this is to once again value work and excellence over pleasure and materialism.

There appears to be a world-wide concern about this decline (*Fortune*, January 1992). There is a sense of diminished expectations with the potential to effect profound changes in how people value work, wealth, family, and community. There are good reasons to believe that the 1990s will be harder than the preceding decades and that people should adopt a prudent defensive strategy in managing their affairs.

This renewal of vitality in our values, attitudes, needs, and expectations cannot be done simply by bringing in consultants. Nor can we achieve success by bringing back the "old values" or religious beliefs. According to the European Values Study, an international report prepared by a number of scholars and social scientists, secularism is flourishing in Western Europe. The study reported that Europeans see religion as less significant to their lives than family, friends, work and leisure activity. The study shows that traditional religious beliefs, as well as the influence of the church on daily life, is waning. The impact of religion declined most sharply in Scandinavia and northwest Europe, where less than half the population views it as very important or quite important. Fewer than half of all Belgians, Britons, Dutch, French, Germans, and Scandinavians expressed confidence in their churches. The highest confidence level–80%–was found in Northern Ireland. Are Western societies becoming less religious or are their practices changing?

The problem is also evident in developing nations. Many societies are now in the process of transforming from totalitarianism to freedom and may lack the internalized value systems that are needed to make the shift to free enterprise and free politics. A country's values, which are shaped by its cultural formation and historical experience, play a central role in its willingness or ability to accommodate democracy and capitalism. Political freedom evolved in the West on the basis of more than three centuries of experience, including the Protestant experience following the Reformation in the sixteenth century. Whether democracy can emerge quickly enough, especially in Latin America, Africa, and the states of the former Soviet Union which lack the traditions of a strong work ethic, individual responsibility, and understanding of capital formation is doubtful (Colson, p. 35). Is it, in fact, even desirable?

This paper is not an attempt to list concerns with no possible redress. It is encouraging that so many understand that the way out–the deliverance, if you will–must come from an educational approach to the problem: an educational approach that is confluent in nature, calling together affective, behavioral, and cognitive components in nations, corporations, and individuals to establish a new foundation for the search for meaning.

It is true that many people have forgotten the ideals of the work ethic which include thrift, industry, diligence and perseverance. *Restoration* of the work ethic requires *teaching* it to children in the home, reeducating the churches and the culture at large, emphasizing the educational system. Six values, according to Colson's study, should be emphasized. They include: the value of the worker, the value of leaders, the value of responsibility and the pursuit of excellence, the value of training, the value of economic and humane profit, and the value of adopting leadership that enables others to meet goals (Colson, 1992).

Educationally, these problems are considerable. What we are speaking about in today's culture is the belief that all values are subjective functions of the individual rather than principles rooted in the wisdom of the ages. Children are taught to let their conscience be their guides, *but* they are given no idea what their consciences should hold dear. This trend represents a surrender to the notion that one cannot hope for any kind of unified moral vision. This is often held up as "pluralism" and "diversity". However, this is an abuse of the meanings of these words since pluralism and diversity suggest valuing differences only. They do not suggest, nor have ever suggested, a lack of parameters which circumscribed correct, morally educated behavior (Neff, 1992).

The president of the Association for Humanistic Psychology in addressing the 30th annual conference (1992) wrote that the values that lie at the core of the humanistic psychology movement have a great deal to offer a pluralistic culture. In the early days of the movement, the emphasis was on self-realization through inner work, but it is now clear that people must reconnect and make a commitment to each other to their communities, and to the earth they share. To achieve a peaceful pluralistic world, there must be a new sense of common purpose. If people can create a shared story that values individuals, cherishes and protects individual subjectivity in all of its diversity, and establishes norms of mutuality and civility that bind people, then there is the possibility of an advance in human consciousness beyond anything yet experienced (O'Hara). (These positions have been eloquently anticipated by Bob Perloff, immediate past president of APA, and Dr. Lee Richmond, president of ACA.)

These goals are not so easily achieved. According to a study of the Public Agenda Foundation, educators and business leaders seem to agree on goals for America's educational system, but they disagree about current performance levels and strategies for reform. In a survey of more than 800 teachers, principals, superintendents, school board presidents, and business executives, 4 out of 5 respondents said that schools must teach students the fundamental values of society, sound work habits, self-esteem, grammatically correct English, science and math, and the abilities to work cooperatively and to be flexible learners. While business executives contend that schools fail to accomplish these goals, most educators still evaluate schools' performance as fair, good, or excellent in all seven areas (*USA Today*, periodical, 1992).

The problems are genuine and filtered through any number of subject areas ranging from Artificial Intelligence to gender roles. However, at the base of the artifice, we believe the problems are fundamentally philosophical.

The discussions on the meaning of work revolve around two centers. One is the question of the most adequate account of the nature of moral reasoning and judgment. The other is a debate about the role and responsibilities of corporations, governments, and others with large scale effective influence on work and the economic system.

Conflicts arise in both centers of discourse. In the discussion of moral theory, what chiefly emerges is conflict between a classical and perennially asserted view of totality–or, at least, complex interrelatedness–in moral reasoning and judgment. This is in distinction from those views which place an emphasis upon application of sets of rules or upon assessment of specified values in making ethical decisions. The case-study analysis is the method often employed for immediate resolution in a concrete context. Much, however, is lacking in this approach.

In the social and economic debates, tension exists between ways of understanding the meaning of work. Work can be seen in one context as an aspect of production or "productivity" and, thus, a separable element in economic calculations. In the larger social context of the real world, work emerges as a vital factor demanding to be seen in a different perspective.

A fruitful project has been to study work in its complex interrelatedness. It is a search for assessment of what is lost in more prescriptive means-to-ends approaches (DesJardins, pp. 96-100). Emerging from these endeavors have been a number of works addressing those philosophical problems arising out of the role of work in society and the situation of workers (Atwater, pp. 21-28). The role of work should be to satisfy the needs of society in such a manner that quality is achieved. At the same time the worker, in theory, benefits through the actions leading to quality. Thus quality becomes a primary virtue of work. The course of all these considerations can lead to profound insights about what elements should characterize human working society when it is rightly constituted and functioning (MacIntyre, 1981).

Consider, for instance, the teaching of Aristotle about the living of the good life or the virtuous life. Virtue lies in the direction of reason: correct reason expertly exercised after having been properly developed. It is reasoning about the realities of life and about particular situations from the perspective which sees their true value in a complex context of relations to family, to the community, and to the whole project of an individual's life. This life project is the overall state of happiness which humans seek by nature, and which is defined in general by what it is to be human (MacIntyre, 1988). These virtues are not mere abstractions but elements of expertise, of highly rational habits in the *practice of living*. *Phronesis*, practical wisdom, or prudence, is that special pervasive element in this life of virtue which is composed of exquisite rationality, seasoned understanding, and effective analysis (MacIntyre, 1981). It is this practical wisdom which underlies the acquisition and effective exercise of all virtues. It is this applied wisdom by which one plays out a life project and it is this applied wisdom that births the skills necessary to do so.

Others would disagree with this model. However, it cannot be denied that the teleological mode of approach avoids in the discussion of morality, and in our discussion of work, the prevalent tendency to *fragment* thought about things human. This fragmentation is at the root of the exaggerated attention given to abstracted elements whose rootedness in the whole of human life is so perilously downplayed. Diet has frequently become less and less a concern about the place which nutrition has in the overall healthy development of a body and the place which meals have in the overall social texture of living. Instead, focus is more intensively upon which foods–or which invisible and untastable elements within foods–are important to keep the arteries unclogged, the effects of stress manageable, the signs of aging to a minimum, the length of one's life to a maximum, etc. Education has become increasingly viewed as the pursuit of a course of studies leading to what will be most profitable economically, or most current in a field of specialization, or to, acquisition of specific cognitive skills which are thought to have the most utility (utility, of course, meaning applicability to business or technology). The attempt to fill a mind with knowledge of the world in which we live and with humanizing insights diminishes.

We are asking what work *means* in the total context of a worker's life. Other considerations about workers' rights, treatment of workers, design of workplaces, work safety, etc., continue to have immense importance for our understanding. But we may rightly give a priority to the endeavor to understand work comprehensively: its *telos* or, more precisely, its place in the teleological dimension of the good life. A very great portion of one's life is spent working. A very great percentage of the effort and energy which one expends and of the skill and intelligence which one acquires in life, and brings to bear on concrete matters, is developed and used in one's work. The idea that one works simply to find the wherewithal to support whatever other effort is personally important in life is misconceived in at least two ways. Firstly, the amounts of time and of resources within one's person which are demanded in doing one's work are simply too great to constitute something on the sidelines of life. Work is woven massively into the fabric of life today often running nearly its whole length.

Secondly, the development of moral character requires constant *application* and *practice*. This is of crucial importance when it is understood to be a necessity to acquire virtue and practical wisdom in order to achieve happiness in both a personal and social context (Atwater). Virtues are skills and strengths habitually embedded in character. How much of this character development can be accomplished in the "after hours" of the life of a worker? Much of the necessary time and many of the concrete opportunities to exercise judgment and practical reasoning, as well as to reinforce virtue and acquire new virtues, must be found in work time. It is vital that these very skills must not atrophy from lack of exercise (Atwater). These skills, these virtues, this practical wisdom constitute the tools with which we pursue happiness. They are our only real avenues to it. As Aristotle insists, its attainment cannot be left to chance (Aristotle).

Work remains, however, for many people doing what one is given as a task to be done and is not, therefore, typically an exercise of practical wisdom. Even when the task is given in general terms and the method of doing it is left up to the employee, the case is still largely the same. It is also the same when the task is generally and simply to improve or enhance this or that element in the corporation or make it more profitable or competitive. This will be done by the use of one's best wits. But, what is missing, of course, is the means-to-end judgment in the context of a community or a whole life.

For many a work project is still a task *set by* the employer for ends or purposes *determined by* the employer, and whose worthwhile nature is a *judgment of* the employer. The fact that a project's design is ingeniated by the worker does not alter this (Atwater). Even the attempt to have workers redesign jobs or work spaces or find the way to quality–total quality–in products is not truly using one's applied skills or *phronesis*–though it touches its boundaries. The perduring questions are: how does one learn practical wisdom? When? If the answer does not involve one's work to some significant degree, then is there an answer at all?

We ask how work is tied to the end point of establishing the good life for the person (MacIntyre, 1988). What is true happiness and how does it interphase with our work? Aristotle is not highly specific about this. The concepts of human nature and its ideal fulfillment remain matters culturally defined to a high degree and variously understood across history.

The resulting answers to the questions about human nature and the good life can always be tested in terms of their reflection of the good life as situated in one's experience. The proposition that the good can be seen in the determination of benefit and harm, pleasure and pain, or *ad hoc* in this or that situation or policy and evaluated in terms of direct and particular consequences, will never be enough. It will fall short of understanding the totality or goal of life, however it is determined. Pleasure or generally described advantage are insufficient substitutions for an overall life project.

Understanding what it means to be truly human is illumined by investigating the person teleologically. The person as an artist exemplifies some highly similar truths about our nature. The crafting and development of excellence of character, the acquisition of the virtues composing a happy life through their concerted exercise: these are features of an art of living. In work, as in other important ways, one develops this art for one's self, one's family, one's community.

It is only by exploring these day to day occurrences that we begin to be able to understand the engines that drive us and the directions in which we go. For human persons live on the twin points of memory and expectation–memory of things past and expectation of things to come. It is, perhaps, this vantage point that provides the most insight into the meanings of work:

> Work is doing what you now enjoy for the sake of a future which you clearly see and desire. Drudgery is doing under strain what you don't now enjoy and for no end that you can now appreciate. (Richard C. Cabot)

References

Andersson, M.L. (1992). "The Meaning of Work and Job." *International Journal of Value Based Management*, 5:2, 89-104.

Antony, Michael, (1993). "Social Relation and the Individuation of Thought." *Mind*, April, pp. 37-61.

Aristotle. (1962). *Nicomachean Ethics.* Translator, Martin Oswald. The Library of the Liberal Arts. New York: Bobbs-Merrill Company, Inc.

Atwater, O. Thomas. (1991). "Virtue and the Workplace." *International Journal of Applied Philosophy*, 6:1, Summer, pp. 21-28.

Billingsley, K.L. (1992). "Good Ministries, Bad Business." *Christianity Today*, 14 December, 36:6.

Braude, Lee. (1975). *Work and Workers.* New York: Praeger Publishers.

Bresler, Robert, J. (1991). *USA Today*, 120:9, Summer.

Brickley, Rosemarie (1987). "God Isn't Finished with Me yet." *Commonweal*, 114, 17 July, 410-411.

Byrne, Edmund F. (1990). *Work, Inc.: A Philosophical Inquiry*. Philadelphia: Temple University Press, 1990.

Cabot, Richard C. (1977). *On Practice, Training, and the Doctor-Patient Relationship*. Labor-Science Pub.

Cherrington, David J. (1980). *The Work Ethic*. New York: Amacom Publishers.

Colson, Charles W., Jack M. Eckerd. (1992), "Why Has Hard Work Fallen on Hard Times?" *Christianity Today*, 34-36.

DesJardins, Joseph R. (1992), "Virtues and Business Ethics." In *Moral Issues in Business*. William H. Shaw & Vincent Barry, eds. Belmont, Cal.: Wadsworth, Inc., pp. 96-100.

Drummond, Robert J. (1991). "Job Satisfaction and Work Values." *Psychological Reports*, December, 1116-1118

Duran, Randall Robert. (1988). "Education for Workers in the Robotics Age: Communication Patterns in the Workplace." Doctoral Dissertation. University of San Francisco.

Farnham, Adrian. (1990). *The Protestant Work Ethic*. London: Routledge.

Farnham, Alan. (1992), "The Lure of Leisure." *The Economist*, 2 May.

Grant, P. (1982). "Why Employee Motivation Has Declined." *Personnel Journal*, 905-909.

Hall, Richard H. (1986). *Dimensions of Work*. Beverly Hills: Sage Publishers.

Haughey, John C. (1990). *Converting 9 to 5*. New York: Crossroads Publishers.

Hollencamp, Patricia K. (1985). "What Is the Experience of the Meaning of Work." Doctoral Dissertation, The Union for Experimenting Colleges and Universities.

Inks, Lawrence Wayne. (1992). "An Interactionist Perspective on Work Value Change." Doctoral Dissertation, Ohio State University.

Jargenen, Clifford E. (1978). "Job Preferences." *Journal of Applied Psychology*, 63, 267-276.

Kaylin, Walter. (1979). *The Power Forward.* New York: Atheneum Pub.

Loscocco, Karyn Anne. (1985). "The Meaning of Work: An Examination of the Determinants of Work Commitment and Work Orientation Among Manufacturing Employees." Doctoral Dissertation, Indiana University.

Luttwak, E.N., R.L. Bartley. (1992). "Is America on the Way Down?" *Commentary*, August 94:2.

Machloviwitz, Abraham. (1980). *Workaholics*. New York: Mentors Publishers.

MacIntyre, Alasdair. (1981). *After Virtue*. Notre Dame, Ind.: University of Notre Dame Press.

MacIntyre, Alasdair. (1988). *Whose Justice? Which Rationality?* Notre Dame, Ind.: University of Notre Dame Press.

Neff, David. (1992). "American Babel." *Christianity Today*, 36, 18-19, 17 August.

Oates, M. (1971). *Confessions of a Workaholic*. New York: World Publishers.

O'Hara, Maureen. (1992). "If Not Now, When?" *Vital Speeches of the Day*, 59, 41-45; 1 August.

O'Reilly, Brian. (1992). "Preparing for Leaner Times." *Fortune*, 125, 40-43; 27 January.

"Performance Fails to Meet Goals." (1992). *USA Today*, Periodical. 121, 8-9.

Ronco, W. & L. Peattie. (1990). *Making Work.* New York: Random House.

"Secularism's Persistence (European Values Study)." (1991). *The Christian Century* 108, 962.

Terkel, Studs. *Working*. (1974). New York: Avon Publishers.

Yankelovich, David. (1982). *New Rules: Searching for Self-Fulfillment in a World Turned Upside Down*. New York: Bantam Publishers.

Zaleznik, Abraham. (1989a). "Real Work." *Harvard Business Review*, 57-64, January.

Zaleznik, Abraham. (1989b). *The Managerial Mystique*. New York: Harper & Row.

SECTION I

Chapter One

A PERSON OF INTELLIGENCE: THE CENTRAL INGREDIENT FOR ETHICAL BEHAVIOR

Gene A. Burns

The Harvard Business School in 1984, just ten years ago, celebrated its 75th Anniversary. Recognizing that Harvard was founded more than 300 years ago, the Business School is still only a freshman in the University. At the time of the celebration, the media broke the carefully nurtured academic quiet in Cambridge to remind us of the division that had developed between the president and faculty. The dichotomy arose from a challenge to the time-honored case-method approach to teaching. In its place, the president had suggested the school should put greater emphasis on teaching ethics.

The mention of the word "ethics" conjures up numerous meanings and definitions of moral standards and conduct. In part, ethics deals with perceptions, with values, or what is often referred to today as "social actions which have redeeming features."

Harvard University President, Derek C. Bok, is a recognized thoughtful, elegant scholar. What provoked him to suggest the Business School should take a more academic approach to business studies? Did Professor David Riesman, a noted sociologist and education expert at the University, sum it all up when he said: "But there is a feeling, especially in Cambridge, that there is something nonintellectual about management?"

From time to time, surveys are made of the attitude of the general public towards the professions and disciplines. Perhaps greater attention is focused on these surveys today because of the whole issue of ethics in business and the professions.

As a young man, I can recall that in the small community where I grew up, the clergy held the number one position in terms of respect and admiration. Closely following the clergy were the physicians, lawyers, teachers and artists–in that order. In a report issued in 1983 by McGraw Hill, the order of this listing changed quite remarkably and additional disciplines and functional activities were added. Somewhat near the bottom of the listing were politicians and business executives. As I recall the survey, only real estate brokers and used-car salesmen were more ill-regarded than the business executive and politician.

With that revelation, I began to do some research to understand better why there is this grave development of disrespect for business managers in particular. Perhaps there may well be a bit of truth in Professor Riesman's statement "that there is something nonintellectual about management."

This concern led me to think back on the career of Albert J. Nock. Now, for those of you not familiar with Nock, it will suffice at this time just to characterize him as the nineteenth-century William F. Buckley, Jr. I shall expand on this later. Nock's views on such subjects as education and the place of the individual in society could well be timely and shed light on attitudes and prejudices regarding management and ethical standards in business.

Accordingly, and with this background, the chapter will discuss:

1. how one can recognize a person of intelligence,
2. how education and ethics are interrelated, and, finally, consider:
3. how an appreciation of intelligence, education and ethics may help explain a seeming paradox between:

- the spectacularly successful goods-producing capabilities of a free-enterprise society, and,
- the less-than-sanguine view by the public of the custodians of business resources, namely, management.

Albert Nock was born in Brooklyn in 1870, the only child of an Episcopal minister. He came from a large family and grew up in a secure, established environment. The family later moved to a lumber town in Michigan on the shores of Lake Huron, where Nock spent the rest of his boyhood. From the time the lake froze in the fall until the spring thaw, the town was completely isolated. He described it affectionately as a self-reliant, independent place, full of characters; it seems to have been an ideal community for such a person as Nock to grow up in. He was sent to a boarding school in Illinois where he received good training, and then to a small college in New York State, St. Stephen's, which was a no-nonsense sort of place. (Today, St. Stephen's is Bard College on the Hudson.) Students were expected to have a fluent reading knowledge of Greek and Latin on arrival; the course of study consisted, in Nock's words, of "readings and expositions of Greek and Roman literature; mathematics up to differential calculus; logic; metaphysics; and a little work on the sources and history of the English language." That was all; there were no courses in English, for instance. English was one's mother tongue and a student was expected to use it properly; as for English literature, that was in the library.

After college Nock played professional baseball for several years while doing graduate work, and at the insistence of his mother, who is reputed to have been a rather purposeful woman, became, as his father had been, an Episcopal minister. He served in several parishes, but never seems to have been entirely satisfied with the calling of pastor, and in 1909 left the ministry to join the staff of the American magazine.

In 1920, Nock became the founding editor of the Freeman, a weekly journal of comment and criticism. According to Nock, when a young writer asked him about the magazine's editorial policy, and particularly whether there were any "sacred cows," he replied that there were three, "as untouchable and sacred as the Arc of the Covenant." These, he said, were as follows: "You must have a point; you must make it out;" and finally, "you must make it out in eighteen carat, impeccable, idiomatic English."

With the wreckage of the liberal theory of education about us today, it is refreshing to go back to Nock's rather heretical views on the subject. Much of his writing is devoted to education such as a series of lectures he gave at the University of Virginia in 1931, entitled "The Theory of Education in the United States." Nock's views on education begin with a sharp distinction between intelligence and what he called "sagacity." It was the gift of sagacity and cleverness, he said, which made it possible for frail, weak humans to survive in a hostile environment; it was sagacity which "enabled man to build up the prodigious apparatus of civilization." He seemed rather doubtful that intelligence or wisdom had much to do with this process. Intelligence, on the other hand, is required if man is "to civilize himself, or even to understand what civilization means." Unfortunately, Nock thought, having been given the sagacity and cleverness to build the elaborate mechanism of civilization, man has never had at his disposal the intelligence to give civilization sufficient direction and purpose; it is the lack of balance between these two gifts which makes human societies so unstable. Corresponding to his distinction between sagacity and intelligence, Nock distinguishes between two kinds of training–that which is functional and that which is formative. It is only formative training which can, in his opinion, truly be called education, but only the intelligent are capable of being educated. Functional training, he said, can produce an Edison, while education may produce an Emerson. These two pairs of distinctions between intelligence and sagacity on the one hand, and education and training on the other, were central to Nock's critique of contemporary education in America.

Today we are in an age of specialization, computerization–call it "the machine age." There is even the expectation that robots will perform much of the work to be done. It is in this connection that Nock may have given us the clue as to why management's motives and objectives are sometimes little understood. There may well be a lack of understanding of the different kinds of individuals resultant from functional and formative training.

It should be understood that Nock had no objection to what he called "functional" training, nor did he deny it its proper place in society. What he did object to was confusing training with education, which he thought was detrimental to both, in fact placed real education in danger of extinction.

The title Nock chose for his autobiography was The Memoirs of a Superfluous Man. He was superfluous because, having belonged to the last American generation offered what he considered to be a proper education, he was an educated man, and America had no place for such a man–he was an anachronism. A society devoted to what he called "economism"–the social philosophy "which interprets the whole sum of human life in terms of the production, acquisition, and distribution of wealth"–needed Edisons, Henry Fords, Andrew Carnegies, all clever, sagacious men, but none of them educated, nor in his opinion intelligent, but what was such a society to do with an educated man?

It should not be assumed that because of his use of the word "economism" to characterize the dominant attitude in the United States that Nock would have had anything in common with John Kenneth Galbraith. It is true that he didn't have a high opinion of men typified by Henry Ford, Andrew Carnegie, or Jay Gould. His objection to them was not that they had been spectacularly successful in producing goods and making money, but that for them these were the principal aims in life. (Sounds like the parable in the Book of St. Matthew.) Nock believed that man/woman should strive to create a society which would bring the various aspects of life into a harmonious whole. By this he meant a blend of workmanship, intellect and knowledge with an instinct of social life and manners.

Nock, as we have observed, questioned whether our acquisitive society had a place for an educated or educable person which a trainable person could not fill. No doubt, his concern was justified when one compares a prestigious university offering courses in beginning and advanced fly casting with Nock's curriculum at St. Stephen's College! But what for Nock were the marks of intelligence? "The person of intelligence," Nock wrote in his Theory of Education in the United States, "is the one who always tends to 'see things as they are,' the one who never permits his views of them to be directed by convention, by the hope of advantage, or by an irrational and arbitrary authoritarianism." To this he added, "...and thus we may say that there are certain integrities at the root of intelligence which give it somewhat the aspect of a moral as well as an intellectual attribute."

Wyndham Lewis, another writer and philosopher, came close to saying the same thing in the observation, "...the ability to perceive the true–which is under everybody's nose but not seen by everybody–it is confined to people of considerable intelligence." If it is only those of intelligence, those who "always tend to see things as they are" who are capable of being educated, what did Nock understand education to be? For him, the purpose of education is to produce a disciplined and experienced mind. Has the great spirit of education disappeared in America? Nock suggested education has become the victim of Gresham's law which, he thought, applied not only to money, but to everything else.

It was the America which seemed to be dominated by "economism" which troubled Nock. "It [economism] can build a society which is rich, prosperous, powerful–even one which has a reasonably wide diffusion of material well-being. It cannot, however, build one which has a savour and depth." Can the attitudes toward management which pervade a large part of our society be attributed to Nock's concern; that is, a lack of depth or culture or ethics–in short, nonintellectual?

If this is the case, then what are managers to do about it? It is not sufficient to reply in the words of the French essayist, Montaigne: "Human beings are very much what they are, and their collective society is very much what it is, and nothing of any conceivable consequence can be done about either." And, in the case of a financial manager in particular, one ought not be content to be viewed as Elbert Hubbard described those in the profession: "Cold, passive, noncommittal, with eyes like codfish...minus bowels, passion or sense of humour."

In reality, we are pretty much left to ourselves. A first step to change perception, however, could be by the individualist's method–that is, by example-setting. A part of example-setting could follow what Nock and, more recently, Bill Buckley, referred to as "Isaiah's Job." It is the notion that some individuals by the force of intellect are able to apprehend the principles coming from what we know as the humane life. And, by force of character are able, in some measure, to adhere to those principles. Again, it is the earlier distinction Nock made of intelligence and sagacity. In carrying out "Isaiah's Job," one represents that element of society which maintains standards and thereby keeps our civilization going.

Successful management demands intelligence–seeing things as they are; and education–to understand the context in which business operates. A concrete example of where intelligence and education could have worked together is the automotive industry in the United States. Was the industry guilty of seeing the auto market as it used to be?

To assert that "there is something nonintellectual about management" is a critical and serious indictment. Ought management to have a periodic self-evaluation process? Should it be left almost entirely to the Securities and Exchange Commission to admonish our colleagues for letting professional management fall so low in public esteem? I shall continue to probe the interrelationships of intelligence, ethics and education, and see how these disciplines could better relate to management in industry.

As William F. Buckley, Jr. wrote in his book, *God and Man* at Yale: "I am dedicated to my cause. At the same time, I cannot claim to have approached this project with the diligence and patience of a professional scholar. As far as pure scholarship is concerned, it is best said of me that I have the profoundest respect for it, and no pretense at it."

The challenge is always to know what is going on–where we are going–and to understand the trend and direction of our times. And, importantly, to return to the theme of this paper–to recognize a "person of intelligence"–to know what is expected of the individual with a formative versus a functional education.

To conclude, one could sum up in a very practical way the purpose and meaning of education. In my research I could find no better definition than the advice given to the Chancellor of Oxford University, Harold MacMillan, when he went up as an undergraduate, at his first lecture: "Let me make this clear to you. Nothing that you will learn in the course of your studies will be of the slightest use to you in after life–save only this–that if you work hard and intelligently you should be able to detect when a man is talking rot and that, in my view, is the main if not the sole purpose of education."

References

Nock, Albert J. *An Appreciation.*

Regnery, Henry. *Modern Age,* Winter 1971.

Chapter Two

THE ROLE OF AFFECT AND THE ROLE OF UNCONSCIOUS PROCESSES IN THE PREVENTION OF WORK-RELATED PSYCHOSOMATIC DISORDERS

Joel R. Gavriele-Gold

1. Introduction

As a culture we have moved from the belief that the mind and body exist as separate entities toward a general belief that the mind and body are one. Recent findings in the field of neurobiology demonstrate that the mind and intelligence exist in every cell of the body. We know today that the cells of the human body communicate with each other through the emotions. When emotions are ignored or not experienced, the body begins to dysfunction. The latest neurobiochemical findings confirm what psychoanalysts have known for the past 50 years through our subjective explorations of the psyche.

THE MIND EXISTS IN THE BODY
THE MIND IS THE BODY
THE BODY IS THE MIND
MIND AND BODY ARE ONE
IT IS THE EMOTIONS
THAT MAKE IT ALL WORK

Nevertheless, despite these recent findings, a great part of the medical world maintains a mind-body split. This relegates workplace health to the emergency room where symptoms are tended to, rather than recognizing that physical and mental health require acknowledgment of the whole person. The average doctor, the average workplace health professional, and the average person, upon hearing that a condition is psychosomatic, believes there is no real physical condition but merely an imagined one existing in the person's head. This is a misconception and not at all the case. In psychosomatic dysfunction there is real physical damage. We must keep in mind that "psycho," mind, and "soma," body, mean nothing more or less than mind-body. Traditionally, psycho-somatic indicates two directions: one from the mind to the body and the other from the body to the mind. When a physical condition is classically labeled psychosomatic it means that to a greater or lesser degree there is an emotional component involved in the genesis and development of the condition.

This chapter asks for a consideration of the advantages of acknowledging and incorporating individual and group emotions in everyday work activities as part of reacting to the accommodation and assimilation of new experience and information. The question remains: how do we stay in emotional contact and emotional balance with ourselves and negotiate the corporate world? Certainly, allowing emotions to live in the world of business implies that people will experience themselves as more empowered and less compliant which may be unsettling to the existing corporate structure.

Let us look at some of the everyday language of mind-body connections commonly in use: he's giving me a headache; white with rage; a sight for sore eyes; a pain in the neck; tongue-tied; all knotted up; itching for a fight; bad blood between them; stuck in my craw; broken heart; takes my breath away, and on and on. What happens, however, when the emotions connected to these expressions are not experienced?

I have observed in my practice that when people ignore the emotional content contained in the expression: "he's giving me a headache," the headache becomes a migraine, or the emotions connected to "white with rage" are disregarded and culminate in a stroke; "a sight for sore eyes" becomes a detached retina; "a pain in the neck" requires the chiropractor; "tongue-tied" moves into epilepsy; "all knotted up" becomes arthritis; "itching for a fight" becomes psoriasis; "bad blood" becomes leukemia; "stuck in my craw" becomes ulcers; "a broken heart" becomes heart disease; "takes my breath away" becomes asthma or tuberculosis, and so on.

Traditionally, somatic responses are regarded as resulting when an unacceptable affect or impulse is not admitted to consciousness, allowed to be felt consciously and discharged. When feelings are not connected to thoughts and incidents, but held in the mind or psyche, energy or libido is accumulated, causing uncomfortable disconnected expressions. In order to avoid these expressions, a predisposed organ or body part is unconsciously chosen as a metaphor, encapsulating the individual's psychic conflict, in an unconscious attempt at partial discharge.

Emotions have to be physically experienced to avoid somatic dysfunction. The physical experience of an emotion must be attached to thought otherwise we would have feelings without names and they would be unconnected to incidents in our lives. If feelings related to personal conflict are not connected to thoughts or if thoughts related to personal conflicts are not connected to emotions, those feelings, disconnected from corresponding thoughts, ultimately depart from psychic experience and lodge in the body where they form a physical dysfunction reflecting a metaphor representing the unacknowledged psychic conflict.

When we speak of work-related psychosomatic disorders we are referring to emotions related to work that are ignored and remain unprocessed, unexperienced and unintegrated into the personality. Perhaps the clearest, if not the most elegant, metaphor I have encountered involved a lawyer employed as a junior partner of a major law firm. (Names and some facts have been changed to protect patient confidentiality.) He was extremely obsessive and held a high regard for his intellect while paying little or no attention to his emotional life. The senior partner to whom John, my patient, directly reported was a man named Fisher. Mr. Fisher was intolerant, contemptuous, arrogant, demanding, and impatient, not unlike John's father. Although John was working 12 hours a day it was never enough for, and certainly never appreciated by, Mr. Fisher. In his second year at the firm, John collapsed during an important presentation and was rushed to the hospital. He was diagnosed as having developed a fissure in his rectum which had to be surgically corrected. John's unconscious choice of dysfunction and its location said it all about Mr. Fisher.

We have two paths to arriving at feelings: one is to have a set of thoughts and conclude from our thoughts that we are feeling a particular feeling, thereby arriving at a feeling through our cognition. The other is experiential: to have the physical experience of a feeling in a here and now situation and then to name the experience through our thoughts.

We know how tissue, muscle, and organ damage occur when unexperienced feelings leave the realm of the psyche and lodge in body parts as metaphors for unspoken language connections and psychic conflicts. We have long been aware that unacceptable thoughts and feelings, too painful or powerful or traumatic to experience, find refuge in the body. We know that preverbal experiences live on in the body-mind.

Once emotions have disconnected and left the realm of psychic processes, they exist like ghosts as somatic manifestations. Migraines, ulcers, asthma, heart and respiratory conditions, skin ailments, intestinal disorders, lupus, tuberculosis, cancer, and arthritis are but a few of these psychosomatic disorders, to say nothing of the separate but more classical hysterical conversion reactions described early in this century by Freud and his followers. Psyche and soma are intricately intertwined–acting and reacting one upon the other in an organized fashion and harmony.

Franz Alexander stated: "Psychological processes are fundamentally not different from other processes which take place in the organism. They are at the same time physiological processes and differ from other body processes only in that they are perceived subjectively and can be communicated verbally to others."[1]

2. Psychoanalysis and Psychosomatic Illness

While training as an analyst in the late 1960s and early 1970s, I often found myself asking patients why they needed a cold, or a flu or an asthma attack. Why had they made themselves ill? Always there was the implication that illness was the person's fault. A well-analyzed person did not get ill, a well-analyzed person did not need illness. If you got ill, you were not dealing with some unconscious piece of something and were ultimately made to feel guilty. It is a mistake we analysts made then that is still being made by some. Thanks to the writings of Georg Groddeck, the real father of psychosomatic medicine, and Franz Alexander, mistakenly regarded as the father of psychosomatic medicine, I learned that the patient was not guilty but rather the patient's unconscious choices reflected the defenses and somatizations he or she needed to survive childhood.

Georg Groddeck rediscovered or reinvented psychoanalysis on his own, perhaps by osmosis, without being terribly aware of the existence of Freud in Vienna until 1913. Groddeck was a character, a troll (by his own description) and an *enfant terrible*. His first mentor, Ernst Schweninger, was a famous physician known for demanding complete authority and absolute servitude of his patients. From him, Groddeck learned that the physician is a mere catalyst, setting curative processes in motion.

At his Sanitarium, at Baden-Baden in the early 1900s, Groddeck discovered the Unconscious, independent of any knowledge of Freud. By the end of World War I, Groddeck had made contact with Freud and they developed a correspondence which continued until Groddeck's death. It was Groddeck's IT that became Freud's ID in psychoanalytic theory. Groddeck prepared a paper for the Psychoanalytic Society entitled "The Psychic Origin and Psychoanalytical Treatment of Organic Disease," which was the first paper to explore what was to become psychosomatic medicine. He affirmed that people can become susceptible to infection because of the changing process of the Conscious and Unconscious which affect blood composition, digestion, cardiac activity–all of the organic life of the person. Many of us might suppose Groddeck was speaking only of hysterics. However, he emphasized: "I consider it a basic and dangerous misconception to suppose that only the hysteric has the gift of making himself ill for whatever purpose."[2] He regarded conversion of emotions to symptoms as quite separate from hysteria.

Groddeck believed, as do I, that a person may ask him/herself: "What purpose does the symptom serve?" He saw the sore throat to force the whispering of secrets; a cold hand to hide hot emotions; early morning coughing as putting aside "the impressions of the past night's dreams and blow away the intertwined small and great fear fantasies and embarrassments of the coming day"; the common cold as a reaction to "the evil smell of a word or thought"; and headaches as "the most widely used means of the unconscious for the halting of thought and drive." You will love reading his Book of the It, for Groddeck has a wonderful little-boy quality in him, coupled with a depth of honesty and insight which inspired Lawrence Durrell to include Groddeck in his Studies in Genius.

Groddeck's attempts to reunite mind and body into a psychosomatic whole created a parallel body of knowledge separate and apart from the rest of the medical world. His work greatly impacted on the development of psychoanalysis, very gradually spreading within the scientific community over the next 40 years until Franz Alexander took Groddeck's work a step further-teaching that all physical body processes are either directly or indirectly influenced by psychological stimuli and the entire organism is a unit of interconnected parts.

In Psychosomatic Medicine: Its Principles and Applications, Alexander regards conditions of specific illnesses and specific organs and muscles of the body as metaphors for unspeakable thoughts and feelings. He speaks of emotional factors in gastrointestinal, respiratory, and cardiovascular disturbances; in metabolic and endocrine disturbances; in disturbances of the skin, joints and skeletal muscles; in sexual disturbances–all the parts of the body in which we now know large quantities of neuropeptides and their receptors reside outside the brain.

Alexander reported early on, although no one listened for 45 years, that reference to emotions in such general terms as anxiety, tension, and emotional imbalance was outdated. I would add stress to his list. Alexander emphasized that "Every bodily process is directly or indirectly influenced by psychological stimuli because the whole organism constitutes a unit with all of its parts interconnected. The psychosomatic approach therefore can be applied to every phenomenon which takes place in the living organism."[3]

Listen now to what he went on to say when no one was listening:

> All our emotions we express through physiological processes...all emotions are accompanied by physiological changes: fear, by palpitation of the heart; anger, by increased heart activity, elevation of blood pressure, and changes in carbohydrate metabolism; despair, by a deep inspiration and expiration called sighing. All these physiological phenomena are the results of complex muscular interactions under the influence of nervous impulses, carried to the expressive muscles of the face and to the diaphragm in laughter, to the lachrymal glands in weeping, to the heart in fear, and to the adrenal glands and to the vascular system in rage. The nervous impulses arise in certain emotional situations which in turn originate from our interaction with other people. The originating psychological situations can be understood only in terms of psychology—as total responses of the organism to its environment.[4]

Alexander preceded modern knowledge by 45 years; Groddeck by nearly 40 years before that. They both believed the mind controlled the body and they may be right. What is becoming increasingly more difficult to ignore is the reality of emotions as the mediating factor in determining the psychological and physiological well-being of the organism as a whole.

3. Recent Findings and the Role of Emotions in Psychosomatic Functioning

In the last eight years startling medical evidence has been uncovered, particularly in the fields of endocrinology, immunology, and neurology. In some ways these discoveries confirm what psychoanalysis has always known. The mind is intimately connected to the functions of the body. These recent discoveries go a step further in reporting that the mind is in the body.

Neurotransmitters are the chemical substances produced by brain neurons. They transmit information across the gap separating nerve cells. Nerve cells produce neuropeptides, or chemicals in the brain. We now know that neuropeptides are produced in other parts of the body as well as the brain. At the present time there are some 65 different neuropeptides, each distinguished from the other by its amino acids. Each neuropeptide with its own amino acids has a specific receptor. The receptor of one type of neuropeptide cannot receive information from another type of neuropeptide. Large clusters of receptors have been found in the intestine, the gonads and a neurotransmitter in the kidneys.

Dr. Candace Pert, a biochemist who studied the distribution of neuropeptide receptors, makes no distinction between mind and body. Pert believes neuropeptides are the language of the mind and body, and goes so far as to say the mind is in the body. Neuropeptides and their receptors organize and integrate the internal life of the body. In 1985, Pert focused on isolating neurotransmitters and mapping the receptors of these natural chemical substances in the brain.

She found an extremely high density of receptors in the limbic system of the brain; traditionally regarded as the system responsible for the expression and possibly the creation of emotions. Both the hypothalamus and the pituitary gland are located within the limbic system. Together the hypothalamus and pituitary regulate hormonal activity and the body's autonomic nervous system.

Associated with the limbic system is the amygdala. Stimulation of the amygdala evokes sexual behavior, anger, powerful reactions of grief, pain, and pleasure associated with profound memories accompanied by total somatic emotional states. (Interestingly, Freud had extolled the use of the couch in reviving long-term memories because he believed a little curvy hooked piece of the amygdala flipped open when people lay in a horizontal position.)

To reiterate, receptors for the brain chemicals responsible for regulating the physiology of the body are concentrated in the limbic system which is the location of our perception of emotions and perhaps where emotions connect to memory. A second concentration for these receptors is found at the dorsal horn of the spinal cord where all sensory information enters our bodies for processing by the brain. Touch, sound, sight, smell and taste information is sent directly to the brain from the dorsal horn. The brain and spinal cord together form the central nervous system.

Pert now believes the dorsal horn is a part of the limbic system. Of vital importance is that Pert also believes the constant deluge of sensory information entering the dorsal horn is ordered and prioritized by the emotions. The emotions determine what will be acted upon, what will be discarded, and in what order. She explained this simply by saying emotions tell you what to do and the receptors put the message into practice.

Perhaps of greatest importance is the discovery of a cluster of receptors in the immune cell called a monocyte. This led to the conclusion that there is a bodywide network of neuropeptides and their receptors traveling from the limbic system and the dorsal horn to the gastrointestinal system, the reproductive system and the immune system. The neuropeptide network is designed to integrate the work of the immune system throughout the body. The emotions put the neuropeptides into action. Pert is convinced that the brain speaks with the immune system. The neuropeptides from the brain alert the monocytes of the immune system and tell them where they are needed. The monocytes respond somewhat like homing pigeons and zero in on macrophages needed to destroy alien bacteria. It seems that Freud's view that, "in time, everything will be found in biology" may indeed be correct.

For Pert, emotion is a physiological experience which can be as subtle as a mood or a tone, an affect or feeling. She speaks of breathing as moving toward emotion and describes thirst as being capable of functioning as an emotion.

Recently interviewed by Bill Moyers on The Mind Body segment of *Healing and The Mind*, Dr. Pert said, "The currency between mind and matter interconnections are emotions."

During the Moyers interview, Pert stated:

> The me that is me is the whole body. Intelligence is in every cell of the body. The mind is throughout the brain and the body. The mind is some kind of enlivening energy throughout the whole body that enables cells to talk to each other and enables the outside to talk to the whole organism. There are emotional messages on all levels of consciousness... I believe emotions have the potential to play a role in this process and influence process. Emotions transform themselves into how well your liver is working and how well your heart works.... Fluctuations in emotional status are influencing health and illness. The chemicals running our body and running our brain seem to be the same chemicals that are involved in emotion and that says to me we better pay more attention to emotions in respect to health.

The Actors' Study was conducted by Dr. Margaret Kemeny to determine the effect of specific emotional states upon the immune system. Accomplished actors were asked to put themselves in specific emotional states: rage, sadness, happiness, grief and depression. Results indicated a significant enhancement of the actor's immune system when he or she felt sad, as well as a significant enhancement when happy states were experienced. The same held true for states of rage and grief. The main finding was emotions of sadness, grief, and other so-called negative feelings do not have a negative effect on the body. While it appears that grief has a positive effect on the immune system, depression seemed to have a significantly negative effect. Therefore, it appears that *any* feelings that are experienced are good for us although we are often afraid of negative feelings. In thinking about this, I believe that depression has a negative effect on the immune system because within depression, we find hopelessness and, hopelessness is devastating to our mental and physical well-being.

Dr. Robert Ader, of the University of Rochester, conducted a number of studies on the classical conditioning of the immune system in rats. He found nerve fibers in the cells of the immune system. He believes the immune system retains memory of past insults to the system and this memory is connected to memory in the brain. In a taste aversion experiment with rats Ader injected them with cyclophosphamide immediately followed by a saccharin-flavored drink. While he knew cyclophosphamide produces a form of nausea in rats, he did not know that it also suppresses specific reactions in their immune systems. This he learned when a number of the rats mysteriously died. He then discovered the rats had been conditioned to weaken their own immune systems by associating the drinking of the saccharin with the cyclophosphamide. In effect, each drink of saccharin produced nausea and immune suppression as if the rats "believed" the saccharin was the cyclophosphamide. Ader demonstrated that the immune system could be impacted by what the organism believed.

In the study of a young female patient suffering from Lupus, Dr. Karen Olness and Dr. Ader employed classical conditioning in the administration of a powerful, ultimately life-threatening experimental drug with the smell of rose water. After a number of classical associations, achieved by taking the drug while simultaneously smelling the rose water, the patient was ultimately able to continue to achieve the effects of the drug on the immune system by smelling the rose water without taking the medication and by having the mind tell the immune system it was receiving the drug. For Drs. Olness and Ader, the mind and body are inseparable.

4. Psychoanalysis and Psychosomatic Dysfunction Today

We now know specific changes take place in the brain and organs when feelings change. What seems important to me in terms of helping people experience their emotions is that there is no substitute for listening to and talking with them. You can help a person reach an emotion by talking about the content related to the emotion. You can even help a person name an emotion (it is surprising how many people do not have names for their emotional experiences), but the person has to arrive at the internal experience of the emotion on his or her own. Sometimes by simply asking a person to describe an incident and then asking, "what was it like?" or "what were you feeling at the time?" you can observe someone attaching a feeling to that incident for the first time in his/her life.

Ella Freeman Sharpe, a psychoanalyst, points out something I would like you to think about. In speaking about a piece of developmental psychology that is a wondrous connection, she pointed to the child's learning bowel control and said when the ego stabilizes this achievement of body control and it becomes automatic, the emotions of anger and pleasure which accompanied body discharges must be dealt with in other ways.

At the same time that sphincter control is established, the child is acquiring speech and the discharge of anger and pleasure, no longer accompanied physically, can now take place through speech.

> The activity of speaking is substituted for the physical activity now restricted at other openings of the body, while words themselves become the very substitutes for the bodily substances. Speech secondly becomes a way of expressing and discharging ideas. So that we may say speech in itself is a metaphor, that metaphor is as ultimate as speech. ...It often appears in practice that the placement of an affect or feeling in the soma is nothing more than a metaphor for what the psyche has rejected.[5]

Sharpe says, "It is a fact that a live metaphor reveals a past forgotten experience and that this was originally a psycho-physical one."[6] We certainly find this to be the case with patients who have been abused physically and/or sexually in childhood and who have repressed the memories of the experience. In some way it seems that people choose their illnesses to reflect their emotional conflicts. On the other hand, I noticed during my internship at a state mental hospital that psychotic mental patients hardly ever suffered somatic complaints. It is as if they had no need of organ dysfunction.

For Freud, "an affect is the qualitative expression of the quantity of instinctual energy and of its fluctuations."[7] Freud believed each instinct expresses itself in terms of affects or ideas. An affect is any feeling, painful or pleasant, vague or well defined, manifested in a massive discharge or in the form of a general mood. When emotions have disconnected from events in a person's life, therapy helps the individual re-establish the relation between the memory of the event and the emotions by restoring the connection and thereby facilitating the discharge of the affect known as abreaction.

Most of us are afraid to look at our feelings because we fear they will be too powerful, too painful, or too threatening to bear. We fear experiencing these feelings will overwhelm us and we will never be able to function again. We don't usually worry about feeling too much joy or too much happiness or too much contentment, for we know that these good feelings last however long they last and then go on to become other feelings. The same holds true for our more difficult feelings, although it is hard to convince people of this. The experience of emotions has a beginning and an end. Emotions contain an energy which ultimately dissipates. Emotions exist along a continuum. For example, a feeling of being ignored may turn to a feeling of hurt, and move on to become a feeling of humiliation, and continue to become anger or even grow into rage which may become so frightening the person turns the rage against him or herself and allows the feeling to become one of sadness or depression.

Some therapists believe in facilitating the discharge of feelings by talking about the feelings, or by hypothetically talking to the people to whom the feelings are connected, *i.e.*, a parent, a sibling, or a friend, during the patient's session. Other therapists believe it is important to physically discharge the feelings by punching a punching bag or hitting an inflatable toy, or by hugging a teddy bear or doll. Still other therapies ask the patient not to discharge the emotion but rather to contain the feeling within the body and experience the emotion physically. In containing and experiencing the feeling one gives the feeling a name and connects it to the memory of the body as well as to the memory of the mind. Personally, I believe it is important to have people both contain the feeling and give life to it through language and verbal expression. I also acknowledge the advantage in physically acting out feelings in cases where an individual is extremely emotionally repressed or disconnected.

In working psychoanalytically no attempt is made to break down the patient's resistance or defenses. A resistance indicates a defense as it appears in the course of treatment. Resistances and defenses are understood to be the person's unconscious methods of dealing with the environment in order to have survived childhood. As a person comes to understand the purpose of the defense he/she can gradually surrender the less successful defense for a more operative defense. The therapist offers himself/herself as a "good object" giving the patient the opportunity to use a different kind of object from the one available in childhood. During the course of treatment, the individual comes to know what his or her needs are and what cannot be made up for in treatment and has been lost, must be mourned. During this process an inauthentic self gradually is replaced by an authentic self.

In working with people with psychosomatic disorders, we often find people who, on the surface, do not suffer from mental distress. Instead we discover organic damage instead of specific neurotic or psychotic components. In other words, psychosomatic reactions are an attempt at self cure as are neurosis and psychosis. Psychosomatic patients are typically not verbally communicative and have little or no affect, imagination or humor. They are neither in psychic pain nor experiencing great levels of anxiety or depression. It is as if these mental expressions have left the psychic realm and lodged themselves within the body. Psychological issues must be brought back to the psyche and treated.

Alexithymia is a non-feeling, non-emotional response to experience. The experience gets pulverized and is not available to thought. Alexithymia was developed as a concept by Nemiah and Sifneos in 1970 and by Nemiah in 1978. In actual alexithymia feelings are lost: (1) because they occurred before the individual had words to attach to and process the emotions, or (2) as a result of trauma in which the feelings were too overwhelming to be internalized and processed psychically, or (3) they occurred in situations where the individual lacked conscious experience of emotions which then unconsciously and quite automatically moved into the body.

Marty and de M'Uzan speak of *la pensée opératoire*, or operatory thinking, which Joyce McDougall, a French psychoanalyst, regards as "a pragmatic and affectless way of relating both to oneself and to other people, a form of relationship that appears to be largely delibidinized."[8] In these scenarios, the individual is out of contact with any inner psychic reality and the emotions are not actually lost but depart from the psyche and lodge in the body.

McDougall says of patients employing operatory thinking, "When I came to recognize the unconscious need, in a number of my patients, to *preserve* these illnesses, not only as a reassurance of one's bodily limits but also as proof of psychic survival, this was for me a notable discovery."[9]

McDougall developed the concept of "normopaths" or people she describes as:

> People obliged to maintain a camouflage of "Pseudonormality" in order not to think or feel too deeply about inner pain and conflict that might otherwise be experienced as overwhelming and mentally disorganizing. Although many of these patients suffered from a variety of well-recognized psychosomatic maladies, they had rarely any connections between the somatic manifestations and psychologically disturbing events in their lives, much as though perceptions of physical and psychological warning signals were totally ejected from consciousness...such a capacity for destroying meaning became analyzable when events that were strongly tinged affectively but not acknowledged resulted in temporary somatic manifestations or disturbed perceptual functioning.[10]

I believe that normopaths comprise a large part of our society. Having had more therapy than I care to remember, and with many friends who have been in therapy, it is easy to forget that the vast majority in our country believes that therapy is either for the very crazy or for people without friends. I always get shocked into reality when I go upstate to my little cottage, only 85 miles from New York City but in another world. The people there are usually alcoholic, extremely overweight, and almost without exception, fond of telling me about one illness or another. To be physically ill is almost a norm.

Every year I attend a wonderful fish supper at the Dutch Reform Church. Perhaps 150 people show up and sit at long, community-style tables much like an Italian mensa. Although these people have grown up together and have known each other for generations, you can hear a pin drop throughout the meal. The entire conversation consists of: "Hello, how have ya been? ... Nice seeing ya, see you again next year." Looking at the scene you would guess you were in the middle of an isolated Scandinavian village as described by Ibsen. These are not people who would seek out therapy.

The patients with psychosomatic problems, I do see in treatment find their way to me because their doctors have suggested therapy. It is sad to note that often these people are physically ill by the time they come to me. These people exhibit no sense of introspection or curiosity about their psychic reality. They show no desire to let their feelings live. They often say, "Just tell me what to do and I'll do it." Working with them is slow and I always feel a tinge of anxiety wondering how I can touch them in some emotional way to help these patients express their feelings. Often I describe my own experience and emotions in relation to whatever we are talking about. When I attempt this at the beginning of treatment I am often met with annoyance over taking the patient's time to talk about myself rather than telling them what to do. As treatment progresses, with any luck, some curiosity about my feelings may be expressed and I feel hopeful.

One patient, in telling me her trip to Russia was ruined when her colitis acted up, said, "I couldn't get to do what I wanted to do when I wanted to do it." Prior to her trip this patient of two years would come close to a feeling and then not want to talk about it, as if that would cause her to lose her physical and psychic boundaries. I asked her what it was that she couldn't do when she wanted to as a child. For the first time, there was a sign of tears and she began to describe a borderline mother who wanted a porcelain doll for a daughter instead of the tomboy the patient yearned to be. This theme followed her in her career of college professor. She didn't get her sabbatical when she wanted it; she almost never got to teach the courses she wanted or to chair her department. This was a moving session and I felt like I had made a real inroad. In the following session there was no mention of the material from the previous session. When I inquired about this the patient replied, "then was then and now is now." I found myself secretly hoping for her to have an attack of colitis at that moment as I sat in silence. It would seem that her psychosomatic infantile defenses, needed to survive childhood, are still too difficult to surrender in exchange for real adult pleasure.

I see a huge conflict growing within our society that is visible in the workplace. On the one hand, society encourages us to exclude our emotions when interacting with each other, thus reinforcing normopathic behavior. On the other hand, we know how vital it is to experience emotions in some real physical thoracic and visceral way, as well as to give life to them through language. I believe an organic and psychic integration takes place as we verbally describe our affective experience.

In our own society we have been re-evaluating: women's rights, gay and lesbian rights, the rights of minorities, of children and animals, as well as the rights of future generations to inherit a clean environment. All these issues have stirred our emotions and our thoughts as we re-feel and re-think what we believe to be true.

Now we have an opportunity to reconsider the role of emotions and work. Not only do we need to find ways of bringing emotions into the workplace, we need also to find ways of helping men become more in touch with their emotions–a men's liberation. Most of us come from cultures endorsing the idea that men cannot express emotions openly. Emotions are women's work, and men are supposed to be strong and able to take on whatever it is that has to be taken on. Women have the luxury of feelings (although their entry into erstwhile male careers already seems to threaten us with more normopathy) and, generally speaking, men have the honor of dying at an earlier age (statiscally about seven years earlier). Let's think about this for a moment. Do men die younger than women because they work harder or because they have more responsibilities, or because they are more `stressed' out than women? No, I believe men die earlier than women because they spend so little time acknowledging their emotional experience.

Men have a double burden. Our culture tells us emotions are for women and our work world tells us there is no room for emotions in a setting where the object is efficiency and getting the job done. Getting the job done is primarily intellectual or physical rather than emotional. How many memos ask the recipient what they feel about the content? It is almost always, "Pete, let me know what you think about this," instead of, "Pete, let me know what you feel about this."

I have noticed something interesting with male patients in management, investment, the professions, politics, and all levels of corporate life. When I ask these men what they are feeling they respond with, "I feel" and then proceed to tell me what they think. Often, when I point this out, they say,"I just told you what I feel." "No," I reply, "You just began a sentence with 'I feel' and then told me what you think." Also interesting to me is how often I ask business people what they feel and they tell me what someone else is thinking or doing to them.

"How do you feel about this decision to put three new people on the sales force?" I'll ask and the response may be, "I feel they are trying to take some of my commissions away and they won't be so interested in my policy suggestions." "Yes, and what does that leave you feeling?" "I just told you." "No you told me what you think." "I don't know, I guess I feel hurt." "Anything else?" "Hurt, maybe angry, yes angry, I've worked my rear end off to get to where I am with them and just as I am starting to make it, and figured I can afford the mortgage on the house we want, they add on these men who will be calling on accounts I built from scratch for this damn company. I'm furious. I can't afford to get hit in my pocket now with a new kid and a new house. I'm scared and I'm angry."

So finally, we get to feelings. It takes time and work to help these people know it is OK to let themselves know and express what they are feeling. This is very difficult for most of us. We have all kinds of ways of avoiding our emotions. We use everyday ego defenses to protect us from uncomfortable feelings and thoughts. We can dream away our emotions and forget our dreams in the morning. We can daydream and engage in fantasy without consciously acknowledging the emotions we experienced or if we have conscious awareness, we can acknowledge these emotions and integrate them into our personality organization.

The role of experiencing emotions is vitally important in maintaining our health as living human organisms. This is not to suggest that experiencing emotions will completely prevent physical dysfunction. All of us have a genetic predisposition to a physical and mental inheritance, but having a genetic predisposition to organic dysfunction, and a genetic clock, does not necessarily mean the dysfunction will emerge. It is possible that the degree to which we experience our emotions determines whether our genetic predisposition toward dysfunction can be temporarily or permanently postponed. We do not know enough.

The world is changing very quickly and massive amounts of new information are coming our way at an alarming rate. New discoveries are being made in almost every field: biology, medicine, neurophysics, and the study of the environment, to name but a few. The world of business is undergoing enormous change. As a result of the role of artificial intelligence in the Post Industrial Revolution, our whole conception of time is changing. Our view of time last changed at the beginning of the Industrial Revolution when people trooped off to factories and offices and had to get to where they were going on time. Now we must learn to deal with computer time or computime which plays a profound role in experiencing emotions. Even the way we look at time has changed in that we now read it digitally. For me, as a psychoanalyst and psychologist, the most profound changes are occurring in understanding the role of emotions in terms of how we experience ourselves as total living human organisms.

Jeremy Rifkin's book, *Time Wars*, is a fascinating study of time and efficiency. Rifkin speaks of how we have become less able to enjoy the present and reflect upon the past. He refers to the new Postindustrial or Information Age resulting from mass development and employment of artificial intelligence. The computer introduces a new time perspective different from the clock. One patient, a top management person in an organization known for its bureaucracy, says that with all the new advances in technology he feels he has become a slave of the computer. His ID card contains a computer chip. The chip informs the computer when he enters or leaves the building. It tells the computer what entrance or exit he used and whether or not he took his car from the organization's garage. He has electronic voice mail which follows him throughout the building as well as leaving messages for him. His computer is full of memos awaiting replies throughout the day. Everything has a time attached to it: his electronic mail, his computer, and his ID card. He says, "I feel like I don't have time to think things through the way I did in the past. I can't find the time to know what I'm feeling. I barely have time to know what I'm thinking. One thing I do know I feel – I feel victimized by efficiency."

Measuring time with a clock is well within our comprehension. We can experience a second, a minute, an hour, a day. What happens, however, when we begin to deal with the nanosecond as the primary way of measuring time? A nanosecond is a billionth of a second and cannot be measured by human experience. Rifkin points out that the snap of a finger is equivalent to the passage of 500 million nanoseconds. For him, "The new 'computime' represents the final abstraction of time and its complete separation from human experience and the rhythms of nature."[11]

We hear and talk a lot about stress. I don't believe in stress. Stress is a catch-all phrase much like: meaningful relationships, family values, appropriate behavior, interfacing, and sound bites. Stress does not sufficiently define what is going on within the person. If you want to talk about stress, you might as well talk about frustration; and if you mean the frustration of not knowing the unknown and feeling insecure, you have to acknowledge the defenses that go along with frustration such as anxiety, tension, and irritability. If you want to talk about stress then stress in relation to what? In relation to unresolved childhood conflicts? To unconscious ways of operating in the world? To wondering what others think about us? To what will happen next? To sitting on the edge of not knowing and calming one's self by constructing self-made realities to cope with frustration?

Rifkin reports a 1980 study by sociologist Louis Pratt showing 90 percent of American business companies granted official leave for bereavement. Most of these companies determined three days was the official amount of time for grief. Pratt believes changes in societal norms are a product of changing business practices. In 1927, Emily Post said the formal mourning period for a widow was three years. By 1950, formal mourning shrank to six months and in 1972, Amy Vanderbilt suggested widows should be back on their feet within a week or two.[12]

Psychologists know the grieving process consists of a number of stages over a period of three to five years, totaling an enormous number of nanoseconds. While no one is suggesting that official leave for bereavement should be three to five years, our internal experience of the grieving process has not shortened. People must explore ways of experiencing their emotions unless we are to become a nation of normopaths.

Rifkin further points to psychological studies of computer compulsives, people who have become impatient with the traditional clock culture. These studies find subjects are less tolerant of reflective, meditative, digressive personality types. The computer compulsives prefer direct yes-no responses and do not like face-to-face open ended conversations. Efficiency is lessening human interaction as well as emotional interaction. A colleague and dear friend, Jean Getoff, has said it quite well: "For the sake of short-term efficiency we are killing off long-term life. The more efficient we make them, the deader we make them."

What happens to emotions in a world of nanoseconds where personal reflection and pondering the past are met with contempt? Recovering memories and reliving them will eventually be regarded as an archaic waste of time. Reading for pleasure and experiencing one's accompanying fantasies will be regarded with disdain. We will be more removed from our inner psychic experiences than ever before. I do not watch the 11 o'clock news anymore because I cannot digest it. In the first ten minutes my senses are flooded with scenes of starving people in Africa, a pitbull who ate the neighbor's kid, a family of five perishing in a Harlem fire, the biggest drug bust in the city's history, a sound bite of nine words from President Clinton on the health bill, and last but not least, Mary-Jo Buttafuocco still protesting Joey's innocence.

This is an age in America in which the role of middle management is drastically changing. An age in which business ethics and practices related to hiring and termination, retirement, and health care issues are being applied quite differently from the traditional American perspective.

Fergus, a senior official in an international organization, was three years away from retirement when he was informed that his contract would not be renewed at his top level. As a result of budget cutbacks, he was told he could continue to be employed at a lower level. Fergus had a long and distinguished career with the organization and was well-known and respected both at headquarters and in the field. He could not tolerate the humiliation of employment at a lower status and could not afford to accept early retirement. Humiliation mounted and combined with unfelt, silent rage as word began to spread about his demotion. Fergus's belief in loyalty and his notions of dedication and hard work were now unfounded and left him depressed, helpless and hopeless. Within months, Fergus suffered a mild stroke which left his speech and gait impaired. The stroke became a metaphor reflecting Fergus's feelings that further talking was pointless and he was not ready "to walk" away from his career. It seems obvious had someone taken Fergus's humiliation into account in light of his distinguished career or had Fergus been able to deal more productively with his emotions, his resulting physical dysfunction might have been averted. There is an upheaval occurring in corporate management which, once again, as in past upheavals, appears to exclude some important psychological facts of life.

In a recent U.S. televised panel discussion on health care, it was estimated that by the year 2000, health care for each employee in the U.S. will cost $17,000 per year. It may be time for business to consider taking greater pre-emptive measures to reduce work-related health problems before they develop into full blown catastrophe.

I had lunch with a friend who is a family doctor. He complained of a new phenomenon regarding great numbers of people in his practice whom he regards as malingerers coming to him for doctors' notes. He believed people with nothing wrong with them paid him visits because it only cost them two dollars per visit on their health plans. He wanted to know why so many people were lazy and didn't want to work. I asked what kind of dysfunction they reported and he replied, headaches, insomnia, skin conditions, gastrointestinal and bowel problems.

Upon asking more about his practice, I learned a large number of his patients were blue collar workers and lower management people. My friend is a sensitive fellow and I know in the past he would ask patients what was happening in their families and at work. He finds he doesn't ask anymore because patients are assigned to him through health plans and the old doctor-patient relationship is quickly disappearing. I asked if any of these "malingerers" talked about their work. He replied that they were worried about job security and complained with big businesses buying out smaller ones and takeovers common, old notions of loyalty did not hold anymore.

I asked him if these people could be cutting off their feelings and having psychosomatic reactions. After a moment's thought he said, no, they just didn't want to work. This bright, sensitive, caring friend of mine does not want to consider the possibility that his patients are not dealing with their feelings about their jobs and instead are having psychosomatic reactions as real responses. He still regards psychosomatic dysfunction as malingering and is not alone in that position. Many corporations requiring doctors' notes for sick days regard employees' psychosomatic complaints as malingering.

In my practice, I have patients who are lawyers putting in 14-hour days, accountants who do not take vacations, housewives who have not been out to dinner and a film in months, couples in couples counseling who can't get to me as a couple, management people who cannot keep lunch time appointments with me because there is no lunch. About 95 percent of my practice does not take time out of their week to acknowledge what they feel. Many report that therapy is the only time they catch up with themselves. All these people are processing a bombardment of external stimuli without giving much of it any emotional meaning. We are just beginning to know that the emotions are physiologically responsible for prioritizing external reality.

When we feel our achievements are unrecognized and unrewarded, when we are bypassed for a promotion or feel unappreciated or misunderstood, when we are excluded from a conference or a convention, do not get an expected perk, or have unresolved feelings of hate, jealousy, envy, greed, or are looking for love instead of respect, we activate feelings consciously or unconsciously for which there may be no outlet within the structure of the organization.

Most of these feelings are not integrated into the work environment in any systematic manner. Going home and yelling at the kids, kicking the dog, or having an affair with the secretary at the office, may be a discharge or acting out of feelings. However, discharging or acting out the feeling is not the same as feeling the feeling. Discharge or acting out is instead of feeling. One may feel better temporarily but the feeling remains unexperienced.

Aldo, a patient of mine, has worked for many years in the restaurant business with his father. Aldo was never good enough for his father who put him down whenever he could. His father could not tolerate a son who might surpass him. Father and son fought constantly over business matters without ever arriving at their feelings about each other. After some 15 years of working with his father, Aldo was diagnosed with Leukemia. He underwent great doses of chemotherapy and became clinically depressed. He and his wife became more estranged. When I first met Aldo he was depressed and almost void of emotions. As Aldo and I worked together over a period of two years and he permitted himself to experience his emotions, he unraveled the story of the relationship with his father and it became quite clear the Leukemia was indeed a metaphor for the bad blood between them. Shortly after Aldo began experiencing his emotions he went into remission and became eligible for bone marrow transplants.

Forty years ago when I was in elementary school, we plodded through without teachers paying much attention to our emotions. Both teachers and kids knew whose parents were divorced, which kids had a parent who had died, who the abused kids were, and so on. None of these issues were ever talked about and everyone was expected to just do their work. Now schools are actively involved in dealing with childrens' emotions. Feelings have been brought into the classroom and children talk about them. School went from an institution which had nothing to do with feelings to one which invited emotions into many phases of education. I believe it is time for the corporation to do the same.

Many years ago I was in a corporate management training program. The program was terrible, the pay was terrible, the hours were terrible and no systematic training or evaluation took place. We were overworked and often ignored and I felt depressed, disappointed and afraid for my future. The people who were responsible for training us regarded us with resentment and secretly saw us as a threat. Many of the trainees had left and I was debating if I should remain in the program or return to school for a higher graduate degree. I met with Ted Bates, founder and President of Ted Bates Advertising. I presented my situation to him and asked for his advice. Mr. Bates told me to stick with it, keep a smile on my face, never complain and in 15 years I would be a vice president. That week I began applying to graduate programs in psychology. Ted Bates was absolutely correct. My colleagues who stayed in the program and kept smiling without complaint all became vice presidents within 15 years. The only problem was that some of them had developed hypertension, high blood pressure, ulcers, colitis, and heart disease within those same years.

We are fostering the genesis and development of work-related psychosomatic responses and disorders in individuals and groups by not allowing emotions to live. A patient employed as a social worker developed breast cancer some time after her mother died. The patient's mother had abandoned her when she was ten years old. The patient was terrified of connecting to her feelings of abandonment for fear that she would emotionally disintegrate and fall into a depression from which she would never return. The patient worked at a hospital with AIDS patients and was surrounded with death and dying. She wanted desperately to move to another area of work after her mother died and was informed that no positions were available within the hospital. The patient felt hopeless and trapped because looking for another job would mean she would not be eligible for continued health care benefits related to her cancer. A new job would mean a new health care insurance company that would not cover future cancer treatments which would be regarded as a pre-existing condition. Her superiors were unsympathetic and began questioning her performance as her hopelessness and despair continued to grow. Within that year the patient developed a deep depression, terrible migraines, and arthritis in her hands.

The stereotypic structure of the conventional workplace relies primarily upon logical, rational responses and a spirit of friendly competition where everyone works toward the goal of achieving what is best for the organization. Work offers a structured area in which stereotypic behavior is defined quite specifically, *i.e.*, we all know how to respond to situations stereotypically. This behavior aligns itself along a number of typical groupings which conform to society's expectations: men-women, white-people of color, young-old, boss-worker, white collar-blue collar, Christian-Jew, American-British. In all these categories social and professional responses may be anticipated without many surprises and conform to accepted expectations and norms. Often, individual responses, both cognitively and emotionally, conform to these cultural and economic splits. The anticipated, "correct" response may be predicted with near certainty depending where the responder falls on the socio-economic status ladder.

I hope I have not left you with the impression that we should surrender our intellect and spend our days experiencing our feelings. In any given situation the ideal would be to integrate what we think with what we feel. When we know what we think and feel about something we are able to formulate decisions using all our knowledge, intellectual and emotional.

Logical, rational, intellectual responses are the primary conscious operatives which basically disregard (or at best pay lip service to) the emotions and ignore unconscious individual and group dynamics occurring within the structure. One patient, a middle-management supervisor in an organization undergoing a large layoff, speaks of his fears: "I'm frightened all the time. I have been with this outfit for 30 years. I still have two kids in college. My daughter is getting married in August and my wife wants to return to school. I don't know what to do. I like my job and I can't afford to take an early out." "Is there anyone you can talk to?" I ask. He tells me he could talk to his supervisor but doesn't feel comfortable doing so. He then adds, "There is this 800 number you can call but then they treat you like you are unbalanced and recommend talking to their therapists. This is not my idea of empowerment if I can't even choose my therapist. No one talks to anyone about the situation because there is a general distrust of management."

Emotions are transmitters which permit the cells of the mind and body to communicate with each other. We must wonder what happens to this process of individual molecular cell communication within the individual while he or she operates within the confines of the workplace where, for the most part, people are asked to put their emotional lives on hold for some eight or more hours per day. Individuals are expected to respond to work experiences and situations with logic, rationality, and a determination of what is best for the organization. What does it do to us when we bar our emotions from consciousness where they might be processed? What effect does this demand for a kind of emotional animated suspension have on our vegetative organs and immune systems and in the possible creation of psychosomatic disorders which often begin with the appearance of anxiety, tension, and agitated depression as a result of the frustration of the workplace? While intellectual activity falls within the realm of socially accepted workplace responses, affective activity is either regarded as a professionally unacceptable response or is given insufficient credence.

In addition to our idiosyncratic defenses, we all operate with two major intellectual defenses which may be labeled: "negative predictions" and "mind reading." These serve the purpose of reducing one of the worst and most painful of anxieties, the anxiety resulting from not knowing. Rather than sitting on the edge and experiencing the anxiety accompanying the unknown, we prefer to engage in negative predictions that see the unknown outcome culminating in a negative conclusion. "They are laying off people and I know I will be one of them because of my age and high salary." Yvonne Agazarian, a Systems Centered psychotherapist, said that once one engages in negative predictions a mental map has been drawn in which the inevitability of a negative outcome is ensured. One has only to follow the map.

Mind reading serves much the same purpose. It also reduces anxiety over the unknown. Mind reading often constitutes a distortion of reality, confounds feelings by treating them as facts, and often disregards the collected data or assumes there is data where none exists. "The boss has never had a high regard for my work. He keeps me on because he feels sorry for me." If we inquire what the boss said or did to justify this statement by the mind reader, we may discover inconclusive evidence and elicit this typical response: "I don't know, it feels that way." The employment of negative predictions and mind reading defenses kills off experiencing the here and now.

If each of us were to take a few moments to develop an inventory of our own physical ailments and attempt to attach emotional meaning to them, we might come to realize which ailments are work-related and which hold elements of our life history. Many of our present-day ailments may appear in a workplace context where the crisis emerges although not necessarily where the cause exists, and therefore may require a psychological development data base for cure. Many psychosomatic ailments, emerging in adulthood, have their origins in childhood and adolescence which are unearthed during psychoanalysis.

Let us examine some of the emotional factors and personality constellations relating to early childhood and adolescence which develop into specific functional disturbances, using Alexander's psychodynamic groupings plus examples from my practice. Keep in mind that each person handles anxiety in a manner characteristic of him/herself, reflecting the specific defenses that person required to survive childhood. This is the meaning of the theory of emotional specificity in the etiology of vegetative diseases.

5. Cardiovascular Dysfunction

Howard came to see me at the insistence of his girlfriend Margaret who had been in treatment with me. He had once almost killed them both by slowing down in the left lane of a four-lane highway to make a u-turn. Margaret believed he was totally unaware of his hostility, his rage toward women, and his self-destructiveness. After meeting Howard, I knew she was correct.

Howard was an exceptionally bright, highly articulate, well-groomed, distinguished looking, upper echelon executive. Feeling physically exhausted, he would often call in sick and take to his bed for a day or two to restore himself. He experienced panic attacks at work when he believed his activities with prostitutes would be found out. He knew he was not liked and his level of production would come into question from time to time. He had read Freud and the more complicated Fenichel and believed therapy was only for those who had trouble functioning. According to Howard, functioning was not his problem.

Shortly after Howard began treatment, Margaret broke up with him. (This is often the case. The person about to break up gets the mate into treatment to soften the blow and let someone else pick up the pieces.) Howard was not particularly disturbed when Margaret ended their relationship. One might even say he hardly noticed.

Howard came from a wealthy Philadelphia mainline family. Life was quite comfortable for the first three years of his life. Suddenly, Howard's father, a well-known banker and womanizer, had a heart attack and died soon after at the age of 36. Howard and his mother moved into the paternal grandparents' mansion where they remained ensconced until Howard was 5 and his mother remarried. The step-father was not as well-off as Howard's father had been, although he loved Howard's mother and wished to legally adopt Howard.

Recounting his disappointment at moving out of his grandparents' home, Howard recalled a lonely childhood and parents who were neither very verbal nor emotional. An overweight child who retreated into a fantasy world of toy soldiers, Howard did well in school and became known for his intellectual abilities. He was on the debating team and ultimately went onto one of the top Ivy League schools. His college career, however, was undistinguished. Howard reported being depressed and in a free-floating fantasy world while at college. Somehow he managed to raise his grades enough to get into a respectable, though not Ivy League, law school.

Upon graduation, Howard came to New York and took a job with a well-known law firm. He was attracted to politics and prostitutes. Always figuring the angle but never quite on the mark, he was manipulative, controlling, subversive, and vengeful in his secretive, competitive strivings. He had almost no awareness of his effect on other people.

Naturally, the prostitutes and his co-workers did not hold Howard in high regard. He was often contemptuous and condescending. In his sessions with me he often raged about the people in his life, saying his mother and step-father were fools for not regarding his intellect with high esteem; the prostitutes were after all just prostitutes; his professional colleagues were fools who were unaware of his feminine conquests and his ability to run intellectual circles around them all. For all of his ranting in my office, Howard's rage never seemed connected to his inner psychic life. It was a kind of free-floating discharge of anger that made me wonder what he was really feeling.

When Howard raged about this or that person, I would ask if he had confronted the person with his feelings. He would regard me with contempt for asking and then slide into self-deprecation over how inadequate he felt in relation to the people he raged about. I inquired about the prostitutes, who from time to time moved in with him, only to find out they had some true love in their life Howard had been unaware of. I learned that Howard had very passive relationships with these women. They assumed dominant roles in bed and sometimes engaged in sado-masochistic activities in which Howard assumed a traditional passive-feminine role. He wanted the women to talk dirty to him, to urinate on him and to slap, bite, and spit on him. In his sexuality, Howard retreated into an extremely passive dependent attitude. Although not necessarily with regard to sexuality, a passive dependent attitude is frequently found in cardiovascular patients.

In fact, it came as no surprise to me when Howard was rushed to the hospital with a myocardial infarct shortly after learning someone else had received the promotion he had been expecting. In many ways, Howard demonstrated the specific personality structure outlined by Alexander. His anxiety and rages were well-noted as were his aggressive impulses that were never directed toward the people who upset him. To his friends and colleagues, Howard appeared in control of his life although his contempt was not appreciated. Only in his sex life did his passive dependent feminine tendencies emerge. Howard was afraid of expressing real hostility. His fear of his own hostility engulfed him with anxiety. His fear of real competition contributed to his feelings of inferiority and formed a vicious cycle of anxiety and self-deprecation.

When Howard recovered and returned to treatment he was scared but able to begin dealing with the loss of his father and his fears of becoming a man and dying at an early age as his father had done. He began to experience his broken heart and his anger at not having been allowed to grieve the loss of his father. He began to deal with his resentment toward his mother for remarrying and removing him from the bliss of his grandparents' home where he had felt loved. He has yet to work on his passive dependent needs and fear of his own hostility.

6. Chronic Diarrhea and Colitis

Jim was a 28-year-old homosexual, a hustler by profession, suffering from chronic diarrhea and colitis. His physical condition was interfering with his professional life as he was spending more time in the toilet than at the bar. Jim was a good looking, rugged, tall, blond guy who looked tough and in charge of himself which made him attractive to his clientele.

The youngest of three children and from a blue-collar family, Jim had two older sisters. It soon became clear that he was describing a schizophrenic mother with many hospitalizations. His father was a tool maker in a factory and spent his after-hours at the bar before coming home late enough to just say hello to the family and go to sleep. Jim was nine years younger than his next older sister and both sisters had married and moved out of the house before he was 10. Whenever his mother had a breakdown, it was left to Jim to call the police and have her hospitalized. His father and sisters refused to get involved. Miraculously, Jim did well in school and became interested in art. He graduated high school and was awarded a scholarship to a local college. In his last year of college he received a scholarship to study art in Rome. This changed his life.

Jim's first attacks of chronic diarrhea and colitis began when he left home. He returned to the States, settled in New York, and shared an apartment with a woman who had been a fellow student at college. When Jim became aware of the intense competition in New York's art world, he fell into a malaise and did not seek out work in his field. Despite his conscientious expressions of desire for real accomplishment, his reluctance to explore opportunities increased. He spent his nights at gay bars and, as he described it, sort of fell into hustling. As we talked about the life of a hustler, great dependency needs emerged as well as an overpowering wish to be nurtured and taken care of without having to reciprocate in any mutual adult fashion.

Jim adored his mother and felt loved by her. He excused her inability to take care of him because of her illness. He became self-sufficient long before he was developmentally ready and was not consciously aware of any resentment about his home situation. He was not particularly angry with his father who offered some nurturing on weekends when he would take Jim to the bar or fishing with his buddies. He excused his sisters as having lives of their own and families to take care of. Nowhere was there any evidence of his yearning to remain with his mother or any awareness of anyone ever being on his side in dealing with the world.

Whenever Jim talked about his mother he would fall into tears and speak of the tragedy of her life. When asked about the tragedy of *his* life, about his lack of a real childhood, his lack of feeling protected, about the trauma of calling the police to have her hospitalized, Jim would excuse himself to go to the bathroom and only return in time to end the session. These reactions continued throughout the first year of treatment. During that time, it became evident to Jim that I could be depended on and trusted to be there for him. As he came to recognize my role as the available mother he never had, he was able to relive his childhood and feel the loneliness, pain, and despair of having to bring himself up and how these feelings related to his unconscious wishes to find someone at the bars who would take care of him, recognize his artistic talents and carry him to fame.

He came to understand the chronic diarrhea as a metaphor for his inability to hold onto himself and as expressing the fact that he was crapping away his life. The colitis was his internal battle about closing off the possibility of making a life for himself and the conflicting wish to be taken care of as well as the wish to have fame handed to him so that he could take care of his mother, end her suffering, and be with her.

Near the end of the second year of treatment, Jim began to look for a job in earnest and found one as a designer in a major department store. By the end of the third year, he still had his job, was freelancing, and had a number of successful art shows. The chronic diarrhea and colitis diminished and finally ceased. He became ultimately involved with an older man who was a well-known person in the dance world. They became lovers and moved in together. As Jim's unconscious wishes for dependency connected to his emotions he began to feel his pain, his isolation, and his anger. Eventually, he was able to exchange his diarrhea and colitis for real accomplishments in the world.

7. Respiratory Disturbances

Élodie was the youngest of four children born to a French-Canadian bourgeois family residing in New England. She came to New York in pursuit of an acting career without achieving any success. She came to me because, after two years of marriage, she was getting a divorce. Her husband informed her that he had come to realize he was homosexual and had, in fact, recently taken a lover. Élodie did not seem as upset by her husband's announcement as she was by the prospect of divorce. The idea of separation terrified her, so did the idea of being a guilty, divorced woman with a secret in the eyes of the Roman Catholic Church. She wanted to get an annulment on the grounds that she and her husband had not consummated their marriage, but her husband would not agree to this. Almost immediately after learning of her husband's refusal, Élodie began experiencing terrible asthma attacks. She soon revealed a history of asthma from early childhood.

Élodie's father was a musician who worked evenings and her mother was a housewife who was eternally exhausted and found pleasure in her oldest child and only son whom the sisters referred to as The King. Her mother made no effort to conceal the fact that Élodie was unwanted but was the wish of God. She claimed to love Élodie but always reminded her that her birth had been difficult and Mama had nearly died. Mother kept the entire family in a state of guilt. She constantly reminded them that she would have become a nun had she not married their father.

Not surprisingly, by age 3 Élodie had developed asthma. Mama was wonderful: staying up whole nights with her, taking her to specialists with the family's last pennies, preparing special dishes for her and taking her to the seashore for fresh air–while telling Élodie how her medical bills kept her from having the washing machine and fur coat she had always wanted. Nevertheless, she was Mama's favorite daughter and should not tell this to her sisters. Mama was a professional at creating secrets and guilt. Élodie came to believe she would not have survived her asthma without her mother's care and devotion. At the same time she existed in a state of profound guilt over the asthma which she believed kept the family poor and her mother from the other siblings. Being special came with the high price of keeping secrets and experiencing guilt.

I wondered how Élodie had ever managed to separate from this mother and find her way to New York. I soon learned that she phoned her mother six to ten times a day. She had a part-time job with an 800 number phone and could get most of her calls in during working hours. Eventually she came to realize that her husband unconsciously was her mother in his constant criticisms and guilt-provoking statements. Psychically and emotionally, Élodie had never left home and mother.

As treatment progressed, Élodie began to experience her anger at her unconsciously seductive, consciously critical, rejecting mother. She also began to feel angry with her absent, passive father who did not protect her from this mother. Her anger moved into sadness and for the first time in her life, she found herself crying. Alexander reports that most asthmatics find it difficult to cry and asthma attacks often end with crying. The suppression of tears often leads to asthmatic attacks. Élodie's specialness had alienated her from her siblings at the same time it supplied her with a specialness, mixed with tremendous guilt.

Élodie was now able to psychologically separate from her mother for the first time. She learned that her marriage could be annulled without her husband having to say the marriage had not been consummated. With the realization that her husband was a new edition of her mother, she was able to end the marriage without much difficulty. The asthma attacks grew rare. Élodie met John at a biking club and they were married about a year later. The following year Élodie terminated treatment which coincided with the birth of her first daughter. That was about 10 years ago.

A few months ago, I received a telephone call from Élodie. Other than her annual Christmas cards, informing me that all was well and the asthma attacks seemed to occur only during the allergy season, I had not heard from her. She called to inform me that her mother had died and she was having difficulty mourning. Once again the tears would not come. The asthma attacks had become more frequent. I suggested she come in and we are presently engaged in short-term therapy to help her connect to her grief.

With Élodie we see a rather common nucleus of developmental psychodynamic features contributing to the genesis of asthma rather than to some other organic dysfunction: an unconsciously seductive, consciously rejecting, guilt-provoking mother and a nearly absent father; a somatic condition which leads to an excessive dependence on the mother, including a need to feel protected. What is interesting, too, is Alexander's observation that asthmatics improve when the patient confesses to something he or she feels guilty about and expects rejection. He also notes the asthmatic's general inability to cry except after an attack.

8. Migraine Headaches, Hypertension, and Arthritis

Migraine headaches, hypertension, and arthritis are found on a progressive continuum in people who are not consciously aware of their feelings of envy and their destructive hostile impulses.

Amos came to see me when his wife of 35 years announced she wanted a divorce and moved out of their home. He was astonished by her decision which he reported as coming out of nowhere. He owned a large corporation with offices throughout the East coast. Outwardly, he looked like the model corporate owner, chairman of the board type. Internally, he suffered violent migraine headaches, hypertension and severe attacks of arthritis. Now approaching 60, Amos was terrified at the prospect of being alone.

In his marriage and professional life, he was a decisive decision maker. He knew what was best for everyone and tolerated little or no argument. Since he was usually correct in his evaluation of situations, he continued to reaffirm his beliefs and others' belief in him. He seemed quite unaware that his wife and three children resented his self-proclaimed perfection. He was not an easy person to live with or work for.

Amos had grown up in a small town, the eldest of three children. He did well in school but had few friends. His father was a well-to-do business man with one social flaw: he had a mistress in town and everyone knew about her. Amos' mother suffered silently and stoically. His father spent Sundays with his mistress and paraded her to restaurants and the local movie house.

Amos repressed his own humiliation while growing up and devoted himself to his mother and two sisters. He loved his mother dearly and wished to become wealthy enough to take her away from his father and the shame that had been thrust upon the family. Amos did become rich but could not save his mother. She died during his last year of college.

Although Amos had superior intelligence, he never regarded himself as a "naturally smart" person. He saw professional people–doctors, lawyers, academics–as the truly smart people and had great envy and contempt for them. Amos's contempt for me was profound. He hated having to come to therapy and hated me for knowing about emotions and unconscious processes which he referred to as "bunk." He hated the idea that people could know something he didn't, unless they were exceptionally powerful, well-known men. Amos had never been able to confront his father about the consequences of his behavior upon the family. He feared his father and envisioned him as an extraordinarily powerful man within the confines of their small hometown.

Amos married his college sweetheart directly after graduation. He was a model of fidelity, although he left the child-rearing to his wife. One of his great regrets in therapy was that he never got to know his children. His wife was a devoted mother who also pursued her creative development after graduating with a fine arts degree. Although Amos did not take her talent seriously, which she knew and resented, he did buy and present her with an art gallery that she successfully developed.

Amos was proud of Abby as a wife and mother although, as with his children, he barely knew her. Their sex life was a history of premature ejaculations and pretense at orgasms. All her attempts to discuss their sex life were met with embarrassment and silence on Amos's part. Although Amos was exceptionally intelligent about the world, he knew little about sex. He grew up mistakenly believing that people who "touched" themselves were homosexual. He feared touching himself or his wife but could not bring himself to discuss any of these issues with her. After Abby had separated she informed Amos that she had a lover.

I suggested to Amos that he may have unconsciously set Abby up to become like his father, and himself like his mother. He now had a symbolic representation of his father whom he could finally confront while he identified with his mother's despair. Amos had never grieved the loss of his mother.

For the first time, Amos was able to look at his anger at his father and experience his deep humiliation. He allowed himself to grieve his mother. As he gave himself permission to feel, he became more human, experiencing a new-found warmth in relationships. He grew closer to his children and Abby noticed subtle changes in him, and then more distinct changes. About a year later, they reunited. The migraines and hypertension have all but vanished and the arthritis is considerably improved.

I have presented these cases of psychosomatic dysfunction to demonstrate the developmental origins of psychosomatic dysfunction. Our early unresolved emotional issues become intensified as we move into adulthood. The workplace invites a playing field for new editions of old issues. The standard paradigm, impacting on the workplace, consists of rational, logical conscious responses people employ in accommodating and assimilating new information and with little and usually no acknowledgment of emotions. Unconscious activities–with which we all operate all of the time–such as transference, projective identification and the repetition compulsion are nowhere to be found. These on-going unconscious dynamics confound the rational, logical atmosphere of the workplace without ever being acknowledged, much less discussed.

By transference, we mean the unconscious act of transferring past thoughts, moods, feelings, images, impulses, and even actions onto present-day individuals and situations. In projection, we unconsciously ascribe to others thoughts, feelings and deeds we do not like or wish to acknowledge in ourselves. As if the rational, logical world of intellect and comprehension is not interrupted enough by transference and projections, we add still another component, the repetition compulsion, an unconscious acting out of an issue, instead of holding it in and recalling it from memory. With the compulsion to repeat, we unconsciously attempt to create new editions of unfinished business from the past in the present with the goal of finally tacking on a happy ending. Because all of us are engaged in these unconscious dynamics a great deal, if not all of the time, one must wonder how we get any work done at all.

When people fall ill there is not always a spontaneous outburst but rather a slow-growing dynamic, often expressed through a variety of symptoms. Productivity in the workplace slowly diminishes when people are made to feel they are cheating or their discomfort is illegitimate. We hear a lot these days about the problems of productivity in society. We cannot have a hopeless workforce without a loss of productivity. The cry for greater and greater productivity cannot be at the price of the health of our working population. It is not cost-effective for any of the concerned parties. Management must come to terms with what the real costs are in relation to the quality of human life in the world of work. For society to address the current productivity problem, we need to see the person as whole in the workplace and not through myopic stereotyped lenses.

We are learning a great deal about the role of emotions on health. We know we cause our bodies to dysfunction when we are not connected to our emotions and when we are not being listened to. We need to learn how we can bring our emotions to work with us and incorporate our feelings in our work and in our professional interactions. We need to find ways to encourage people to talk about their feelings related to their work and to who they are. The expression of emotion has to become professionally acceptable. Let us make work contribute to health, not detract from it.

Notes

1. Franz Alexander. 1950, p.12.
2. Carl M. Grossman and Sylvia Grossman, p.80.
3. Franz Alexander. 1950, p.35.
4. *Ibid.*, p.38.
5. Ella Freeman Sharpe, pp.154-55.
6. *Ibid.*, p.155.
7. J. Laplanche and J.B. Pontalis
8. Joyce McDougall. 1989, p.23.
9. *Ibid.*, p.21.
10. *Ibid.*, p.27.
11. Jeremy Rifkin, p.2.
12. *Ibid.*, p.62.

References

Ader, Robert. "Experimentally Induced Gastric Lesions: Results and Implications of Studies in Animals." In Duodenal Ulcer. ed. by Herbert Weiner, Kerger & Basel: Switzerland, 1971.

________. ed. *Psychoneuroimmunology.* New York:Academic Press, 1981.

________. "The Placebo Effect as a Conditional Response." *Experimental Foundations of Behavioral Medicine: Conditioning Approaches,* ed. Robert Ader, Herbert Weiner, and Andrew Baum. Hillsdale, N.J.: Erlbaum, 1988.

Agazarian, Yvonne. "A Theory of Living Human Systems and the Practice of Systems-Centered Psychotherapy." Special Presentation at The Thirty-Seventh Annual Meeting of The American Group Psychotherapy Association. 15 February 1993, San Diego, California.

Alexander, F. *Psychosomatic Medicine: Its Principles and Applications.* New York: W.W. Norton & Co., Inc., 1950.

________. *The Scope Of Psychoanalysis.* 1921-1961. New York: Basic Books, 1961.

Banki, Csaba M., Lajos Karmacsi, Garth Bissette, and Charles Nemeroff. "Cerebrospinal Fluid Neuropeptides in Dementia." *Biological Psychiatry*, 32 (1992), 452-456.

Bion, W.R. *Learning from Experience.* New York: Basic Books, 1962.

Breuer, Josef and Sigmund Freud. *Studies on Hysteria*. In *The Standard Edition of the Complete Psychological Works of Sigmund Freud.* Vol. 2. London: The Hogarth Press, 1971.

Burger, Chester. *Executive Etiquette.* London: Collier-Macmillan Ltd., 1970.

Cannon, Walter B. *Bodily Changes in Pain, Hunger, Fear, and Rage.* New York: Harper and Row, 1963.

Chen, Doreen, M.D., "The Traditional Role of Acupuncture in Chinese Medicine: Mind-Body Issues; Points of Therapeutic Contact." A Symposium. Presented by The Institute for Expressive Analysis. New York, Spring 1992.

Cooper, Jack R., Floyd E. Bloom, and Robert H. Roth. *The Biochemical Basis of Neuropharmacology.* New York: Oxford University Press, 1978, pp. 259-281.

Davanloo, H., ed., *Short-Term Dynamic Psychotherapy*. London: Jason Aronson Inc., 1992.

Dienstfrey, Harris. *Where the Mind Meets the Body.* New York: HarperCollins, 1991.

Dunbar, F. *Emotions and Bodily Changes.* 3rd ed. New York: Columbia University Press, 1947.

Groddeck, Georg. *The Book of the It.* London: Vintage Books, 1949.

Grossman, Carl M. and Sylvia Grossman. *The Wild Analyst.* London: Barrie and Rockcliff, 1965.

Laplanche, J. and J. B. Pontalis. *The Language of Psychoanalysis*. London: The Hogarth Press, 1973.

McDougall, Joyce. *Theaters of the Mind: Illusion and Truth on the Psychoanalytic Stage.* New York: Basic Books, 1985.

________. *Theaters of the Body: A Psychoanalytic Approach to Psychosomatic Illness.* New York: WW Norton & Co., 1989.

Moyers, Bill. *Healing and the Mind.* New York: Doubleday, 1993.

Neemeroff, Charles B. "New Vistas in Neuropeptide Research in Neuropsychiatry: Focus on Corticotropin-Releasing Factor." *Neuropsychopharmacology*: 2 (1992), pp. 69-73.

Nemiah, J. "Alexithymia and Psychosomatic Illness." *Journal of Continuing Education in Psychiatry,* 1978, pp. 25-37.

Nemiah, J. and P. Sifneos. "Affect and Fantasy in Patients with Psychosomatic Disorders." *Modern Trends in Psychosomatic Medicine*. London: Butterworth, 1970. Vol. 2.

Pert, Candace B. "The Wisdom of the Receptors." *Advances.* (Summer 1986) Institute of Noetic Sciences, 475 Gate Road, Sausalito, California 94965, USA.

Pert, Candace B. and Solomon H. Snyder. "Opiate Receptor: Demonstration in Nervous Tissue." *Science*, 179:9 March 1973

Pert, Candace B. *et al.* "Neuropeptides and their Receptors: A Psychosomatic Network." *Journal of Immunology*, 135:2 (August, 1985).

Rifkin, Jeremy. *Time Wars: The Primary Conflict in Human History*. New York: Simon & Schuster Inc., 1973.

Rose, Steven. *The Conscious Brain.* New York: Vintage Books, 1976.

Ruff, Michael and Candace B. Pert. "Neuropeptides Are Chemoattractants for Human Monocytes and Tumor Cells: A Basis for Mind-Body Communication." In *Enkephalins and Endorphins Stress and the Immune System*, eds. Nicholas P. Plotnikoff, *et al.* New York, Plenum Publishing Corporation, 1986.

Sifneos, Peter E. "Motivation for Change." In *Short-Term Dynamic Psychotherapy.* ed. by Habib Davanloo. London: Jason Aronson Inc., 1992.

_______. 1975. "Problems in Psychotherapy in Patients Characteristics and Physical Disease." *Psychotherapy and Psychosomatics*, 26, 65-70.

Sharpe, Ella Freeman. *Collected Papers on Psycho-analysis*. New York: Brunner/Mazel, 1950.

Tublitz, N., D. Brink, K.S. Broadie, P.K. Loi, and A.W. Sylwester. "From Behavior to Molecules: An Integrated Approach to the Study of Neuropeptides." *Hormone Research*, 3 (1992), 16-21.

Winnicott, D.W. *The Maturational Processes and the Facilitating Environment*. London: The Hogarth Press. 1965.

Chapter Three

LEISURE AS THE BASIS OF WORK TOWARD A UNIFIED LIFE

Michael J. Naughton

Whenever I ask audiences what the first word they think of when the hear the word *work*, I receive responses along three categories: (1) *Job*: money, income, hard, necessary (evil), Monday, boring, monotonous, toil, and with the proficient and expanded vocabulary of my university students, "yuck." Behind such words lie a meaning and value of work restricted to economic rewards. (2) *Career*: creativity, advancement, opportunity, personal satisfaction, self-esteem, self-reliance, etc. Behind these words lie a meaning and value of work restricted to psychological rewards. (3) *Vocation*: witness, community, contribution to society, vocation, common good, collaboration with God, stewardship, etc. And behind these words indicate the meaning and value of work lies primarily in moral and spiritual terms.[1] This last category, as one might suspect, is the least cited.

The three categories are not necessarily exclusive. One's work can be hard and toilsome but the person can still find personal satisfaction as well as contribute to society (parenting for example). However, work is often understood as having its ultimate meaning in either the financial rewards given (job), or the psychological satisfaction acquired (career).[2] This state of affairs, I argue, is extremely problematic for the Christian life. It is problematic not only because of the obvious materialism and egoism implied in work viewed as a job or a career, but also because of the notion of leisure associated with such understandings of work.

I argue in this paper that to understand the meaning of work, once must provide an understanding of leisure, since both leisure and work constitute the two most essential dimensions of one's life. Karl Rahner points out that both leisure and work mean "not two periods of time in human life, but simply moments in a person's self-realization which exist only in their relation with one another and are the primary constituents of human existence itself."[3] The notion that work and leisure have little to do with each other for certain people may be true, but it is true in a life that represents conflict and disunity (the Catholic in the Mafia or the pacifist in the defense industry). For Rahner as well as the Christian social tradition, self-realization is a unified life of work and leisure.

For many people, the meaning of work stems fundamentally from the leisure one takes. As Aristotle points out, we work to attain leisure. Leisure constitutes a category that describes happiness. It provides the end and purpose of human life (although not for the careerist). It is that time which provides the significance of work, as well as for that which one is destined. This is why an understanding of leisure is so important for the meaning of work. A philosophy or theology of work often has as its basis in a philosophy or theology of leisure. It is precisely a reflection on leisure where the fundamental meaning of one's life is made explicit. The meaning of work is only intelligible in terms of a larger framework where "unity resides in the unity of a narrative which links birth to life to death as narrative beginning to middle to end."[4] This narrative is found fundamentally in leisure, but it is lived in the interrelationship between leisure and work.[5]

Before discussing the various meanings of work and leisure, two general comments may be helpful for the discussion. (1) When people work, they incur two changes: an object in the form of a good or service (transitive), and the subject, namely, the person who works (intransitive). Work is directed toward a specific object outside of the subject who works, whether that object takes the form of a good or a service. At the same time, like all human activity, work has a self-determining dimension that penetrates the subject.[6] A mutual influence exists between the changes of the person who works and the changes that takes the form of goods and services. The object that is created has a dynamic effect on the formation of the worker's character. Not only is the object changed by the subject, but the subject is changed by the object.

Leisure, as an activity, also has a subjective and objective effect. In terms of its subjective formation, leisure as Pieper explains, is a form of contemplation where one opens "one's eyes receptively to whatever offers itself to one's vision, and the things seen enter into us, so to speak, without calling for any effort or strain on our part to possess them."[7] Fundamentally, to have leisure is to have rest in something one contemplates on. This rest has a fundamental effect on who the person is. In terms of its objective formation, leisure forms a significant part of one's culture. In leisure and work both the person and the society in which one resides are taking shape to a significant degree. The shape that takes place is determined in the interrelationship of work and leisure. Work and leisure influence each which determines the normative notion of each.

This mutual influence implies that the line between work and leisure are not distinct.[8] The more interconnected work and leisure become, the more likely one will attain a unified life. A unified life is the harmonization between one's leisure and one's work. One can even say that work becomes more humane and fulfilling the more it becomes like leisure.

The key to this chapter rests in the normative meaning of leisure and work.[9] Below I outline three possibilities of a unified life. The first two I argue are normatively undesirable and in the end destructive of the self as well as society. The first model restricts work to an economic means that serves to maximize consumption in leisure. This is problematic since it makes work an undignified activity with no significant meaning, which if it could be avoided should be. The second model restricts leisure to regenerative function that serves to enhance one's status and self-esteem at work. This is problematic since it makes leisure an undignified activity with no significant meaning except in terms of its enhancement of work. While the economic and psychological dimensions of work and leisure are important, they are deficient by themselves since they are unable to appropriate a meaning of work that links individuals to one another and to God. The third model provides dignity and meaning to both leisure and work, and which I take to be the desirable model for a unified life.[10] The vocational model does not subordinate work completely to leisure nor leisure to work (although undermining the dignity of work is a temptation). Work understood as a vocation and leisure understood in terms of worship provides a unified life on a moral and spiritual level that is not attainable by the other two models.

1. Job: Instrumentalization of Work to Maximize Consumption

In her interview with Studs Terkel, Nora Watson provides a stark and seasoned view of work as a job.

> Jobs are not big enough for people. It's not just the assembly line worker whose job is too small for his spirit, you know? A job like mine if you really put your spirit into it, you would sabotage immediately. You don't dare. So you absent your spirit from it. My mind has been so divorced from my job, except as a source of income, it's really absurd.[11]

For Nora Watson and so many like her, work understood as a job is devoid of any meaning except economic meaning. A job centers on the means by which people make money so as to consume goods. As Robert Bellah *et al.* states, a job "supports a self defined by economic success, security, and all that money can buy."[12] The ultimate value of one's job, then, lies in its ability to further one's consumption. As Mike Royko points out, "If work is so good, how come they have to pay us to do it?"[13] Of course the economic view of work is not always by choice. Because of low wages (real employee wages have decreased since 1973),[14] and poor work design, some organizations eliminate any meaning from work besides an economic one. But either because of this structural reason or some other reason work is often look upon merely as an economic activity.

Work understood only as an economic means has always been around. However, it takes on a systematic meaning in this century with Frederick Taylor's scientific management, who has been considered one of the most influential persons of the twentieth- century organization. According to Taylor, work is fundamentally an economic endeavor. The value of work is judged by the monetary benefits received, consequently, worker motivation is confined to so-called extrinsic rewards. Maximizing these extrinsic benefits is seen as the ultimate value or goal of work for the worker.

For employers, the benefit of tapping worker's economic nature results in increased efficiency, productivity, and profitability. Any sort of intrinsic value, such as a worker's psychological, moral or spiritual satisfaction, is relegated to the non-work life. Work, according to this view, is equated with "making a living,"–exclusively an economic living. Nels Anderson, writing under the sponsorship of the UNESCO Institute for Social Science, articulates Taylor's belief about economic primacy:

> That the workplace does not utilize his whole personality is of little concern: he [the worker] would probably resist that because the major part of his personality finds expression in the nonwork sphere. It is in the nonwork sphere that he looks for the satisfaction which counts for him. What he wants mainly from the work place is money, and in this respect the manager is no different. He too would leave the enterprise for a better job with higher pay.[15]

Since work is only an economic activity, its organizational aspects should reflect this economic reality.[16] Anderson fails to point out that work has a subjective effect on the person which influences how one views leisure. If work is viewed as merely economic rewards, leisure becomes the place in which the rewards are spent. This point is discussed latter in the paper.

The problems with work viewed as a job are many, most notably, its tendency toward materialism. According to a study of several opinion surveys, workers in various occupations are increasingly defining themselves in terms of what they earn and have, what one author calls the "new money maniacs."[17] The value of work is defined by its extrinsic attributes, such as, wages, bonuses, vacation pay, perks, and working conditions. The better the material benefits the better the work. For the worker, labor is reduced to its compensation. Work is nothing more than a commodity, in which the exchange is based on monetary value.

This attitude toward compensation has influenced and has been influenced by an instrumentalist view of management. In this view of management, managers see employees and customers only in terms of efficient means to particular financial ends. Once this role of efficiency is stripped, "the individual means little or nothing."[18] Concerning employee relations, workers are valued simply on their financial worth to the company. For example, in the business ethics class I teach we discuss Jim Sawyer whose alcoholism is negatively affecting his job performance. Most students in the course argue that the company should seek treatment for Sawyer not because he is a human being, but to replace and retrain another employee with Sawyer's qualification would be too costly. One student who had personal experience with this situation told the class that he fired an alcoholic employee because her value (namely, she was unskilled) did not warrant the time and resources of management. What amazed me about the whole discussion was that many students had no other language in which to evaluate the case other than whether the costs of treatment exceeded benefits to the company.[19]

With work described as a monetary tool, leisure often becomes an activity of "having" more not with "being" more. One works for leisure, that is, one works for the weekend. Connected with a job, leisure is often viewed as entertainment (sports–watching and performing, TV watching, video games, movies, bars, etc.) and consumption (shopping). It is valued in terms of its ability to amuse.[20] Jacques Ellul states that leisure is something that distracts the person. "Instead of being the moment when man, because he is no longer in the grip of everyday worries, rediscovers himself, thinking about what he is and what he ought to be, leisure becomes on the contrary the moment when amusements succeed to the maximum in making him forget."[21] Instead of discovering and penetrating the mysteries of one's being, leisure provides an escape from reality through various amusements. Leisure is a time to get away from reality not a time to penetrate it. One enters the activities of sport, music, TV, movies, travel, etc. not to become more human, but to become more isolated in the world of amusement. Leisure, in this way, is understood largely in individualistic terms, that is, how does leisure serve the individual. It has little to do with human flourishing that has any appreciation for the social or spiritual nature of the person.

Juliet Schor points out that since 1948, productivity in the US grew annually between one and three percent. The increase in productivity provided a choice between either more free time or more consumption. Americans choose consumption and consequently more work. The average American owns and consumes twice as much as he/she did in 1948. To maintain such consumption patterns work time could not be reduced. Schor argues that despite conventional wisdom, work hours in the last two decades has actually increased.[22] Surveys report that Americans average 16.5 hours of leisure a week, "which has decreased by as much as one third since the early 1970s" from 26 hours.[23] Of that time they have in leisure, Americans have spent an increasing amount of it shopping and being entertained. Schor points out that in cross-country comparisons, Americans shop more than anyone else. Americans shop three to four times as many hours as Western Europeans. "They also spend a higher fraction of the money they earn. And with the explosion of consumer debt, many are now spending what they haven't earned."[24] Shopping has become the "most popular weekday evening `out-of-home-entertainment.'"[25] Whereas shopping was once a necessary chore, today its a form of entertainment to see the latest fashions. Concerning entertainment, the picture is similar. Gary Burtless points out that,

> In the past 20 years the amount of time devoted to watching television has climbed faster than the average amount of free time. To judge by their actual behavior, most Americans who complain they enjoy too little leisure are struggling to find a few extra minutes to watch Oprah Winfrey and *L.A. Law.*[26]

Ironically, such an increase in consumption and entertainment has come at a price of more work to finance such consumptive habits which has led to less free time to shop and be entertained. Hence shopping has become more entertaining (note the Mall of America) and entertainment more exotic. With limited time, the experience of leisure is intensified to make up for the lack of time.

When leisure is totally restricted to entertainment and consumption, it fails to do precisely what it is supposed to do–provide rest as well as happiness. When people are consumed in a substantial amount of entertainment, they are far from relaxed or rested. Instead, they become restless, dis-eased, or tired. Too much sleep makes one tired, sluggish, and apathetic. Too much entertainment makes one bored, restless, and anxious. It is what Pieper describes as *acedia* (one of the seven capital vices), a spiritual poverty that stems from sloth, despair or boredom. *Acedia* or idleness or sloth is a "deep-seated lack of calm which makes leisure impossible." It is a restlessness that does not mean only inactivity as commonly understood, but rather, as Kierkegaard noted, a "despairing refusal to be oneself."[27] The *acedia* results from failing to ask what things ultimately are. It is a failure to marvel at the ordinary and to experience its mystery.[28]

This is not to say that entertainment or consumption are inherently bad. Instead, it is to say that this form of leisure will not provide rest by itself. Leisure understood only in terms of entertainment lacks meaning that is satisfactory to the human heart. It lacks meaning, since much of its basis lies on the pursuit of pleasure and the avoidance of pain principle. Leisure understood in these terms essentially leads to boredom, which either makes people complacent (the couch potato) or search for more exotic leisure activities.[29]

If leisure is to provide rest, then it is not just a result of external factors. It is not just spare time, amusement, entertainment, free-time, vacation, a weekend, etc. It is not non-activity of the mind. Instead, leisure is fundamentally contemplation. As Pieper states, leisure is an "attitude of the mind and a internal condition of soul that fosters a capacity to perceive the reality of the world." It is a form of silence that serves as a precondition to understanding reality. Silence, however, does not, in this context, "mean `dumbness' or `noiselessness.'" Instead, silence is that power of the soul to receive that answer of reality, not only on occasion, but to live it in every aspect of one's life.[30] Leisure enables one to have wholeness by understanding one's life in terms of reality, namely a created reality. Pieper warns, however, that "unless we substitute true leisure for our hectic amusements, we will destroy our culture–and ourselves."[31]

2. Career: The Glorification of Work and the Instrumentalization of Leisure

With the increasing education and skills of people, work understood as a job is becoming less prominent, although as pointed out above, it is still significant. Particularly with the participative or high involvement management phenomena, work is increasingly becoming valued in psychological terms. The worker is defined "by a sense of expanding power and competency that renders work itself a source of self-esteem."[32] In addition to supplying material goods, work as a career ought to contribute to the development of one's psychological health by being creative, autonomous, and fulfilling. People who perceive work as a career expect more out of their work than those who perceive work as a job. Their career becomes an important means to their own self-esteem.

Articulating work viewed as a career are theorists from the Human Relations School. Reacting to Taylor's extrinsic perspective to work, this school represented by theorists such as Frederick Herzberg, Chris Argyris, Rene Likert, and Douglas McGregor sought to tap the internal potentialities of workers. They stress psychological needs of the person, indicating the person's capacity for growth and self-realization within the workplace. Workers have the capacities to achieve a humane as well as an effective workplace. According to Herzberg, while extrinsic factors are important in the workplace, they are not the factors on which to build a successful organization. Workers need to be organized in such a way as to know that their contribution is significant. No matter what workers are paid, when they are organized in a purely extrinsic way their potentialities are untapped. They are unable to contribute to a more efficient and profitable workplace. Workers who are not satisfied, and for Herzberg this is rooted in the psyche, fail to contribute their full selves.[33]

The corrective Humanism offers to Taylorism is commendable. However, its primary emphasis on the psychological nature of the person suffers from a lack of social vision. When the psychological nature of the person dominates as the primary category of understanding work, work can become subservient or hostage to various sets of individual psychological needs at the expense of social needs.[34] The fulfillment of these needs may or may not serve the public welfare. William F. May points out that the very word *career* points to individualistic tendencies. He explains that the words *car* and *career* have the same etymological root. They both refer to movement, and increasingly a private way of movement. With the massive highway infrastructure in the west, one's "*auto*-mobile" or self-driven car lets the person travel alone. Even though the car drives one out into society, it does so with a "glass-enwrapped privacy" that shields one from travelling with others.

In similar terms, the careerist calculates his/her travels not in public but in private terms. Like the privacy of a car, the careerist is interested in what means, in terms of education, contacts, money, skill, power, etc., are necessary to get from here to there. While the activities of careerists are within the law, they have little connection to the public good. As May points out, "questions of public obligation and responsibility seem marginal and episodic at best, distracting and suicidal at worst. The careerist travels by public thoroughfares and largely obeys the rules of the road, but toward his or her own private destination."[35]

The goal of self-actualization attempted by the notion of a career is noble; however, unless self-actualization is rooted in a correct notion of the human good, its tendency toward selfishness becomes ever greater. The corporate financial officer arranging multi-million dollar mergers or the marketing agents for large tobacco companies may find their work fulfilling, exciting, and creative. But does that mean their supposed self-actualization and personal creativity contribute to the human good? When their labor may contribute to displaced workers, ill-health, and social disruption can they truly be satisfied? In other words, careerists detach their work from the larger social good since they unable to conceptualize a good that transcends their own interests narrowly understood.

Careerists have difficulty in engaging in moral debate over their work. At best they can engage in a therapeutic understanding about their work. Work often becomes personal and private unto which only the individual is able to give meaning. The careerist participates in what MacIntyre calls the emotivist project where "all evaluative judgments and more specifically all moral judgments are *nothing but* expression of preference, expressions of attitude or feeling, insofar as they are moral or evaluative in character."[36] Any discussion of the meaning of work on any public level becomes almost incomprehensible for the careerist, since meaning is a private affair.

With work as the source of personal meaning and self-esteem, leisure often becomes understood as a "regenerative function."[37] This can be seen for two reasons: (1) Internal Intentions: For those who see work as the fundamental locus of meaning and self-esteem, leisure is not only a break *from* work but leisure is also *for* work in order to get rested to go back to work in a more productive way.[38] Leisure serves as a tension release; however, it is not done for its own sake. Whether the coffee break, Sunday worship, or time with the family, leisure is viewed as a means of renewal to be more efficient at work, not as an end in and of itself. Leisure is a means to make better workers for a more productive, efficient and profitable enterprise. It is merely another productive function. For careerists, the dictum is not "we work to live," but, "we live to work."[39] They fear retirement not because of economic necessities but "because of a gnawing fear that their idleness will lower their prestige in a work-oriented society that confers status only on active producers."[40] (2) External Pressures: Careerism can also be foisted upon people. For people to succeed in organizations there is great pressure to work long hours at an intense pace. Leisure is either literally squeezed out or people are so tired that all they wish to do is to rest up for the next day through extra sleep or television watching. Schor notes that the only nation that works more than the USA, Japan, is the only nation to watch more TV than the USA.[41]

The presence of careerism and its apprehension of leisure has had a significant effect on education in the US. Pieper points out that "leisure in Greek means *skole*, and in Latin *scola*, the English school." The person of leisure is the "scholar." Irving Babbitt points out that leisure, for the Greek was the "expression of the highest moments of the mind. It was not labor; far less was it recreation."[42] It was that employment of the mind in which one could penetrate the meaning of creation. It was a time not to flee reality but rather to penetrate its meaning. This contemplation was done within a community. By looking at art, science, math, history, philosophy, literature, theology, etc. one could glimpse at the mystery of creation. Unfortunately the life of leisure for the Greeks was supported by the institution of slavery and a poor understanding of work.

For the careerist, however, school is relegated to the technique of so-called "successful living." When Socrates asks Protagoras the Sophist what he teaches his students, he replies "To be well informed–both in their own affairs, namely how best to manage one's house and run one's estate, effective in speaking and in acting."[43] Pieper characterizes this as pseudo-philosophy which restricts the justification of philosophy and the rest of the liberal arts to techniques of the work world. Rather than a form of leisure, school takes on the form of technique where knowledge is power to provide personal satisfaction, success, markets, and income. This of course is not to deny the place of professional education in the university, but rather that such professional education be better fitted within the larger framework of liberal arts education.

For Pieper, a careerist view of leisure distorts its central characteristic: *celebration.* Careerists students come to see themselves as masters and owners of creation. Their education has instilled a view of the world as "raw material" on which to act on for their own personal purposes. Careerists have difficulty in seeing "the goodness of creation"–in seeing the world as a created order that one participates in and for which one has reverence. They are so busy that they cannot stop to receive anything beyond their own initial preferences.[44] But as Pieper points out, the justification of leisure is not success, better productivity, etc., but rather that the person be given time to "retain the faculty of grasping the world as a whole and realizing his full potentialities as an entity meant to reach Wholeness."[45] For Pieper, this wholeness has at its core a spiritual dimension that is necessary to receive the whole of reality.[46] It is a moment of celebrating that creation is good.

3. Vocation: The Dignity of Work and the Celebration of Leisure

This reflection thus far is not to deny the value of work defined as a job or a career. Instead it is to critique the failure of these perspectives to attain a more excellent value. Work is a job. It is a means to a financial end. If work, in terms of employment, does not generate a good income as well as optimal profits, no matter how noble or psychologically satisfying, in the end it's not doable. Work should also be psychologically rewarding. If workers are psychologically stilted and degraded, work becomes a form of oppression and alienation. Self-esteem is an essential ingredient to any true community of work. A job and career point out the fundamental dimensions of work, namely, work is a means to self-preservation and familial support as well as psychological development. But these dimensions by themselves fail to capture the full meaning of human work. A more excellent good exists than the economic and psychological goods offered by work understood as a job and career. Work fails to be fully human, since the economic and psychological dimensions are not properly ordered to the social dimension which characterize an element of work as a vocation. A vocation must include the fundamentals of the economic and psychological dimensions of work, but it also must order these goods to the common good. A better understanding of the common good in terms of vocation is in order.

A. The Common Good

Vocation within in the Christian tradition is a calling from God. It transcends the materialism of a job and the individualism of a career. It does this by connecting work's purpose with the proximate and ultimate end of a person's moral and spiritual life. As a vocation, work is more than just a source of material and psychic rewards. Instead, a vocation within the Christian tradition is a profession of faith that directs one's work to moral and religious ends. As Walter Brueggeman states, the question is not simply "Who am I" but "Whose am I?"[47]

Unfortunately, the word vocation, particularly in the Catholic tradition, has had a limited understanding. Prior to Vatican II the popular understanding of vocation was restricted to a religious vocation. Only priests, nuns, and brothers had vocations. Spirituality was relegated for the laity to certain times and places.[48] Today there is a similar restriction, namely, only those who are involved in church work, social work, teaching, medicine, counselling, and other so-called people centered occupations can have vocations. If this is the case, vocation becomes restricted to an elite, where those involved in management, law, real estate, manufacturing, and other so-called profit centered occupations, are abandoned to the amorality of the market.

If work as a vocation is to have significant impact, it must be extended to all fields of work, especially to the increasing sector of the business economy. Unfortunately, work understood as vocation has certain barriers within the business community itself. Work, particularly in business, is understood as a series of functions such as finance, marketing, human relations, production, etc. Such functions are often understood to have the decisive meaning to the purpose of the organization, such as finance with maximizing profits, marketing with improved market share, production with better efficiency and productivity or human relations with greater personal satisfaction. Yet, these functions all fall short within the Christian tradition as to the end in which work is directed. While each function done competently is necessary for a successful organization, no one function explains fully the over-arching principle of the purpose and meaning of work. Business functions provide essential tools to the practice of commerce, but they do not answer the two fundamental questions of work: "What kind of subjects do we what to be?" and "What kind of objects ought to be made?" These are fundamentally questions of virtue since people and their communities become the subjects of the acts they performed. As James Keenan, S.J. points out, the key to virtue is that "one's way of acting today will shape one into the person one will become tomorrow."[49] The goods and services provided today, and the reasons for which they are provided, affect the moral characters of those productive persons.[50]

Recognizing the formative influences of work, a vocation calls attention to the contribution of a worker to serve the needs of the larger community. Work is not only a private, that is, financial (job) or psychological (career) affair. Work is done within a particular social and historical context, that if denied, denies the meaning of the individual. Work must be directed toward the common good in which the fulfillment of the worker is intrinsically connected to the fulfillment of the community. In the words of John XXIII, the common good is "the sum total of those conditions of social living, whereby men are enabled more fully and more readily to achieve their own perfection."[51] He maintains that organizations have an important part in creating those conditions which favor the development of the human personality, particularly in light of the products and services they produce as well as the design of work they provide. While organizations have the right to pursue their own particular interests, this cannot be done outside the common good which promotes human dignity.[52] For John XXIII, organizations share the moral call to serve others and contribute to the good of society.[53] They are an indispensable factor in placing workers at the service of the natural law, that is, in the development of the human personality, supporting the family, and achieving the common good through what it produces. It is in this community of work where virtue is practiced and the common good is attained. Hence, the vocation of work is not merely an individual vocation but an organizational one as well.[54]

B. Leisure/Worship as the Basis of Vocation

But what makes a vocation socially conscious, that is, what justifies and sustains a vocation? The answer lies in a Christian understanding of leisure. To understand leisure, it is first important to understand what is meant by rest which leisure is supposed to give. Aquinas points out that there are two forms of rest: (1) The rest from motion: when one stops working he/she rests from the work done. (2) The rest in the fulfillment of one's activities: when the architect designs a building and sees it through to completion, he/she experiences a certain sense of rest at its end. Rest occurs on reflecting upon the completion of the object, and the process it took to accomplish the task.[55]

This second sense of rest is found in Genesis. When God ended His work each day, He looks back on His work and sees that it is good. This form of rest expresses a celebration that what has been made has order and is fundamentally good. Humanity is asked to participate in this celebration fundamentally in terms of worship. In the Judeo-Christian tradition, to leisure is to rest, to rest is to worship, and to worship is to affirm that which is most worthy. Sabbath in Hebrew comes from the verb "to rest," and worship and worth have the same etymological root. In order to have leisure, one must rest in that which the person believes is of most worth.

Rest is not simply idleness *from* work but rest *in* He who gives rest, namely, God. It is a rest to hear God's word, to receive God's sacrament and to be informed by God's grace. Work is not enough in the realization of a person's vocation. Within the very system of a Judeo-Christian notion of work there resounds the commandment "Remember the sabbath day, to make it holy: six days you shall toil and do all your work, but the seventh day is the sabbath in honor of the Lord your God: you shall not do any work. . . . the Lord has blessed the sabbath day and declared it sacred" (Gen 2:1-3).

Pieper points out that this fundamental sense of goodness and order is a precondition to celebration and consequently a precondition to rest in this second sense. For who would celebrate and find rest in a world that is disordered, chaotic, and meaningless. Pieper explains that "Those who do not consider reality as fundamentally 'good' and 'in the right order' are not able to truly celebrate, no more than they are able to 'achieve leisure.'"[56] That is why the deepest form of leisure is the celebration and worship of God, the Creator of all that is good. It is the deepest form of leisure since it is the deepest form of affirming the goodness of creation. Leisure provides the time to allow the person's "inner eye to dwell for a while upon the reality of Creation. He looks and he affirms: it is good."[57]

Precisely in affirming God's creation as good, the person is able to participate in God's ongoing work of creation.[58] The goodness of work is affirmed on the basis of God's created order, not on the basis of one's individual preference. For example, the careerist vocabulary has nothing in his/her vocabulary to call work good. It may be productive, efficient, profitable and even personally satisfying but the criteria of work is either a calculation or at best provides a sense of personal satisfaction (emotivism).[59] For the careerist, entering the vocabulary of goodness becomes a form of oppression of imposing one's good upon another. In a vocation, goodness is based on the created order revealed by a personal God. Leisure in its Christian meaning places work in a created context that gives normative meaning to work. Work within the Christian tradition does not have an independent meaning, but is incarnated with meaning that is received from "divine rest."[60]

C. The Relationship between Worship and Work

It is important to qualify that while worship is at the center of the meaning of leisure, leisure means more than just worship. Miroslav Volf points out that good leisure is indicated by four basic traits: (1) enjoyment of nature (aesthetic act); (2) the free exercise and development of one's talents, abilities, and meaning (philosophical act[61]); (3) fellowship and development of community (social act[62]); and (4) friendship with God (religious act).[63] Pieper points out that such acts (he does not mention the social act) "break through and transcend the workaday world."[64] Leisure is a time for the person to be open to the whole of reality. But Pieper does not expand on how these acts of leisure, especially the religious act, are shot through and transform work itself.[65] Leisure is not an escape from the work world, but rather a time to reflect on the ultimate meaning of all that is in the world including one's work. Connecting what happens in leisure to what happens in work is the essence of a unified life.

Within the Christian tradition, a certain tendency to relegate work to a sphere of insignificance in one's personal development has always existed. When work is relegated to this sphere, the extent of the relationship between work and leisure is that work ought to allow time for leisure by providing adequate wages to allow people to take time off.[66] However, this basic level of integration is inadequate. The kind of work that occurs has a significant effect on the kind of leisure that is done, since work has a formative effect both on the person and the culture in which one resides (this works the other way as well–the kind of leisure done affects the kind of work done). Pieper points out that leisure is that place and time where people "are enabled to remain fully human."[67] It is as he states "the basis of culture." But leisure by itself cannot sustain culture. Work forms also an important component to culture in that it forms both persons and society. People are not able to remain human in leisure alone nor work alone, but rather in an integration of the two. Again, as Rahner points out, human fulfillment is the relationship between work and leisure.[68] While Pieper states that "true culture does not flourish except in the soil of leisure," it might be better to state that true culture does not flourish except in the soil of an integration of leisure and work.[69] To this relationship I now turn.

To have rest, that is to celebrate God's creation through worship, provides a new sense of reality that does not discolor reality but penetrates its meaning. It penetrates reality by giving the perspective of the Creator. It corrects one's vision of life's meaning as a new pair of glasses with the right prescription corrects one's vision of the physical reality.[70] This correction does not come from within, however, just as the correction of the eyes does not come from within. It comes from grace, the gift of freedom (the fundamental inclination towards God) that provides a sensitivity to how things ought to be. To rest in God is not to escape one's work, (although it has certainly been misinterpreted to mean such a thing), but rather to penetrate the meaning of work and its relationship to creation ever more clearly. Worship, particularly in terms of its sacramental meaning, is not an escape from the world, "rather it is the arrival at a vantage point from which we can see more deeply into the reality of the world."[71] This incarnational view of worship points out that spirit pervades materiality, grace perfects nature, and worship makes holy one's work. As Volf explains, "Communion with God in worship establishes the context of meaning that gives work ultimate significance."[72] Work is not only a means to consumption or personal satisfaction, but also a collaboration in an on-going created reality with a distinct moral order. Values in the workplace, then, are embedded in a larger framework than the workplace itself. It is embedded in a life story or narrative that attempts to make sense of one's life as a whole by integrating what one rests in, with one's work.

A unified life for the Christian lies in the unity that one is able to rest in the work one performs in a way that enables one to rest in God's friendship. This relationship between one's work and one's leisure occurs at various levels. At a minimum, what is done at work should not contradict or bring disrespect to what is done in leisure. However, the relationship of work and worship is not only on a non-contradictory level. It is also a relationship that is transformative. Worship is a moment in which the one who works can rediscover the sense of his/her work. It is not restricted to the limited times in which worship takes place. As Michael Schmaus points out, worship proves its fruitfulness in the world in its "effort to re-shape the world in a way more worthy of man, so that the whole of Christian life has the character of worship, while worship is sterile when it is not prolonged in everyday life, when divine service does not become service of others."[73] Worship penetrates the world of work and transforms it. As Brian Hehir points out, "it is in the midst of the liturgical movement" that the social vision of the Church developed.[74]

Worship provides one with a new direction, a new way in which to look at work, in a sense a new end. Work is no longer, at its core, a means to consumption, or to personal satisfaction. Rather, it is centrally a way of collaboration of the friendship formed in leisure. Leisure is not only a transcendence from work but it is also a transformation of work. This is important to note since it is work where personal and social change takes place. Characters are shaped in the workplace. Work provides an opportunity for a significant degree of self-determination where one can in a sense become "more of a human being" and as a consequence more of a reflection of God's image.[75] Civilizations are built from the workplace which can contribute to God's Kingdom. As Volf explains: "the presence of God in worship transforms people so that they can advance through work that transfiguration of the whole universe which is the coming of the Kingdom of God."[76] Grace is not an occasional activity that happens every once in awhile through rare moments of inspiration. But grace is transformative of persons and all their human actions. It is what Edward Vacek, S.J. describes as the "Gospel of the acting person."[77]

To rest in God, that is to receive God's grace, then, "is not a call to leave the place one is in but rather an invitation to live out the very same existence in a new way – as a consequence of a light which allows one to appreciate that this existence has divine dimensions which previously had been hidden."[78] A vocation integrates the divine into the activity of human work, namely, one's work becomes graced. God calls all workers, doctors, factory workers, managers, lawyers, farmers, etc., to work to build the kingdom, to be stewards of the earth, to collaborate, and have dominion over the land because they are made into God's image.

The reason why people are asked to collaborate is that creation is not finished. Creation is not a one time event. It is a continuing process, sustained through God's power and love, in cooperation with people. Teilhard de Chardin states that

> We may, perhaps, imagine that the creation was finished long ago. But that would be quite wrong. It continues still more magnificently, and at the highest levels of the world. *Omnis creatura adhuc ingemiscit et parturit*. And we serve to complete it, even by the humblest work of our hands. That is, ultimately, the meaning and values of our acts.[79]

Work can actually place the person in a relation with his/her ultimate destiny, "becoming an ally with the living God."[80] People continue to develop and perfect creation in collaboration with God by participating in God's continual creative activity. Through their work they provide further form and order to what has been given in nature's raw materials. John Paul II maintains that people participate in God's creative activity by carrying out God's command to subdue and have dominion. In this way, they reflect "the very action of the creator."[81] He asserts that God has given people the command to subdue the earth, and God has provided work as the means to attain this dominion.[82] This command to subdue the earth is an invitation to participate in God's creative activity.

This theme of collaboration is key to Catholic social thought, especially for John Paul. He perceives the relationship of the workers' activity with God's creative activity as extremely personal. There is an intimate calling and invitation to participate and carry on God's work every day in the organization. He points out that humanity's talent and progress which emanate from their work is not in competition or in opposition with God's creation; instead, quoting *Gaudium et Spes*, "the triumphs of the human race are a sign of God's greatness and the flowering of his own mysterious design."[83] For John Paul II, Christians are called to build up the kingdom, that is, to perfect creation, through their work as collaborators within the Creator's order and design. Work as collaboration entails a personal vocation to build the world not only in a technological and scientific way, but primarily in a moral way–as partners in establishing God's kingdom of peace, love, and justice. As a collaborator, the worker has been given a religious reason to participate in furthering the perfection of creation. This elevation fulfilled through Christ's grace makes work not only good but holy.[84] Work is not an option for those who can work, even if one has enough money not to work. People are made to work ("as a bird is to fly"–see *Quadragesimo Anno*, 61), since it is through work that people realize, in a partial way, their relationship to the Creator as collaborator.

However, as Hauerwas points out, the collaboration theme runs the danger of becoming a form of idolatry. And yet, idolatry is not a necessary dimension of collaboration.[85] On the contrary, the collaborative theme gives meaning and dignity to work. The problem occurs when work becomes the only activity with God. That is, people lose perspective when work is performed in a life without leisure, even when it is supposedly done for God. Work must pattern divine work. This pattern is an alternative one between work and leisure. The pattern itself is learned and given in leisure (the creation story in Genesis). Leisure provides reflection and grace on the meaning of work (its end and purpose) as well as a relationship to work in terms of the relationship to the creator. And work provides a manifestation of what is given in leisure.[86] But leisure in terms of worship is not only done for work. Volf points out that God did not only create people to be servants but also friends. "As much as they need to do God's will, so also they need to enjoy God's presence."[87]

4. Conclusion

The understanding of leisure as worship, generates an understanding of work understood as vocation. While worship is an end in itself (friendship with God is the highest good), it does not mean that worship has no relationship to work. Friendship has certain behavioral claims on friends. As an act of friendship, worship inspires people to collaborate in the moral order of God's creation. The failure to live the unity between work and leisure is characterize by *Gaudium et Spes* "among the more serious errors of our age." The council fathers go on to say "Let there be no false opposition between professional and social activities on the one part, and religious life on the other. The Christian who neglects his temporal duties, neglects his duties toward his neighbor and even God, and jeopardizes his eternal salvation."[88] Friendship with God has certain claims on one's work. Not to take such claims seriously, means God's friendship can be lost.

Leisure and work then are intimately related. One is incomplete without the other. Leisure disconnected from work tends toward a spiritualism that becomes disconnected from the world thereby becoming corrupted. Worship becomes a form of modern gnosticism that flees the material world where matter has little to do with the spirit. Work disconnected from leisure tends to turn the activity of work into an end in itself at the exclusion of one's ultimate end. This is why Augustine for example is critical of people of commerce not necessarily by what they do (exchanging goods), but for their inability to find rest in God. According to Augustine, people of commerce "occupy their minds with the anxiety of possessing."[89] Their hearts fail to rest for which it was created to rest in. This prevents them from their final end.[90] For Augustine, the wealth acquired by work is meant to be relinquished for the good of all so the person does not become possessed by wealth preventing him/her from resting in God.[91]

The more leisure intersects with work at every level, the more work becomes a vocation and the more one's life becomes unified. Or in more theological language, the more work becomes an act of worship, of praising the creator, of collaborating with God, the more one comes to see the mystery and wonder of a created reality. This of course does not mean that all work is a worship of God. Work can be designed in such a way (80-hour weeks, poor wages, non-participation, etc.) and directed to such ends (pornography, marketing dubious products, etc.) that by its very nature it excludes such worship as well as human fulfillment. But it is precisely in leisure that one can perceive such problems to be problems.

Notes

1. These categories are taken from Robert Bellah, *et al., Habits of the Heart* (New York: Harper and Row, 1985), see ch. 3. Karl Rahner also hints at similar categories in "Theological Remarks on the Problem of Leisure." In *Theological Investigations*, vol. 6 (Baltimore: Helicon, 1969), pp. 368-390.

2. See Arthur Anderson, "America's Money Maniacs," *Business & Society Review*, 66 (Summer 1988): 13-17 and Kenneth Kovach, "What Motivates Employees? Workers and Supervisors Give Different Answers," *Business Horizons* (September-October 1987): 58-65.

3. Rahner, "Theological Remarks," 379.

4. Joe L. Wallis, "The Relevance for Social Economics of Alisdair MacIntyre's Conception of a Practice," *Review of Social Economy* 50 (Spring 1992): 5; quoted from Alisdair MacIntyre, *After Virtue* (Notre Dame, Ind.: University of Notre Dame, 1984), p. 205.

5. This is not to say that work cannot provide its own internal meaning. The pursuit of the excellence of one's work has a certain claim of commitment which gives meaning to the practitioner (Wallis, "Relevance of Social Economics," p. 5). Yet, it is difficult for the meaning of work to be self-contained. This is the problem of the careerist. While every person who enters a particular work subjects himself to the attitudes and standards which define the work, such attitudes and standards are subjected to various temptations of exploitation (MacIntyre, *After Virtue* , p. 190). Without a clear direction of purpose imbued with the virtues of justice, courage and honesty, workers tend to cave into such temptations.

6. Karol Wojtyla, *The Acting Person*, Analecta Husserliana Series, ed. Anna-Teresa Tymieniecka, vol. 10 (Boston: D. Reidel Publishing Co., 1979), p. 150. Wojtyla speaks of the subject as the primary and principle object of the subject's activity. While this is true, the language becomes cumbersome and circular to use.

7. Joseph Pieper, *Leisure as the Basis of Culture* (New York: A Mentor Book, 1952), p. 25.

8. A intentional dimension exists to work and leisure. What may be leisure to one may be work to another (volunteering vs. a social worker or fishing for leisure and fishing for a livelihood). While the acts may be the same, the purpose for doing so is different.

9. See Aristotle, *Politics*, 8, 3, 1337 b.

10. I take here Juliet Schor's description of work and leisure in carving out the time frames of work and leisure, *The Overworked American* (New York: Basic Books, 1992)]. Work has essentially two major time frames: "The first is hours of paid employment . . . The second is hours of household labor–a category whose major components are cleaning, cooking, and child care . . . the combination of these two forms of work make 'total working hours.' Leisure is then the residual" (*ibid.*, p.13).

This is not a perfect description since there are exceptions to it.

11. Studs Terkel, *Working* (New York: Avon Books, 1975), p.675.

12. Bellah, *Habits of the Heart*, p.66.

13. See Yves Simon, *Work, Society, and Culture* (New York: Fordham University Press, 1971), p.18 for the etymology of work. Work understood as a job can stated in the following: "Something people do not like to do, but it allows them to do what they like." That is, work is an activity that they do for half their waking hours that they vehemently dislike, in order to enjoy the other half of their waking hours.

14. See Schor, *The Overworked American*, p. 80.

15. Nels Anderson, *Dimensions of Work: The Sociology of a Work Culture* (New York: David McKay, 1964), p.89; quoted in Ronald Mason, *Participatory and Workplace Democracy* (Carbondale, Ill.: Southern University Illinois Press, 1982), p.115.

16. Taylor's understanding of work is complemented by the prevailing theory of management that restricts the vision of management solely to comply with organizational goals, which are economic in nature. In the arena of the organization, the manager's primary and sole function is to conform to the strict economic obligations of the owners of capital within the confines of the law. Any sense of moral obligations to themselves, employees, the environment, the community and the larger good of society are secondary to obligations of owners.

17. Arthur Anderson, "America's Money Maniacs," p.15.

18. Joseph DesJardins, "Virtues and Business Ethics" in W. Michael Hoffman, Jennifer Mills Moore, and David A. Fredo, eds., *Corporate Governance and Institutionalizing Ethics*. (Washington: D.C. Heath and Co.: 1984), p.100.

19. This attitude also carries to customers. All goods and services (the object) are produced solely to gain financial benefits. Reference to the common good as a purpose for the production of goods of service only arise if they best serve this economic endeavor. A crude example of work restricted to extrinsic rewards is of the doctor who performs c-sections simply because they are more profitable and more efficient than vaginal birth. The meaning of his/her relationship to the patient becomes restricted to financial benefits gained. Or think of the example of the Ford Pinto case, where safety of customers is based primarily on costs and benefits to the financial performance of the company.

20. If one takes salaries as an indicator to the importance and value a society places on people, entertainers (this includes sports figures) win hands down.

21. Jacques Ellul, "Reflections on Leisure," *Interplay* (December 1967): 54. An essay in the *Saturday Evening Post* (11 January 1958) entitled "Holiday for Howie" describes how when faced with the real meaning of leisure, Howie has difficulty in accepting it. He discovers that leisure provides him the time to reflect and open him to reality. "He hurries home to explain this to his wife—a large order—and to tell her he has decided to take a second job, one which will fill two of his three free

days, because: 'Time is not for me. Some people can handle it. I can't. . . .' 'Oh, Howie' [says his wife]. There was love and admiration in her muffled voice,. And vague regret.' 'Cheer up, Doll. Think what we can do with the extra money—lots of things. Think what we can get—a new car, with all the gadgets! Color TV! Air conditioning! We'll really be living! Smile, Doll!'" Quoted from Harvey Swados, "Less Work—Less Leisure," in *Mass Leisure* eds. Eric Larrabee and Rolf Meyersohn (Glencoe, Ill.: The Free Press, 1958), pp.353-363.

22. This is the result of moonlighting, overtime, increased travel time, and downsizing (Schor, *The Overworked American* pp.31, 33-34).

23. This is the time left after sleep, employment and household chores are taken care of; see *ibid.*, pp. 1, 5, 22.

24. *Ibid.*, p.3.

25. *Ibid.*, p. 107.

26. Gary Burtless, "Are We All Working Too Hard? Its Better than Watching Oprah," *Wall Street Journal* (4 January 1990), 1. Burtless goes on to argue that people in general do not want to work less since it would be less consumption and entertainment. For him, leisure is a cost. In order to enjoy leisure one needs money. There is little doubt that this is true, but as it stands its materialistic and consumeristic and fails to capture the full meaning of leisure. As the saying goes, one can know the price of everything and the value of nothing.

27. Pieper, *Leisure*, p.38.

28. *Ibid.*, pp.99-102.

29. Such a life as Plato points becomes indistinguishable from that of animals. Like grazing animals, people who only seek entertainable pleasures "look always with their heads bent to the ground like cattle, at the banquet tables they feed, fatten, and fornicate" (*Republic* 586a). While Plato's words are harsh they point seriously beyond the materialism implied in this notion of work and leisure.

30. Pieper, *Leisure*, p.41.

31. The key to a unified life lies primarily in a qualitative rather than quantitative sense. John Ryan states that a unified life "consists in thinking, knowing, communing, loving, serving, and giving, rather than in having or enjoying. Its supreme demand is that we should know more and love more, and that we should strive to know the best that is to be known and to love the best that is to be loved. It demands that we satisfy the cravings of our senses only to the extent that is compatible with a reasonable attention to the things of the mind and the spirit." John Ryan, *Declining Liberty and Other Papers* (New York, 1927), p.323. To rise above such materialism would not be found simply in better entertainment, but rather to enter into that which ought to be loved and known best.

32. Bellah, *Habits of the Heart*, p.66; see James Donahue, "Jesuit Education and the Cultivation of Virtue," *Thought* 67 (June 1992):198-205 on his discussion of career

particularly as it relates to college students.

33. Frederick Herzberg, *Work and the Nature of Man* (Cleveland: The World Publishing Co., 1966), p.12.

34. It should be pointed out that not all the psychologists mentioned above fail to recognize this. McGregor for example is aware of the social dimensions to human nature. See Douglas McGregor, *The Human Side of Enterprise* (New York: McGraw-Hill Book Co., 1960).

35. William May, "The Beleaguered Rulers: The Public Obligation of the Professional." *Kennedy Institute of Ethics Journal* 2 (1992): 31.

36. MacIntyre, *After Virtue*, p.12. MacIntyre points out that in the public realm of the organization, careerists (he speaks of managers) can only approximate the "truths of fact and mathematical relation." Public meaning of the organization cannot extend beyond such techniques. In the realm of the organization, according to the careerist, one can speak only of means. "About ends it must be silent" (*ibid*., p.54).

37. See Rahner, "Theological Remarks," p.372.

38. Pieper, *Leisure*, p.43. Pieper calls this second reason "the total work mentality approach." He was primarily responding to marxists on this point when he wrote his book *Leisure as the Basis of Culture*, but it is applicable to the careerist, which in certain respects seem little different that the marxists. Schor points out that it is those with this "total work mentality" that set the pace of the organization and create the external pressures mentioned above–Schor, *The Overworked American*, p.70. This type of forced careerism can happen on a macro level as well. For example, Germany, which has more holidays (most of which are Catholic) than most industrialized countries, is experiencing pressure from international competition to cut its holidays and work longer hours. In *The Wall Street Journal* it was reported that "A holiday cost German industry an average of 5.5 billion marks [$3.5 billion]" Industrialists and others are lobbying to have some holidays abolished, but most are Catholic feasts which has caused considerable resistance ("Germany Is Troubled by How Little Work Its Workers Are Doing," *The Wall Street Journal* [6 May 1993], 1).

39. Recent studies indicate that more and more people are getting tired of the career track; see Schor, *The Overworked American*, p.132. They find that work as a single source of meaning finds itself unfulfilling. What they thought it would do for them, it did not. As careerist, they became functionaries, and as functionaries they became sterile and vapid.

40. "Leisure," *New Catholic Encyclopedia*, "Leisure," p.624; this may be a partial result for those who die or have acute depression after they retire.

41. Schor, *The Overworked American*, p.161. Those who are over-worked are those who leisure in those things that demand the least energy as well as the least personal engagement. It is also true that the kind of work done that partially affects the kind of leisure. Ronald Mason points out that employees that are involved in highly participatory workplaces often are involved in other communities outside the workplace such as community, church, civic, and humanitarian groups.

42. Irving Babbit, *Literature and the American College: Essays in Defense of the Humanities* (Los Angeles, 1956), p.169.

43. Pieper, *Leisure*, p.75. Careerists of today see school as a means to the furthering of their own career. One can hear them in the halls "tell me only what I need to know to get a job." "This is not relevant to my life" (as if they know, particularly at such a young age what is relevant). See Dr. Richard Pring's excellent chapter in S. Natale and B. Rothschild (eds.), *Work Values: Education, Organization, and Religious Concerns* (Amsterdam and Atlanta: Rodopi 1995), for a discussion on the integration of liberal arts and vocational education.

44. See Pieper, 81. The danger here in criticizing the careerist is disconnecting the life of leisure from the life of work as too often has been done particularly on religious as well as philosophical bases. The careerist understands correctly that work is made for his/her fulfillment or perfection. Work must be seen beyond just its financial dimension. What the careerist has a difficulty with is what the normative nature of the fulfillment or happiness is. At best the fulfillment is a matter of personal preference that can only be individually determined. Without this normative end, the careerist is in danger of what Ken Goodpaster calls teleopathy, in S. Natale and B. Rothschild (eds.), *Work Values: Education, Organization, and Religious Concerns* (Amsterdam and Atlanta: Rodopi 1995), namely, a sickness of ends. The careerist becomes fixated on particular limited ends whether they are their own or the organizations to such an extent that other larger ends such as human dignity or the common good become thwarted.

45. *Ibid.*, p.44.

46. *Ibid.*, p.88.

47. Walter Brueggeman, "Covenanting as a Human Vocation," *Interpretation* (1979): 126; quoted from May, "The Beleaguered Rulers," p.28.

48. There were of course many exceptions to this, such as Dorothy Day, Peter Maurin, and the Catholic Worker Movement, Jesuit Labor Priests (see Joseph McShane, "The Working Class Spirituality of the Jesuit Labor Priests," S. Natale and B. Rothschild [eds.], *Work Values: Education, Organization, and Religious Concerns* [Amsterdam and Atlanta: Rodopi 1995]), and Josemaría Escrivá's Opus Dei movement. Such movements were attempts to integrate work and leisure in a meaningful way for the laity. See Volf for other problems on the relationship between work and leisure in the Christian tradition (Miroslav Volf, *Work in the Spirit* [New York: Oxford University Press, 1991], p.138); see also May, "The Beleaguered Rulers."

49. James Keenan, S.J., "Virtue Ethics: Making a Case as It Comes of Age," *Thought* (June 1992): 119.

50. It important not to lose sight of this virtue dimension of a vocation, particularly in a result-oriented culture such as ours. Let me illustrate. "Why are corporations socially responsible?" Many of my students argue that it is out of self-interest (narrowly understood). They maintain that corporate good acts are extensions of the

public relations division – they are motivated by the desire to create a good image. The students then go on – argue that the intentions of the agents in the corporations for such good corporate acts are irrelevant anyway. What matters are the consequences, that is, does it contribute to the greater good of society. The problem with their argument is they simply focus on the object changed and not the subject who is performing the object. That is, they only have half the story or half the reality. They fail to understand that motives or intentions are forming those subjects who act. Not to be concerned about the intentions of the agents in the corporations, is not to be concerned about whether the subjects of the corporations are transformed into virtuous people.

51. *Mater et Magistra*, p.65.

52. *Ibid.*

53. Benjamin Masse, *Justice for All* (Milwaukee: Bruce Publishing Co., 1964), p.91.

54. It is important to note that vocation is not understood here only in personal terms. One also has to understand vocation in organizational or institutional terms as well. Organizations, for example, are an indispensable factor in placing workers at the service of the natural law, that is, in the development of the human personality, supporting the family, and achieving the common good through what it produces. It is in this community of work where virtue is practiced and the common good is attained. Hence, the vocation of work is not merely an individual vocation but an organizational one as well.

55. Sylvester Killeen, *The Philosophy of Labor According to Thomas Aquinas*, Ph.D. Dissertation, The Catholic University of America, 1939, p.108; see *Summa Theologica*, II. 179-182. "Come to me, all who labor and are heavy laden, and I will give you rest. Take my yoke upon you, and learn from me; for I am gentle and lowly in heart and you will find rest for your souls. For my yoke is easy, and my burden is light" (Mt. 11:28-30).

56. Joseph Pieper, *An Anthology* (San Francisco: Ignatius Press, 1989), pp.141-142.

57. At the center of the Judeo-Christian tradition meaning of rest is worship (individual and communal). Certain days (holy days – holidays or feast days), and times are set aside for worship. It is an essential element in one's self-realization. This leisure time points out that the most important activity in one's life is not what one produces, but what one rests in. It is not to say that what one produces is unimportant, rather, its importance stems from what one rests in. As John Haughey pointed out in his book, *The Holy Use of Money* (New York: Doubleday & Co., 1986), pp.70-79, to worship literally means that which one gives worth to. It is from resting in God, whether at eucharist, prayer, meditation, retreat, etc., that one opens his/her life to the reality of God.

58. God rests in the goodness of his own creation. We too can only rest when the work we do is a participation in that goodness.

59. In describing the manager as a careerist, MacIntyre explains that "the manager treats ends as given, as outside his scope; his concern is with technique, with

effectiveness in transforming raw materials into final products, unskilled labor into skilled labor, investments into profits." Managers, according to MacIntyre are unable to engage in moral debate. "They are seen by themselves, and by those who see them with the same eyes as their own, as uncontested figures, who purport to restrict themselves to the realms in which rational agreement is possible—that is, of course from their point of view to the realm of fact, the realm of means, the realm of measurable effectiveness" (MacIntyre, 30). Reason is merely calculative; "it can assess truths of fact and mathematical relation but nothing more. In the realm of practice therefore it can speak only of means, about ends it must be silent" (MacIntyre, *After Virture*, p.54). Management thus understood is part of the emotivist project.

60. Edwin Kaiser, *Theology of Work* (Westminster: The Newman Press, 1966), p.51.

61. The Greeks notion of schola or what Haughey calls discipline reflection is a good example of this. Other examples are the Aspen Institute, the University (the meaning of a liberal arts school and the nature of a Catholic University especially within the business curriculum), meditation (good reading), etc.

62. The most obvious example here is the family. But it also means service to the community especially the poor. Jesus' works of mercy on the sabbath caused great conflict with the Pharisees (Mt 12:1-4; Mk 2:23-28; Lk 6:1-11; 13:10-16; 14:1-5; Jn 5:9-18; 7:22f; 9:14-16). As McKenzie points out Jesus is not rejecting the Sabbath observance, but rather challenges the casuistic interpretations of the Pharisees ("Sabbath," *Dictionary of the Bible*, p.752). Because the sabbath is holy one cannot evade the goodness one owe's to another. Jesus states that "The sabbath was made for humankind, and not humankind for the sabbath; so the Son of Man is lord even of the sabbath" (Mk:27-28). It is interesting to note that since 1970s volunteer time has decreased and the family unit has apparently become weaker (Schor, *The Overworked American*, p.161).

63. Volf, *Work in the Spirit*. p.136.

64. Pieper, *Leisure*, p.73.

65. There are points where Pieper develops this, such as in his desire to deproletarize the worker and his distinction between *ratio* and *intellectus*. For Pieper, we do not live in two distinct worlds, one of leisure and one of work. "On the contrary, it is the same tangible, visible world that lies before him upon which a genuine philosophical reflection is trained. . . . things are questioned regarding their (things of the world) ultimate nature and their universal essence, and as a result the horizon of the question becomes the horizon of reality as a whole" (*ibid*., p.97).

66. Some argue that work is insignificant to one's life and needs little reflecting on. This is similar to Karl Barth who points out that "Man does not do anything special by working . . . Nor is it God's work that he continues, completes and executes." Quoted from Edward Vacek, S.J., "John Paul II and Cooperation with God," *The Annual: Society of Christian Ethics* (1990): 91-92; see Karl Barth, *Church Dogmatics* 3(4): pp.472-74, 526, 536. See Hauerwas's critique of John Paul II, Gilbert C. Meilaender, *Friendship*, pp.96-99. Meilaender writes, "Whatever its defects, it is one of the virtues of capitalism that it must allow people simply to work for money

and seek fulfillment elsewhere" (p.98). Work is not an important dimension to self-fulfillment. At its best according to these authors, one works not to be a burden to others, and to serve one's neighbors. This is why Meilaender seems to deny the possibility of a unified life and prefers to see work in terms of what he calls *ambulando* (pp.102-103). This is in contrast to papal social thought. In *Mater et Magistra* (256) states, "That a man should develop and perfect himself through his daily work–which in most cases is of a temporal character–is perfectly in keeping with the plan of divine providence. The Church today is faced with an immense task: to humanize and to Christianize this modern civilization of ours. The continued development of this civilization, indeed its very survival, demand and insist that the Church do her part in the world. That is why, as we said before, she claims the co-operation of her laity. In conducting their human affairs to the best of their ability, they must recognize that they are doing a service to humanity, in intimate union with God through Christ, and to God's greater glory. And St. Paul insisted: 'Whether you eat or drink, or whatsoever else you do, do all to the glory of God.' [1 Cor. 10:31] 'All whatsoever you do in word or in work, do all in the name of the Lord Jesus Christ, giving thanks to God and the Father by him.'" [Col. 3:17]

67. Pieper, *Anthology*, p.140.

68. Rahner, "Theological Remarks," p.379; see also Simon, *Work, Society, and Culture*, pp.182-188.

69. John Paul II points out in *Christifideles Lacia* (p.59) "there cannot be two parallel lives in their existence. . . . Every activity, every situation, every precise responsibility . . . are the occasions ordained by providence for a `continuous exercise of faith, hope and charity.'"

70. See Otto Herman Pesch, "The Theology of Virtue and the Theological Virtues," *Concilium*, 191 (1987): 81-100.

71. Joseph Woodill, "Virtue Ethics: An Orthodox Apreciation," *Thought*, 67 (June 1992): 186. He is quoting Alexander Schmenmann, *For the Life of the World* (New York: St. Vladimir's Seminary Press, 1973), p.27.

72. Volf, 140. Or as Teilhard de Chardin notes: "by virtue of the Creation, and, still more, of the Incarnation, *nothing* here below *is profane* for those who know how to see." Pierre Teilhard de Chardin, *The Divine Milieu* (New York: Harper and Row, 1960), p.66.

73. In *Encyclopedia of Theology*. ed. Karl Rahner. (New York: Seabury Press, 1975), p.1841; see Virgil Michel, *The Social Question* (Collegeville, Minn.: Office of Academic Affairs Saint John's University, 1987) for ways of incorporating liturgy and social justice. Michel explains that "When twenty persons receive Communion at Mass and go back to their separate pews, this would almost imply that there were now twenty Christs extant among the pews. We know, of course, that this is not the Catholic doctrine. When twenty or more individuals receive Communion they have all been intimately united to one and the same sacramental Christ. Christ is not divided or really multiplied among them after Communion: rather they are all contained in one and the same Christ, and thus united most closely into a single supernatural fellowship with Him. The early Christians understood this very well.

And therefore they had no difficulty in transferring this intimate fellowship of love that was wrought among them in holy Communion into every action of their daily lives." Michel summarizes this section of the book with a syllogism: The liturgy is the indispensable source of the Christian spirit; the true Christian spirit is indispensable for social regeneration; consequently, the liturgy is the indispensable basis of Christian social regeneration (p.6). See also *Liturgy and Social Justice*, ed. Edward M. Grosz (Collegeville, Minn.: The Liturgical Press, 1989) as well as *Liturgy and Social Justice* ed. Mark Searle (Collegeville, Minn.: The Liturgical Press, 1980). Also see *Mater et Magistra*, p.258ff on the Mystical Body of Christ and its relationship to work. John XXIII states: "We most earnestly beg all our sons the world over, clergy and laity, to be deeply conscious of the dignity, the nobility, which is theirs through being grafted on to Christ as shoots on a vine: 'I am the vine; you the branches.' They are thus called to share in his own divine life; and since they are united in mind and spirit with the divine redeemer even when they are engaged in the affairs of the world, their work becomes a continuation of his work, penetrated with redemptive power. 'He that abideth in me, and I in him, the same beareth much fruit.' Thus is man's work exalted and ennobled—so highly exalted that it leads to his own personal perfection of soul, and helps to extend to others the fruits of redemption, all over the world. It becomes a means whereby the Christian way of life can leaven this civilization in which we live and work—leaven it with the ferment of the gospel."

74. *Liturgy and Social Justice* (1989), p.43.

75. *Laborem Exercens*, p.9.

76. Volf, 140. As John Paul II pointed out, "Let the Christian . . . uniting work with prayer, know the place that his work has not only in earthly progress but also in the development of the kingdom of God" (*Laborem Exercens*, p.27).

77. It is important to work out the relationship between theological virtues (grace) and work. John Paul II points out "The dimension of work and the dimension of faith, are not two separate things, any more than the dimension of the world and the dimension of the Kingdom of God. They have been joined together in the eternal thought and will of the Creator. From the beginning, the path of faith passes through work, and the path of work through faith. . . . So it is not true that the life of faith and hope in the kingdom of God draws man away from work. The opposite is true: it is precisely this faith and hope that shed full light on human work, it is they that completely reveal its meaning and true value. It is the Gospel of work which fully restores his work to man. It alone enables man to realize himself as man, while with the work on his hands he transforms nature. It alone gives work its dignity. And, at the same time, the Gospel leads up to the summit of a 'transfiguration: through which work shares in man's immortality, becoming the path to his salvation.'" (Homily, 18 March 1984).

78. José Luis Illanes, *On the Theology of Work* (Dublin: Four Courts Press, 1980), p.39.

79. Teilhard de Chardin, p.62. He goes on to state that "Our work appears to us, in the main, as a way of earning our daily bread. But its essential virtue is on a higher level: through it we complete in ourselves the subject of the divine union; and

through it again we somehow make to grow in stature the divine term of the one with who we are united, our Lord Jesus Christ. . . . God is inexhaustibly attainable in the *totality* of our action" (p.63).

80. John Paul II, Homily, 13 December 1986.

81. *Laborem Exercens*, 4.1.

82. *Ibid.*, 9.1.

83. *Ibid.*, 25.4; quoted from *Gaudium et Spes*, 34.2.

84. *Laborem Exercens*, 25.5. John Paul II's vision of workers as collaborators raises the importance of the work process to a theological level, highlighting the religious structure of the worker's place in the production process. He explains that the capacity for creativity, self-reflection, invention, and innovation in people constitute in part their likeness or image of God as well as the means to further perfect creation. If people are created in God's image and if God's first act is creation, then the characteristics of creativity on the part of workers has an important part to play in their work. Their creativity is an image of divinity that ought to be expressed in the workplace. The whole person should be involved—the physical, the intellectual, the emotional, and the spiritual aspects of the person. Work ought to be designed to use the whole person and not merely one part, as for example, in certain types of assembly-line and bureaucratic structures. Although John Paul II does not offer specific or obligatory models for the workplace, he perceives a moral obligation on the part of employers and experts in the field of organizational behavior and resource management to search for ways of incorporating the full person into the production and service process. For him, the key to utilizing the full person is to recognize the participatory character of each person as well as through worker ownership.

85. John Paul II explains that idolatry occurs precisely when collaboration is lost, since collaboration contextualizes the relationship of humanity within the created order. He states: "The human person, therefore, is a collaborator and craftsman, but not the absolute master, neither of himself nor of things, which he is called in turn to mold so that the garden may become more bountiful. The earth which he has received as a gift must be subjected to the `dominion' of the human person in the framework of the divine plan, or else his role as collaborator will be compromised" (Homily, 9 January 1988).

86. This integration of work and leisure, or the liberal arts and vocational training has much to say about university education, particularly at a Catholic University. Business education within a liberal arts school is not a contradiction in terms but makes sense. The more business education is immersed and integrated in liberal education, the more likely that leisure and work will find a meaningful relationship.

87. Volf, p.137. As Augustine points out, "no one ought to be so leisured as to take no thought of his neighbor, nor so active as to feel no need for the contemplation of God" (*The City of God*, xix, 19).

88. *Gaudium et Spes*, p.43. What is important to note here is that it is wrong to imagine, as John XXIII states, "that a life of activity in the world is incompatible

with spiritual perfection. The two can very well be harmonized" (*Mater et Magistra*, p.255).

89. Kaiser, *Theology of Work,* p.116.

90. In the first paragraph of the *Confessions* Augustine states, "You stir man to take pleasure in praising you, because you have made us for yourself, and our heart is restless until it rests in you." For Augustine rest is not idleness, but the full meaning of the sabbath–to rest in God. See also Pieper, *Leisure*, p.77ff.

91. This should not be interpreted as a careless or unthoughtful relinquishing of wealth. It is relinquished for a dual purpose. To serve others and to let one rest in God. In order to serve others and to continue to serve in the future, wealth must be relinquished prudently. Leisure points out the importance of the eschatological dimensions of the Christian faith which plays into what has been said above concerning virtue. Our ultimate end in life is to rest in God. The significance of our work must be directed to this end. The work we do partially forms us into particular kinds of people. This formation along with a spiritual formation opens or closes us to our heavenly destination. If in this world we reject God's grace in the work and leisure activities of our life, what makes us think that we will accept God's love in our next life. Few books show this more clearly than C.S. Lewis's *The Great Divorce* where several characters fail to enter heaven by the inability to overcome the habits (vices) they have acquired in their earthly life. "'Blessed are the dead who from now on die in the Lord.' 'Yes,' says the Spirit, 'they will rest from their labors, for their deeds follow them'" (Rev 14:13).

Chapter Four

WORK AND PLAY: ARE THEY OPPOSITES OR A CONTINUUM?

Carole A. Rayburn

The meaning of "work" has often been defined in its contrast to "play," which is also in need of a better honed definition. Seen as the effort, exertion, labor, task, duty, or sustained activity that affords a person a livelihood, "work" may also be viewed as any purposeful activity regardless whether or not it is remunerative. "Drudgery" may be irksome or dull labor, while "grind" may be labor that is exhausting to body or mind. Work usually involves monetary compensation, accountability to others, a goal of competency and recognition. Work is often associated with stress and strain (Osipow & Spokane, 1983; Rayburn, Richmond & Rogers, 1983, 1986). Intrinsic and extrinsic values are important in defining work (Kaplan & Tausky, 1974; Kazanas, 1978). Too, the state of mind of the individual must be taken into account. Work is often pictured as serious, goal-oriented activity in which people engage for financial and sometimes intellectual survival. Play, on the other hand, is seen as fun, recreation and sport, release of energy and pent-up frustrations, self-expression, and recuperation and refreshment.

Related to play is "leisure." Bundy (1977) has defined "leisure" as synonymous with free time that must be productive. Largely identified with recreation and amusement for Bundy, leisure is not an end in itself but has meaning in work (the center of life around which everything else revolves). In an older concept, leisure is an attitude of mind, connoting enjoying things for their own sake. In this second view, work is the temporary absence from leisure and has the goal of entering into leisure. Here, work has meaning only in connection with leisure because leisure is the very center of life and the basis of culture.

Neulinger (1981) proposed that intrinsic motivation and perceived freedom are necessary before a healthy leisure experience may be experienced within and outside the work environment. Csikszentmihalyi (1975, 1982) sees the crux of the matter as not whether individuals are at work or leisure but whether they can escape boredom and anxiety by having the freedom to optimally use their skills in relation to challenges and thus being able to have enjoyment and "flow" (positive subjective states, especially when people perceive high challenges and high skills as attaining a balance). Jahoda (1986) spoke of work as having not only the opportunity of providing money through earning a living but also involving social experience, social identity, time structure, activity, collective purpose. She identified what she considered opposites of work needs: Leisure needs or unstructured time, privacy, individual effort, personal identity, and periods of passivity. Thus, for Jahoda, work and play involve complementary sets of needs but they are opposites and cannot substitute for each other. However, for Haworth and Ducker (1991) and Haworth and Hill (1992), some individuals do not experience a strict division between what they obtain in work and what they obtain in leisure.

Kanchier and Unruh (1989), comparing work values of managers who voluntarily left their jobs with those who stayed, used the 1970 definition of D. E. Super for work values as qualities, rewards, or satisfaction that persons desire to seek from their work. Most people saw work as a means of developing and maintaining their sense of identity and self-esteem.

Abramis (1990) studied play in work with an adult population 18-71 years of age. He found two types of play in work: Play as a Game (a sense that work feels like a game, sport, or puzzle) and Play as Goofing Around (a sense of more unstructured play). Play as a Game (PGM) involves challenge, skills, autonomy, and feedback, and it is more structured and focused, as well as being significantly affected by job design. PGM may increase job satisfaction, a sense of competence and a mastery of life. However, Play as Goofing Around had little effect on individuals' lives and was unrelated to job design. Play as a Game was viewed as assisting learning and mastery, acting as a coping mechanism to lessen fears, stress, and strain and having a positive effect on creativity and initiative. Play as Goofing Around may also serve to lower stress. Abramis suggested that play may increase arousal and attentiveness, being especially helpful to people who have boring jobs. He concluded that some kinds of play need to be encouraged, sometimes as an integral part of work, and not simply "accepted."

1. Work and Play Questionnaire

To better understand the relationship between work and play, a specially devised five-item questionnaire was presented individually to 35 people. The questions were as follows:

1. Do you consider any of your work "play"?
2. What part?
3. What is your definition of "work"?
4. What is your definition of "play"?
5. When does "work" become "play"?

These questions were presented in an open-ended form to better tap the pool of possible responses. One additional question was asked after item 5: Do you think work and play are opposites or a continuum?

(a) The population: The population of 35 people was comprised of 13 males (37%) and 22 females (63%). There were 30 Caucasians (86%), four Blacks (11%), and an Asian-American (3%). In terms of age, the mean age was 52.06 years, with a range from 17 to 75 years. There were 25 professionals (79%), with nine psychologists, four educators, and one each of the following: editor, engineer, dentist (plus two dental assistants), anthropologist, physicist, hospital administrator, attorney, program analyst, economist, and architect. The white-collar workers made up 25% or 8 persons in this population (two secretaries, an office manager, two contractors, a grant specialist, a pharmacy clerk, and a private investigator). There were two people in the blue-collar group (6%), a waitress and a mechanic. Sixty percent (21) were married, one was widowed (3%), four were divorced (11%), and nine (26%) were single.

(b) Results: There were 25 persons (71%) who indicated that they do consider at least some part of their work as play. Four reported that they enjoyed their work so much that virtually all of it was play. Ten individuals (29%) did not consider any of their work as play, indicating that their work was far too serious to be thought as "play" in any way.

On item 2, for the 71% indicating that at least part of their work was "play," eight (23%) mentioned social interaction; seven (20%) communicating with others; three doing experimental research; two "playing" with computers; five (14%) joking with co-workers; three meditating while driving on the job; two making hypotheses, two helping others–especially family members in a family business; and one person mentioned each of these–having a positive attitude, teaching others, seeing the results of your work, and being involved in creativity, intuition, and problem solving, as the part of work which was considered "play."

To the question, "What is your definition of work?", ten individuals defined work in terms of "something to make money needed to live and pay bills." Some subjects had more than one definition, or at least an answer with several aspects of "work." Three of the subjects defined work as accomplishing a goal with competence, three mentioning fulfillment of professional activity needs, nine defined it with regard to the routine effort, demanding tedium, obligations and constraints, with constant worry, pressure and stress. Generally, work was viewed as something done for monetary reward, whether one liked to do the work or not. Seven people saw work as serious, purposeful, goal-oriented behavior. One person mentioned work as creating something new, as being judged or evaluated, and as having a definite beginning and end.

Responding to the item on how they would define "play," 11 people (31%) mentioned that play was that which provided leisure, recreation, a sense of relaxation without pressure. Defining play as "what I enjoy," fun, pleasure, enjoyment, or satisfaction were 19 subjects (54%). Three spoke of playfulness, humor and telling jokes. Seven talked about doing what comes naturally or spontaneous non-goal-directedness. For one person, "play" involved not having to be responsible or to take care of others; purposeful goal-directedness; renewal of spirit–"a recharge of one's batteries"; and challenging, inventive, creative, joyful activity.

On the fifth question, "when does 'work' become 'play'?", five (14%) said when social interaction is involved; 21 subjects (60%) said when they were enjoying their work, having fun or pleasure; five (14%) reported it was when they experienced relaxation and had no pressures, were free from anxiety and worry; two said when they were joking with coworkers; one mentioned not having to take ourselves too seriously; two said when a person has fun because a goal is achieved; and one person mentioned having no outside demands and being in charge or control of goals or plans; having the freedom to create something new and different; looking forward to something with anticipated pleasure; and doing something challenging.

It is noteworthy that those who considered part of their work "play" saw work and play as a continuum and had some difficulty unraveling what was work and what was play. Those who took themselves and their jobs too seriously to see any part of their jobs as "play" saw "work" and "play" as opposites. Many of these individuals admitted to being tense and stressed much of the time. Thus, the majority (71%) of the sampled population–though quite modest in size–considered "work" and "play" to be a continuum.

2. Work as a Continuum

While work as stress, strain, and exertion may be seen by some persons as the opposite of play–seen as rest, relaxation, fun, satisfaction, and enjoyment–work and play may be seen as operating on a continuum as well. When we vacation, play sports, or engage in expressive activities for which we are not paid, we may still be exerting ourselves and competing to set new records of competency (doing more or better in less time). To enjoy our work more and suffer less "burnout," we might plan more flexibility, creativity, and play/fun in our work schedules. Play in our work might become even more focused, meaningful, and healthy and become the coping resource for us to become more efficient and skillful in the work periods of our lives.

There does seem to be an ever constant shift in our life schedules from "work" to "play," with one phase deriving greater meaning and enjoyment from the presence of the other phase: each gives the other special meaning. There may be several such shifts from "work" to "play" states and back again during an eight-hour work day. Thus, there seems to be much justification for conceptualizing "work" and "play" along a continuum rather than envisioning them as opposites. For this continuum, we could define "work" and "play" as feeling states that are the independent variables. "Work" could be defined as "activity that is goal-oriented or has an objective toward accomplishing a particular goal or mission, with some extrinsic reward." "Play" would be defined as "an activity that is done for fun, pleasure, satisfaction, enjoyment, challenge, creativity, and refreshment and renewal, with intrinsic reward." The dependent variable would be the measure of the feeling states or performance over time, location, personality variables, etc. The picture would look like this:

```
Feeling States               |
Over Time, Location          |
or Personality Type          |
                             |
  Minutes/Hours              |
                             |
                             |
                             |______________________________________________
                           <----------WORK --------------- PLAY -------->
                                         FEELING STATES
```

An expansion of the "work" portion of the continuum would possibly look like the following:

Boring Work	Laborious Work	Tedious Work	Serious Work	Efficient Work	Mastery and Control Work

The expansion of the "play" portion of the continuum might possibly look like this:

Goofing Off	Social Interaction	Playing Games	Solving Puzzles (Specific)	Creativity	Intuiting

"Joking around with others" might lie between "Goofing Off" and "Social Interaction," and "Communicating with Others" might lie between "Social Interaction" and "Playing Games." Because of the constant interaction, interplay, and shifting from the "work" to the "play" states, the definitions of each might be applicable in part to the other under certain conditions of location (site of the activity), time (of the year, month, day), personality variables (type of personality, attitudes, values, etc.), and any other pertinent conditions. Intuiting is seen as part of the "play" portion of the continuum, since it is most often a spontaneous, effortless activity associated with very high-level thinking or pulling together of several facts at a very high, insightful rate of speed. It is thought by the present researcher that conceptualizing "work" and "play" along a continuum would better accommodate the experience of more people than would a schema of "work" and "play" as opposites.[1]

Note

1. I wish to thank Drs. Bradley and Phyllis Burson for their encouragement and help in writing this chapter.

References

Abramis, D. I. (1990). "Play in Work: Childish Hedonism or Adult Enthusiasm?" *American Behavioral Scientist*, 33:353-373.

Bundy, R. (1977). "Leisure: The Missing Futures Perspective in Educational Policy." *Journal of Education*, 159:93-104.

Csikszentmihalyi, M. (1975). *Beyond Boredom and Anxiety: The Experience of Play in Work and Games.* San Francisco: Jossey-Bass.

Csikszentmihalyi, M. (1982). "Toward a Psychology of Optimal Experience." *Review of Personality and Social Psychology*, 2:13-36.

Haworth, J. T., and J. Ducker. (1991). "Psychological Well-Being and Access To Categories of Experience in Unemployed Young Adults." *Leisure Studies,* 10:265-274.

Haworth, J. T., and S. Hill (1992). "Work, Leisure, and Psychological Well-Being in a Sample of Young Adults." *Journal of Community and Applied Social Psychology,* 2:147-160.

Jahoda, M. (1986). "In Defense of Non-Reductionist Social Psychology." *Social Behavior*, 1:25-29.

Kanchier, C., and W. R. Unruh. (1989). "Work Values: How Do Managers Who Change Jobs Differ from Those Who Do Not?" *Journal of Employment Counseling,* 26:107-116.

Kaplan, R. H., and C. Tausky. (1974). "The Meaning of Work Among the Hard-Core Unemployed." *Pacific Sociological Review*, 17:185-198.

Kazanas, H. C. (1978). "Relationship of Job Satisfaction and Productivity to Work Values of Vocational Education Graduates." *Journal of Vocational Behavior,* 12:155-164.

Neulinger, J. (1981). *To Leisure: An Introduction.* Boston: Allyn & Bacon.

Osipow, S. H., and A. R. Spokane. (1983). *A Manual for Measures of Occupational Stress, Strain, and Coping.* Columbus, Ohio: Marathon Consulting and Press.

Rayburn, C. A., L. J. Richmond. and L. Rogers, (1983). "Stress Among Religious Leaders." *Thought*: Fordham University Quarterly Review, 58:329-344.

Rayburn, C. A., L. J. Richmond, and L. Rogers, (1986). "Men, Women, and Religion: Stress Within Leadership Roles." *Journal of Clinical Psychology,* 42:540-546.

Chapter Five

WOMEN'S WORK: THE RE-NEGOTIATION OF MEANING

Georgia M. Keightley

In his 1981 encyclical letter, *Laborem exercens*, Pope John Paul II called for "the discovery of the new meanings of human work."[1] He did so in recognition of the new developments in technology, economics and politics effectively re-shaping the world of work and production forces, he asserts, as significant as those accompanying the industrial revolution of the last century. For the pontiff, the explication of meaning will necessitate the "formulation of the new tasks that in this sector face each individual, the family, each country, the whole human race and finally the church itself."[2]

One of the important new developments in the realm of work has been the large scale entry of women into the labor market across the world. According to a U. N. report on women published in 1991, "as officially measured, 41% of the world's women 15 and over–828 million[3]–are economically active."[4] The document goes on to acknowledge that an additional 10-20% of the world's women fit the category "economically active" but that because of inadequate measurements, these are not officially counted as part of the labor force.[5] In the United States, current estimates are that 55% of all women over the age of 16 are at work, with about 70% of these in the 20-44 age range and 30% in the 45-54 age range.[6] Not only is women's presence and involvement in the workplace affecting the world's economies in a significant way; women's increased, more formal partipation in economic life has also been the source of far reaching social and cultural change. The purpose of this chapter is to explore some of the ways in which women's active engagement in this way has affected classic understandings of work. The basic question to be examined here is this: In what way does women's experience call for a re-evaluation–and a re-valuing–of the meaning of work, of economic life? To put it in another way, what particular insights respecting work accrue to the disciplines of economics, ethics and spirituality from the study of contemporary women's experience in the workplace?

In the U. S. context, women's presence in the labor force has sparked a series of public debates in respect to a variety of issues. By examining and considering two of these, I will argue that the controverted points are in reality indicative of fundamental disagreements about meaning and value, that these issues are problematic precisely because they are about the need to re-think and re-negotiate accepted understandings of work and their social consequences.

The two issues I examine are those of pay equity and sexual harassment. In both cases, I provide a brief description of the public discussion and then go on to identify the matter of meaning/value that is at stake. I then indicate the specific points of conflict as well as the insights that devolve from women's experience. Finally, I discuss the implications of these, what they contribute to the renewal of a contemporary ethic of work and what they suggest for the development of an authentic Christian spirituality.

1. The Need to Attend to Meaning

For sociologists Berger and Luckmann, meaning has to do with "the objectivations of subjective processes...by which the intersubjective commonsense world is constructed."[7] By means of language and concepts, the different areas of human experience are named, delimited and ordered. But meaning is not only constitutive; it is also functional in that it serves as a frame of reference in which one can locate the particular experiences and events of existence.[8] More to the point, it is only within some specific framework of meaning that one can interpret and understand one's life.

A. Meaning and Women's Experience

Contemporary feminist studies show that typical understandings and construals of work do not always coincide with women's actual experience, that in reality many of the accepted meanings mislead and misinterpret. Therefore, uncovering the dissonances is vital to achieving an accurate understanding of social reality. Arriving at a proper grasp of meaning–the definitions of experience that are operative as well as the manner in which they function–will ultimately make possible better judgements as to what is effective or ineffective public policy, of what is just or immoral practise.

Feminists are quick to point to the many myths about women and work upon which workplace and government policy have often been based. A first such myth has to do with the assumption that by nature women are not fitted for the public workplace. Instead, a woman's work is presumed to flow from her biological capacity to bear and nurture children; her work is properly "private and family centered rather than social and kin focused."[9] Indeed, the papal document cited above strongly suggests that by God's design, gender predetermines the kind of work one must do.[10] But as feminists point out, it is precisely this kind of thinking that has served to justify women's exclusion from the workplace altogether, that has led to their segregation in the job market, and has justified their lower wages.[11]

To illustrate further: Feminists point out that traditional models of work are based on and draw almost exclusively upon men's occupational experiences and that this data is assumed to be fully explanatory of women's situation's as well.[12] As critics point out, however, such analysis actually obscures what may be unique or even central to women's situation's. For instance, such male models do not take into account the career interruptions women experience because of child-birth and subsequent parenting responsibilities. And, when male experience is presumed to be the norm, women invariably suffer in the comparison. Thus, present theory tends to categorize women as being secondary sector workers who show little interest in acquiring occupational training or in moving ahead.[13]

Finally, the theoretical exclusion of women from the category "work" has occurred in connection with a definition central to economics, that of work being "the production of goods and services." Under this classification, women's domestic work receives no place or status; neither is it assigned any economic value. And, when a woman does enter the workforce, it is taken for granted that she does so out of less serious motives than her husband.[14] It is presumed that she takes a job only to get extra spending money or that she is brought here merely by the need to supplement her husband's income. But whatever the reason, women's presence in the workplace is taken to be an exception rather than the norm.

Again, the point to be made here is that meanings are important because they are functional and constitutive of both theory and policy. And, for this reason, study of "the meaning that women make of their own experiences," is indispensable in light of the fact that larger sets of research data generated through the government census bureau and social science research centers are frequently used to imply that women's lot as workers has greatly improved with regard to opportunities, conditions and pay. Such conclusions, however, can give rise to a false optimism that in the end can be particularly damaging for minorities, the poor and/or single parents.[15]

B. Meaning and Economic Theory

The importance of attending to meaning and its explication is also the thesis of economist Robert Heilbroner's *Beyond the Veil of Economics*.[16] He argues that far from being a value-free science, economics can actually obscure the truth of how society functions. For one thing, economic theories contain premises and value judgements, i.e., meanings concerning human nature, history, society, etc., that are never made explicit.[17] For another, theory overlooks that the human forces–affect and obedience, the universal products of the socialization of humankind–continue to serve the market as an important orchestrating means.[18] And, while Heilbroner would agree that the term capitalism refers to a specific process of provisioning, he would insist that capitalism is also a regime, a vision of a definite sociopolitical order with an agenda and the coercive power to enact it.[19] As he says, "the market presents a wholly new means of social orchestration."[20]

On this basis he goes on to argue that a true understanding of modern work is possible only when considered within the context of capitalism. He asserts that work as we know it comes with the advent of civilization, that while primitive societies were obviously engaged in the necessary tasks of producing and reproducing the material requirements of life, nonetheless these activities were "so radically different in motive, rationale, organization, and social control that the term 'work' is inappropriate by our standards."[21]

Heilbroner defines work as being a social relationship, one distinguished by those tasks "carried out in a condition of subordination imposed by the right of some members of society to refuse access to vital resources to others."[22] Work in its modern sense then appears when control over resources becomes one of society's defining characteristics.

From this vantage point, the time and energy spent on production are seen to be matters of paramount interest to those who are the beneficiaries of others' work. As Heilbroner notes, the labor hours commanded by ruling classes are an index of their power as are the work energies at their disposal.[23] Again, when seen in this light, Adam Smith's description of the waged labor contract as an instance of "perfect" or "natural" liberty actually obscures the truth that the need for employment provides a disparity in social power "from which arose the rights to payment called *rent* or to claims to a residual called *profit*" and, "without which the access to resources called *employment* would not be offered."[24] It was Marx, of course, who called attention to capitalism's ability to conceal the exploitative nature of its gains.[25]

Just as was true in the case of women cited above, Heilbroner argues that a failure to consider work as a purposeful type of social relationship can easily result in misdiagnosis of problems associated with the market place. His work reiterates the thesis that by attending to meaning, not only will a better grasp of social reality accrue, so will the ethical implications of economic life and activity become apparent. In effect, this is precisely what U. S. Catholic bishops had in mind when they asked Catholics to evaluate economic systems in terms of what they do *to* people, *for* people, when they argued that this should be a criterion for judging a system's effectiveness as opposed to looking at productivity only.[26]

To develop this thesis about meaning and its significance in relation to human economic activity, I now want to look at two issues that are currently being raised by the increased presence of women in the contemporary workplace.

2. Pay Equity as a Question of Meaning

The debate over pay equity centers on the efforts of women "to get employers to equalize the wage rates for women in traditionally female jobs with wage rates for men in traditionally male jobs requiring equivalent abilities."[27] In other words, the aim is not simply to gain for women "equal pay for equal work"; it also has in view the achievement of equal pay for work of comparable worth.

Research shows sex-based discrimination to be the primary cause of the wage gap between women and men. And, as one scholar notes, the division of labor by sex and "the historical undervaluation of 'women's jobs'" are virtually universal phenomena.[28]

Those who research and study work issues indicate that the wage gap is at bottom, culturally rooted. The visible cause, gender-based discrimination, has its matrix in human consciousness. And, despite all efforts to improve women's human capital by developing skills through educational and job training, by enacting equal employment opportunity and antidiscrimination measures,[29] it is ultimately attitudinal bias that explains why "an increasing prevalence of women or nonwhites within a job is most likely to taint a position, depressing its relative standing."[30]

One author argues that what is fundamentally at stake in the pay equity debate is the question of value. She notes that the effort to define value strictly in terms of the skill, effort and responsibility needed to do a job overlooks the specific social matrix out of which such a definition necessarily comes. Consequently, analysis must also involve "the social reexamination of value."[31] "Pay equity asks not only to have the skills of women that are as useful in society as the skills of men compensated equivalently but also that in calculating value, the experiences and *values* of women [themselves] are equally integrated into the calculation process."[32]

When one begins to speak about value, however, one begins to speak about meaning. And despite theorists efforts "to tie the surface phenomena of economic life to some inner structure or order,"[33] economic realities are inevitably subject to the exigences of history as well as to the desires and intentions of human beings. And, when construed from the standpoint of meaning, the pay equity issue presents a rather different dynamic. As opposed to being a matter of sexual discrimination *per se*, the problem now centers on the more fundamental question of time and it's intrinsic worth. To illustrate, I refer again to the interpretation set forth in Heilbroner's *Beyond the Veil of Economics.*

As previously noted, Heilbroner describes the term "work" as denoting a social relation, that of subordination/domination. Work as the restriction of human freedom occurs once some individuals are able to gain control of resources vital to life's sustenance. To get access, those without these goods must surrender their time plus a portion of their work product to those in control, *i.e.*, the owners.[34]

Heilbroner notes that once this situation arises, a radical re-valuing of time occurs. That is, for those engaged in what anthropologists call "the domestic mode of production," time and energy are matters of small importance.[35] In primitive society, little time separates the gathering of food from its use; and because competition for nature's resources is virtually non-existent, tasks have no special priority or pressure. Life is instead leisurely and confident. And while there is no material wealth, there *is* material well-being. What is missing, above all, is the competition to win access to nature's resources.

Once permission to secure the necessaries of life becomes a matter of course, however, the individual's time becomes of the essence. It becomes a constitutive element of the new relation created between owner and hire.

More to the point, one's time is no longer one's own. Much of it now belongs to an employer whose command of labor hours becomes an index of power. The work energies at the employer's disposal not only become the means by which nature's resources are translated into the products of culture; they also become the means to profit.[36]

Even in the modern workplace, the employer strives to exercise total control over the employee's time. As Heilbroner observes, it is the owner's prerogative to require surrender of personal autonomy, the submission of both body and mind, to the pace and movements, of a complex schedule designed to meet capitalism's own ends.[37] Here one thinks of the reduction of labor's activity to the dismembered dull, monotonous gestures of the assembly line or the interminably long hours today's employee spends staring at the computer screen.

At the same time, implicit to capitalism are powerful incentives to increase work time. In truth, some have argued that "the logic of capitalist labor relations points in the direction of jobs becoming all-consuming."[38] As if to confirm, recent statistics show that "the average employed person is now on the job an additional 163 hours, or the equivalent of an extra month a year."[39] The advent of the fixed annual salary has allowed employers to extend the work day; they are able to demand longer hours knowing full well there are far more candidates than there are jobs to fill.[40] Coincident with this, it has become part of the corporate culture that long hours are a barometer of the professional manager's dedication and commitment in addition to being a good indicator of the caliber of his/her work.

But this increase of work time has not been without its cost. Stress and the loss of sleep are constants of life today as are neglect of spouse and children, the difficulties of maintaining a balance between the demands of work and private life plus a host of stress-related illnesses. This issue of time now exceeds the workplace: it has become a crisis of American life and culture. And nowhere is this more evident than in the lives of women who must cope with the double burden–the traditional duties of home and children and a growing responsibility for earning a paycheck.[41]

It is my thesis that this clash between the public and private that occurs in women's lives is "at bottom" about time, its meaning and valuing. And this is why.

As it has developed historically, women's time has been–and even continues to be–rooted in an entirely different order than men's. That is to say, public perception of a woman's time is in terms of that earlier period of human social life when "tasks associated with the physical sustenance of the group are not distinguished by organization or esteem from other tasks and activities also required to maintain collective life, such as the rearing of children."[42] But in particular, her life relates to–and reminds of–a context where such tasks are not carried out for any extrinsic purpose or reward.

While man's time has long been regulated by the market's demands–he has been obliged to surrender the use of his body and mind to the time and space configurations required by his employer–woman, either ideologically or really, has not. And it is precisely here that the tension between woman's time and the workplace reveals itself. For one thing, woman's bodily rhythms are determined by and continue to be subject to nature. The fact is, the cycle of pregnancy and childbirth, the socially assigned responsibility for nurturance and parenting simply refuses to bend to the rhythms and whims of market time. In other words, a woman simply cannot transfer complete autonomy over self to her employer. This then presents a direct challenge to the subordination/domination pattern central to the employer/employee relation. And it is from this that the current difficult struggles between women and the workplace on the basic issue of pay equity and such related issues as child care, parental leave, flexible hours, etc. ensue.

One may further argue that a woman in her prescribed role as wife and mother in a most visible way serves as society's memory as well as its conscience. After all, the longstanding restrictions placed on her sexuality and her family responsibility in effect encode values that have been important to–even essential to–human flourishing, namely, those of home and children, love and friendship, of vision and hope for the future.

What is at stake as work threatens to consume all of our waking hours is the value of woman's time and the values that she in her person has for so long symbolized and manifested. Now recognition or agreement about this should by no means be construed as an argument that women must leave their workplaces and return to full-time domestic duties. It is simply to say that in this instance woman's dilemma symbolizes that of contemporary humanity. Rather, it is to argue that as a society we are being pressed to re-examine the way in which we use and manage our time, we are increasingly obliged to reconsider the meanings that we currently attribute to time. What is needed is a public discussion as to whether or not as a community we wish our lives to be the context within which work's time fits or whether instead we shall continue on in the direction of trying to squeeze all of life into the narrow confines delimited by work's time. Together we must decide whether time is to be the objective force within which *homo oeconomicus* increasingly finds himself–or for that matter, herself–imprisoned. Or whether to the contrary time is to be–as it was for past generations–the comfortable milieu within which all society's members are allowed to live out their lives in a creative, fulfilling–and meaningful–way.[43]

3. Sexual Harassment as a Question of Meaning

A basic concern of feminist scholars has been provision of a definition of sexual harassment. Generally speaking, the term refers to one of the ways men exert social control over women. More narrowly, "sexual harassment" has been used to specify a range of behaviors that are publicly embarassing to women, especially those that occur in the workplace.[44] But however it is defined, common to all is recognition that sexual harassment has to do with "unwanted sexual attention".[45]

According to Rosemarie Tong, in the workplace this attention normally takes one of two forms.[46] On the one hand, sexual harassment can be *coercive* in that either a reward or threat is proffered in exchange for a sexual favor. On the other hand, harassment may be *non-coercive*. It can be behavior that is merely annoying or offensive, in this case taking the form of lewd comments and/or inappropriate gestures or physical contact. But again, what both types of behavior have in common is that "they are unsolicited, unwelcome, and generally unwanted by the women to whom they are directed."[47] In the workplace both "interfere with the ability of the person who is their target to work, or they make that person feel uncomfortable or frightened."[48]

Peggy Crull notes that these two behaviors are prototypes and create a continuum in relation to which other behaviors may be placed and evaluated.[49] These two types have also been subject to the most legal and popular attention.[50] For our interest, Crull calls attention to the power configurations associated with each, suggesting that the different types of harassment are expressive/reflective of the different levels of power men exercise over women.[51] For example, "the very essence of the *quid pro quo* dilemma lies in the fact that the harasser has the power to fire the woman to whom he directs his attention."[52] Those normally subjected to this kind of attention are persons in jobs typically held by women. In contrast, "atmosphere harassment" tends to occur in those situations where women do work not traditionally theirs. But while in this case a woman's male co-workers have little direct economic power over her, their behavior nonetheless creates a hostile, even intimidating environment. Whether rooted in a fear of competition and/or a recognition of the loss of power over her, this exercise of covert power by her male co-workers invariably has negative consequences, sometimes making it necessary for a woman to leave her job altogether.[53]

As was the case with pay equity, sexual harassment too is best understood when treated within the larger context of meaning. While public relationships between men and women appear to be the primary issue, when approached in another way, sexual harassment raises the question about the very end and purpose of work itself. The question is: Is work simply a matter of exploitation, that of the many by the few, that of the collective by the market system? Or should work be instead a significant means to personal growth and well-being for all human beings?

As Heilbroner suggests, work's meaning has been played out within the historic drama of power's exercise. To reiterate, at some point in time and with the emergence of private property, work appears as a relationship of subordination/domination. And as feminist scholars have been quick to point out, man's early domination of woman actually anticipates capitalism: under the social system of patriarchy, woman not only becomes man's property; he acquires the right to both her daily labor as well as to the product of her reproductive labor, her children.[54] The feminist position here–contra

Heilbroner–would be that, as far as women are concerned, work as we know it puts in an appearance long before the emergence of capitalism.

Much has been written on patriarchy which has been defined as "a system of social relationships in which males dominate females in certain ordered hierarchical ways."[55] And while there has been a tendency to see "the family as patriarchy and the rest of the social and economic relations of society as not-patriarchy," one scholar argues that today perhaps the most significant exercise of male power takes public form, and this has to do with the degree to which men control and are the beneficiaries of woman's work and its produce.

"Women's work is patriarchally determined to the extent that women work under the auspices of and to the benefit of men."[56] Carol Brown points to a shift that has occurred wherein "control of women's labor is moving from the private patriarchy of individual men within families to the public patriarchy of hierarchical, male-dominated work institutions that are part of the profit-making system."[57] Thus she holds that while women continue to provide the bulk of unpaid household labor and child care upon which the paid economy is utterly dependent, women's work outside the home too comes increasingly under the collective control of men in the guise of an "industry and government-centered public patriarchy of a high-technology monopoly capitalist economy."[58]

Under public patriarchy, men not only retain effective control of woman's labor, they have even expanded it. In effect, the conditions regulating woman's place in society "are now set less by husbands or for the sake of husbands, and more by employers and public policy makers for the sake of male-dominated society in general or specifically for the sake of profit making employers."[59] At the same time, management of the labor force has become the prerogative of elite white male professionals. These not only manage; they also set forth and implement the policies of programs and business, public administration, education, medicine and other fields.[60] And as indicated above, male control of women's participation in the workplace manifests itself in such things as job segregation, low wages, poor-working conditions, little chance for advancement; it shows itself in "a lack of stability" as well as "employer/employee relations conducive to arbitrary and capricious work discipline."[61] On the other hand, studies show that while woman's work takes place increasingly outside the home, the fact is that from the 1880s to the present the work women do for pay is the same kind of work they have historically been expected to do as wives and mothers; moreover, their work tends to be done under the same conditions of inequality and subordination.[62]

Brown emphasizes that not only do women do for the public the same kind of work they once did for the men of their families, they now do it for society as a whole. Women's low paid work not only serves some men who are employers, clients, customers, or coworkers. Thanks to public patriarchy, all men are now able to obtain women's services without the necessity of marriage. Thus, poorer men who could never afford homemaker wives now receive the services of working women. The fact is, "the jobs of many working women are oriented to giving 'service with a smile,' and are directed toward making life nicer for men at all levels."[63] As Brown asserts, "Waitresses, nurses, and housecleaners are among the effective replacements for workers within the home."[64]

As shown in the example of coercive harassment, the workplace often replicates the family hierarchical relationship in job structure. For example, the executive secretary has long functioned as the boss's "wife."[65] To develop this analogy–and to press the point about meaning–sexual harassment might well be described as public patriarchy's version of spouse abuse. While certainly all of the instances of subordination and inequality associated with the workplace underscores man's power over woman, perhaps none symbolizes its exploitative character more than does sexual harassment. For as feminist scholars show, there is no more basic form of man's oppression of woman than his claim to, or his possession of, her sexuality and bodily integrity whether this be physical or conceptual.

If the use of power to exploit is the discernible norm in today's workplace, analysis of women's experience focuses attention on two of power's other, positive uses. That is, besides being the occasion of the exercise of power over others, human work can also provide an opportunity for the "power to," the empowerment of both self and others.

In regard to the first, a recent study shows that work plays a central role in most women's personal development today. Work provides "a crucial impetus" in that a woman is here given an opportunity not only to test her skills and abilities. Depending upon the situation as well as the availability of employer-sponsored education and job training, she also has the possibility of enlarging them.[66] From her work experience can emerge a satisfying sense of mastery and accomplishment that is reinforced by positive feedback from others about the value they place on her work, and their notions of her as worker. A woman comes to realize that her work not only makes it possible for her to take responsibility for herself, it is also the means by which she contributes to society's own good functioning. Finally, the workplace provides a rich variety of relationships to be negotiated. Scholars show that the experience of colleagueship, the give-and-take involved in team work, collaboration with others is a major way by which individuals come to a clearer understanding of who they are.[67] But women find that not only can work provide for their personal empowerment, it is also an important instrument to be wielded in the empowerment of others. A study of ten women working in non-traditional jobs revealed that a primary difference in the way men and women approached their work manifested itself in the way in which each group used power. While men have been socialized to think of power mainly in terms of "power over," the women interviewed were concerned to use the power at their disposal for helping others. This the author attributed to the women's own socialization, *i.e.*, their earlier preparation for the roles of mother and homemaker.

From interviews with women physicians, lawyers, engineers, stockbrokers, legislators, etc. women were shown to use power in four common ways. First of all, they were consciously oriented to serving their clients. Theirs was a willingness and an ability to listen and respond to others.[68] Secondly, concern for their co-workers well-being was also marked. Above all, these women wanted to ensure that their workplaces were collaborative, emphathic and egalitarian, allowing the free exchange of ideas and feelings.[69] Thirdly, the women were insistent about the need for a balanced worklife. This was something they wanted not only for themselves; time for family, leisure, pursuits of one's own interests outside was something they wanted to ensure for others as well. Finally as managers, the group was unanimous in its desire to use power well. Most of all, the women wanted to create a good work environment where the power at their disposal would be directed to serving the group's good rather than that of any one individual.[70]

What the results of this study suggest–and what Heilbroner's work confirms–is that while the power dynamic will ever be a condition of work within the market system, it is the end to which power is directed that becomes key.

When considered within the framework of that vision a society has of itself–a community whose goal is justice and equality and the well-being of all its members–then the challenge becomes one of trying to maximize the freedom that exists within work to the extent that the regulating principle subordination/domination is replaced with "the free act of obedience of all members of society" directed to their own purposes rather than to those of a small minority.[71]

The challenge, in other words, is that work–which originated as a basic form of social subordination–should become instead the first and perhaps most emancipatory form of social responsibility. Heilbroner argues that this goal can be achieved by lessening all of those things within work that limit personal freedom–e.g., the division of labor as we know it, the hierarchical ordering of jobs– and in turn, by maximizing all of those elements of work that invigorate, excite, that produce a sense of self-esteem and fulfillment, that foster comunity and thus strengthen the bonds of social solidarity. Work, in this case, becomes a reality that not merely "expresses human dignity but increases it." Even more than this, it provides the means to the achievement of human responsibility to bring all created reality to its fruition.

4. Implications for Economics, Ethics, and Spirituality

Consideration of women's experience in the contemporary workplace, the specific issues of pay equity and sexual harassment, and examination of the meanings implicit thereto yields a variety of insights pertinent to economics and ethics.

Some of these are general and methodological. For example, this study shows that because of their direct affect on individual lives· all social systems–as opposed to being mere abstractions or objectifications–have an intrinsically human, practical dimension. In fact, it is exactly in this that their moral character resides. Heilbroner insists that a nation's economy actually represents the embodiment of morality and politics[72] in that it implicates a vision of human community as well as proposes a strategy for achieving it. When approached in this way, it becomes evident that economic theory depends on assumptions about persons, society, history, assumptions that are indispensable to the system's successful functioning. Such suppositions need to be made explicit for only on this basis can an adequate moral analysis be made. This in turn underscores the fact that because of the degree of human complicity, systems can, and must be, adjusted to better facilitate and regulate human social interaction for the well-being of all rather than accommodate the wishes of the few. And lastly, in that meaning is both constitutive and functional, attention to that which persons attribute to and/or discover in economic realities has to be integral to both theoretical and moral assessment. Without this more comprehensive look, one risks putting forth public policy that is ineffectual, of recommending solutions that are morally inadequate.

In addition to the general, study of the pay equity and sexual harassment debates bring to the fore some specific justice issues. As this study indicates, these include: the matter of job discrimination and its consequences for women and minorities; the number of hours that comprise the just workday and conversely, the wage that reflects a job's actual time demands; the matter of workplace environment; the humane workday schedule; the overall time and space configurations to which the worker is obliged to adapt.

More importantly perhaps, this study has highlighted the considerable consequences of power and its use. Specifically at issue is frank acknowledgement that men have used power over working women in inappropriate ways, that this is not to be discounted or trivialized and that to do so is itself morally wrong. In fact, analysis of women's situation raises the very question of the continuing viability of hierarchically structured relationships given the ease with which these can become exploitative. This study also calls attention to the inherent moral responsibilities of corporate leadership as well as to power's privileged role in fostering the personal development and well-being of workers. Lastly, it becomes obvious that while the work of all society's members is essential to achievement of the common good, the availability and easy access to good work is itself requisite to and even constitutive of the common good.

Finally, it is in terms of the questions of meaning posed that the spiritual dimension of the social realities examined here comes to the fore. Recent Roman Catholic documents stress the significance and dignity of the human being, the need to protect life and respect dignity; they also point to the collective responsibility to enable personal growth and creativity. The question of work figures large here: What, after all, can be said about work's ultimate purpose? Is it strictly to keep up with the rapacious demands of our consumerist economy? Or, is it instead to provide the wherewithal to a meaningful, satisfying life for all?

Today, work has very much become a question of society's priorities. Should it be allowed to consume all of our waking hours and energies, so much so that our other human tasks and interests necessarily fall by the way? But this in its turn poses the fundamental question of value itself. In the case of pay equity, at issue is the value of time, and in particular that women spend doing what they have traditionally done. Although this appears to be a matter of women's concern, in reality it is very much about the entire community and its future. Are children and parenting important enough, of such value that we are willing to restructure our economic life so as to allow them the time and community suppport so essential to their good flourishing?

In terms of sexual harassment, at issue is power and the structure of human relationships. Are work relations to be designed so to empower or to control? The above review also calls attention to the critical importance of social structures in promoting human creativity, productivity, development.

Certainly there are other questions which this scrutiny of women's experience, modern work and its meaning raises. The object here has been to specify only some and to recommend an approach for future research.

Notes

1. *Laborem exercens*, p.2.

2. *Ibid.*

3. *Ibid.*

4. *The World's Women: Trends and Statistics 1970-1991*, United Nations Publication E.90.XVII.3, p. 4.

5. *Ibid.*

6. Nia Lane Chester and Hildreth Grossman, eds. in *The Experience and Meaning of Work in Women's Lives* (Hillsdale, N.J.: Lawrence Erlbaum Associates, Publishers, 1990), p. 1.

7. Berger and Luckmann, *The Social Construction of Reality* (New York: Doubleday and Co., 1966), p. 20.

8. Hans Mol, *Meaning and Place: An Introduction to the Social Scientific Study of Religion* (New York: The Pilgrim Press, 1983), pp. 20-21.

9. Heidi Hartmann, "Capitalism and Patriarchy" in *Women and the Workplace*, eds. Martha Blaxall and Barbara Reagan (Chicago: University of Chicago Press, 1976), p. 146.

10. *Laborem exercens*, p. 4.

11. See Barbara R. Bergmann, *The Economic Emergence of Women* (New York: Basic Books, Inc., 1986), pp. 88-89.

12. Grossman, *Experience and Meaning of Work*, p. 7.

13. Veronica Beechey, "Rethinking the Definition of Work" in *Feminization of the Labor Force: Paradoxes and Promises*, eds. Jane Jenson, Elisabeth Hagen, and Ceallaigh Reddy (New York: Oxford University Press, 1988), p. 47.

14. Grossman, *Experience and Meaning of Work*, p. 2.

15. *Ibid.*, p. 5.

16. Robert L. Heilbroner, *Beyond the Veil of Economics* (New York: W. W. Norton and Co., 1988).

17. *Ibid.*, p. 185.

18. *Ibid.*, p. 34.

19. *Ibid.*, p. 196.

20. *Ibid.*, p. 23.

21. *Ibid.*, p. 83.

22. *Ibid.*, p. 85.

23. *Ibid.*, p. 87.

24. *Ibid.*, p. 91.

25. *Ibid.*, p. 92.

26. National Conference of Catholic Bishops, *Economic Justice for All: Pastoral Letter on Catholic Social Teaching and the U.S. Economy*, 1986.

27. Bergmann, *The Economic Emergence of Women,* p. 173.

28. Mary Rubin, "Equal Pay for Work of Comparable Worth: The Role of Research in Shaping an Equity Strategy," *Women's Studies Quarterly,* (1985): 8.

29. *Monthly Labor Review* 115 (November 1992): 40.

30. James N. Baron and Andrew Newman, "For What It's Worth: Organizations, Occupations, and the Value of Work Done by Women and Nonwhites," *American Sociological Review*, 55 (1990): 172.

31. Gay Binion, review of Steven L. Willborn, *A Secretary and a Cook: Challenging Women's Wages in the Courts of the United States and Great Britain* (Ithaca, New York: Industrial and Labor Relations, 1989) in *American Political Science Review*, 85: 603.

32. *Ibid.*

33. Heilbroner, *Beyond the Veil of Economics*, p. 105.

34. *Ibid.*, p. 86.

35. *Ibid.*, pp. 80-84.

36. *Ibid.*, p. 87.

37. *Ibid.*, p. 97.

38., Juliet B. Schor, *The Overworked American: The Unexpected Decline of Leisure* (New York: Basic Books, 1992), p. 65.

39. *Ibid.*, p. 29.

40. *Ibid.*, p. 71.

41. *Ibid.*, p. 20.

42. Heilbroner, *Beyond the Veil of Economics*, p. 82.

43. A paraphrase of a quotation by historian E.P. Thompson found in Schor, *The Overworked American*, p. 50.

44. Janet E. Stockdale, "Sexual Harassment at Work" in *Women at Work*, eds. Jenny Firth-Cozens and Michael A. West (Philadelphia: Open University Press, 1991), p. 54.

45. *Ibid.*, p. 55.

46. Rosemarie Tong, "Sexual Harassment" in *Gender Basics: Feminist Perspectives on Women and Men*, ed. Anne Minas (Belmont, California: Wadsworth Publishing, 1993), p. 365.

47. *Ibid.*

48. Peggy Crull, "Searching for the Causes of Sexual Harassment: An Examination of Two Prototypes" in *Hidden Aspects of Women's Work*, ed. Christine Bose, Roslyn Feldberg, Natalies Sokoloff, *et al.* (New York: Praeger, 1987), p. 227.

49. Crull uses different terms to describe the two behavior patterns identified by Tong. Crull uses "quid pro quo harassment" to refer to what Tong calls "coercive," and "atmosphere harassment" instead of "non-coercive." See Crull, "Searching for the Causes," pp. 228-229.

50. *Ibid.*, p. 227.

51. *Ibid.*, p. 233.

52. *Ibid.*, p. 232.

53. *Ibid.*, p. 235.

54. Carol A. Brown, "The New Patriarchy," in *Hidden Aspects*, ed. Bose *et al.*, p. 140.

55. *Ibid.*, p. 138.

56. *Ibid.*, p. 140.

57. *Ibid.*, p. 137.

58. *Ibid.*, p. 142.

59. *Ibid.*

60. *Ibid.*, p. 143.

61. *Ibid.*, p. 146.

62. *Ibid*,.

63. *Ibid.*

64. *Ibid.*, p. 153.

65. *Ibid.*, p. 147.

66. Eileen M. Brennan and Julie M. Rosenzweig, "Women and Work: Toward a New Developmental Model," *Families in Society* (November 1990): 528.

67. *Ibid.*, p. 531.

68. Bose, Christine *et al.*, eds. *Hidden Aspects of Women's Work* (New York: Praeger, 1987), p. 3.

69. *Ibid.*, p. 45.

70. *Ibid.*, p. 147. See also p. xviii.

71. Heilbroner, *Beyond the Veil of Economics,* p. 103.

72. *Ibid.*, p. 34.

Chapter Six

VALUING WOMEN EDUCATORS

Ailsa M. Watkinson

1. Introduction

The *Oxford English Dictionary* defines values as "that amount of some commodity, medium or exchange . . . which is considered to be an equivalent for something else; a fair or adequate equivalent or return."[1] It is, as Marilyn Waring notes, an economic definition–a definition that had changed from its original Latin meaning of "to be strong or worthy." The change in definition reflects a societal change in what is valued: economics over worth. This difference in the meaning of value is also evident in the practice of educational administration which is closely tied to the world of commerce rather than the world of children. The world of commerce has traditionally been occupied by men and the world of children has traditionally been occupied by women.

Carol Gilligan's work on the ethic of justice and the ethic of care provides a compelling backdrop to the differing views of value. The ethic of justice values equality, reciprocity and fairness, characteristics that fit neatly into the economic definition of value. The ethic of justice is formal and abstract: value in a three–piece suit. The ethic of care values connection and is concerned with problems of detachment, abandonment and indifference. It is more contextual.[2] But within the economic definition of value it finds no place: it is of worth but of no value. Research shows that more men than women use the ethic of justice and more women than men use the ethic of care.[3]

The purpose of this chapter is to question our expectations of and assumptions about what makes a good educational administrator. Expectations and assumptions developed from questionable theories of leadership and organizational design which have placed little value on characteristics often associated with women, the values of women and child centered pedagogy. Expectations and assumptions that are counter to legal obligations and interpretations concerning the democratic rights of equality and fundamental freedoms both in Canada and on the international scene.

The first part of the chapter begins with an introduction of the framework informing this chapter: the ethic of care and the ethic of justice. Carol Gilligan's seminal works redefined for many of us our understanding of moral development. She gave voice to the historically undervalued voice of women. As Robin West said, "I don't know any woman who hasn't recognized herself somewhere in this book...."[4] Gilligan's theory of the ethic of care and justice forms the background to a discussion on the maleness of educational administration which is demonstrated, not only in numbers, but in theory and organizational practice. The effect is a practice of educational administration that is congruous with the ethic of justice. However, as will be argued in the second section, these practices and theories are the antithesis of good pedagogical practices and possibly even litigious. Our ability to meet the educational rights of the child, especially in terms of dealing with such foundational matters as inequality and democratic rights provided for in *The Canadian Charter of Rights and Freedoms*[5] and *The Convention on the Rights of the Child* [6] requires decision makers to employ, and to value, the ethic of care. The legal interpretation given to Canada's eleven-year old *Charter* is a contextual one–an interpretation which calls on decision makers to abandon, in legal terms, the rigid Rule of Law and in educational terms, the paternalistic-authoritarian paradigm. Finally, I will report on the findings of a study which analyzed the moral orientations of women and men educators in dealing with conflicts of inequality and democratic rights.[7] The conclusion draws some challenges worthy of our attention.

2. The Ethic of Care and the Ethic of Justice

Alasdair MacIntyre's first chapter in *After Virtue* is entitled "A Disquieting Suggestion."[8] In it he asks us to imagine a world in which all knowledge is destroyed. Later, in his imaginary world, parts of knowledge are retained and strung together, becoming new but incomplete knowledge. There are gaps, but worse yet, no one knows what, if anything, is missing.

MacIntyre uses this metaphor to advance his hypotheses "that in the actual world which we inhabit the language of morality is in the same state of grave disorder as the language of the natural sciences in the imaginary world."[9] He states further that we have "lost our comprehension"[10] of morality, not even aware that our view of morality is riddled with omissions.

MacIntyre's metaphor could be used another way: It could be used to describe the missing voice of women in history, education, science, psychology, philosophy, moral theory, and education.[11]

Implicit in their absence is their lack of value. The voice of women, their experiences, their knowledge, and their ways of knowing are black holes in what is considered "knowledge": That, I submit, is a "disquieting" reality.

The missing voice, to expand on MacIntyre's metaphor, is an overwhelming catastrophe because very few recognize it as a catastrophe at all. Like the inhabitants of Plato's cave, they view their world as the truth, and know nothing of the missing knowledge. MacIntyre uses his metaphor to decry the state of morality. His metaphor is referred to here to decry the gap created by ignoring the experiences and thoughts of women, a gap that even MacIntyre has overlooked.

In recent years, however, the missed voices of women have been heard. The listening has been due in large part to other women.[12] One such woman is Carol Gilligan whose own work, and the work of others inspired by her research, has evolved into an inclusion of the "other voice." Gilligan, an educational psychologist from Harvard University developed the theory[13] of two moral orientations, an ethic of care and an ethic of justice, in response to the work of Lawrence Kohlberg, best known for his theory of moral development.[14] Kohlberg's theory, which Gilligan terms the ethic of justice, describes a sequential progression of moral development which begins with a focus on "avoiding punishment and unquestioning deference to power" and progresses to self chosen ethical and abstract principles such as the Golden Rule and categorical imperatives.[15]

Kohlberg developed his theory of moral development by studying the moral judgement of males from childhood into adulthood. His study group consisted of eighty-four white boys whom he studied over a period of twenty years. The fact that his study was developed from observing only white males has put his theory of moral development into doubt. Gilligan is one who has doubted his theory saying, "Although Kohlberg claims universality for his stage sequence, those groups not included in his original sample rarely reach his higher stages."[16]

Gilligan noticed that women did not progress beyond the third stage of Kohlberg's six-stage sequence of moral development.[17] The third stage is characterized as the "good boy - nice girl" orientation, it good behavior is that which pleases or helps others and is approved by them."[18] Gilligan points out that Kohlberg and Kramer[19] considered this stage to be functional in the lives of most women who remain in the home and "only if women enter the traditional arena of male activity will they recognize the inadequacy of this moral perspective and progress like men toward higher stages where relationships are subordinated to rules (stage 4) and rules to universal principles of justice (stage 5 and 6)."[20] In other words, according to Kohlberg and Kramer, maintaining interpersonal relationships is morally inferior to abiding by the rules, and that for women's morality to advance they must "progress like men."[21]

In response to the alleged error in research methodology, which missed the voice of women, Gilligan conducted new research, listening to women speak of their own moral decisions and concluded that there is another moral orientation that has been ignored, the ethic of care.[22]

The care perspective is based on the premise that hurting others is to be avoided. Listening to others is considered vital as is building and sustaining trust and relationships. It develops from a focus on oneself to an acceptance of the interconnectedness between self and others.[23]

3. Contrasts between Care and Justice

Contrasts between these moral orientations can be seen in a number of areas. First, each orientation displays a difference in the perception of the self. Lyons has shown that those who describe the self as separate from others, show a predominance for the ethic of justice in moral reasoning.[24] The ethic of justice, which reflects Kohlberg's theory of moral development, values autonomy.[25]

The perception of the self as separate from others in turn views relationships as contractual. Relationships are necessary primarily because of the mutual benefit each party derives from them. The contractual nature of relationships is based on reciprocity and grounded in duty and obligation.[26] In contrast, the perception of the self as connected to others and valuing connectedness is associated with a predominance for the ethic of care, recognized through Gilligan's work. It is centered in responsibility, connectedness, compassion and inclusion.[27]

Another contrast can be seen in how individuals perceive moral problems. The ethic of justice focuses on competing rights, the ethic of care focuses on conflicting responsibilities. The ethic of justice, in Gilligan's words, is "formal and abstract . . . the conception of morality as fairness ties moral development to the understanding of rights and rules." The ethic of care "requires for its resolution a mode of thinking that is contextual and narrative,"[28] and centers around an understanding of responsibility and relationships. It is, in Gilligan's words, "an activity of relationship, of seeing and responding to need, taking care of the world by sustaining the web of connection so that no one is left alone."[29] The ethic of care recognizes the importance, of connection between one's self and others and is centered in the need for compassion and care.

Another contrast is evident in gender preference. Gilligan and others[30] have provided empirical data to suggest that these two views of morality, the ethic of care and the ethic of justice, show a predominance, "although not gender specific . . . gender related, suggesting that the gender differences we currently observe in moral reasoning signifies differences in moral orientation which in turn are tied to different ways of imagining self in relationships."[31] (See Table 1)

Table 1. Contrast Between Care and Justice

	ETHIC OF JUSTICE	ETHIC OF CARE
SELF	separate, autonomous	connected
RELATIONSHIPS	contractual, reciprocity	interdependence, connectedness
GENDER PREDOMINANCE	more male	more female
MORAL PERCEPTIONS	competing rights, rules and rights, formal and abstract	conflicting responsibilities, contextual narratives

4. The Maleness and Moral Orientation of Educational Administration

The field of educational administration is overwhelmingly occupied by men. In Saskatchewan, for example, only 19.2% of the administrative positions (principals, vice-principals, and district staff) are held by women.[32] This raises the question: Is there a connection between the maleness of educational administration and its practice–a practice that, according to some, is based on rational objectivity and almost void of heart?[33]

The late Thomas Greenfield was one of the best-known commentators in the discourse over what he refers to as the loss of the humane element from educational administration. What Greenfield refers to as the humane element could also be labelled the care perspective. He believed that the scientific study of organizations, adopted by educational administrators, has led to the loss of humanity. He wrote that educational administration is based on power, objectivity and the utility of science so much so that all human passion is lost.[34]

Greenfield was particularly contemptuous of Herbert Simon, whose if "adult" and "most fashionable" work brought the methods of science to administration.[35] Simon's vision, adopted by educational administration, was to build a theory of administration on scientific knowledge. According to Greenfield, once Simon had convinced others in the field that science was on their side, his aim was to ensure that administrators made efficient and effective decisions. To do this, Greenfield says, they had to rid themselves of value, humanity and passion.

> The horror of Simon's neutered science appears only with the realization that it conforms, almost perfectly, to the view that administrators seem to want to have of themselves: that they are instruments of an objective, selfless rationality. Administrative science . . . has done much to establish the belief that devalued, but rational, decision making is desirable, attainable, and scientifically verifiable. This belief relieves the anxiety of decision making and removes the administrators sense of responsibility for his decisions.[36]

Greenfield is describing the justice perspective. The logic of the justice perspective is "an impartial logic . . based on impersonal standards or universal principles . . . ."[37] Decision-makers who rely on universal principles as guides to decision making, transcend and thus remove themselves from the complexities of the context of another's situation. The result is that a decision, which may have untold consequences for another, is made in almost total disregard of the person's unique circumstances. To illustrate the point, Greenfield refers to corporations which, when faced with large numbers of layoffs, are encouraged to consider the health of the organization rather than the impact of their decision on the lives of the workers and those who depend on them.[38] Decision-making of this type is bound by considerations affecting the health of the organization thus limiting the scope of other possible decisions. And, as Greenfield points out, such decision-making can effectively eliminate one of the *most* important components of the care perspective: responsibility.

"[The] view that administrators seem to want to have of themselves"[39] is instructive in another sense. Greenfield's description coincides with the traditional characteristics ascribed to men but is the inversion of the characteristics ascribed to women.[40] Characteristics often associated with women such as nurturing, empathy, compassion, cooperation and connectedness–or the care perspective–are undervalued or seen as an impediment in the arena of administration.[41] Instead, leadership implies the masculine qualities of aggression, toughness, abrasiveness, and competition.[42]

Writers have discussed the maleness of administration saying that the requisites of management are constructed from popular beliefs of the stereotypical male.[43] After all, leaders have historically been men. The effect is that many organizational theories, concepts and models of organizational behavior have been developed from studying men in leadership. Thus the characteristics associated with leadership are those that describe maleness. According to Gareth Morgan, the qualities of leadership fits the western stereotype of maleness. Qualities such as analytical, rational and instrumental are valued while the qualities of nurturing and empathic support, often associated with women, are undervalued. Leadership, he writes, "define a man's world."[44] Tom Sergiovanni agrees. Management literature, he said, was traditionally written "by men for men, and its values–individualism, competition–define success in a masculine way."[45]

As a consequence, decisions "grounded in considerations of sympathy, caring and an assessment of differentiated need are defined as not rational, not 'objective', merely sentimental."[46] What counts in decision-making *is* rational, objective, impartial decision making.

The maleness of leadership and structure, assumed as a given within the educational system and other bureaucracies, was developed from studying the military, corporations and other institutions that had or have little, if anything, to do with children or women. The military connection to educational administration theory is especially troubling. Noble traces the military's interest in the contribution of the "human factor" during times of conflict and aggression to organizational theorists such as Herbert Simon, the development of organizational theories and their application to the education of children.[47]

Charol Shakeshaft, in her book *Women in Educational Administration,* has devoted an entire chapter to the topic of "Androcentric Bias in Education Administration and Research."[48] In it she examined a number of theories and concepts which are commonly referred to in educational administration textbooks but which were developed by studying organizations virtually devoid of children and women. For example, an important theory on leadership was developed from observing the behavior of air force bomber commanders and crew members, commissioned officers, non-commissioned personnel and civilian administrators in the Department of Navy.[49] The definition of what makes a leader and thus what is valued in a leader was predetermined by the almost exclusive male samples they chose.

Another well known theory of leadership effectiveness was developed from male-centered activities such as "radar bomb scores, the percentage of company net income over three years, stock controls, the percentage of basketball games won, creativity ratings and time to hit targets."[50] Further, leadership effectiveness theory has developed from these roots to "a consciousness that prizes the drive to compete, to win, to beat everyone else"[51] which is viewed by some as contrary to women's leadership style.[52] Shakeshaft notes that the most common weakness of organizational theories, concepts and models of organizational behavior is the fact that women are not included. She sums it up by saying, "females are viewed as `other' or rendered invisible in this male-defined perspective."[53] An even more sinister weakness of organizational theories, concepts and models of organizational behavior, developed from studying the military, is the fact that they are applied to children who are compelled to attend schools.

The bureaucratic design of work is considered another male defined perspective. In the beginning, schools were organized as one room centers of teaching. By the late nineteenth century these schools were reorganized into "cost-efficient models of business."[54] Today, according to Hodgkinson:

> Modern state-financed education is essentially bureaucratic in its structure. The characteristic features of such structure are a hierarchy of personnel, tenure and careerism, role formalism, record keeping and paperwork, impartial and impersonal rules and regulations, professionalism and technical competence, committees–and collective decision making, judicial process and unresponsiveness to changes in external or internal environment.[55]

Hodgkinson further states, "the fact is that bureaucracy works."[56] This premise is disputed by others. Smircich writes that the bureaucratic design of organizations, with its stress on impersonality, fairness, rights, and hierarchy, is congruent with the male mode of perceiving the world and while "no one may be happy with bureaucracy, men are more at home there."[57]

One of the many characteristics of a bureaucracy is "a horizontal division of graded authority or hierarchy, entailing supervision from above."[58] Inherent in their design is domination at the top and graded submission on the way down. Ferguson believes bureaucracies epitomize the unequal distribution of power and dominance between men and women.[59] By this she is referring to the domination by men on the lives of women and children. These forms of domination exist in family lives, within the justice system, the medical system, the education system and others.[60]

A de-humanized organization does not value the characteristics Gilligan and others have ascribed to women, such as nurturing, empathy, compassion, cooperation and connectedness.[61] Working within a de-humanized environment is unappealing to many women. Thus the very essence of a bureaucracy, its inherent domination and de-humanized environment, act as a systemic barrier[62] to women. A de-humanized educational environment also effects students. School violence has been blamed on the impersonal and detached conditions of school life which are manifested by bureaucracies.[63] As Ferguson points out, bureaucracies "damage people in different ways at its different levels."[64]

Even though there have been attempts to change the organizational structure of educational institutions, with attention paid to school culture, systems theories, and effective schools, the it modern education is essentially bureaucratic.[65] And, I would add, paternalistic and authoritarian.[66]

5. A Legally Inspired Change

The lack of any real change in the organization and administration of schools is all the more surprising considering the research that demonstrates learning opportunities for students are enhanced within a humane environment.[67] A humane or humanistic school setting is characterized by the ethic of care: it is defined as a student-centered environment with small classes, student input in decision making and attention to individual needs. It is an atmosphere under which students and teachers get to know each other well–a community of teachers, administrators and students working cooperatively, nurturing "fundamental humane and creative educational thinking, enabling them to bestow upon their pupils the happiness of school life and the joy of exchanging ideas with the teachers."[68] In addition, a nurturing, positive and supportive environment promotes social networking, cooperative behavior and creative and self-enhancing independence.[69]

Nevertheless, the humane child centered educational system has not developed. Perhaps, as I believe, it is because it does not fit "the view that educational administrators seem to have of themselves."[70] A view that fits the masculine stereotype of impersonal competitiveness, power and control. It is clear that as long as educational administration is controlled by men who are comfortable with the status-quo, little will change. Amonashvili believes that the reason for the resistance is that "the moment of truth" has not arrived.[71] She states that "an idea can become a reality only if it finds its moment of truth, that is, if it can help people solve the vitally important problems facing them in specific historical circumstances."[72]

The moment of truth for Canadian educators and in particular educational decision-makers has been hoisted upon them, ready or not by the Canadian Supreme Court's interpretation of the rights and freedoms contained in the *Canadian Charter of Rights and Freedoms*.[73] The Canadian Supreme Court is one of the most influential decision-making bodies in Canada. Their decisions are of national import, so too is the reasoning behind their decisions and the interpretation given to the law. The interpretation given to the *Charter* directly effects all those in decision making roles including educators. In addition, the interpretation given to the young *Canadian*

Charter will undoubtedly influence the interpretation given to another new and parallel human rights law, *The Convention of the Rights of the Child.* It is worthwhile then to examine briefly the way in which the *Charter* has been interpreted.

6. The Canadian Charter of Rights and Freedoms

The formal and abstract characteristics describing the ethic of justice are central to the Rule of Law doctrine[74] which requires if equality before the law or the equal subjection of all classes to the ordinary law of the land administered by the ordinary courts. . . ."[75] It provides that all people, regardless of their status are to be treated the same. The Rule of Law is epitomized by the image of the blindfolded lady justice. Its most restrictive interpretation has meant the impartial administration of rules without regard to social, economic or political status of a citizen.[76] Blind justice refuses to consider anything that could detract from an impartial decision, "[no] circumstances. No special cases. No emotions. Everything must be rational, objective, legalistic...."[77] The effect has been that the rule of law has eclipsed the historical and entrenched inequalities that have caused suffering for many disadvantaged groups and individuals such as women, children, and other minorities throughout history.[78]

Recently, however, the Canadian courts have demonstrated an alignment with the ethic of care in their interpretation of cases dealing with the democratic rights of equality and fundamental freedoms. The courts former reluctance to get too deeply into a case had, according to former Justice Wilson, caused them "to reduce the context of the dispute to its bare bones through a complex system of exclusionary evidentiary rules."[79] But things have changed. The change is especially apparent when courts are faced with the *impact of* denying or limiting the rights and freedoms of those who "suffer social, political and legal disadvantages in our society."[80] The Canadian Supreme Court has stressed the need to contextualize in order to draw meaning from the words of the *Charter.* They have stressed this point in two important ways. First, in determining the purpose of a *Charter* right or freedom[81] and, second, in considering *the* limits that can be placed on rights and freedoms.[82] It is the need to contextualize that draws the interpretation of the *Charter* into the realm of the ethic of care. The ethic of care, according to Gilligan, conceptualizes a moral problem as a conflict between responsibilities rather than between competing rights and "requires for its resolution a mode of thinking that is contextual and narrative rather than formal and abstract."[83] A contextual approach to interpreting the *Charter* considers the particular other rather than the generalized other[84] and enhances empathy and compassion. As an example of the Courts use of contextual reasoning, let us consider the Court's definitions of equality and discrimination.

Historically, equality has meant treating everyone the same–giving everyone the same opportunity. Treating everyone equally in order to realize equality is consistent with the ethic of justice. It is reciprocal, "I'll treat you the same if you treat me the same." But it is based on the naive assumption that all are equal in the first place.[85] Viewing equality in this manner rarely allows for a consideration of the effect of inequality that some groups have suffered throughout history.

Clinging to the view that in order to be fair we must treat everyone equally, obfuscates any consideration of the social, political and legal conditions of disadvantaged individuals and groups. Equality is considered in the abstract rather than in its context.

The difference between a contextual caring approach and an abstract justice approach to equality was illustrated in a recent Ann Landers column. There appears to have been a letter to Ann Landers complaining about the lack of consideration given to pregnant women on buses. One reader responded to the original letter and wrote :

> This is for Sally in Toronto who figured she is entitled to a seat on the bus because she is seven months pregnant: Get real lady, this is the '90s. You women have been screaming about equal rights, so now you've got 'em. Live with your equal rights and stop beefing.[86]

The writer's notion of equality is an abstract one: equating equality with equal treatment regardless of the context of the woman's situation. If he considered the discomfort pregnant women often feel when they are seven months pregnant (fatigue, swollen ankles, maneuvering with an extra thirty or so pounds) and added to this the discomfort of standing on a bus (stretching to hold onto a bar while maintaining her balance which is already stressed by the additional pounds she is carrying), perhaps he could understand the difference between equal treatment and the more contextual approach to equality; equality of results. Even though all men and women are treated equally, the discomfort a pregnant woman feels standing on a bus would not be equal to the discomfort of another man or woman; the pregnant women would suffer more. It appears the writer was not the "wise man" referred to in the following quote; "It is a wise man (*sic*) who said that there is no greater inequality than the equal treatment of unequal."[87]

The first equality case arising out the *Charter* reached the Supreme Court in 1989.[88] The interpretation given to equality recognized that realizing equality includes an analysis of equality of results as well as equal treatment, "the difference in treatment between individuals under the law will not necessarily result in inequality and, as well, that identical treatment may frequently produce serious inequality."[89]

The Court rejected an exclusive legalistic, ethic of justice interpretation of equality saying:

> It is not every distinction or differentiation in treatment at law which will transgress the equality guarantees of the Charter . . . for the accommodation of differences, which is the essence of true equality, it will frequently be necessary to make distinctions.[90]

Thus equal treatment or equal opportunity is not enough. In fact, treating everyone the same can exacerbate inequality. An interpretation of equality that includes equality of results forces decision–makers to consider the particular individual and her/his circumstances.

The courts' interpretation of discrimination also connotes a caring approach. In the same case the Court said that not every distinction made by law can be termed discrimination. First it must be shown that those who claim discrimination are members of groups who have and do suffer social, political and legal disadvantages. The Court said, "the analysis of discrimination in this approach must take place within the context of the enumerated grounds and those analogous to them."[91] For the courts to determine who is disadvantaged, and how, the Courts must listen to the voice of the fit other." In addition, the adoption of the words "suffer" and "disadvantages" to describe those protected from discrimination will necessitate an examination of the specific circumstances of individuals and groups to eliminate those who do not suffer and are not disadvantaged.[92]

The *Andrews* decision, along with other recent equality and democratic freedom cases[93] have begun the process of weaving a contextual approach to the interpretation of Canada's young *Charter.* Put another way, the care orientation has weaved its way into the *Charter*'s interpretation.

7. The Convention on the Rights of the Child

A caring, contextual approach to interpreting the *Charter* is also instructive in our consideration of *The Convention on the Rights of the Child.* On 20 November 1989 the United Nations General Assembly unanimously adopted The Convention which came into force on 2 September 1990. On that date it became international law meaning that States which ratified the *Convention* must review their laws to make sure they are in line with the provisions of the *Convention.* If a signatory to the *Convention* fails to comply with the it, the state is answerable to the international community.[94] Some of the highlights from the *Convention* include the recognition that a child needs freedom to develop his or her intellectual, moral and spiritual capacities and that these capacities depend on a healthy and safe environment, access to medical care, and minimum standards of food, clothing and shelter, protection from all forms of exploitation and the obligation of the State to help in carrying out the duties. The wording of the *Convention* calls upon decision makers to consider the child, the particular circumstances of children and to take steps to ease their burden. It recognizes the disenfranchisement of children and their vulnerability to exploitation.

Article 29 provides direction on the education of the child. It states:

1. States Parties agree that the education of the child shall be directed to:

(a) The development of the child's personality, talents and mental and physical abilities to their fullest potential;
(b) The development of respect for human rights and fundamental freedoms, and for the principles enshrined in the Charter of the United Nations;
(c) The development of respect for the child's parents, his or her own cultural identity, language and values, for the national values of the country in which the child is living, the country from which he or she may originate and for civilizations different from his or her own;
(d) The preparation of the child for responsible life in a free society, in the spirit of understanding, peace, tolerance, equality of sexes, and friendship among all peoples, ethnic, national and religious groups and persons of indigenous origin;
(e) The development of respect for the natural environment.

Of particular interest is section l(d). As we have seen, some of the principles necessary for the preparation for a responsible life, such as tolerance, equality and friendship require familiarity, knowing others well, empathic understanding or what Gilligan calls a web of connectedness – those values that describe the ethic of care. The wording of the *Convention* along with the Canadian interpretation of a free society, equality and tolerance requires educators to take seriously the value of the ethic of care–a moral orientation that, as we shall see, women educators are capable of employing at work and in a valuable manner.

8. Moral Orientation of Women and Men Educators

Thirty two educators, who worked in a public urban school division, were given two hypothetical equality cases to consider and discuss, prior to being asked: "Can you tell me about a time when you faced a conflict concerning an equality matter and you had to make a decision?" The narratives of the 32 educators: 16 teachers and 16 administrators with an equal representation of males and females, were taped, transcribed and analyzed using A *Guide to Reading Narratives of Conflict and Choice for Self and Moral Voice.*[95]

The process of analysis involved reading each narrative four times, first to listen to the narrator's voice as s/he tells the story; second, to listen for the narrator's "self"; third, to listen for the care orientation; and fourth, to listen for the justice orientation.

Each narrative was coded according to the three dimensions of presence, predominance, and alignment. Presence of the justice or care orientation is evident if, in the telling of the story, the narrator considers care, justice or both orientations. Predominance is the most salient voice in a narrative. It is "the degree to which a person focuses or elaborates a moral voice"[96] in his/her entire narrative. The third dimension, alignment, is decided by interpreting which moral orientation the "self" favors. Each narrator either explicitly or implicitly aligned with one moral orientation or both.[97]

The study's most suggestive finding was the difference in moral orientation used by women and men. The data collected in this study show that women's narratives were predominantly care oriented and more women aligned with care. Men's narratives were predominantly justice oriented and more men aligned with justice. Justice predominated in the narratives of seventeen educators. When these numbers were broken down by sex, justice predominated almost twice as often in men's narratives as in women's (11:6), care predominated almost three times as often in women's narratives as in men's (8:3). The findings of this study portray an even larger difference between women's and men's alignment with a moral voice. Of the 15 educators who aligned with justice, 12 were men and three were women. Put another way, men aligned with justice four times more than women. Of the 13 educators who aligned with care, 10 were women and three were men. (See Table 2)

Table 2. Moral Orientation of Women and Men

	Care		Justice		Both		Neither	
	W	M	W	M	W	M	W	M
Presence	0	0	0	6	16	10	0	0
Predominance	8	3	6	11	n/a	n/a	2	2
Alignment	10	3	3	12	3	1	0	0

The study also showed that the difference between men's and women's moral orientation in dealing with dilemmas of equality and other democratic rights was as prevalent when the groups were broken down into classroom teachers and educational administrators.

All the narratives of women educators revealed both care and justice, exemplifying the bilingualism of which Ann Wilson Sharf has written.[98] Ten of the male educators also understood both orientations but six showed no understanding of the care orientation.

Overall it can be said that, not only in general discussions of equality issues but within those areas protected by the *Charter*, more women educators than men are care oriented. This is particularly important and of value considering the Courts alignment with the care orientation in their interpretation of the *Charter*. Their abilities in this regard give them an edge over their male counterparts in the equality dilemmas they face and the decisions they make. But there is more at stake than merely avoiding *Charter* litigation. The feelings of exclusion and isolation experienced by many minorities has been the root cause of racial violence.[99] The face of Canada's population is changing as it is throughout the world. Recent reports say that more of the worldwide population is moving and mixing. In Canada, there are more Aboriginal and immigrant students attending our schools.[100] Canada's commitment to a multicultural society, the entrenched rights of minorities and women in Canada's constitution, and the international obligations outlined in the *Convention* compel teachers and administrators to do better.

9. Conclusion

The research discussed in this chapter serves as evidence that former expectations and practices of educational administration, organization and leadership, which are closely tied to the justice orientation, are inappropriate, harmful and possibly litigious in light of the *Charter*'s interpretation, Canada's changing demographics and the international communities obligations under the *Convention on the Rights of the Child.* The maleness of educational administration and the justice orientation respond counter to the principles and values of a free and democratic society and the aspirations of students, minorities and women.[101] Caring, or the care orientation is constitutionally and internationally demanded of educators, giving judicial clout to Noddings contention that caring must become a necessary credential to teach.[102] In addition, other research shows that children and young adults learn better in a caring environment.[103]

The educational implications to be drawn from this research underscore the need for major changes in the educational administration and teacher education programs to address the lack of the care orientation in dealing with equality issues; the need for the inclusion of the characteristics of caring, compassion and empathy as necessary requirements for the job of educator; and the need for the conscious and forthright appointments of women to positions of educational administration so that the intentional or unintentional perpetuation of male leadership can be broken and women will be given a chance to make a difference.

The question now is "Will these Legal Obligations Build a New School Order?"[104] The new school order would be informed by the care orientation, demonstrating through its educators, respect for the dignity of all students, commitment to social justice and the equality rights of all citizens, acceptance of a wide variety of beliefs and respect for diverse cultures and group identity.[105] Only when educational institutions do that can we have faith in them and honestly say that educational institutions "enhance the participation of individuals and groups"[106] who come to our schools and universities to learn and to work.

Notes

1. Marilyn Waring, *If Women Counted: A New Feminist Economics* (San Francisco: Harper, 1988), 21. The latter definition is found in the *Oxford English Dictionary.*

2. Carol Gilligan, *In a Different Voice: Psychological Theory and Women's Development* (Cambridge, Mass.: Harvard University Press, 1982).

3. Carol Gilligan, "Remapping the Moral Domain: New Images of Self in Relationship" in Carol Gilligan, J.V. Ward, J. McLean Taylor, *et al.*, eds. *Mapping the Moral Doman: A Contribution of Women's Thinking to Psychological Theory and Education* (Cambridge, Mass.: Harvard University Press, 1988), p. 8; Nona Plessner Lyons, "Two Perspectives: On Self, Relationships, and Morality" in *Mapping the Moral Domain,* p.21.

4. Robin West, "Jurisprudence and Gender" *University of Chicago Law Review* (1900) 55 p.2, referring to Gilligan's *In a Different Voice*.

5. *The Canadian Charter of Rights and Freedoms,Constitution Act*, 1982, as enacted by *Canada Act*, 1982 c.11.

6. *The Convention on the Rights of the Child*, 28 I.L.M. 1448 (1989). The Convention was adopted by the United Nations on 20 November 1989. It entered into force on 2 September 1990.

7. Ailsa M. Watkinson, "Caring and Justice in Education: A Charter Challenge." Unpublished Doctoral Dissertation, University of Saskatchewan, 1992. Inequality, in this context, includes any issue that involves at least two parties one of which has more power than the other.

8. Alasdair Maclntyre, *After Virtue* (Notre Dame, Ind.: University of Notre Dame Press, 1984). Maclntyre uses male pronouns and "man" throughout his book. Little mention is made of woman, except to say that the key virtue for women is fidelity, "so in women, who constitute the crucial relationships within a household, fidelity is the key virtue." Fidelity includes the quality of being faithful: chastity. For a critique of *After Virtue* see Donna Greschner, "Feminists Concerns with the New Communitarians: We Don't Need Another Hero" in Allan C. Hutchinson and Leslie J.M. Green, eds., *Law and the Community: The End of Individualism* (Toronto: Carswell, 1989), p. 119.

9. *Ibid.*, p. 2.

10. *Ibid.*

11. See Iris Murdoch, *The Sovereignty of Good* (Boston: Routledge & Kegan Paul, 1970); Carol Gilligan, *In a Different Voice: Psychological Theory and Women's Development* (Cambridge, Mass.: Harvard University Press, 1982); Angela Miles and Geraldine Fenn (eds.), *Feminism From Pressure to Politics* (Montreal: Black Rose Books, 1989); Mary O'Brien, *The Politics of Reproduction* (Boston: Routledge & Kegan Paul, 1981); Irene Poelzer, *Saskatchewan Women Teachers, 1905-1920: Their*

Contributions (Saskatchewan: Lindenblatt & Hamonic, 1990); Charol Shakeshaft, *Women in Educational Administration* (London: Sage Press, 1989); Judith S. Glazer, "Feminism and Professionalism in Teaching and Educational Administration" *Educational Administration Quarterly* 27(1991), p.321.

12. *Ibid*.

13. Ann Wilson Schaef, *Women's Reality: An Emerging Female System in a White Male Society* (San Francisco: Harper & Row Pub., 1985), warns that theories (especially in the area of psychoanalysis) have been used as weapons. She views theory as a tool to help us explain and conceptualize.

14. Kohlberg's theory of moral development consists of six sequences within three levels. The preconventional level (stages 1 and 2) confront moral dilemmas with an "egocentric understanding of fairness based on individual needs." This develops upward in a hierarchical progression to the conventional level (stages 3 and 4). At this level "a conception of fairness is anchored in the shared conventions of societal agreements." The post-conventional level (stages 5 and 6) culminates in principled moral reasoning which demonstrates an "understanding of fairness that rests on the free standing logic of equality and reciprocity." Kohlberg's theory is referred to extensively in the exploration of ethics and morality in educational administration. See for example Christopher Hodgkinson, *Towards a Philosophy of Administration* (Oxford: Basil Blackwell, 1978); Ralph B. Kimbrough, *A Course of Study for Educational Leaders* (Norfolk, Va.: American Ass. of School Administrators, 1985); Kenneth A. Strike, *Educational Policy and the Just Society* (London: University of Illinois Press, 1982).

15. Lawrence Kohlberg, *The Philosophy of Moral Development: Moral Stages and the Idea of Justice* (San Francisco: Harper & Row, 1981) pp. 17-19.

16. Gilligan, *In A Different Voice,* n. 2, p. 18.

17. Gilligan's claim that women appear to be stuck at the third level is disputed by at least two authors who both claim that women are more likely to be clustered at level four. See, Lawrence J. Walker, "Sex Differences in the Critical Development of Moral Reasoning: A Critical Review" *Child Development* 55(1984), pp.677, 697, and Diana Baumrind, "Sex Differences in Moral Reasoning: Response to Walker's (1984) Conclusion that There Are None," *Child Development* 57 (1986), pp. 511, 516.

18. Kohlberg, *The Philosophy of Moral Development*, p. 18. In Nel Noddings's book *Caring: A Feminine Approach to Ethics and Moral Education* (Berkeley: University of California Press, 1984), p.97, she writes: "a consideration of caring and an ethic built upon it gives new meaning to what Kohlberg assesses as 'stage three' morality. At this stage, persons behave morally in order to be thought of–or to think of themselves as– 'good boys' or 'good girls'. Clearly, it makes a difference whether one chooses to be good or to be thought of as good. One who chooses to be good may not be 'stuck', as Kohlberg suggests, in a stage of moral reasoning. Rather she may have chosen an alternative route to moral conduct."

19. Lawrence Kohlberg & R. Kramer, "Continuities and Discontinuities in Childhood and Adult Moral Development" *Human Development*, 12(1969), p.93, referred to in Gilligan, *In a Different Voice*, 18.

20. *Ibid*.

21. Waring notes that, in addition to women being morally inferior as Kohlberg and Kramer claim, the labor of women homemakers is considered of no value according to the influential United Nations System of National Accounts (UNSNA): "A woman who supplies such labor [as child birth, growing and processing food, nurturing, educating and running a household] . . . are unacknowledged as part of the production system. A woman who supplies such labor is not seen by economists as performing work of value," Waring, *If Women Counted*, p.28. UNSNA is the method of measuring production and growth throughout most of the world. This system measures the value of all goods and services that actually enter the market. See *ibid.*, p.33, n.1.

22. Gilligan, *In a Different Voice* , p. 78, describes a sequence in the development of the ethic of care. The initial focus is on caring for one self, followed by a transitional phase in which one is critical of this focus as being selfish. The criticism leads to a focus on self and others; a notion of responsibility. This too is criticized as being altruistic thus leading to the third perspective which focuses on an understanding of the dynamics of relationships and the acceptance of the interconnectedness between self and others.

23. *Ibid.*

24. Lyons, "Two Perspectives."

25. *Ibid.*

26. *Ibid.*

27. *Ibid.*

28. Gilligan, *In a Different Voice,* p. 19.

29. *Ibid.,* p. 62.

30. *Ibid.,* n. 6; Diana Baumrind, "Sex Differences in Moral Reasoning," p. 516. See also the collection of writings in E.D. Kittay and D.T. Meyers, eds., *Women and Moral Theory* (New Jersey: Rowman & Littlefield, 1987); Gilligan *et al.,* eds. *Mapping the Moral Domain.*

31. Carol Gilligan, "Remapping the Moral Domain: New Images of Self in Relationship" in Gilligan *et al.*, eds., *Mapping the Moral Domain,* p.8.

32. "Women Teachers in Saskatchewan, Statistical Data 1990-91," Saskatchewan Teacher's Federation. Within the context of the economic definition of value there can be little doubt that educational administrators are valued more than classroom teachers. Educational administrators make an average of $13,000.00 (Canadian) more a year than classroom teachers. In some large urban areas the administrators

are "released" from teaching. Ailsa M. Watkinson, "Savings Possible if School Administrators Properly Labelled" (Saskatoon) *Star Phoenix* (7 May 1993.) The information for the article was pulled from the 1993 Budget of the Saskatoon Public Board of Education.

33. Shakeshaft, *Women in Educational Administration*, p.11; Glazer, "Feminism and Professionalism"; Linda Smircich, "Toward **a** Women Centered Organizational Theory," Symposium co-sponsored by the Women Management and Social Issues in Management Division of the Academy of Management, San Diego, Cal. 11-14 August 1985.

34. Thomas B. Greenfield, "The Decline and Fall of Science in Educational Administration" *Interchange* 17:2 (1986), pp. 59-60. Greenfield is referring to the work of Herbert Simon whose book, *Administrative Behavior* "offered . . . a method of value-free inquiry into decision making and administrative rationality" (p.58).

35. *Ibid.* Greenfield is reporting Simon's own description that his and March's work was "adult" and "most fashionable."

36. *Ibid.*, p. 62.

37. Lyn Mikel Brown, ed, A *Guide to Reading Narratives of Conflict and Choice For Self and Moral Voice* (Cambridge, Mass.: Harvard, Center for the Study of Gender, Education and Human Development, 1988), p.111.

38. Greenfield, "Decline and Fall," p.63, referring to W.G. Scott & D. Hart, *Organizational America* (Boston: Houghton Mifflin, 1979) pp. 46-47. The reporting of the Gulf War also illustrates the point. The censoring of information on human suffering was replaced with information on "smart bombs," "collateral damage" and a "new world order." The language used to describe and report on the war was such that it kept the public's attention away from the suffering and horror caused by the war and its impact on the lives of children, women, and men.

39. *Ibid.,* p.62.

40. The Chinese constructed feminine and masculine traits according to Yin and Yang. Yin: female, negative, passive, weak, destructive, earth, completion; and Yang: male, positive, active, strong, constructive, heaven, beginning. Wing-tsit Chan, *A Source Book in Chinese Philosophy* (Princeton: Princeton University Press, 1963) pp. 244-248, referred to in Mary Vetterling-Braggin, Frederick A. Elliston, and Jane English, eds. *Feminism and Philosophy* (New Jersey: Littlefield, Adams & Co., 1977), p.98. For a discussion of the positive aspects of these differences see, Gilligan, *In a Different Voice;* Gilligan *et al.*, eds. *Mapping the Moral Domain*; Sara Ruddick, *Maternal Reasoning: Towards a Politics* of *Peace* (Boston: Bracon Press, 1989).

41. Catherine Marshall, "The Stigmatized Woman: The Professional Woman in a Male Sex-Typed Career" *The Journal of Educational Administration* 23:2 (1985), p.131. The article discusses the attempts some women administrators make to compensate for the "stigma" of femaleness in order to make it easier for their male colleagues to accept them. She points out that these attempts are women's ways of

fitting into a profession based on the male as model. See also Gilligan, *In A Different Voice;* Gilligan *et al.*, eds. *Mapping the Moral Domain*; Ruddick, *Maternal Reasoning*.

42. J. Heam and P.W Parkin, "Women, Men, and Leadership: A Critical Review of Assumptions, Practices, and Change in the Industrialized Nations" (1988) in N.J.Adler and D.N. lzraeli, eds., *Women in Management Worldwide* (London: M.E. Sharpe Pub., 1988), p.21. Marilyn Loden, *Feminine Leadership or How to Succeed in Business Without Being One of the Boys* (New York: Times Books, 1985), ch. 2. Shakeshaft, *Women in Educational Administration.* See also Kathy E. Ferguson, *The Feminist Case Against Bureaucracy* (Philadelphia: Temple University Press, 1984); R. Moss Kanter, *Men and Women of the Corporation* (New York: Basic Books, Inc., 1977).

43. *Ibid.* See also, Gareth Morgan, *Images of Organizations* (London: Sage Publications., 1989); Ron Brandt, "On Rethinking Leadership: A Conversation with Tom Sergiovanni," *Educational Leadership*, 409:5 (1992), p.46.

44. *Ibid.*, at p. 211.

45. *Ibid.*, p. 47. Thomas J. Sergiovanni, "Why We Should Seek Substitutes for Leadership," *Educational Leadership* , 47, 49:5 (1992), p. 41 talked about new ideas of leadership and admitted to reading feminist scholarship and being taken aback by it. He stated that "when I first began to read the feminist literature, I thought, 'who are these arrogant people?' But it turns out they were right." For further insight into Sergiovanni's changes in thought about leadership.

46. Iris M. Young, "Impartiality and the Civic Public" in Seyla Benhabib and Drucilla Cornell, eds., *Feminism as Critique: On the Politics of Gender* (Minneapolis: University of Minnesota Press, 1987), p.63.

47. Douglas D. Noble, "Education, Technology, and the Military" in Landon E. Beyer and Michael W. Apple, eds. *The Curriculum: Problems, Politics, and Possibilities* (Albany, N.Y.: State University of New York Press, 1988), 241. Noble despairs (p.251) that the processing of the mind, like the processing of a technical instrument has lost, "any consideration of the possibility that things could have been different-that our present `cognitive' understanding of the mind, and of its role in society, is an historical invention whose hegemonic influence keeps us from considering alternative approaches to intellect, and . . . to the meaning of intellectual development within education." As noted earlier, Thomas Greenfield, "Decline and Fall," was extremely critical of the willingness of educational administration to accept the "scientific" theories of Simon.

48. Shakeshaft, *Women in Educational Administration,* p.148.

49. *Ibid.*, p.160. The theory referred to is The Leadership Behavior Description Questionnaire initially developed by Hempill and Coons and later revised by Halpin and Winer whose research was supported by the Air Force Personnel and Training Research Center, the Office of Naval Research, Rockefeller Foundation, International Harvester, and the Kellogg Company.

50. *Ibid.*, p.161. Fred Fielder's research was funded in part by the Office of Naval Research. In his book *Leadership and Effective Management*, he acknowledges their funding.

51. Shakeshaft, *Women in Educational Administration*, p.161.

52. *Ibid.*; Judith Blackmore, "Educational Leadership: A Feminist Critique and Reconstruction" in John Smyth, ed., *Critical Perspectives on Educational Leadership* (London: The Falmer Press, 1989); Flora Ida Ortiz and Catherine Marshall, "Women in Educational Administration" in Norman J. Boyan, ed., *Handbook of Research on Educational Administration: A Project of the American Educational Research Association* (New York: Longman, 1988) p.126; A. Fishel & J. Pottker, "Performance of Women Principals: A Review of Behavioral and Attitudinal Studies" in J. Pottker & A. Fishel, eds., *Sex Bias in the Schools: The Research Evidence* (Rutherford, N.J.: Fairleigh Dickinson University Press, 1977) p.289.

53. Betty Lehan Harragan, *Games Mother Never Taught You: Corporate Gamesmanship For Women* (New York: Warner Books, 1977). p.42. The book's main objective is to persuade women to play men's games in order to fit into a man's world. She warns women that business and the organization of work is based on male characteristics: militarism and sports.

54. Shakeshaft, *Women in Educational Administrators*, p.31.

55. Christopher Hodgkinson, *Educational Leadership: The Moral Art* (Albany, N.Y.: State University of New York Press, 1991) p.54.

56. *Ibid.*, p.55. Hodgkinson eventually develops his thesis into a critique of the bureaucratizing of education. But even his premise that bureaucracies work in other institutions is questionable.

57. Linda Smircich, "Toward a Women-Centered Organizational Theory," Symposium cosponsored by the Women Management and Social Issues in Management Division of the Academy of Management, San Diego, Cal., 11-14 August 1985, p.9. See also, Judith S. Glazer, "Feminism and Professionalism in Teaching and Educational Administration," *Educational Administration Quarterly* 27(1991), p. 321.

58. Ferguson, *The Feminist Case Against Bureaucracy*, p. 7.

59. *Ibid.*

60. *Ibid.* See also, Angela Miles and Geraldine Fenn, eds., *Feminism from Pressure to Politics* (Montreal: Black Rose Books, 1989); Robin West, "Jurisprudence and Gender," *University of Chicago Law Review* 3 55:1 (1988), pp.64-65; Susan Moller Okin, *Justice, Gender, and the Family* (New York: Basic Books, Inc., 1989); R. Moss Kanter, *Men and Women of the Corporation* (New York: Basic Books, 1977).

61. Gilligan, *In a Different Voice*; *Mapping the Moral Domain*; see also Sara Ruddick, *Maternal Reasoning.*

62. Systemic barriers are institutional norms, which are considered harmless and neutral but which have a discriminatory or exclusive effect.

63. Ferguson, *The Feminist Case Against Bureaucracy*, pp.42-46.

64. *Ibid*., p. 88.

65. Hodgkinson, *Educational Leadership.*

66. Wayne MacKay, "The Judicial Role in Education Policy-Making: Promise or Threat?" *Educational Law Journal*, (1988-1989), p.127; Fazal Rizvi, "In Defence of Organizational Democracy" in John Smyth, ed. *Critical Perspectives on Educational Leadership* (London: The Falmer Press, 1989), p. 235; A.A. Morris, *The Constitution and American Education,* 2nd. ed. (St. Paul, Minn.: West Publishing Co, 1980), p.253.

67. Doris B. Matthews, "The Effect of School Environment of Intrinsic Motivation of Middle-School Children," *Journal of Humanistic Education and Development*, (1991), p.30. Matthews reports that the intrinsic motivation in academic teaming of girls and boys is increased in humanistic school settings as compared to students in more structural school environments; Edward W. Schultz *et al*., "School Climate: Psychological Health and Well Being in School," *Journal of School Health*, 57(1987), p.432.

68. Shalva Amonashvili, "Non-Directive Teaching and the Humanization of the Educational Process, " *Prospects* 19(1989) p.585..

69. Schultz, "School Climate," p.32.

70. Greenfield, "The Decline and Fall of Science in Educational Administration," p.62.

71. Amonashvili is from the former U.S.S.R. She argues, "Non Directive Teaching," p.582, that "the democratization of society, the humanization of social life, the renewal of the political structure, the introduction of glasnost and the new forms of economic and agricultural development are just some of the factors that are creating a moment of truth for the realization of humane education policies in the Soviet Union."

72. *Ibid.*

73. Prior to 1982, the provincial governments had exclusive jurisdiction over education, allowing them to make any laws relating to education. In effect, they were supreme in matters of education. All of that changed with in inclusion of the Canadian Charter of Rights and Freedoms in Canada's supreme law, the Constitution. The decisions of educational decision makers are now subject to Charter challenges.

74. West, "Jurisprudence and Gender," pp.59-60.

75. A.V.Dicey, *Introduction to the Study of the Law of the Constitution,* 10th ed., by E.C.S. Wade (1959), p.202, referred to in Dale Gibson, *The Law of the Charter: Equality Rights* (Toronto: Carswell, 1990), p.32.

76. William E. Conklin, *Images of a Constitution* (Toronto: University of Toronto Press, 1989), p.22.

77. Thomas I. White, "Business, Ethics; and Carol Gilligan's 'Two Voices,'" The Society for Business Ethics Annual Convention, San Francisco. 10-12 August 1990.

78. West, "Jurisprudence and Gender." Canada's Prime Minister and former Justice Minister, Kim Campbell, believes that the justice system openly discriminates against many women. In 1991 she organized and sponsored a national symposium on "Women, Law and the Administration of Justice" and said, "every once in a while, justice has to lift up her blindfold and take a gander at what is under her and understand the human reality and the complexity of what's before her." "Equality in Justice System Likened to `Weird Trip for Women'" The (Saskatoon) *Star Phoenix* (14 June 1991) p.E 3. In other words, blind justice must descend from the pedestal and wallow in the misery of others.

79. Madame Justice Bertha Wilson, "Will Women Judges Really Make a Difference," The Fourth Annual Barbara Betcherman Memorial Lecture, Osgood Hall Law School, York University, Toronto, 8 February 1990.

80. *Ibid.*

81. Edmonton Journal v. Alberta (Attorney General) [1990] 102 N.R. 321 at 347.

82. Rocket v. Royal College of Dental Surgeons of Ontario [1990] 2 S.C.R. 232 at 246-247; R. v. Keegstra, (1991) 117 N.R. I at 38.

83. Gilligan, *In a Different Voice*, p.19.

84. *Ibid.*, p.11. See also, Seyla Benhabib, "The Generalized and the Concrete Other" in Eva Feder Kittay and Diana T. Meyers, eds., *Women and Moral Theory* p.154; Lawrence Blum, "Particularity and Responsiveness" in Jerome Kagan and Sharon Lamb, eds., *The Emergence of Morality in Young Children* (Chicago: University of Chicago Press, 1987), p.306.

85. MacKinnon puts it succinctly when she writes that the only equality in this argument is that "men's differences from women are equal to women's differences from men. There is an *equality* there." Catherine A. MacKinnon, *Feminism Unmodified: Discourse on Life and Law* (Cambridge, Mass.: Harvard University Press, 1987).

86. "Pregnant Woman on Bus Draws Sympathy, Outrage", The *Star Phoenix* (5 November 1990), p.A-10. One reader responded that she was boiling mad when she read about the woman being left to stand and suggested men try an "Empathy Belly:" "It's a plaster stomach strapped on over the arms, which weighs about 35 pounds and is used by therapists to give men an idea of what it's like to be pregnant."

87. Andrews v. Law *Society of British Columbia* [1989] 2 W.W.R. 289 p.299 quoting from Dennis v. U.S., 339 U.S. 162 at 184.

88. *Ibid.*

89. *Ibid.*, p.299.

90. *Ibid.*, p.303.

91. *Ibid.*, p.313.

92. Deciding what "groups . . . suffer social, political and legal disadvantages" invites an examination of dominance. Catherine MacKinnon, *Feminism Unmodified: Discourses on Life and Law,* advocates a "dominance approach" for analyzing equality. An examination of the distribution of power would take into account the sex segregation of poverty, violence against women and children, job ghettos and pornography.

93. *Ontario Human Rights Commission and Simpson-Sears Ltd.* (1985), 23 D.L.R. (4th) 321 (S.C.C.); *Bhinder v.C.N.R.*,[1985] 2 S.C.R. 561; *C.N.R. v. Canadian Human Rights Commission* [1987] 1 *S.C.R.1114; Ontario Human Rights Commission v.Etobicoke*, [1982] 1 S.C.R. 202; *Alberta Human Rights Commission v. Central Alberta Dairy Pool* [1990] 2 S.C.R. 489; *Brooks v. Canada Safeway Ltd.,* [1989] 1 S.C.R. 1219; *R. v. Swain* [1991] 125 N.R. *1; Mahe v. Alberta* [1990] 1 S.C.R. 342 at *362; Rocket v. Royal College of Dental Surgeons of Ontario* [1990] 2 S.C.R. 232 at 246-247; R. *v. Keegstra,* [1991] 117 N.R I at 34; *R. v. Turpin*, [1989] 1 S.C.R. 1296 at 1331-32; *Edmonton Journal v. Alberta (Attorney General),* [1990] 102 N.R. 321 at 350; *United States of America v. Cotroni; United States of America v. El Zein* [1989] 1 S.C.R. 1469 at 1489-1490; *Zylberberg et al v. Sudbury Board of Education,* (1988) 290 A.C. 23 (Ont. C.A.) at 34.

94. The Canadian government ratified the *Convention* in November 1991. Most developed and developing nations have ratified the Convention. Notably absent from the list of ratifying states is the United States.

95. Brown, ed., *A Guide to Reading Narratives.*

96. *Ibid.*, p.132

97. For a more detailed description of the method and methodology employed in the research see, Watkinson, "Caring and Justice."

98. Anne Wilson Schaef, *Women's Reality: An Emerging Female System in a White Male Society* (San Francisco: Harper & Row, 1985), p.13. While conducting a workshop on racial issues, Wilson found that the black participants could describe clearly the characteristics that they perceived to be uniquely Black and uniquely white. The white participants could not,"because they knew nothing about the Black system." The Black participants knew the white system because they had to survive in it, but the white participants did not need to know the black system.

99. Marci McDonald *et al.*, "Streets of Hate," *Maclean's* (11 May 1992). The issue highlights the 1992 Los Angeles and Toronto race riots.

100. By the year 2011, approximately one-third of the school population will be of Aboriginal ancestry, almost doubling the number of children of Aboriginal students.

Saskatchewan School Trusties Association, "Saskatchewan 2000" (Regina: Saskatchewan School Trustees Association, 1991).

101. Rosemary Brown states that education is, "an institution [that] plays at maintaining the status quo. . . . Education is indeed part of the reason why sexism and racism flourish." Rosemary Brown, "Overcoming Sexism and Racism-How?" in Ryszard L. Cholewinski, ed., *Human Rights in Canada: Into the 1990's and Beyond* (Ottawa: Human Rights Research and Education Centre, 1990), p.233.

102. Nel Noddings, *Caring: A Feminine Approach to Ethics and Moral Education* (Berkeley: University of California Press, 1984), pp.197-200. See also, Nel Noddings, "The Gender Issue" *Educational Leadership*, 49(1992), p.65, in which she argues for an inclusion of women's culture in educational planning.

103. Noddings, *Caring;* Alfie Kuhn, "Caring Kids: the Role of the Schools," *Phi Delta Kappan* (March 1991); David E. Purppel, *The Moral and Spiritual Crisis in Education: A Curriculum for Justice and Compassion in Education* (Boston, Mass.: Bergin & Garvey Pub., Inc., 1989).

104. The question is my revised version of George S. Counts's *Dare the School Build a New School Order?* (New York: Arno Press, 1969).

105. R. v. Oakes (1986) 65 N.R. 87 at 125.

106. *Ibid.*

Chapter Seven

THE NOTION OF HUMAN WORK AS "SELF-UNDERSTANDING" AND ITS RELATION TO SOLIDARITY

John E. Kelly

In his book, *The Spirit of Solidarity*, Fr. Józef Tischner argues that any coherent approach to the meaning of work must be analyzed within a theory of society in which the transcendent values of love and justice have become immanent and prevail in all of our social and political endeavors. He notes that the significance given to the solidarity movement is intimately connected with the reality of human work. Focusing upon human work as having the capability of being personally transformative as well as socially fulfilling, Tischner suggests that work should be considered a particular form of "conversation" that serves to sustain and develop human life. He writes:

> From the exchange of meaningful sounds–words–one person grows to understand another. Working people do something similar. The objects of their exchange are not ordinary words (although this also may happen) but other products of work that in their structure are similar to words. Just as words are the synthesis of the raw material of the senses (for example, sound) with a meaning, so the product of work is a synthesis of some kind of raw material (for example, clay, ore, or iron) with a meaning (as results of this come pots, hardware, plows). Owing to work, raw material acquires a meaning. The individual meanings of things fuse, overlap, touch, and form the general world of the products of work. Only the one who is capable of grasping meaning of these products knows how to behave in this world. [1]

The author emphasizes the positive and objective elements with respect to the reality of modern work; yet he does not overlook or minimize its *de facto* negative qualities, its dehumanizing fragmentation, its brutalities toward and exploitation of broad segments of the population:

> Solidarity turns out to be a communion of working people who strive to free human work from the hardships and suffering caused by other human beings, that is, from the hardships that are not inherent in the process of converting raw materials into a product. [2]

Tischner considers the basic sign of exploitation in the work place to be "needless suffering" where "the basic project of work went one way," and working peoples' "actual work went another." The result is that "the work contract has not borne reciprocity." What follows is that "work for man has been replaced by "man for work."[3]

Tischner's reflections upon the positive and negative elements in work help to pinpoint the considerable ambiguities surrounding the reality of work in our modern industrial setting. This issue has also been addressed by the current Pope; for in his encyclical devoted exclusively to the theme of human work, John Paul II, while not overlooking the negative elements in human work, the various alienations of labor which are the result of the different acts of injustice which can be committed against labor, draws upon scripture and the western religious and philosophical traditions to place greater emphasis upon the positive value of work.[4]

Through work man/woman makes actual the freedom of his being. The Pontiff goes so far as to consider man/woman as a "co-creator" through his/her work.[5] Yet this extremely positive interpretation of work has not gone unchallenged. John Paul II has been sharply criticized for not having understood the ambiguity of technologically enhanced work. Stanley Hauerwas, for example, is critical of *Laborem exercens* in that it confers an unrealistically high theological status on work as a self-fulfilling activity.[6]

The ambivalence and ambiguity of work which has been experienced in the religious tradition, is similarly felt in contemporary society at large. On the one hand, work is seen as indispensable for man's personal and social development. On the other hand, there is evidence of an increasingly instrumentalist attitude toward work whereby the inherent dignity of work itself becomes subordinated to its rewards.[7] For example, it has been advanced in some quarters that by increasing humanity's domination over nature, modern technology will increase humanity's leisure and cultural pursuits to the point where self- realization can be achieved through the spiritual activities of leisure.

With an increasing significance given to leisure along with a decreasing significance to work the question can legitimately be raised whether such an approach to work does not too easily make leisure meaningful in itself and the culmination of human activity. Is there not the danger then, that work will be reduced to a merely functional preparation for leisure, thereby bifurcating the human person, where neither work nor leisure can be meaningful? Such a technical or merely functional approach to work seems to underlie the thinking in many circles today. Gregory Baum, for example, suggests that we might be faced with the need to develop a whole new approach to unemployment by moving toward a spiritual and cultural stance which gives increasing significance to leisure and decreasing significance to work:

> In some countries the Church is confronted with a pastoral question, the answer to which is by no means easy. Should the Church in the face of a society with chronic unemployment demand full employment and continue to promote a piety that leads to dedication and diligence, or should the Church recognize that there is no return to full employment and hence produce a spiritual outlook that enables people to remain humanly and psychically well even if they do not work? Has the time come when the Church must transcend the work ethic?[8]

Historically this tension between the positive and negative attitudes toward the subject of work is deeply embedded in the West's cultural tradition. In the ancient classical period a positive approach to labor is evident in the epics of Homer and Hesiod. In this epoch the theme of work is considered not only as basic to humanity, and as personally transforming of the subject, but it also is conceived as religious in its expression.[9] Xenophon, for example, looked upon farming as providing scope for moral development.

> The land, which is a god, teaches justice. Whosoever best cultivates the land, will receive the most from the gods. In cultivating the land, the farmer participates in an order that is natural and divine and is taught humility and justice.[10]

Yet in the literature of ancient Greece there is ample evidence of a much less sanguine account of the significance that should be accorded to work. A quite negative and instrumentalist approach to work can be found in the philosophical writings of Plato and Aristotle. Documents of both philosophers capture aristocratic Athens's conception of manual work and the crafts as illiberal, if not slavish, however necessary they may be to meet the city's needs. In both *Politics* III, 5 and VII, 9-10, for example, Aristotle emphasizes the importance of leisure and the absence of repetitive labor for the development of man's ethical and intellectual life. The constraints placed upon those who are preoccupied with work to secure the necessities of life prevent their participation in the life of the polis, or city state.[11] Texts of this sort are responsible for the prevalent view that "to the Greeks work was a curse and nothing else."[12]

Aristotle sets an extremely high standard for citizen status in the polis. He is reluctant to consider hired laborers, craftsmen, or those involved in sustained activity in the world of business as suitable candidates for participation in the judicial and legislative offices of the city. His argument is that the leisure required to participate in political discourse makes it impossible for those preoccupied with providing for the day-to-day necessities of life (whether for the individual or for the city) to make significant contributions in civic affairs. In addition, he considers a life of political involvement incompatible with private gain.[13] A truly free and human life, then, is reserved for the elite of society. Hannah Arendt writes:

> "The good life," as Aristotle called the life of the citizen, therefore was not merely better, more carefree or noble than ordinary life, but of an altogether different quality. It was "good" to the extent that by having mastered the necessities of sheer life, by being freed from labor and work and by overcoming the innate urge of all living creatures for their own survival, it was no longer bound to the biological life process ... No activity that served only the purpose of making a living, of sustaining only the life process, was permitted to enter the political realm, and this at the grave risk of abandoning

> trade and manufacture to the industriousness of slaves and foreigners so that Athens indeed became the "pensionopolis" with a "proletariat of consumers" which Max Weber so vividly described.[14]

Today, we would surely consider Aristotle's requirement of complete leisure for full participation in the community to be extreme. While appreciating his insistence on high standards to qualify for citizenship, we would tend to fault him for not exploring how improved economic conditions might make it possible to bridge the class difference of his day by making leisure and education available to a broader segment of society, rather than relegating so many in the polis to the status of instruments or support groups to satisfy the needs of the citizen class. Indeed, Aristotle's own argument in the *Politics* which focuses on the obligation of the rulers to all who reside in the city, would tend to justify a more inclusive sense of responsibility to those under their charge. On this issue Aristotle has this to say: "Now it is evident that the form of government is best in which every man, whosoever he is can act best and live happily."[15]

The rather restrictive and hierarchical policy regarding the qualifications for full status in the community, together with the downplaying of the significance of the world of work are rooted in the prevalent socio-political setting in which Aristotle lived and wrote; for in the ancient Hellenic world-view there exists what Polanyi has referred to as an "embedded economy," where the economic is not a detached discipline, but rather integral to the broader moral and social climate of the society.[16] It is a setting in which economic activity is confined to the household. Productive labor is considered a mere tool for freeing citizens, and especially the master of the household, for political activity, that properly social space in which freedom can be given due expression. Arendt notes that the distinctive trait of the Greek household or oikos economy "was that in it men lived together because they were driven by their wants and needs. The driving force was life itself." But the fitting place for the practice of virtue and achieving the good life will only be realized at the political level; for according to Arendt:

> What all Greek philosophers, no matter how opposed to polis life, took for granted is that freedom is exclusively located in the political realm; that necessity is primarily a prepolitical phenomenon, characteristic of the private household organization.[17]

Labor and the pursuit of economic gain, then, is looked upon merely as an indispensable instrument for meeting the needs of the free members of Athenian society.[18]

But the "embedded" state of the ancient economy is not the only reason for Aristotle's negative attitude toward wealth and his downgrading of the world of work. He argues also that the world of exchange and other economic pursuits should not be pursued as ends in themselves. Economics has an important social and ethical role to play, and therefore must be subordinate to the primary function and end of the polis.[19] This must include providing and coordinating the means for the full virtuous development of its citizens. It is important, therefore, that adequate consideration be given to the material as well as the institutional conditions needed for the proper functioning of all members of the community.[20] For it is the city that has the potential to enable people to be their best.

Aristotle, then, does not have a problem with trade and the general expanding world of exchange of goods in the interest of personal and communal self sufficiency. But he does have serious misgivings with the redirection of the economy toward limitless acquisition of property and other forms of wealth as ends in themselves.[21] It is clear that Aristotle's argument that the economic realm must be rooted in an ethical context, that it must be an instrument for the full human development of its citizens, will appeal in no small measure to later political theorists. G.W.F. Hegel, for example, will speak of political economics as a "human science," not a science that studies impersonal forces or natural laws, but one that takes "man" as its subject, insofar as men are distinguished from subhuman animals in their ability to satisfy their own needs in an economic way and in a social way.[22] Karl Marx too would be indebted to Aristotle for having advocated an economic policy which was "subordinated to human rule, and its being in the service of an end outside of production and circulation."[23]

Aristotle must still be faulted, however, for not having more vigorously addressed the obstacles to full participation in the life of the city for a wider segment of society. It is true that he does give hints of envisioning a work setting in which different modes of production might develop whereby entirely new institutions of social life could arise; for example, in *Politics*, I, 3, he notes that perhaps slavery would be unnecessary if automatic tools were available, as was the case with the machines of the mythical Daedalus or Hephaestus, where the shuttle would weave of itself and a plectrum do its own playing of the lyre.[24] Presumably these innovative productions would result in economic and personal liberty not only for the head of the household and for those fortunate enough to have the financial means to be involved in the political and cultural works of this "preferred society."[25] Yet, Aristotle seems to be incapable of anticipating how more expanded and sophisticated industrial and commercial activity might provide scope for the material and spiritual development of a larger proportion of the population.

The transformative role that labor is capable of playing is severely confined in Aristotle's purview to the work of politics and culture.

His analysis of social conditions takes for granted preindustrial forms of life. He is set against an exchange environment that would intensify accumulation and oligarchy whose fruits could be taken advantage of by only a few in society.[26] Due to Aristotle's limited vision with regard to the creative potential in the field of work, the mechanics, the farmer, the craftsmen, the business man, are looked upon as instruments, not of *poiesis*, or production, but of praxis, or human action done for its own sake; that is, the workers produce, but not for the sake of production itself. In Aristotle's purview there is no inherent value in these kinds of work. Their primary role is to provide for the necessities of the household economy so that its free members will not have to occupy themselves with the time-consuming tasks of production. Abraham Edel examines in some detail this reluctance on the part of Aristotle to recognize greater continuity between *poiesis* and praxis. He writes:

> When he gets close to any applied field it is only from the point of view of the people who will have to administer and govern the producers–those mechanics and tillers of the fields and slaves–as well as to make proper use of or appreciate the product, but not to engage in such production itself.[27]

It has been noted above that Aristotle does not seem to have been able to anticipate how an improved economic climate might provide leisure and education for a broader base of the community. Had he not been so much a product of his own time he would have recognized a much wider area where work could be a humanizing activity in itself, and not simply an instrument that allows the privileged classes to enjoy the "good life." Further still, his vision of the role that the polis should play in helping to create the material and social conditions necessary for its citizens to realize their full potential provides an intellectual and social framework for reform.

The gradual development of the humanizing and transforming possibilities of work has been addressed in great detail by Adam Smith. He traces the expanded role that can be found in labor to the end of the feudal period. Demand for increased productivity placed a premium on the efficiency, creativeness, and skill of the workers, with the result that, with increased bargaining power, there emerged a keen sense of the worker's independence.[28] By providing for increased productivity as well as by reducing costs, the specialization of labor not only became a source for economic development and a higher standard of living for a greater cross section of society, but it also had the potential for encouraging worker creativity.[29] At the same time, however, Smith recognized the danger, as would Marx, of labor's specialization restricting, if not enslaving, the worker's sphere of action.[30] Nevertheless Smith was convinced that the pitfalls of specialization could be dealt with through broadly based educational and cultural programs. On this point, Patricia H. Werhane notes:

> It is education, according to Smith, that will enhance the lives and character of laborers, the idea being that the progression of the mind will help one to judge one's work rather than being identified with it. Whether education alone is enough to prevent this phenomenon of identifications is surely questionable. But Smith's more important point is that it is the separation of the laborer from his/her productivity, not its identification, that creates the conditions for liberty.[31]

Smith, then, would oppose Marx's view that the identification of the laborer with his labor is a mark of progress; for this kind of identification marks a return to the precommercial stage, where the serfs had little flexibility and scope for personal self development. Werhane notes that both Smith and Marx recognize that "the laborer is never paid fully for his/her productive contribution"; Smith, however, would insist that it is in the laborer's best interest "to control his/her own labor productivity as a commodity for which she can get the best price."[32]

Smith clearly could not anticipate the extreme vulnerability facing the industrial worker in our advanced productive system nor, as Werhane notes, "did he predict the kind of negative alienation" which, since Marx, we have taken as a serious problem.[33] But his response, as noted above, would tend in the direction of regulation and education rather than in the dismantling of the institution of private property;[34] in a setting of free enterprise, properly administered, productive labor can move beyond merely practical know-how or mechanical operation to become a means not only for transforming the subject matter, but the worker as well.

If Aristotle had been able to grasp the expanded opportunities for self-growth on the part of the worker in our mechanized commercial atmosphere, he undoubtedly would have been able to assess the role of work in a new light.

Once labor is viewed as more than unthinking repetition and a technical mastery over nature, but rather as a transformative activity, Aristotle's social and political principles would be able to provide the basis for whatever reform might be necessary to allow all capable members of society to participate in labor's newly found potential. For nowhere in the literature of pagan antiquity has the virtue of justice been more keenly examined or more accurately described than in the *Nicomachean Ethics*, and nowhere have the implications of that virtue for social and political life been more thoroughly canvassed than in the treatise on *Politics*.[35]

With the discovery of labor's humanizing potential, Aristotle would have been quick to insist that society's role is to provide the means whereby all capable members of the community would be provided with the resources needed to effectively participate in the labor force.

This assessment is based on the major thrust of this political thinker's commitment to a fair allocation of the city's resources. The redistribution that Aristotle has in mind extends not only to the resources required for those in need of the basic necessities; it would also include adequate educational resources to provide effective vocational and character development. For example, it has been noted that in *Politics*, II, Aristotle is emphatic in his criticism of law givers (theoretical and actual) for their neglect in providing the means whereby its people might function to the best of their potential.

> *Nicomachean Ethics* X, 9, argues that if people are to become capable of functioning well, education must be publicly and not just privately instituted, and that the public sphere must provide not only for the initial development of capabilities in the young, but also for their maintenance during adulthood.[36]

Aristotle's political science, then, focuses upon creating a city whose primary responsibility must be to provide its people with all the necessary and sufficient means for living a fully human life. The city must organize its resources so that its citizens can, without unnecessary obstacles, achieve self-sufficiency; for Aristotle, a truly self-sufficient life requires that all of our actions be informed, disciplined and organized by practical reason (*phronêsis*), that unifying virtue which includes not only an understanding of one's proper end but also an ability to secure in ever-varying situations reasonable means to reach this end. It is the view of Aristotle, then, that

> Truly human living requires performing all one's natural activities in a way infused by human choice and rationality; and that the capability to function in this human way is not automatically open to all humans, but must be created for them (brought forward from more rudimentary capabilities) by material and social conditions. [37]

From Aristotle's perspective, the transformative character of the good life is not achieved without considerable planning and leadership on the part of the city's lawmakers. But the "natural place" in which this development might be created and nourished is limited to the domain of political and judicial affairs, and reserved for those who enjoy the necessary leisure required to function on this level. It will be necessary to wait until a later epoch before the domain of work in all its forms is seen as a feasible transformative path to inner freedom for a more broadly based segment of society.

Unlike Aristotle, who would relegate the world of work in all of its forms to a lower sphere because, from his perspective, it seemed incapable of fostering self-determination, G.W.F. Hegel considered work in all of its modes as the path to inner freedom. Hegel's range of vision or horizon allowed him to understand the meaning of the tradition out of which Aristotle was writing on its own terms; but at the same time he was able to see it within a larger whole and in truer proportion.[38] He was perhaps the first modern thinker in the West to thoroughly examine what work could mean for man/woman's personal development.

Hegel argues that it is through work, in all of its forms, that human development is shaped. We define ourselves insofar as we are productive.[39] Work becomes the mediating principle whereby the self achieves identity and a sense of permanence. Through productive work Hegel sees a grounding for the development of culture; for in work man/woman transforms nature, and in the process, transforms him/herself.

> Through work the raw material directly supplied by nature is specifically adapted to these numerous ends by all sorts of different processes .... [40]

Work serves as a vehicle for the development of culture. On the theoretical level the innovative advances in the work place create an atmosphere of intellectual excitement:

> This education consists in possessing not simply a multiplicity of ideas and facts but also a flexibility and rapidity of mind, ability to pass from one idea to another, to grasp complex and general relations and so on. It is the education of the understanding in every way, and so also the building up of language.[41]

With regard to its practical ramifications, Hegel points out that work not only develops character traits of discipline, and concern for the needs of others, but it also confirms for the worker a keen sense of her/his own abilities.

> Practical education, acquired through working, consists first in the automatically recurrent need for something to do and the habit of simply being busy; next, in the strict adaptation of one's activity according not only to the nature of the material worked on, but also, and especially, to the pleasure of other workers; and finally, in a habit, produced by this discipline, of objective activity and universally recognized aptitudes.[42]

Work for Hegel, then, can have this educative effect because of its formative activity. Through work the self is capable of withdrawing into self, and in this reflective withdrawal begins to think differently. The result of work's power is that the self comes out of its immediacy and begins to achieve a new and enlarged self-certainty. Commenting on work's liberating effect on consciousness, Hans-Georg Gadamer writes:

> Only in this is there contained the confirmation proper to the self consciousness of ability, namely, that it comes to be "for it as its own," this not only in the single existent which it produces, but beyond this, in its own being-for-self as ability ... when it "puts out" the form as its own (when it produces), it recognizes itself. And thus precisely in work it has a mind of its own: That, I can do![43]

Gadamer hastens to point out that this reflective breakthrough for the self is not yet the full encounter with self which, for instance, the work of art affords and which allows us to recognize, "that's me!" Yet the relationship between the former and latter stages is only a question of degree; for "Hegel is not worried about the specific form which working consciousness has given the thing." What is decisive, Gadamer suggests, is that the self be able to discover the creative potential in the field of work. On this point Gadamer writes: "Thus self-confirmation is not achieved in viewing any particular existent as such, but only in the form which is one's *own* and which precisely for this reason brings out the pure being-for-self contained in the freedom of one's ability."[44]

In the *Phenomenology of Spirit* Hegel develops in a more dramatic way the transformative capabilities of work. As the five stages (struggle until death, master/slave, and the interiorizing of the master/slave relationship in stoicism, skepticism, and unhappy consciousness) of the self's desire for recognition and identity unfold, it becomes progressively more clear that to be truly conscious of self is to be conscious of being free, and that one must grasp that freedom is something more than absolute independence from the other, or more than mere self-assertion or mastery over the other. Instead, the self must come to realize that its freedom and identity is inextricably linked with the other who also must be capable of preserving independence.

> Each is for the other the middle term, through which each mediates itself with itself and unites with itself; and each is for itself, and for the other, an immediate being on its own account, which at the same time is such only through this mediation. They recognize themselves as mutually recognizing one another.[45]

Hegel will point out in the ensuing pages of the section pertaining to Lordship and Bondage, however, that consciousness is a slow learner with regard to the truth that to exist for oneself one also must exist for another; that the being of the other is not a threat to one's independence but is dialectically necessary for one's self-revelation.

> Self-consciousness exists in and for itself when, and by the fact that, it so exists for another; that is, it exists only in being acknowledged.[46]

In his analysis of the master-slave relationship (or lord and bondsman) Hegel begins to uncover how work makes a significant contribution toward "ones self-revelation," or to self-understanding. Involved here is a consideration of the complicated struggle for recognition. At the previous level, the "struggle unto death," the relation of the two self-conscious individuals focused on attempting to prove to each other that "it is only through staking one's life that freedom is won."[47] But with the eventual death of one of the parties in this struggle, all that has been proved is that each held mere life (or "natural existence") of no account; the result, however, is the destruction of consciousness and with it, the collapse of the dialectical interplay; consequently "the two do not reciprocally give and receive one another back from each other consciously, but leave each other free only indifferently, like things."[48] Hegel is suggesting that things cannot "look back"; that one truly "sees oneself" in the eyes of another independent consciousness who highlights one's own deficiencies and can be a source of encouragement and self-development. An advance is made at this point with the recognition that the act of struggle unto death is only an "abstract negation"; it is clearly not the "negation" coming from a consciousness which supersedes in such a way as to preserve and maintain what is superseded, and consequently survives its own "supersession."[49] At this point in the struggle two opposed shapes of consciousness" (*Gestalten des Bewusstseins*) insist upon radical independence. If confronted with the choice of freedom or life, the lord will opt for freedom. The attitude of the other (the bondsman), however, considers mere life to be essential; given the choice of freedom or life, this "dependent consciousness" chooses life.[50] In the conflict which unfolds between the master, who prizes independence (his properly human life) over subservience to the point where he is willing to sacrifice his life, and the slave, who is willing to subordinate his autonomy in order to survive, the process of self-realization can continue.

On a first reading it would appear that the master, through his dominance, has achieved a privileged position. Yet his triumphant gain is short lived; for while it is true that the lord or master achieved "recognition" as the truly independent party in the relationship, it is the slave who will be afforded the opportunity to give more concrete expression to what it means to be a self.[51] In his fear of death and desire for survival the slave gives over his freedom to the master; yet paradoxically, there continues to be in place a field wherein the slave can secure independence and identity within his dependence:

> In fear, the being-for-self is present in the bondsman himself; in fashioning the thing, he becomes aware that being-for-self belongs to him, that he himself exists essentially and actually in his own right.[52]

Indeed as the drama unfolds, contrary to what would have been expected, it is the master who comes to realize his own inferiority in comparison to the slave. It is the slave who begins to think with new awareness of self; for it is the slave, who through work on behalf of the master, tests and explores new possibilities. It is quite evident, of course, that, since the bondsman continues to be under the control of the lord, he is not objectively free. The result is that the relationship remains precarious and compromised; yet this work setting "transforms the subject's consciousness of the object into a more authentic consciousness of self."[53]

In paragraph 196 of the *Phenomenology* Hegel presents three necessary moments for the proper development of consciousness: fear, service, and construction (*Bilden*). Hegel will demonstrate that the slave, and not the master, will be the agent who is provided with the opportunity to "work through" these three moments in hopes of becoming a freely acting subject.

The negative moment of fear or experience of death is the experience of the self's total dependency in existence. By resisting this "alien reality," even if it be only a "skilled cancellation," the slave begins the process of liberation through focused and disciplined service.

> The moment of obedient service transforms chaotic activity into work, which affects the transformation (construction) of both reality and the consciousness of the slave.[54]

It becomes increasingly clear, then, that it will be the slave and not the master who is in a position to exercise the transformative activity which work allows. The master's status never moves beyond that of being a consumer; it is the slave who is in the more privileged position of being a producer. The master simply takes what is given for his own enjoyment; his relation to things is "purely destructive"; it involves simply a "non-mediating negation," whereas the slave is in a position to construct, to impose his personality on the object. The slave's actions, then, are not destructive like the master's, but rather are a means for development. The slave negates the given natural being of things by raising it to a higher order through the mediating efforts of his creative workmanship.

> Through the rediscovery of himself by himself, the bondsman realizes that it is precisely in his work wherein he seemed to have only a alienated existence that he acquires a mind of his own.[55]

Gadamer pursues the transforming role of work by drawing upon Hegel's employment of the concept of *Bildung*. He notes that initially *Bildung* was associated with the idea of culture–the developing of one's natural talents or capacities. But if the idea of work as a major contributing factor in the self's learning process is restricted to this one sense of the term, one would not necessarily move beyond the notion of "technical ability."[56] Hegel, instead, conceives of work as being a much more interior phenomenon. It is true that "in acquiring a 'capacity,' a skill, man gains the sense of himself;"[57] still, the transformative character of work is the result of recognizing "one's own in the alien" or unfamiliar. In this consists the basic movement of spirit, "whose being consists only in returning to itself from what is other."[58]

This "returning to itself from what is other" is the result of the process of transformation, or self-understanding, on the part of the worker. By working on the alien or unfamiliar subject matter, the worker is tested, challenged, questions himself more profoundly, and, in the process, achieves self understanding.

> Every single individual who raises himself out of his natural being to the spiritual finds in the language, customs, and institutions of his people a pre-given body of material which, as in learning to speak, he has to make his own.[59]

This inner dynamic which characterizes work is reinforced by Gadamer in his comparison of the movement or process of *Bildung* to play; for play, as well as any productive work setting, entails the element of risk and fascination, a movement beyond ourselves and an experiencing of the alien, the unfamiliar.

> Thus we say of someone that he plays with possibilities or with plans. What we mean is clear. He still has not committed himself to the possibilities as to serious aims. He still has the freedom to decide one way or the other, for one or the other possibility. On the other hand, this freedom is not without danger. Rather the game itself is a risk for the player. ... One enjoys a freedom of decision which at the same time is endangered and irrevocably limited.[60]

Play, like work is *Bildung*; in getting involved in participating in a game, for example, the player begins to learn more about himself/herself, his/her strengths, his/her weaknesses. In competitive play, as in any "resistant work setting," the player recognizes, perhaps for the first time, his/her limitations and strengths and also the need of cooperating with others in the team effort or project at hand.[61]

In questioning the subject matter, whether it be, for example, the challenge of the game on the playing field, or the obstacles which must be overcome before a worker can resolve a particular problem, the participant begins to question himself/herself; in understanding the material s/he understands himself/herself. The workplace, then, becomes a region where the worker learns by transcending the narrow confines of his/her own opinions; consequently, the subject matter, as well as the agent are "opened up." On this point Kojève writes:

> Work is *Bildung*, in the double meaning of the word: on the one hand, it forms, transforms the World, humanizes it by making it more adapted to Man; on the other, it transforms, forms, educates man, it humanizes him by bringing him into greater conformity with the idea that he has of himself, an idea that–in the beginning–is only an abstract idea.[62]

The "double role" that Kojève assigns to the notion of work is very much in keeping with the connection between labor and human consciousness which has been advanced by Hegel and Gadamer. In applying his/her ideas and insights to the task at hand, the worker shapes the object and at the same time "shapes himself/herself"; he/she gains additional perspective and awareness of the possibilities for future growth. Involved here is a questioning, not only of the subject matter, "but of ourselves with respect to ourselves and our circumstances";[63] for questions always assist the person in drawing out the yet undetermined possibilities of a thing, of exploring new connections and thereby reaching a position where conclusions can be drawn. On this point Gadamer writes:

> To understand the questionableness of something is already to be questioning. There can be no tentative or potential attitude to questioning, for questioning is not the positing but the testing of possibilities .... Questioning opens up possibilities of meaning, and thus what is meaningful passes into one's own thinking on the subject.[64]

It becomes increasingly more evident, then, that the notion of work as "practical knowledge" will be conceived too narrowly if it is looked upon simply as "technical skill," where the worker assumes a detached, objective stance, skillfully responding to clear cut plans. This "technological attitude" seems quite removed from the viewpoint advanced by the authors above, *viz.*, that work, given the proper circumstances, can rise to the spiritual level. Gadamer argues that the differences are patent:

> It is obvious that man is not at his own disposal in the same way that the craftsman's material is at his proposal.[65]

It is important, therefore, that man/woman acquire another kind of knowledge that s/he would have of himself/herself in his/her moral being. It will be practical knowledge; but a type of practical knowledge distinct from the technical skill or knowledge that guides the making of something. Aristotle captures the difference in question when he refers to this kind of knowledge as "self-knowledge"–knowledge for oneself (*phronêsis*).[66] He distinguishes theoretical knowledge (*epistêmê*) from the two types of practical knowledge, *viz.*, moral knowledge (*phronêsis*), and technical knowledge (*technê*); but he also makes the further distinction between *technê* and *phronêsis*. It is practical knowledge in the form of the virtue of *phronêsis* (prudence, self knowledge) that can provide for the spiritual possibilities of work. *Phronêsis* or practical wisdom provides the self with a clean grasp of the right ends as well as insight into how to achieve those ends. It disposes us to discover the appropriate means for the circumstances. The person who has acquired the virtue of *phronêsis* does not appeal to fully determined rules that are then automatically applied to a particular dilemma as is the case with *technê*. The person of *phronêsis* recognizes that "the concrete and unique reality of human freedom when lived with others through time constitutes a distinctive and ever changing process."[67] Hence the person of *phronêsis* must develop the habit of good judgment in situations where there is no possibility of clear cut solutions. Further still, Gadamer points out that the person of *phronêsis* exercises also the virtue of "sympathetic understanding" or *sunêsis* ("fellow-feeling, forbearance, forgiveness"). It entails the capacity for moral judgment especially in one's relation to other persons:

> The question here, then, is not about knowledge in general but its concretion at a particular moment. This knowledge also is not in any sense technical knowledge or the application of such. The man of the world, the man who knows all the tricks and dodges and is experienced in everything there is, does not really have sympathetic understanding for the person acting: he has it only if he satisfies one requirement, namely that he too is seeking what is right–i.e., that he is united with the other person in this commonality.[68]

Phronêsis, unlike *technê*, disposes the person to think for himself/herself and to make responsible choices in settings that are often extremely complex and ambiguous. It cannot be taught in the manner of a technical craft. It requires a learning process tempered by experiencing situations that force upon the subject considerable personal reflection before judgments can be rendered.

> The image that a man has of what he ought to be–i.e., his ideas of right and wrong, of decency, courage, dignity, loyalty, and so forth ... are certainly, in some sense, images that he uses to guide his conduct. But there is still a basic difference between this and the guiding image the craftsman uses: the plan of the object he is going to make. What is right, for example, cannot be

> fully determined independently of the situation that requires a right action from me, whereas the *eidos* of what a craftsman wants to make is fully determined by the use for which it is intended.[69]

Phronêsis, then, is the type of knowledge that can provide for authentic personal growth; it prompts the self to become involved in complex situations in which solutions do not come automatically by an appeal to clear cut rules. And, as Hegel and Gadamer have argued, it is the work setting that can provide the creative space in which this type of knowledge can be nurtured.

Hegel's reflections on the significance of work contributes in no small measure toward a fuller appreciation of its spiritual potential; at the same time it becomes abundantly clear that society has a heavy responsibility to foster an atmosphere in which work can exercise its integrative role in the personal development of all members of the community.

If the mode of production in modern industry and the form of human commerce in our currently structured industrial society do not allow scope for all members of society to find personal significance in the workplace, serious questions necessarily arise as to whether we are not becoming unfairly restrictive regarding who will be allowed to be really free in the contemporary work-setting.

Indeed, the argument has been advanced that, unless the major industrialized nations, such as the United States, begin to consider more carefully the transformative role that work can play in the current commercial market place, not only for its managers and professionals, but also for its front-line workers as well, they will continue to find it increasingly more difficult to compete in the world market.

The enviable economic strides made by the United States, for example, early in the century can be attributed to our achievements in utilizing the mass production system. A nucleus of well educated and well trained workers were able to break down the work to be done on the assembly lines into little pieces which could then be handled by workman with little education and training. With every new advance in technology, it was possible for these same workers to become the most productive in the world.

But it was inevitable that this same equipment would eventually be able to be sent anywhere in the world. And workers were sure to be found to manage this technology at a fraction of the wages demanded by American workers. Hence:

> The only way high-wage countries like the United States can compete in this game is to respond to the needs of customers all over the world who are willing to pay top prices to get first-quality goods and services, customized to their requirements and delivered quickly.[70]

But to respond to this demand for quality will require front-line workers capable of taking on much more personal responsibility than was required in the past. And this new form of work organization will require a greater percentage of this work-force who have acquired a broad education as well as increased technical skills.[71] Indeed it will be necessary for firms to treat their front-line workers as they now treat their managers and professional staff.[72] Further still, what with the restructuring and down-sizing which necessarily will follow, a program which draws the formerly unskilled labor force into areas of greater responsibility, the ranks of middle management will be affected in no small measure. It will be the responsibility of government as well as industry to guarantee that a new marginalized segment of the work-force does not emerge who are denied the opportunity to participate in the nation's productive capabilities. If work has the ability of truly transforming the self, then it is quite clear that:

> A job ... is not like a piece of pie that someone gives me, or like a paycheck that I take home with me. A job is not a consumer good. It is something I go to, something I engage in with many others in highly complex, structured activity that is linked with a vast interlocking system. From this point of view it is really more accurate to speak of participating in the work of society than of having a job. The distribution of jobs, therefore, concerns the way that participation in the economic process is structured–how it provides access to work for all or just for some, whom it excludes and whom it includes.[73]

Perhaps under the pressure of economic survival we will begin to probe more deeply the foundations of our understanding of the meaning and value of work for human life.

Notes

1. Józef Tischner, *The Spirit of Solidarity*, trans. Marek Zaleski and Benjamin Fiore, S.J. (San Francisco: Harper & Row, 1984), p. 14. In addressing both the positive and negative elements of work, Tischner draws upon the Platonic-Aristotelian conception of "knowledge of the good", which consists in seeing things under certain aspects which constitute intrinsic reasons for engaging in them. It is a type of knowledge that is intimately connected with caring about something, and does not seem to be merely a technical or instrumentalist type of knowledge or "know-how" centering upon power, utility, and expediency. On this theme see also Hans-Georg Gadamer, *The Idea of the Good in Platonic-Aristotelian Philosophy* trans. P. Christopher Smith (New Haven: Yale University Press, 1986), Shaun Gallagher has noted that genuine exchange entails social agreement. This agreement requires some type of conversation or collaboration; for, "in a genuine dialogue or conversation one remains open to the thoughts of the other and, in principle attempts to stay with the subject matter." Shaun Gallagher, *Hermeneutics and Education* (Albany, N.Y.: State University of New York Press, 1992), p. 148.

2. *Ibid.*, p. 13.

3. *Ibid.*, p. 21.

4. John Paul II, *Laborem exercens*. John Paul II emphasizes that the creative potential of the worker can only be realized if work is for man's development rather than man being reduced to being for work, a mere cog under the control of others. Hence, his emphasis upon the priority of labor over capital. The pontiff considers this theme of work to be the essential key to the "social question".

5. *Ibid.*, "Man has to subdue the earth and dominate it, because as the 'image of God' he is a person, that is to say, a subjective being capable of acting in a planned and rational way, capable of deciding about himself and with a tending to self realization.... Understood as a process whereby man and the human race subdue the earth, work corresponds to this basic biblical concept only when throughout the process man manifests himself and confirms himself as the one who 'dominates.' This dominion, in a certain sense, refers to the subjective dimension even more than to the objective one. This dimension conditions the very ethical nature of work. In fact there is no doubt that human work has an ethical value of its own, which already and directly remains linked to the fact that the one who carries it out is a person, a conscious and free subject, that is to say, a subject that decides about himself."

6. Stanley Hauerwas, "Work as Co-Creation: A Critique of a Remarkably Bad IDEA," in John W. Houck and Oliver F. Williams, C.S.C., eds., *Co-Creation and Capitalism: John Paul II's Laborem Exercens* (Washington: University Press of America, 1983), pp. 48-49. "No doubt John-Paul II's account is motivated by an attempt to call attention to the dignity of the common man's labor. But in so doing he underwrites what can only be described as a romantic and elitist view of work."

7. David Hollenbach, "Unemployment and Jobs: A Theological and Ethical Perspective," in John W. Houck and Oliver E. Williams, eds., *Catholic Social Teaching and the U.S. Economy: Working Papers for a Bishops' Pastoral* (Washington: University Press of America, 1984), pp. 118-119.

8. Gregory Baum, ed., *Work and Religion* (New York: Seabury, 1980), pp. vii-viii.

9. F.S. Fiorenza, "Work and Critical Theology," in W.J. Heisler and John W. Houck, eds., *A Matter of Dignity: Inquiries into the Humanization of Work* (Notre Dame, Ind.: University of Notre Dame, 1977), pp. 26-28. Fiorenza notes that Hesiod continues to praise farming as a religious act, even after the small farmer, caught in transition, was losing his land and autonomy: "In farming, everything must be done at the right time and in the right form. Only then can the farmer trust divine justice and expect that the divine earth will yield its fruits. Justice, the favorite daughter of Zeus, blesses and rewards those working in accord with the laws of nature and justice."

10. *Ibid.*, p. 26. See also J.P. Vernant, *Mythe et Pensée chez les Grecs* (Paris: François Maspero, 1968).

11. Artistotle, *Politics*, VII, 9, 1328 b33-a2. "Now since we are speaking of the best form of government, i.e. that under which the state will be most happy (and happiness, as has already been said, cannot exist without virtue), it clearly follows that in the state which is best governed and possesses men who are just absolutely, and not merely relatively to the principle of the constitution, the citizens must not lead the life of mechanics or tradesmen, for such a life is ignoble, and inimical to virtue. Neither must they be a farmer, since leisure is necessary both for the development of virtue and the performance of political duties." In an attempt to present a more nuanced picture of Aristotle's severe treatment of the status of the productive arts, Hannah Arendt argues that Aristotle's comments regarding the status of those involved in manual labor, the crafts and commercial trade are not due to contempt for these endeavors but rather are based on the fact that these activities allow little time for more liberal pursuits. She writes: "Coulanges, in distinction from other authors, stresses the time—and strength—consuming activities demanded from an ancient citizen, rather than his "leisure", and sees rightly that Aristotle's statement that no man who had to work for his livelihood could be a citizen is a simple statement of fact rather than the expression of a prejudice"—Arendt goes on to argue that, in contrast to the ancients where citizenship is defined in terms of capability which only can be fostered with adequate free time, "it is characteristic of the modern development that riches as such, regardless of the occupation of their owner, became a qualification for citizenship: only now was it a mere privilege to be a citizen, unconnected with any specifically political activities." Hannah Arendt, *The Human Condition* (Chicago: University of Chicago Press, 1958), p. 65, n. 68. See also Fustel de Coulanges, *The Ancient City* (New York: Doubleday Anchor Book, 1956), pp. 335 ff.

12. Adriano Tilgher, *Homo Faber: Work Through the Ages*, trans. D.C. Fisher (Chicago: Henry Regnery, 1958), p. 3 (cited in Fiorenza, "Work and Critical Theology, p. 25). See also John Paul II, *Laborem exercens*, p.6: "The ancient world introduced its own typical differentiation of people into classes according to the type of work done. Work which demanded from the worker the exercise of physical

strength, the work of muscles and hands, was considered unworthy of free men and was therefore given to slaves."

13. Aristotle, *Politics*, III, 9, 1280 a31. "But a state exists for the sake of the good life, not for the sake of life only: if life only were the object, slaves and brute animals might form a state, but they cannot, for they have no share in happiness or in a life of free choice. Nor does a state exist for the sake of alliance and security from injustice, nor yet for the sake of exchange and mutual intercourse; for then the Tyrrhenians and the Carthaginians, and all who have commercial treaties with one another, would be the citizens of one state."

14. Arendt, *The Human Condition*, pp. 36-37.

15. Aristotle, *Politics*, VII, 2, 1324 a 24-26.

16. Shaun Gallagher, "Interdependence and Freedom in Hegel's Economics" in William Maker, ed., *Hegel on Economics and Freedom* (Macon, Ga.: Mercer University Press, 1987), p. 160. Gallagher cites Polanyi's description of an embedded economy as one in which the elements of the economy are "embedded in noneconomic institutions, the economic process itself being instituted through kinship, marriage, age groups, secret societies, totemic associations,. and public solemnities. The term 'economic life' would here (that is, in such a society) have no obvious meaning." Karl Polanyi, "Primitive, Archaic, and Modern Economics," ed. George Dalton (New York: Anchor, 1968), p. 84. See also Polanyi, "Aristotle Discovers the Economy," in K. Polanyi, ed., *Trade and Market in the Early Empires* (Glencove, Ill.: 1957), pp. 60-94. Gallagher also notes that: "a different concept of the economy results from the recognition that economic factors are distinguishable from a moral and social infrastructure and that they can be scientifically controlled. Such a disembedded economy presupposes the establishment of a market system following laws different from those of non-economic institutions." Gallagher argues that Aristotle had only a vague notion of how economic considerations might transcend the private world of domestic life.

17. Arendt, *The Human Condition*, pp. 30-31.

18. Aristotle, *Nicomachean Ethics*, I, 4, 1096 a6 ff. "The money maker's life is in a way forced on him [not chosen for itself], since it is [merely] useful, [choiceworthy only] for some other end."

19. In his introduction to his translation of the *Politics* of Aristotle, Ernest Barker, commenting on Aristotle's economic theory writes: "wealth on this basis, is a means to a moral end; as such a means, it is necessarily limited by the end and it must not be greater—as equally it must not be less— than what the end requires. This is not socialism; but it is a line of thought inimical to capitalism (which involves the unlimited accumulation of wealth), and through the influence of Ruskin and others it had, in its measure, tended to foster modern socialism." Ernest Barker, *The Politics of Aristotle*, trans. with notes and appendixes (New York: Oxford University Press, 1958), p. lvi. See also William J. Booth, "Households, Markets, and Firms," in George E. McCarthy, ed., *Marx and Aristotle: Nineteenth-Century German Social Theory and Classical Antiquity* (Savage, Md.: Rowman and Littlefield, 1992), p. 249. Booth notes that Aristotle's focus on the economy as subordinate to more basic

human and societal ends appealed to Karl Marx. He writes: "The *oikos* economy's quality of being subordinated to human rule, and its being in the service of an end outside of production and circulation, unquestionably appealed to Marx and gave him a part of the foundation of his theory of communism."

20. Aristotle, *Politics*, II, 6, 1265 a38 ff. On this theme Martha Nussbaum maintains that "interpreters who stress Aristotle's role as theoretician of civic virtue often forget that the Aristotelian virtues are, for the most part, dispositions concerned with the reasonable use of external goods: they are not "moral" in the sense of being occupied with a noumenal realm that is totally cut off from or independent of the material circumstances of life ... good functioning, and even good thinking and good desiring, are not independent of the resources people have and the institutions in which they live. It is the job of political thought to imagine such conditions." Nussbaum observes that interpreters of Aristotle among the more affluent nations often forget and underemphasize Aristotle's concern for and interest in the questions of hunger and scarcity, of property and its distribution. Martha Nussbaum, "Nature, Function, and Capability: Aristotle on Political Distribution," in George E. McCarthy, ed., *Marx and Aristotle:* , pp. 194-195. See also Peter Simpson, "Making the Citizens Good: Aristotle's City and Its Contemporary Relevance," *The Philosophical Forum*, 22:2 (1990), p. 156. Simpson reminds us that when Aristotle considers the *polis* a "perfect society," the Stagirite is not suggesting that the state is without faults, but rather that only here does one find a natural place for full human development. He writes: "This communal living is initiated at the level of physical or biological needs; but if it were to stop there an element of human nature would either be left undeveloped or distorted into subhuman perversions. This element, the element of *logos*, is moreover the decisive or determinative element because it is what makes human beings distinctive and different from other animals. If this element of *logos* is to be properly developed, that is if human beings are to realize their natural perfection, they must choose a life of *logos* for its own sake, not for its incidental advantages; and their communal living must advance to the level of the city understood as something distinct in kind and purpose from either household or village on their own."

21. *Politics*, I, 8, 1256 b26-37. "Of the art of acquisition then there is one kind which by nature is a part of the management of a household, in so far as the art of household management must either find ready to hand, or itself provide, such things necessary to life, and useful for the community of the family or state, as can be stored. They are the elements of true riches; for the amount of property which is needed for a good life is not unlimited, although Solon in one of his poems says that `No bound to riches has been fixed for man'. But there is a boundary fixed, just as there is in the other arts; for the instruments of any art are never unlimited, either in number or size, and riches may be defined as a number of instruments to be used in a household or in a state."

22. Gallagher, "Interdependence and Freedom in Hegel's Economics," p. 172.

23. Booth, "Households, Markets, and Firms," p. 249. "Men once again gain control of exchange, production and the way they behave to one another," Karl Marx and Frederick Engels, *The German Ideology*, vol. 5 of Karl Marx - Frederick Engels, *Collected Works* (New York: International Publishers, 1976), p. 48 (cited in Booth, p. 268).

24. Aristotle, *Politics*, I, 4, 1253b34-1254a1. "For if every instrument could accomplish its own work, obeying or anticipating the will of others, like the statues of Daedalus, or the tripods of Hephaestus, which, says the poet, 'of their own accord entered the assembly of the gods;' if, in like manner, the shuttle would weave and the plectrum touch the lyre without a hand to guide them, chief workmen would not want servants, nor masters slaves."

25. Abraham Edel, *Aristotle and His Philosophy* (Chapel Hill, N.C.: University of North Carolina Press, 1982), p. 339.

26. Stephen White, *Sovereign Virtue: Aristotle on the Relation Between Happiness and Prosperity* (Stanford, Cal.: Stanford University Press, 1992), p. 217.

27. Edel, *Aristotle and His Philosophy*, p. 217.

28. "The property which every man has is his own labor, as it is the original foundation of all other property, so it is the most sacred and inviolable. The patrimony of a poor man lies in the strength and dexterity of his hands; and to hinder him from employing this strength and dexterity in what manner he thinks proper without injury to his neighbor, is a plain violation of this most sacred property. It is a manifest encroachment upon the just liberty both of the workman, and of those who might be disposed to employ them. As it hinders the one from working at what he thinks proper, so it hinders the others from employing whom they think proper." Adam Smith, *The Wealth of Nations* (hereafter cited as WN), ed. R.H. Campbell and A.S. Skinner (Indianapolis: Liberty Classics, 1976), I, X, c.12. Cited in Patricia H. Werhane, "Freedom, Commodification, and the Alienation of Labor in Adam Smith's *Wealth of Nations*," *The Philosophical Forum*, 22:4, (1991), p. 384.

29. *Ibid.*, p. 389. See also WN, I. i. 8, cited in Werhane, "Freedom, Commodification," p. 398, n. 14.

30. *Ibid.*, p. 390.

31. *Ibid.*, pp. 391-392.

32. *Ibid.*, p. 397.

33. *Ibid.*

34. Smith issues a warning with regard to the possible negative effects of the specialization of labor if education and regulation are not present as integrative factors in the productive process." But the understandings of the greater part of men are necessarily formed by their ordinary employments. The man whose whole life is spent in performing a few simple operations, of which the effects too, are perhaps always the same, or very nearly the same, has no occasion to exert his understanding, or to exercise his invention in finding out expedients for removing difficulties which never occur. He naturally loses, therefore, the habit of such exertion, and generally becomes as stupid and ignorant as it is possible for a human creature to become.... His dexterity at his own particular trade seems, in this manner, to be

acquired at the expense of his intellectual, social, and martial virtues." WN, V, i, f. 50, cited in Werhane, "Freedom Commodification," p. 390.

35. Aristotle, *Nicomachean Ethics*, V, VIII.

36. Nussbaum, "Nature, Function, and Authority," p. 187. See also *Nicomachean Ethics*, II, 1, 1103b3-6; *Politics*, VIII, 2, 1337a8. In *Nicomachean Ethics*, X, 9, 1180a1-4, Aristotle comments: "But it is surely not enough that when they are young they should get the right nurture and attention; since they must, even when they are grown up, practice and be habituated to them, we shall need laws for this as well, and generally speaking to cover the whole of life."

37. Nussbaum, "Nature, Function, and Authority," p. 205. See also Aristotle, *Nicomachean Ethics*, VI, 12, 1144a1-35. In an attempt to clarify the importance of practical reason (*phronêsis*) for the self's proper formation, Aristotle (1144a24-37) writes: "There is a faculty which is called cleverness; and this is such as to be able to do the things that tend towards the mark we have set before ourselves, and to hit it. Now if the mark be noble, the cleverness is laudable, but if the mark be bad, the cleverness is mere smartness; hence we call even men of practical wisdom clever or smart. Practical wisdom is not the faculty, but it does not exist without this faculty. And this eye of the soul acquires its formed state not without the aid of virtue, as has been said and is plain; for the syllogisms which deal with acts to be done are things which involve a starting–point, viz. 'Since the end, i.e. what is best, is of such and such a nature,' whatever it may be (let it for the sake of argument be what we please); and this is not evident except to the good man; for wickedness perverts us and causes us to be deceived about the starting-points of action. Therefore it is evident that it is impossible to be practically wise without being good."

38. Hans-Georg Gadamer, *Truth and Method*, 2nd rev. ed. (New York: Continuum, 1993), p. 302, (cited hereafter as TM). Gadamer has examined how the awareness of being affected by history is primarily an awareness of the hermeneutical situation. He defines the concept of "situation" as that which "represents a standpoint that limits the possibility of vision." Therefore the concept of "horizon" is essential here. Gadamer writes: "The horizon is the range of vision that includes everything that can be seen from a particular vantage point. Applying this to the thinking mind, we speak of narrowness of horizon, of the possible expansion of horizon, and so forth. Since Nietzsche and Husserl, the word has been used in philosophy to characterize the way in which thought is tied to its finite determinacy, and the way one's range of vision is gradually expanded." See also Rudolf Siefert, "Work and Religion in Hegel's Thought," in Gregory Baum, ed., *Work and Religion*, pp. 117-128.

39. Karl Löwith, *From Hegel to Nietzsche: The Revolution in Nineteenth-Century Thought*, trans. David E. Green (New York: Holt Rinehart and Winston, 1964), p. 265. Commenting upon Hegel's discussion of the theme of work in the Jena lectures, Löwith writes: " ... he describes its spiritual character as being primarily a 'negative attitude' toward nature. Work is not an instinct, but a product of 'reasonableness,' a `mode of spirit.'"

40. G.W.F. Hegel, *Philosophy of Right*, p. 196, trans. T.M. Knox (London: Oxford University Press, 1967), pp. 128-129 (hereafter cited as PR). In his discussion of Hegel's analysis of the transformative character ingredient in work, Alexandre

Kojève has noted that, with work, "there is necessarily change, progress, historical evolution. For what changes as a result of Work is not only the natural World; it is also–and even especially–Man himself ... It is only by rising above the given conditions through negation brought about in and by work that Man remains in contact with the concrete, which varies with space and time. That is why he changes himself by transforming the World." Alexandre Kojève, *Introduction to the Reading of Hegel*, trans. J.H. Nichols (Ithaca, N.Y.: Cornell University Press, Agora edition, 1980), p. 51. Kojève, p.51, n.3 gives a helpful example with regard to how work shapes a distinctly human world: "A manufactured object incarnates an idea (a 'project') which is independent of the material 'hic et nunc'; that is why these objects can be 'exchanged.' Hence the birth of an 'economic,' specifically human World, in which money, capital, interest, salary, and so on appear."

41. PR, 197, p. 129.

42. *Ibid.*, p. 129.

43. Hans-Georg Gadamer, *Hegel's Dialectic: Five Hermeneutical Studies*, trans. P. Christopher Smith (New Haven: Yale University Press, 1976), p. 71.

44. *Ibid.*, p. 72.

45. G.W.F. Hegel, *Phenomenology of Spirit*, 184, p. 112. Texts of the *Phenomenology of Spirit* will be cited from *Phenomenology of Spirit*, trans. by A.V. Miller (Oxford: Oxford University Press, 1977). This translation has been made from the 5th edition, of *Phänomenologie des Geistes*, ed. by J. Hoffmeister (Hamburg, Felix Meiner Verlag, 1952), hereafter cited as PS.

46. Hegel, PS, 178, p. 111. It has been noted that Jean-Paul Sartre's approach to the dialectic of interpersonal relationships takes a quite different turn, in that for Sartre, the "look" of another results in the other party in the relationship being reduced to a "thing" (see "Le Regard," *L'Etre et le néant* [Paris: Gallimard, 1944]). Hence the subjectivity of the one being scrutinized is lost; hence, "the very being of the other as a self, then, is a threat to one's own selfhood." See Quentin Lauer, *A Reading of Hegel's Phenomenology of Spirit* (New York: Fordham University Press, 1993), p. 125, n. 39.

47. Hegel, *Ibid.*, 187, p. 114.

48. *Ibid.*, 188, p. 114.

49. *Ibid.*, 188, pp. 114-115.

50. *Ibid.*, 189, p. 115.

51. Lauer, *A Reading of Hegel's Phenomenology of Spirit*, p. 130.

52. Hegel, PS, section 196, p. 118.

53. Lauer, *A Reading of Hegel's Phenomenology of Spirit*, p. 133. See also Hegel PS, section 195, p. 118: "This negative middle term or the formative activity is at the

same time the individuality or pure being-for-self of consciousness which now, in the work outside of it, acquires an element of permanence. It is in this way, therefore, that consciousness, qua worker, comes to see in the independent being (of the object) its own independence."

54. Lauer, *A Reading of Hegel's Phenomenology of Spirit*, p. 134. See also Hegel, PS, section 194, p. 117: "Furthermore, his consciousness is not this dissolution of everything stable merely in principle; in his service he actually brings this about. Through his service he rids himself of his attachment to natural existence in every single detail; and gets rid of it by working on it." Commenting on this insight, Lauer notes that Hegel emphasizes that, to put order into the fleeting and chaotic world, consciousness is pushed back onto itself; "but awareness ... is not an adequate ground for self awareness as the locus of reality; creating reality is required." See Lauer *A Reading*, p. 134, n. 53. P. Christopher Smith has pointed out that Gadamer sees parallels between Hegel and Heidegger with regard to the fear of death's impact on the self's enlarged sense of itself. He writes: "If Gadamer is correct in his interpretation, death has the same role in Hegel's understanding of the transition from consciousness to self consciousness as it has in Heidegger's understanding of the transition from inauthenticity to authenticity. The higher stage for both Hegel and Heidegger would be *Sein-zum-Tode*, being towards death, for it is only death which can put the individual in authentic relationship with himself." Cf. Martin Heidegger, *Sein und Zeit* (Tubingen: Niemeyer, 1960), pp.46-53. See translator's note 12, in Gadamer, *Hegel's Dialectic,* p. 69.

55. Hegel, PS, section 196, p. 119.

56. Gadamer, TM, p. 11. "The concept of *Bildung* transcends that of the mere cultivation of given talents, from which the concept is derived."

57. *Ibid.*, p. 13. Commenting upon the scope of work as a form of transcendence and appropriation of consciousness, Gadamer writes: "*Bildung* here no longer means 'culture'—i.e., developing one's capacities or talents. Rather, the rise of the word *Bildung* evokes the ancient mystical tradition according to which man carries in his soul the image of God, after whom he is fashioned, and which man must cultivate in himself....In having no goals outside itself, the concept of *Bildung* transcends that of mere cultivation of given talents, from which concept it is derived. The cultivation of a talent is the development of something that is given, so that practicing and cultivating it is a mere means to an end. In *Bildung*, by contrast, that by which and through which one is formed becomes completely one's own." TM, p. 11.

58. *Ibid.*, p. 14.

59. *Ibid.*

60. *Ibid.*, p. 106.

61. *Ibid.*, p. 102. Referring to the importance of play as a means of learning, Gallagher (*Hermeneutics and Education*, p. 49) notes that educational researchers know that in the process of play children learn about "the nature of materials and begin to form concepts of weight, size, texture, softness, hardness, plasticity, impermeability, transparency and so on." Of equal, if not greater importance,

"children begin also to discuss the possibilities and limitations of their own powers." See John Blackie, "How Children Learn," *NEA Journal*, 47 (1968), pp. 40-42, cited in Gallagher, *Hermeneutics and Education*, p. 359, n. 20.

62. Kojève, *Introduction to the Reading of Hegel*, p. 52.

63. Gallagher, *Hermeneutics and Education*, p. 157.

64. Gadamer, TM, p. 375.

65. *Ibid.*, p. 316.

66. *Ibid.*, p. 316. See also Aristotle, *Nicomachean Ethics*, VI, 8, 1141b33-1142a30.

67. George F. McLean, "Hermeneutics, Historicity, and Values" in George McLean and Olinto Pegoraro, *The Social Context and Values: Perspectives of the Americas* (Lanham, Md.: University Press of America, 1989), p. 24.

68. Gadamer, TM, p. 323.

69. *Ibid.*, p. 317.

70. *Ibid.*, p. 5.

71. Nussbaum, "Nature, Function, and Authority," p. 201 cites the discussion of public education found in *General Education in a Free Society: Report of the Harvard Committee*, ed., Paul Buck, John H. Finley, Jr., *et al.* (Cambridge, Mass.: Harvard University, 1945). The authors of this report draw upon ancient Greek models of education, and argue that: "a national plan for general education should specify in extremely general terms certain capabilities that we wish to develop in all citizens: for example, social awareness and responsiveness, the ability to construct and understand a scientific argument, intellectual and emotional responsiveness to great works of literature, music, and art. After discussing these general capabilities at some length, they then argue that it should be left to each local region and institution to specify a curriculum more concretely in these areas, on the basis of concrete reflection about how its particular students, in the context of their particular ways of life, might best realize the capabilities in question."

72. Brock, "What America Needs: A License to Skill," p. 105.

73. Hollenbach, "Unemployment and Jobs: A Theological and Ethical Perspective," p. 130.

Chapter Eight

CHRISTIAN ETHICS AND SEXUAL HARASSMENT

J. Milburn Thompson

Sexual harassment is not a new phenomenon. It is as ancient as the stories of Potiphar's wife and Joseph (Genesis 39) and Susanna and the elders (Daniel 13; Moore 1992). Yet sexual harassment was named only in the mid-1970s; before that it was literally unspeakable (CWC/UPC 1982, 3; S. Martin 1989, 57). Now, however, women are speaking up and sexual harassment is being widely discussed and debated.[1]

A watershed event in the contemporary awareness of sexual harassment was Anita Hill's accusation against Clarence Thomas during his confirmation hearings for Supreme Court Justice in October 1991. Events such as the resignation of Dr. Frances Conley from her senior faculty position at Stanford Medical School, the Tailhook Convention scandal, the suit by women workers at Stroh's Brewery, and the accusations against Senator Robert Packwood have kept the issue in the public eye. Although this national debate has surely raised consciousness about sexual harassment, the issue remains ambiguous and muddled.

The rather extensive literature on sexual harassment falls into several overlapping categories: feminist denunciations (Dworkin 1992) and anti-feminist responses (Davidson 1991), advice for victims (Bouchard 1990; CWEALF 1991), legal explorations (MacKinnon 1979; Tong 1986; Bowman 1993), social science attempts to uncover the extent and nature of sexual harassment (Collins 1981; S. Martin 1989; Marks and Nelson 1993) and advice for business or the academy on prevention (Deane 1986; J. Martin 1992). There is very little explicit ethical analysis in the literature on sexual harassment, and there is very little on sexual harassment in the literature on Christian ethics. This chapter endeavors to begin to fill these two gaps. Is sexual harassment wrong? Why is it wrong? When is it wrong? What resources does the Christian tradition offer for analyzing and responding to sexual harassment?

This chapter will have four sections: The first section will define and describe the phenomenon of sexual harassment. The second section will explore the meaning and morality of sexual harassment by distinguishing between two perspectives–the feminist and the real world. It will contend that, based on Christian faith, the feminist perspective tells the truth about sexual harassment. The third section will examine the resources of the Christian tradition for understanding and responding to sexual harassment. The fourth section will reflect on some of the ethical ambiguities regarding sexual harassment. The focus will be on sexual harassment in the workplace, although these reflections should apply to the phenomenon wherever it appears–at work, on campus, on the street, in the parish.

1. The Phenomenon of Sexual Harassment

The following four vignettes raise the issue of sexual harassment:

A woman applies for a position as an architect. She is desperate to have a job in the midst of a recession, and she is excited about the possibility of working for this firm which has a very good reputation. When she is called back for a second interview, the man who is the personnel director assures her that she is the best qualified of several good candidates for the position, and he will hire her if she will have sex with him.

An attractive young woman is hired to be a receptionist for a medium-sized office building. This is her first job. She is bright and helpful. A married man in his early thirties who works in one of the offices constantly comments on her body. Every encounter with him is filled with sexual innuendo and subtle propositions. It makes her anxious and angry, but she is not sure how to respond to the situation.

A woman works in an office space that is divided into short cubicles. She is a stylish dresser. She often catches the man in the cubicle in front of hers looking at her. When she looks up at him he looks away. He has never made sexual comments or touched her, but the way he looks at her makes her uncomfortable.

A male college professor is discussing a poor paper with its female author. During the lengthy discussion he shares some of his personal history, tries to dismiss the pressure of grades, uses a sexual analogy to make a point–all in a sincere effort to help this student. She perceives his comments to be sexual harassment, and, with the support of a campus women's group, files a formal complaint (based on *Oleanna*, a 1992 play by David Mamet).

Sexual harassment is illegal sex discrimination. Guideline 1604.11(a) of the Equal Employment Opportunity Commission (EEOC) states that,

> Harassment on the basis of sex is a violation of Sec. 703 Title VII. Unwelcome sexual advances, requests for sexual favors, and other verbal or physical conduct of a sexual nature constitute sexual harassment when (1) submission to such conduct is made either explicitly or implicitly a term or condition of an individual's employment, (2) submission to or rejection of such conduct by an individual is used as the basis for employment decisions affecting such individual, or (3) such conduct has the purpose or effect of unreasonably interfering with an individual's work performance or creating an intimidating, hostile, or offensive working environment. (CWC/UPC 1982, 7)

Often the employer can be held liable for sexual harassment by his/her employees (see Chalfie 1993 for an overview of the law regarding sexual harassment). While the EEOC definition is accurate and comprehensive, Lin Farley seems to get to the heart of the matter: "Sexual harassment is best described as unsolicited non-reciprocal male behavior that asserts a woman's sex role over her function as a worker" (1978, 14-15). It is the "inappropriate sexualization of an otherwise nonsexual relationship" (Langelan 1993, 34 quoting the National Council for Research on Women). The harasser treats the other as a sex object rather than a co-worker or colleague.

The types of behavior that might constitute sexual harassment include: staring at, commenting upon, or touching a woman's body; requests or demands to acquiesce in sexual behavior; pressure for dates; sexual innuendo or lewd remarks; sexist or pornographic jokes, cartoons, posters; sabotaging women's work; retaliation for refusing a request or for complaining about sexual harassment; inappropriate gifts or invitations; insisting that workers wear revealing clothing; and sexual assault (Langelan 1993, 25-26; L. Farley 1978, 15).

Typically the first two conditions in the EEOC definition are referred to as "quid pro quo" harassment and the third as "hostile environment" or "condition of work" harassment (MacKinnon 1979, 32-42; S. Martin 1989, 58-59). Rather than *quid pro quo* (something for something, this for that), I prefer the term sexual extortion (L. Farley 1978, 11; Paul 1991, 6). Sexual extortion seems to better capture the coercive nature of demanding sexual favors in exchange for a job, a promotion, or a good performance review, and it more clearly highlights the seriousness and the immorality of this form of sexual harassment. Although sexual extortion is normatively unethical, one could imagine situations where it could be subtle or even ambiguous.

Hostile environment sexual harassment can cover a wide variety of situations from a constant, brutal barrage of incidents designed to intimidate a woman out of a previously male workplace to an off-color joke, a sexist remark, or a look. It can be coercive or non-coercive (Tong 1986, 150-53), sexual or sexist. Sometimes sexual harassment can take the form of "microinequities," subtle acts that seem hardly worth protesting but which accumulate into a very uncomfortable, even intimidating work environment (Chester 1987, 164; L. Farley 1979, 15). There is more room here for ethical ambiguity. The same action might be meant and perceived differently. It might be wanted or unwelcome. While this distinction between sexual extortion and hostile environment is helpful, it is important to remember that life experience is more complicated and nuanced than is the distinction.

Susan Erlich Martin begins her survey of the social science and statistical studies of sexual harassment with the following statement: "Knowledge is still limited about the frequency of various types of sexual harassment, the characteristics of victims and harassers, the conditions under which it occurs, its psychological and physical effects on the victims, and their responses to it" (1989, 59). The rather subjective nature of sexual harassment makes it difficulty to study. Perceptions about what constitutes sexual harassment, its frequency and seriousness can differ widely. Most agree that it is pervasive in the experience of women (S. Martin 1989, 59-60, but see Paul 1991, 5 and Morgenson 1990, 65 for opposing views). General trends garnered from the social science studies are the following:

Sexual extortion happens less frequently than hostile environment harassment. Sexual harassment happens to women in all racial and ethnic groups, of all ages, no matter their class or educational background. It happens more frequently to young, single women and to women who enter previously all male workplaces or who work in predominantly male work environments. The typical harasser is a male, and he tends to harass habitually (S. Martin 1989, 59-62). There is a recognition that sexual harassment can happen to males and that harassers can be females, but the consensus is that the overwhelmingly predominant pattern is for males to harass females. Feminist interpreters contend that sexual harassment has a different meaning when a male is the victim (Lebacqz and Barton 1991, ch. 6). "The harassed women tend to feel that the incident was their fault and that they were individually responsible as well as demeaned" (S. Martin 1989, 62). The emotional stress that women suffer from sexual harassment often manifests itself in physical illness. Women think they will not be believed and will be retaliated against if they protest or complain about sexual harassment. "Fear of reprisals and negative outcomes appears to be well founded" (S. Martin 1989, 66). Sexual harassment costs women emotionally and financially, and it costs employers considerably through lost productivity and financial liability (Moskal 1990, 62).

2. The Meaning and Morality of Sexual Harassment

It seems to me that there are basically two perspectives on the meaning of sexual harassment, the feminist perspective and the "real world" perspective. These perspectives lead to contrasting interpretations and conclusions. Each of these perspectives will be explained, then I will reflect on their truth and ethical implications.

A. The Feminist Perspective

The feminist perspective sees sexual harassment as an abuse of power, a manifestation of a sexist, patriarchal social structure in which men dominate women. In theological terms (not often employed in the literature on sexual harassment), sexual harassment is a sinful personal choice that is expressive of a sinful social structure – sexism (NCCB 1992, #46, 49). "It [sexual harassment] demeans and destroys the dignity of the victim. Rather than affirming women as whole persons as Jesus did, it reinforces the idea of women as sexual objects. It challenges women's humanity, undermining their self esteem, job satisfaction and self-confidence; and it keeps women at lower status in the workforce" (United Methodist Church 1991, 16).

Feminist literature tends to see sexual harassment as one category on the spectrum of sexual violence perpetrated by men on women in the interest of domination (Kelly 1987, Randall 1992, 20-21). Carole Sheffield says that, "It [terrorism] is the common characteristic of rape, wife battery, incest, pornography, harassment, and all forms of sexual violence. I call it sexual terrorism because it is a system by which males frighten, and by frightening, control and dominate females" (1989, 3). Terrorism and violence are key ingredients in the social structure of male domination. "Male domination is a system of power that renders women inferior to men, and is constructed from a basic domination/submission understanding and structure of gender relations" (Smith 1992, 66). Christine Smith further argues that the two processes of male "objectification" of women and female "identification" with men allow the system of male domination to continue. "There is such a distancing in the process of objectification that *use* and *abuse* seem normal and natural" (Smith 1992, 67; cf. MacKinnon 1982, 541; MacKinnon 1983, 635-36; Bianchi and Ruether 1976). Male identification by women is a sort of colonial mentality, an internalization by women of the system and the stereotype so that women place men above women (Smith 1992, 67-8).

This system of male domination is eroticized to form the social construction of sexuality in patriarchal culture. "Rather the key factor is that male power has become *eroticized*. Men and women alike are socialized not only to think that being a man means being in control but also to find male domination sexually arousing" (Lebacqz 1990, 7; cf. Smith 1992, 71; MacKinnon 1979, 220-21). Men think of themselves as sexual predators. "Men have been taught that they are the hunters, and women – all women – are fair game. The mythology about the workaday world abounds with sexual innuendo" (Sheffield 1989, 16; cf. Smith 1992, 72). (As we shall see, while the feminist perspective finds this system morally outrageous, the real world perspective sees it as normal and natural.)

Sexual harassment, then, is an abuse of power. Men use sex and sexuality in order to dominate women and keep women in a subordinate position. "A feminist approach to sexual harassment views this behavior as the use of power derived from the economic or occupational sphere to gain benefits or to impose punishments in the sexual sphere" (S. Martin 1989, 63). "Sexual harassment is nevertheless an act of aggression at any stage of its expression, and in all its forms it contributes to the ultimate goal of keeping women subordinate" (L.Farley 1978, 15; cf. Dworkin 1992, 6). Thus, feminists argue that sexual harassment gets its meaning from its social context (MacKinnon 1979, 2). It is one of the tools in the arsenal of sexual violence that men use to dominate and control women (Thistlethwaite 1991, 329). And it works. Sexual harassment (along with rape, battery, and assault) frightens and terrorizes women, intimidates women when they walk down the street or ride a bus, keeps women out of traditionally male work, forces women to quit their jobs, maintains women's economic and social subordination. Sexual harassment is a malicious and evil form of sex discrimination. Standing up to sexual harassment is a necessary step in the liberation of women and the equalization of social structures.

B. The Real World Perspective

On the other hand, some contend that feminist ideologues simply do not understand the real world. In real life, workplaces are unpleasant and ripe with sexual tension, and some people are rude and annoying. Naomi Munson approvingly describes the work environment at a weekly magazine: "The men were a randy lot, dedicated philanderers, and foulmouthed to boot; the women, having vigorously demanded–and been granted–absolutely equal status, were considered fair game . . ." (1992, 49). The workplace is the field for the battle of the sexes, and women should be expected to hold their own (Munson 1992, 50). Ellen Paul thinks that the sexual harassment issue needs to be "de-ideologized"; distinctions have to be made. "Statements that paint nearly all women as victims and all men and their patriarchal, capitalist system as perpetrators, are ideological fantasy. Ideology blurs the distinction between being injured–being a genuine victim–and merely being offended" (Paul 1991, 5).

Real world proponents admit that sexual extortion is wrong and deserves legal redress. They are less sure, however, about hostile environment harassment. "For women to expect reverential treatment in the workplace is utopian, yet they should not have to tolerate outrageous, offensive sexual overtones and threats as they go about earning a living" (Paul 1991, 5). In the real world instances of male insensitivity, such as "sexual innuendo, ogling, obscenity, unwelcome opportuning, nude pinups," and the like may not be wrong (Munson 1992, 5). Even if these behaviors are morally reprehensible or merely inconvenient, are they illegal? Should the company be held legally liable (Paul 1991, 5, 6)? The real world perspective is concerned about the intrusion of the law and government regulation into the workplace and private matters (Cohen 1991, 11; Morgenson 1990, 65). "Should people have the legally enforceable right not to be offended by others? At some point the price for such protection is the loss of both liberty and privacy rights" (Paul 1991, 7). They suggest that the so-called pervasiveness of sexual harassment in the workplace is hyperbole based on polls that are finding what they are seeking (Paul 1991, 5; Morgenson 1990, 65).

At the heart of the real world perspective is the acceptance of gender differences as being natural (Davidson 1991, 39-41). "Sexual harassment is traditionally explained as either biologically based, 'natural' behavior or as the idiosyncratic personal proclivity of a minority of men" (S. Martin 1989, 62). Males have a stronger sex drive and are naturally aggressive, and males and females are naturally attracted to each other, even in the workplace. Boys will be boys, and girls should and can fend for themselves. In the context of the battle of the sexes, sexual harassment becomes a very slippery concept, a matter of subjective perception or miscommunication, notoriously ill-defined (Cohen 1991, 8; Paul 1991, 5). A man's clumsy attempt at courtship can be called sexual harassment by a hypersensitive or even disgruntled woman. Perhaps women can be subject to sexual extortion, but men can be wrongfully accused, blackmailed, and retaliated against as well (Morgenson 1990, 67; Davidson 1991, 44; Munson 1992, 49). Furthermore, to suggest that women need special protection in the workplace is to patronize them, deny their equality, and perpetuate the victim syndrome (Davidson 1991, 44; Morgenson, 1990, 66; Munson 1992, 50-51; Paul 1991 7; Roiphe 1993 makes a similar argument regarding date rape). To survive and prosper in the workplace women need to develop a thick skin and a sense of humor. "Meanwhile, women should 'lighten up,' and even dispense a few risque barbs of their own, a sure way of taking the fun out of it for offensive male bores" (Paul 1991, 7; cf. Reich 1993). Hypersensitive feminist ideologues with chips on their shoulders about sexual harassment are making the workplace a minefield for their confused male colleagues rather than the exciting and enjoyable setting for potential romance that is normal and natural.

In short, the real world is a complex, confusing, ambiguous place. In the real world men aggressively chase women; women tease and manipulate men for their own advantage; and it is best to keep judges and government regulators on the sidelines in this age-old battle of the sexes. Sex, romance, and power are part of real life, but feminist ideologues seem unable to appreciate this. According to Nicholas Davidson, feminists fanatics contend that sexual harassment, "consists in pressure on a woman to submit to sex with a man, backed up by psychological, financial, or physical intimidation, short of actual rape. The presumption is that the man holds power with which he is able to coerce the woman, or which persuades him he is able to do so. The attempt to define and punish a crime of 'sexual harassment' therefore, is part of a larger effort to fundamentally change the ethos of society, as that ethos is understood by feminists: to wrench power from the male oppressors and create an egalitarian society in which sexual difference will no longer be important and in which sexual hierarchy, in particular, will no longer exist" (1991, 41).

Such a program, Davidson insists, denies the reality of gender differences, which are biological and natural, not socially constructed. Sexual extortion can be a real problem, but mostly sexual harassment is an exaggeration concocted by fanatical feminists who are having a hard time coping with work in the real world.

C. Taking a Perspective

It is clear that the feminist and the real world perspectives understand each other fairly well. To a great extent they are reflecting on the same reality, yet their ethical interpretation of sexual harassment differs substantially. Feminists find sexual harassment to be a pervasive and malicious abuse of power, a personal and social sin. Real world proponents, while admitting that sexual extortion is wrong, find sexual harassment to be ill-defined, subjective, ambiguous, rather natural or normal, and mostly trivial. Is sexual harassment a tool in the social structure of male domination of women or is it mostly a natural and normal human behavior? Is sexual harassment evil, wrong, and sinful or more of a romantic game, more of a breach of etiquette than of ethics? Is sexual harassment wrong or amoral? Which perspective tells the truth about the meaning and the morality of sexual harassment?

I am persuaded that the feminist perspective best captures the meaning of sexual harassment, although the real world perspective might offer some caveats and correctives. Sexual harassment is basically an immoral abuse of power. It is wrong and should be stopped and prevented. Justifying this position and countering the real world perspective is, however, surprisingly difficult.

Whether sexual harassment is a manifestation of the patriarchal social construction of sexuality or a natural human behavior is a form of the nurture versus nature debate. In this century the pendulum of that debate has swung from nature to nurture, and now seems to be edging toward a "more nurture but some nature" position. I think the meaning of sexuality is basically a social construct that can differ from one culture to another and can change, but the biological differences in male and female must have some psychological and spiritual repercussions, although I am hardpressed to identify what they are. Even if the two perspectives agreed in leaning toward the nurture side of the debate, they could still disagree on the meaning and morality of the social construction of sexuality. Feminists reject patriarchy as wrong; real world proponents find patriarchy normal and acceptable. The difference is fundamental and difficult to dispute with reasoned arguments. These perspectives are more a matter of faith than of science or reason.

One's judgment about the ethics of patriarchy (I do not think the reality of patriarchy can be seriously questioned) depends upon one's vision of human nature and human life and one's theological anthropology. (This too is influenced by culture or nurture, but one must take a stand somewhere.) Although Christian tradition has been patriarchal in its thought and practice, Christian faith also contains resources for transcending and judging patriarchy. Central to Christian faith is the belief that human persons are created in God's image (the dignity of each person and the equality of all), called to covenant (right relationship in community), and called to justice (fairness, nonviolence, priority to the perspective of the victim). If these beliefs are fundamental, then patriarchy is wrong. Patriarchy denies the equality of male and female and diminishes human dignity. Neither genuine relationship nor community (union) is possible between masters and slaves, dominants and subordinates, superiors and inferiors. Patriarchal domination is based upon violence and violation, injustice and exploitation, objectification and depersonalization. The suffering of victims sunders the bonds of just community and cries out to a just God. Christian beliefs logically lead to the affirmation of the feminist perspective and to naming sexual harassment a sin (Fortune 1983, 76-90).

Taking a perspective is an essential first step. The real world perspective does not think sexual harassment is really a moral problem. A Christian feminist perspective places sexual harassment in the ethical domain, and offers reasons why it is wrong. But a more complete ethical analysis will need to address other questions. What values, virtues, and norms are helpful for analyzing the ethics of sexual harassment and for responding to it? How do moral principles regarding sexual harassment apply to the messy ambiguity of human experience? The Christian tradition also provides resources for this fuller ethical analysis of sexual harassment.

3. The Christian Tradition and Sexual Harassment

The resources of the Christian tradition–Scripture, the history of the Church, and theological reflection–have not, so far as I know, been focused in a way that intends to shed light on the issue of the ethics of sexual harassment. Feminist theologians have reflected on the Christian tradition and on sexual ethics in critical, creative, and insightful ways, but have not focused on sexual harassment. My purpose is to gain insight into the ethics of sexual harassment. It appears that the teaching of Jesus and contemporary theological thought can illuminate the ethics of sexual harassment.

It must be acknowledged from the beginning that, from a feminist perspective, Christian tradition is part of the problem. Feminist theologians have persuasively demonstrated that Christianity is thoroughly patriarchal and sexist. Christian sexual ethics, from Paul through Augustine to the contemporary Church, has been dualistic and patriarchal (Bianchi and Ruether 1976). My purpose, however, is not to critique the tradition from a feminist perspective, but to draw on the tradition for positive insights into the ethics of sexual harassment.

A. The Teaching of Jesus in Relation to Sexual Harassment

The spirit of the Christian tradition would seem to lend weight to the feminist perspective on sexual harassment. The feminist perspective identifies the evil in sexual harassment with the abuse of dominating power to objectify and exploit a human person. Jesus, grounded in the Hebrew traditions of *imago Dei*, covenant, and justice, rejected dominating power and the depersonalization and exploitation of human beings.

Richard Gula, reflecting on Jesus and discipleship, paints a portrait of Jesus in reference to power. He correctly contends that Jesus rejected dominating power and embraced instead the liberating power of love. "In doing so [rejecting the temptations to use demonic power in the desert], Jesus rejects structures of domination based on the superiority of some and the inferiority of all the rest. Structures of domination thrive on the never-ending competition for the place at the top. They are supported by manipulation, coercion, and violence, . . . Jesus' message and use of power call for something radically different. Jesus constantly challenged any use of power that promoted superiority/inferiority as the paradigm in human relations" (Gula 1989, 193). Instead, Jesus opted for liberating power (cf.

Lebacqz 1985, 128-36). Jesus establishes a community of service where domination has no place. "When Jesus deliberately reverses social positions by becoming a servant [at the footwashing scene at the last supper], he witnesses to a new order of human relationships in the community whereby the desire to dominate and establish superiority has no place" (Gula 1989, 194). Jesus establishes a discipleship of equals, a community characterized by service, hospitality, forgiveness, and reconciliation. "The reign of God ushers in a new way of life whereby power is not for cruel exclusion, but for hospitable inclusion" (Gula 1989, 195). On the cross, Jesus empties himself and in doing so reveals the emptiness of all oppressive power. "The cross expresses his ultimate dispossession into the arms of God whose love has already conquered the powers of the world (Gula 1989, 196)." Rather than a theology of ownership (Bohn 1989), harassers need to hear this theology of the cross with its message of dispossession and renunciation of domination and control, its message of service and hospitality, equality and inclusion. The harassed, however, who have been sold self-servingly the self-sacrifice of the cross, need to hear this theology of liberation (Bloomquist 1989, 68; Bianchi and *Ruether* 1976, 108-9). Jesus' rejection of the structures of domination and his embrace of service, hospitality, and liberation seem directly relevant to the phenomenon of sexual harassment as understood by the feminist perspective. This sort of discipleship would call the harasser to conversion and the community to support the victim. This understanding of power, consistent with creation in God's image and God's call to covenant and justice, can be articulated in the moral norm of *right relationship* (Fortune 1983, 81-83).

In perhaps the only passage in the Gospel directly related to sexual ethics, Jesus seems to reject the objectification and depersonalization at the heart of sexual harassment. "You have heard that it was said, 'You shall not commit adultery.' But I say to you everyone who looks at a woman with lust has already committed adultery with her in his heart" (Mt. 5:27-28, New American Bible 1990). This is one of the antitheses in Matthew's sermon on the mount. It is clear here and in the whole passage that Jesus is re-directing the focus from external acts to internal attitudes and intentions, to the heart (Harrington 1989, 333; Vaught 1986, 77). Scholars find the literal interpretation of this passage in the context of a theology of ownership, that the husband owned the wife and that another man should not covet his property. To "Lust" was to desire, to possess or to have dominion over (Davenport 1988, 154, cf. the *Good News* version of this text). In the Hebrew culture the sin of adultery is committed against the woman's husband. His property has been stolen from him. "So Jesus' literal meaning might more accurately be expressed: 'Anyone who desires greatly in his heart to sexually possess a woman has already taken possession of her or stolen her'" (Fortune 1983, 57). Jesus is internalizing the violation of the man's property rights involved in adultery.

Marie Fortune wishes to build on this literal meaning of the passage. She sees adultery as an offense against a woman by violating mutuality and the respect owed her. "Thus we can interpret Jesus' teaching to mean that for a man to desire to possess and dominate [lust for] a woman is an offense against her. It is a distortion of human sexuality which is physically and spiritually abusive" (Fortune 1983, 58). I agree with Fortune, and I want to go a step further. It seems to me that the basic dynamic in lust is treating the other as an object of desire, depersonalizing the other. Thus, a man thinks he can have her, possess her, use her, dominate her, control her. All of this depends on the objectification of a person. In the context of Jesus' consistent ethic of love, the transcendent meaning of the passage seems to be a warning against objectification and depersonalization, against lust. If Jesus' warning were expressed in positive terms it would be a call to love, to relationship, fidelity, and union. It is a call to see all persons as the image of God (Bullard 1989, 81-82). "When Jesus modifies the original law, he is making an effort to establish respect for the opposite sex at the level of inner appreciation rather than just outward act: . . ." (Brooks 1985, 42). If this is correct, and if sexual harassment treats a woman as a sex object rather than a colleague, then Matthew 25: 27-28 can be taken as a condemnation of sexual harassment and a call to the norm of *respect* for persons.

B. Contemporary Christian Ethics in Relation to Sexual Harassment

The work of two Christian feminist theologians–Marie Fortune and Karen Lebacqz–is most directly related to the ethics of sexual harassment. They are primarily concerned with sexual violence (rape, assault, battery, incest) and with the relationship of sex and power especially in regard to the sexual abuse of women by clergymen. Theirs is a practical theology focused on issues of sexual and professional ethics from a feminist perspective. Together they develop an ethical framework based on concepts of consent, trust, sin, and justice that is helpful for addressing sexual harassment.

First a clarification is in order. The ethical framework being developed here is primarily one for professional ethics rather than sexual ethics. Fortune (1991, 368) correctly criticizes Lebacqz and Barton (1991) for a lack of clarity on this point. The confusion is understandable. Fortune and Lebacqz are trying to develop a sexual ethic that takes power seriously, and a professional ethic for clergy that is cognizant of power and responsibility regarding sex. Sexual harassment, however, is primarily about how colleagues and coworkers relate to each other in the workplace or classroom (or casual encounters in the street) rather than about sexual relationships per se. Sexual harassment is fundamentally a matter of professional ethics (Fortune 1983, 107).

Marie Fortune establishes the principle of *consent* as primary for both sexual ethics and professional ethics regarding sexuality (1983, 99-111). "Consent to sexual activity, in order to be authentic, must take place in a context of mutuality, choice, full knowledge, and equal power, and in the absence of coercion and fear. When there is an imbalance of power in a relationship, these necessary factors will not be present" (Fortune 1989, 38).

Lebacqz and Barton embrace the principle of consent and expand upon it by drawing on the notion of a valid consent in a medical context. To give a valid consent a person must be informed of the risks and benefits in a way in which they can comprehend the information. The person must be capable or competent and non-coerced or truly free (Lebacqz and Barton 1991, 114-20; Lebacqz 1988, 71). The imbalance of power between a supervisor and a worker or a teacher and a student makes a valid consent virtually impossible because such a relationship is neither equal nor truly free. Indeed, in a patriarchal society male domination of women calls into question the possibility of consent between any man and woman (Lebacqz and Barton 1990, 43-45; 1991, 139-41). Fortune and Lebacqz make this point in reference to pastors and parishioners, but it is equally valid in the workplace or the university. The professional and cultural status of men in the workplace makes genuine consent highly unlikely. Sexual extortion is clearly coercive, and most verbal and physical conduct of a sexual nature in the workplace is coercive and/or controlling, and, therefore is unwanted, inappropriate, and wrong.

Secondly, sexual extortion and harassment are violations of *trust* in the context of a covenant theology of work. Again Lebacqz and Barton make this point in the context of the pastor/parishioner or counselor/client relationship (1991, 121-25; cf. Fortune 1983, 108), but trust applies as well to work relationships. Managers are supposed to develop the skills of workers, and coworkers are supposed to collaborate to accomplish tasks and goals. When a man uses his position to extort sexual favors or treats a woman as a sex object he violates the trust necessary to sustain some sense of community in the workplace. Such behavior generally lowers productivity by distracting and demeaning the victim.

Marie Fortune correctly insists on the importance of naming sexual violence a sin. Sexual harassment is likewise a *sin*. Sexual harassment denies the sacredness of the person. The victim is objectified, dominated, degraded, humiliated, and violated where she is most vulnerable, her sexuality (Fortune 1983, 85). The harasser, too, denies his humanity and God's call to relationship. Sexual harassment alienates one from the other, breaking the bonds of community. In violating God's most sacred creation, sexual harassment sins against God (Fortune 1983, 86). Sexual harassment is a sin against others, self, community, and God.

It is important to point out that sexism and sexual harassment are the sins of men against women, a male problem, like racism and prejudice are primarily a white problem. Since the system encourages the blaming of victims, women too often internalize the shame and guilt of being violated (Tong 1986, 149). But it is male violence and violation that are wrong, and it is men who need to repent, convert, and be reconciled (Bloomquist 1989, 67; Burt 1988, 31,34; Pellauer 1985, 49). Men have created patriarchy and sexism and have a responsibility to change the social structures of male domination. In doing so they not only alleviate the suffering of women, they also redeem their wounded selves. The basic responsibility for making mutuality and community more possible rests with men. Obviously sexual harassment is a violation of *justice*. Sexual harassment is unfair and exploitative; it victimizes women. As such the law recognizes that harassment is sex discrimination. It is a personal sin within the context of social sin, that is, a society characterized by male domination.

Justice, however, not only names the sin, but guides the response of Christians and the Church. Individuals must be converted and culture must be transformed to stop and prevent sexual harassment. Marie Fortune reminds the Church that justice is the foundation for healing and reconciliation. She outlines a framework for doing justice and mercy in response to sexual violence and abuse. "Truth-telling, acknowledgment of the violation, compassion [for victims], protection of the vulnerable, accountability [from the violator], restitution, and vindication [of the victim] are the requirements for doing justice and mercy in the face of violation and injustice" (Fortune 1989, 114; cf. 1983, 87-88; 1988, 47-48). The silence surrounding violence toward and harassment of women must be broken (Pellauer 1987, 55); the truth must be spoken; harassers must be confronted; and claims should be filed. The violator must acknowledge his sin, be held accountable for the consequences of his behavior, and try to repair the damage he has done. Only on the basis of his repentance and conversion can his healing and reconciliation be attempted. Victims must be believed, accompanied, protected, and vindicated. This process of justice reverses business as usual in a patriarchal society where offenses are unreported or not taken seriously, women are disbelieved and retaliated against, and men remain in positions of power where they can abuse others. Christians and Churches have a responsibility to protest the violation of women, stand in solidarity with female victims, and call oppressors to conversion–to work for justice.

From a Christian perspective, then, sexual harassment is an abuse of power in a male dominated society. It violates the God-given sacredness of the human person and the right relationship among persons that is the basis of a covenant theology. It is a manifestation of the domination and depersonalization so clearly rejected by Jesus. Sexual extortion is clearly coercive. In the context of the professional and cultural power of men over women consent can hardly be honored. Physical and verbal conduct of a sexual or sexist nature is coercive or controlling, an abuse of power in the workplace. It violates both the freedom and the trust of the vulnerable. It is unfair and exploitative. Sexual extortion and harassment are sins, and the sexist social structure that gives birth to violence toward and the violation of women is sinful. Christian women and men and the Churches can contribute to creating a just, non-sexist society by bravely breaking the silence about the violation of women and the domination by men, by compassionately standing in solidarity with victims, by steadfastly calling harassers to repentance and conversion, and by effectively advocating for social change.

The Church should consciously form the *character* of Christians to be respectful and just and to seek right relation in community and the liberation of the oppressed. The Church should create men who do not harass women and women and men who do not tolerate sexual harassment. The ethics of sexual harassment is fundamentally a matter of virtue and character, of respect and justice. It is also a matter of *ethos*, of social structure. The Church, a community of conscience, should be an outspoken critic of the injustice of a sexist society and an exemplary model of a just and equal community (DeVogel 1988, 14). The record of the Churches in this regard is mixed at best.

4. Ethical Reflection on Sexual Harassment

Sexual harassment is a manifestation of male domination, an abuse of power, not romantic gesture. It is an ethical issue. Sexism and sexual harassment are normatively wrong and sinful. Christian faith can affirm the truth and rightness of the feminist perspective on sexual harassment, and Christian tradition is helpful in establishing moral norms and outlining an ethical framework. But moral norms–right relationship, respect, consent, trust, and justice–need to be critically applied to concrete and complex human situations, to real life. This section will consider some theoretical complications and caveats raised by the real world perspective and reflect on the ethics of responding to sexual harassment.

First, there is the question of intentionality and subjectivity. The definition of sexual harassment states that the conduct must be "unwelcome" or "unwanted." The real world perspective correctly points out that this makes sexual harassment subjective and ambiguous. The same act can be meant and perceived or interpreted in different ways. The intentions of the actor and the perceptions of the receiver are both subjective and ambiguous. Human communication is notoriously complex, especially between males and females (Burt 1988, 33-34; Wall 1991). The feminist perspective seems to discount the intentions of the actor and to focus only on the receiver's perceptions of the behavior (Garment 1992, 34). Is this adequate ethics?

This question returns us to the meaning of sexual harassment and the difference between the feminist and real world perspectives. The real world perspective asserts that the male intentions behind physical and verbal conduct of a sexual nature in the workplace are pure and good–to aggressively attract women for the purpose of courtship and romance and sex. Martha Langelan responds by pointing out that this so-called courtship behavior is spectacularly unsuccessful, even counterproductive, in actually attracting women: "women react with disgust, not desire, with fear, not fascination" (Langelan 1993, 39). Langelan contends that sexual harassment is not courtship; it serves another purpose entirely–domination and coercion. "Like rape, sexual harassment is designed to coerce women, not attract them" (Langelan 1993, 40). Sexual harassment is an abuse of men's real–economic, professional, and gender-based–power. Its purpose is coercion, not courtship.

Langelan identifies three types of harassers. The "sexually predatory harasser" tries to procure sexual access. The "dominance harasser" tries to put women in their place. He aims at female deference and fear. He uses intimidation to maintain the social structure of male dominance. The "strategic" or "territorial harasser" is protecting male turf. His goal is to eliminate a female competitor or to control access to male territory. All three types of harassers abuse power but for different purposes–sex, power, or territory. "Harassment is a widespread male practice not because it works as a romantic courtship ritual, but because it works so successfully as an exercise of gender-based power" (Langelan 1993, 50). In each case the harasser objectifies and depersonalizes the victim; she is degraded, demeaned, dehumanized. Thus, from the feminist perspective, male intentionality is neither pure nor good; it is, consciously or not, coercive and controlling, exploitative and evil.

While the agent's intentions are an important aspect of morality, so are his actions and their consequences. It is also important to focus on the act itself–behavior such as grabbing a woman's breast, pinching her, propositioning her, or commenting on her body–and the consequences of the behavior–the humiliation, objectification, coercion, control, and victimization of women. Sexual harassment is not an innocent, romantic game; it is an illicit, malicious power play. As feminists suggest, there may be something amiss in the socialization process of a woman who is *not* offended by sexual harassment (Langelan 1993, 58; Lebacqz and Barton 1991, 142-53). The behavior is generally unwelcome, but, unwanted or not, it is offensive. The behavior itself treats a person as a sex object. It has no place in the workplace. Men need to be socialized to see women as persons, in the image of God; and to understand appropriate public behavior toward women (Cooper 1989). Other men (Burt 1988, 31,34), women, and institutions (companies, colleges, and Churches) all have a role to play in raising male consciousness about the purpose of sexual harassment, men's true intentions, and the reality of their behavior. Perhaps sexual harassment is not so subjective after all. This caveat suggested by the real world perspective is more of a cavil.

Second, the real world perspective warns that men can be falsely accused and that women can also be manipulative with their sexuality, using it to succeed. This is an important and realistic caveat, although it needs to be put in perspective. Both research and life experience indicate that the phenomenon that is pervasive, even pandemic, in this patriarchal society is male sexual harassment of women. Given this reality of sexual harassment and given the tendency of the sexist system to blame and punish the victim, it seems to me that female victims claiming harassment should be believed and given the benefit of any doubt until persuasive counterevidence is presented. Harassment is often unwitnessed, and harassers stonewall by simply denying that it happened and using their power to retaliate against the victim. A Christian perspective, with its preference for the perspective of the victim, should have less difficulty with this "guilty until proven innocent" moral norm, but I recognize that the law has the opposite principle deeply embedded in its system. Supervisors and managers, deans and bishops, colleagues and co-workers, however, are not bound by legal principles. They can and should believe the victim until her credibility is seriously called into question. Nevertheless, women are also subject to original sin, and it is certainly conceivable that they could falsely accuse a man or that there could be legitimate ambiguity regarding the interpretation of his actions (see the unpublished off-Broadway play *Oleanna* by David Mamet 1992). False accusations or overreaction also create victims and cause suffering and harm. Although exceptional in claims of sexual harassment, deception, retaliation, vengeance, and manipulation are also wrong and sinful.

There is a myth about casting couches and women sleeping their way to the top. The reality is that this notion is a convenient mask for male sexual coercion (L.Farley 1978, 183-98). Still, given that women are also socialized into the eroticization of male dominance, it is conceivable that women might try to use their sexuality rather than their competence to achieve success at work (Hadditt 1992, 98-99). This is an abuse of powerlessness. Such manipulation is wrong in principle because it also objectifies and exploits, and it seldom succeeds in the long term. Office affairs and flirtations are almost always more damaging and costly to the woman involved (Rapp 1992, 58). Both female manipulation and male coercion are products of a sexist social structure. Both are wrong. Male coercion, however, is the rule, and female manipulation is the exception.

A third caveat from the real world perspective is the idea that feminist fanatics are taking all the fun out of the workplace. Actually, of course, sexual harassment is no fun for the victim, and feminists are trying to professionalize and humanize the workplace. Still, there are two ways in which this caveat might be a valid ethical point.

The first is that feminism must be careful of becoming overly negative and pessimistic regarding sexuality and sexual expression. Certainly, the Christian tradition since Augustine in the fifth century has been dualistic regarding human nature and pessimistic regarding sexuality. Christian practice has been unduly ascetic. Contemporary sexual liberation may be merely the opposite side of the same dualistic coin. Both the ascetic and the libertine debase sexuality and depersonalize women (Bianchi and *Ruether* 1976, 72-75, 104-7). The feminist analysis of an oppressive patriarchal society that eroticizes male dominance and normalizes male sexual violence and abuse can understandably be tempted toward demonizing all heterosexual activity (Edwards 1987, 24-27; Roiphe 1993, 30, 40).

Contemporary Christian ethicists, meanwhile, are laboring to transform Christian sexual ethics by rejecting dualism, affirming the goodness of the body and of sexuality, and celebrating joyful sex as an expression of committed love (Gudorf and Blaney 1988). Most of these reformers, however, do not seem to take seriously enough the power dynamics that exist in a patriarchal social context.

Karen Lebacqz seems to begin to strike the right balance between the reality of male dominance and the hope for genuine intimacy between men and women. "Women are not respected in the sexual arena, but are raped, attacked, and treated as objects. At the same time, heterosexual women seek to trust, love, and be intimate with those who have the power to rape, attack, and be disrespectful" (Lebacqz 1990, 10). She suggests the metaphor "love your enemy" as fitting for a Christian sexual ethic that deals adequately with these ambiguities and ironies. Other feminists use a transformed notion of eros to speak positively of the urge toward mutuality and right relation (Friedman and Irwin 1990).

Lebacqz also wants to make room for love and romance in the realm of professional ethics. Writing specifically about protestant clergymen and relationships with parishioners, she clearly recognizes the professional and gender-related social power of the clergyman, strictly circumscribes ethical behavior, and squarely puts the responsibility for right behavior on his shoulders. But she recognizes that love can happen here. She does not think a man can be both pastor and lover. Therefore, the first step is to clearly relinquish the pastor-parishioner relationship (Lebacqz and Barton 1991, 126-31, 189; cf. Majka 1991, 19). Analagous advice would seem to be ethically fitting for the workplace. While romance is hardly the purpose of the workplace, it can happen there. But an office romance should quickly lead to different offices. This is true because of the principles of consent, trust, and justice, and because of the disastrous consequences for the individuals and the office that can be reasonably expected.

The second way in which the caveat about feminism leading to a joyless workplace might have some validity pertains to ambiguity. Human communication is complex and ambiguous (Wall 1991). Some incidents of sexual harassment, then, might well be open to different interpretations. The ethical response, for example, to the four vignettes near the beginning of this article probably should differ.

The first vignette is a clear example of sexual extortion. Although the job candidate is in a difficult position, she should confront the personnel director and file a complaint with the EEOC. I think the personnel director should be fired. Sexual extortion is a serious sin with very harmful effects.

The married man in the second vignette is clearly creating a hostile working environment for the female receptionist. Again I think he should be confronted, and that she should probably at least file an internal complaint. His behavior is offensive enough to warrant his dismissal, although other remedies might be considered. Neither of these cases is very ambiguous.

The looks of the man in the third vignette, however, are of a less serious nature. I think these looks constitute sexual harassment, but it is conceivable that his looks are being misinterpreted. She should confront him or at least assertively express her feelings. The looks should stop. Perhaps his work station can be moved or re-arranged. Only if the looks persist should a complaint be filed. Protesting sexual harassment has nothing to do with prudishness; it is about power. Still there is some ambiguity in this situation. The response, however, should be proportionate to the offense.

The fourth situation and the play, *Oleanna*, on which it is based, are genuinely ambiguous. The male professor is surely pompous and arrogant, but he may be genuinely intending to help the student, rather than coerce or control or harass her. On the other hand, perhaps her perceptions of harassment are correct. It seems to me that confrontation, even clarification, should have been attempted before a grievance was filed. Such ambiguity calls for caution and care lest this become a case of reverse harassment.

Finally, while sexual harassment is a male moral problem, women have an obvious vested interest and an important role in stopping and preventing it. Women's response to sexual harassment also has an ethical dimension.

Women typically respond to sexual harassment with appeasement, counter-aggression, or avoidance (Langelan 1993, 97-102). Although perfectly understandable given the dynamics of the social pattern of male dominance, none of these is very helpful or effective in stopping or preventing sexual harassment. Much better response strategies include straightforward confrontation tactics, building a support network, and filing official charges (Langelan 1993, 103). The response should fit the situation and be proportionate to the offense, as suggested above.

Martha Langelan is a creative advocate for confrontation tactics in response to sexual harassment. She correctly argues that confrontation is a nonviolent, direct action strategy that is usually effective for personal defense and a potent tool for social change. Confrontation works both personally and politically. She distinguishes between assertiveness and confrontation. "Assertiveness involves defining the problem clearly, stating one's feelings openly, and negotiating a change in behavior or some other mutually satisfactory solution to the problem at hand" (Langelan 1993, 104). Assertiveness might be appropriate with an acquaintance, or a man who has demonstrated a sincere desire to change his attitude and avoid sexist behavior, or in ambiguous situations where the perception of harassment might be questioned by the reasonable woman. Confrontation means specifically and clearly naming the offensive behavior and unequivocally demanding that it stop. Usually confrontation is the necessary response to situations of sexual harassment. For example, if a man in the office puts his hand on a co-worker's thigh, she should grasp it firmly and remove it while looking him right in the eye and saying, "Take your hand off of my leg! That's harassment! I don't like it. No woman does. It is wrong. Stop it!" There is no negotiation. This is a confrontation, not a debate. Nor is it counter-aggression. Cursing, name-calling, or punching are inappropriate, generally ineffective, and much more risky and dangerous. The confronter names the behavior and demands that it stop. She repeats the demand as necessary (Langelan 1993, 115-26). Because the woman unexpectedly refuses to submit to male domination, she publicly names his offensive behavior, and she takes a principled, nonviolent stand, confrontations often stop harassment. The harasser finds that his behavior no longer serves its purpose of controlling women. Other men in the vicinity get their consciousness raised as well. They will be on notice that harassment will not be tolerated. Even if the harassment continues, the harasser and witnesses are now clear that this conduct is unwelcome.

Ordinarily, it seems to me that the victim almost has an obligation to confront the harasser. Although I realize that in nearly all situations confrontation is an act of courage and that in some situations the risk of violence or retaliation might legitimately deter a woman from confronting her harasser, in most instances I think there is a moral obligation to communicate to the harasser that his behavior is unwanted, offensive, and will not be tolerated. Confrontation can work, and it leaves the victim full of self-esteem rather than humiliated, angry and demeaned. As confrontation becomes more common, sexual harassment will become less pervasive. It is a powerful step in making sexual harassment socially intolerable. Martha Langelan's book *Back Off!* is a persuasive witness to the personal and political effectiveness of confrontation.

Besides confrontation, the victim of harassment should seek a support network. Generally there have been other victims. They can be gathered for a group confrontation and/or to file a joint grievance or complaint. Victims need friends who believe them and remind them that they are not to blame for this behavior. Institutions (businesses, universities, Churches) should have well-thought-out grievance procedures for sexual harassment, and victims should use them. Institutions tend to act in their own self interest rather than to seek justice for victims. Thus institutions tend to shoot the messenger, misname the problem, and blame the victim (Fortune 1989, xiv, 120-22). Thus an outside mediator (Crabtree 1991) or an ombudsperson or team (CWC\UPC 1982, 16-17; J. Martin 1992, 44) might be carefully considered by institutions in the interest of justice. Victims should document incidents and seek witnesses. Both will be necessary in filing an internal grievance, an external complaint with the Equal Employment Opportunity Commission (EEOC), or a legal suit (CWEALF 1991; PCSW 1992; Chalfie 1993; Bouchard 1990, 41f). Although complaints and suits remain risky and costly for victims in a patriarchal system, they can be effective and accomplish an imperfect justice. Confrontation, seeking support, and filing complaints can liberate women from sexual harassment, and these can be creative steps toward changing the patriarchal social structure that supports sexual violence and harassment.

5. Summary - Conclusion

Sexual harassment is the inappropriate and unsolicited sexualization of a nonsexual relationship. It is treating a woman as a sex object rather than a colleague. Sexual harassment can take two forms–sexual extortion and the creation of a hostile environment. It is a pervasive reality in the experience of women. There are two ways of understanding sexual harassment, the feminist perspective and the real world perspective. Feminists see sexual harassment as a malicious abuse of power manifesting the patriarchal system of male domination. In the real world, say others, males are the sexual hunters and females the hunted. It is natural and normal for males to aggressively flirt with females, even in the workplace. This is simply the battle of the sexes, and, within bounds, there is nothing wrong with it.

On the basis of the Christian beliefs in creation, covenant, and justice, the feminist perspective best captures the meaning of sexual harassment. It is an abuse of power in the interests of male domination and female subordination. It wrongfully objectifies and depersonalizes women. Given the inequality in professional and gender-based power between men and women, women's free consent to sexual advances in the workplace is hardly possible. Such advances also erode the trust necessary for community and productivity in the workplace. Sexual harassment is unfair and exploitative. It is a personal sin of men that manifests a sinful social structure–sexism. Justice demands that silence be broken; victims be believed, protected, and vindicated; and offenders be called to repentance and conversion, reparation and reconciliation.

Although males, intentionality in incidents of harassment may at first seem ambiguous, further reflection finds that the purpose of sexual harassment is nearly always coercive and exploitative. The behavior itself is also offensive and its consequences harmful and victimizing. False accusations and sexual manipulation by females are possible and wrong. Deception and manipulation also manifest a sexist social structure and are the exception not the rule. The claims of female victims of sexual harassment should be given credibility and the benefit of the doubt unless there is clear evidence to the contrary. The feminist perspective is open to the temptation toward a pessimistic view of heterosexual activity, but it is possible to achieve a healthy sexual ethics that takes power seriously, and a healthy professional ethics regarding sexuality. Although sexual harassment is normatively wrong, the complex nature of human communication does present the possibility of ethical ambiguity regarding particular cases. A proportionate ethical response is called for. Harassers should be creatively and courageously confronted, and victims should seek support and file claims. In responding to sexual harassment women achieve personal liberation from harassment and move toward the political goal of justice and mutuality.

There is little direct ethical analysis in the literature on sexual harassment, and little on sexual harassment in the literature on Christian ethics. This article has attempted to begin to fill these gaps by offering an ethical analysis of sexual harassment from a Christian perspective. Clearly, sexual harassment is a subject ripe for further reflection on the part of Christian ethicists.

Note

1. The *Catholic Periodical Index* does not have a listing for sexual harassment. The *Religion Index* has a listing, but the references are few; popular literature, and church-oriented. Christian feminists have reflected on sexual violence (Fortune 1983), sexual ethics (M. Farley 1978; Pellauer 1985), and professional ethics (Lebacqz and Barton 1991). These reflections provide an important starting point for focusing on sexual harassment from the perspective of Christian ethics.

References

Bianchi, Eugene, and Rosemary Ruether (1976). *From Machismo to Mutuality: Essays on Sexism and Woman-Man Liberation*. New York: Paulist Press.

Bloomquist, Karen L. (1989). "Sexual Violence: Patriarchy's Offense and Defense." In *Christianity, Patriarchy, and Abuse: A Feminist Critique*. See Brown 1989, pp. 62-69.

Bohn, Carole R. (1989). "Dominion to Rule: The Roots and Consequences of a Theology of Ownership." In *Christianity, Patriarchy, and Abuse: A Feminist Critique*. See Brown 1989, pp. 105-16.

Bouchard, Elizabeth (1990). *Everything You Need to Know About Sexual Harassment*. New York: Rosen Publ. Group, Inc.

Bowman, Cynthia Grant (1993). "Street Harassment and the Informal Ghettoization of Women." *Harvard Law Review* 106 (January), pp. 517-80.

Brooks, Oscar Stephen (1985). *The Sermon on the Mount: Authentic Human Values*. Lanham, Md.: University Press of America.

Brown, Joanne Carlson, and Carole R. Bohn, eds. (1989). *Christianity, Patriarchy, and Abuse: A Feminist Critique*. New York: Pilgrim Press.

Bullard, Michael (1989). "Sexual Violence and Coercion." *Church and Society*, 88 (November–December), pp. 78-88.

Burt, Martha (1988). "Cultural Myth, Violence Against Women, and the Law." *The Drew Gateway* 58 (February), pp. 25-37.

Chalfie, Deborah (1993). "Your Legal Options: Sexual Harassment and the Law." In *Back Off!* See Langelan, Appendix B, pp. 340-59.

Chester, Barbara (1987). "Sexual Harassment: Victim Responses." In *Sexual Abuse and Assault*. See Pellauer 1987. pp. 161-71.

Cohen, Lloyd R. (1991). "Sexual Harassment and the Law." *Society*, 28 (May-June), pp. 8-13.

Collins, Eliza G.C., and Timothy B. Blodgett (1981). "Sexual Harassment: Some See It . . . Some Won't." *Harvard Business Review* 59 (March-April), pp. 77-95.

Cooper, Kenneth C. (1989). In *Contemporary Moral Controversies in Business*. ed. by A. Pablo Iannone. New York: Oxford University Press, pp. 190-92.

Crabtree, Maril (1991). "Power and Sex In the Church–Where Is Justice?" *Daughters of Sarah* 17 (May-June), pp. 16-19.

CWC/UPC (Council on Women and the Church/United Presbyterian Church in the U.S.A) (1982). *Naming the Unnamed: Sexual Harassment in the Church*. Louisville, Ky.: Presbyterian Church, U.S.A..

CWEALF (Connecticut Women's Education And Legal Fund) (1991). *Sexual Harassment in the Workplace*. Hartford, Ct.

Davenport, Gene L. (1988). *Into the Darkness: Discipleship in the Sermon on the Mount*. Nashville: Abingdon Press.

Davidson, Nicholas (1991). "Feminism and Sexual Harassment." *Society* 28 (May-June), pp. 39-44.

Deane, Richard H. (1986). "Sexual Harassment–Is Your Company Protected?" *Business* 36 (April-May-June), pp. 42-45.

DeVogel, Susan Harrington (1988). "Sexual Harassment in the Church." *The Christian Ministry* 19 (July-Aug.), pp. 12-14.

Dworkin, Andrea (1992). "Women in the Public Domain: Sexual Harassment and Date Rape." In *Sexual Harassment: Women Speak Out*, see Sumrall and Taylor. pp. 1-17.

Edwards, Anne (1987). "Male Violence in Feminist Theory." In *Women, Violence, and Social Control*, See Hanmer and Maynard. pp. 13-29.

Farley, Lin (1978). *Sexual Shakedown: The Sexual Harassment of Women on the Job*. New York: McGraw-Hill Book Co.

Farley, Margaret (1978). "Sexual Ethics." In *Encyclopedia of Bioethics*. ed. by Warren T. Reich. Vol. 4. New York: The Free Press. pp. 1575-89.

Fortune, Marie M. (1983). *Sexual Violence: The Unmentionable Sin*. New York: Pilgrim Press.

Fortune, Marie M. (1988). "Violence Against Women: The Way Things Are Is Not the Way They Have To Be." *The Drew Gateway* 58 (February), pp. 38-50.

Fortune, Marie M. (1989). *Is Nothing Sacred? When Sex Invades the Pastoral Relationship*. San Francisco: Harper and Row.

Fortune, Marie M. (1991). "Violating the Pastoral Relation: Review of *Sex in the Parish*." *Christianity and Crisis* 51 (18 November), pp. 367-68.

Freeman, Jo, ed. (1989). *Woman: A Feminist Perspective*. Mountain View, Cal.: Mayfield Publ. Co.

Friedman, Sandra, and Alec Irwin (1990). "Christian Feminism, Eros, and Power in Right Relation." *Cross Currents*, 40 (Fall), pp. 387-405.

Garment, Suzanne. (1992) "Why Anita Hill Lost." *Commentary*, 93 (January), pp. 26-35.

Gudorf, Christine, and Robert Blaney (1988). "Recent Works in Christian Sexual Ethics." *Religious Studies Review*, 14 (April), pp. 125-31.

Gula, Richard M. (1989). *Reason Informed by Faith: Foundations of Catholic Morality*. Mahwah, N.J.: Paulist Press.

Hadditt, Marylou (1992). "Nudes in the Workplace." In *Sexual Harassment: Women Speak Out*, see Sumrall and Taylor. pp. 98-99.

Hanmer, Jalna, and Mary Maynard, eds. (1987). *Women, Violence, and Social Control*. Atlantic Highlands, N.J.: Humanities Press International, Inc.

Harrington, Daniel (1989). "Not to Abolish, But to Fulfill." *Bible Today*, 27 (November), pp. 333-37.

Kelly, Liz (1987). "The Continuum of Sexual Violence." In *Women, Violence, and Social Control*, See Hanmer and Maynard. pp. 46-60.

Langelan, Martha J. (1993). *Back Off! How to Confront and Stop Sexual Harassment and Harassers*. New York: Simon and Schuster.

Lebacqz, Karen (1985). *Professional Ethics: Power and Paradox*. Nashville: Abingdon Press.

Lebacqz, Karen (1988). "Pastor-Parishioner Sexuality: An Ethical Analysis." *Explor: A Journal of Theology*, 9 (Spring), pp. 67-81.

Lebacqz, Karen (1990). "Love Your Enemy: Sex, Power, and Christian Ethics." *The Annual of the Society of Christian Ethics*. ed. by D.M. Yeager. Washington: Georgetown University Press, pp. 3-23.

Lebacqz, Karen, and Ronald G. Barton (1990). "Sex, Power and Ministry: The Case of the Normal Neurotic." *Quarterly Review*, 10 (Spring), pp. 36-48.

Lebacqz, Karen, and Ronald G. Barton (1991). *Sex in the Parish*. Louisville: Westminster/John Knox Press.

MacKinnon, Catherine A. (1979). *Sexual Harassment of Working Women: A Case of Sex Discrimination*. New Haven: Yale University Press.

MacKinnon, Catherine A. (1982). "Feminism, Marxism, Method, and the State: An Agenda for Theory." *Signs*, 7 (Spring), pp. 515-44.

MacKinnon, Catherine A. (1983). "Feminism, Marxism, Method, and the State: Toward a Feminist Jurisprudence." *Signs*, 8 (Summer), pp. 635-58.

Majka, Linda C. (1991). "Sexual Harassment in the Church." *Society*, 28 (May-June), pp. 14-21.

Mamet, David (1992). *Oleanna*. An unpublished play.

Marks, Michelle A., and Eileen S. Nelson (1993). "Sexual Harassment on Campus: Effects of Professor Gender on Perception of Sexually Harassing Behaviors." *Sex Roles*, 28:3-4, pp. 207-17.

Martin, Susan Erlich (1989). "Sexual Harassment: The Link Joining Gender Stratification, Sexuality, and Women's Economic Status." In *Women: A Feminist Perspective*, see Freeman. pp. 57-75.

Martin, Justin (1992). "New Tricks for an Old Trade." *Across the Board*, 29 (June), pp. 40-44.

Moore, Carey A. (1992). "Susanna: A Case of Sexual Harassment in Ancient Babylon." *Bible Review*, 8 (June), pp. 20-29, 52.

Morgenson, Gretchen (1990). "Watch that Leer; Stifle that Joke." In *Business Ethics 90/91*, see Richardson. pp. 65-68.

Moskal, Brian S. (1990). "Sexual Harassment '80s Style." In *Business Ethics 90/91*, see Richardson, pp. 62-64.

Munson, Naomi (1992). "Harassment Blues." *Commentary*, 93 (February), pp. 49-51.

NCCB (National Conference of Catholic Bishops) (1992). Called to Be One in Christ Jesus. 3rd Draft. *Origins* 21 (23 April), pp. 761-76.

Paul, Ellen Frankel (1991). "Bared Buttocks and Federal Cases." *Society*, 28 (May-June), pp. 4-7.

PCSW (Permanent Commission of the Status of Women) (1992). *Sexual Harassment in the Workplace*. Hartford, Ct.

Pellauer, Mary D. (1985). "Moral Callousness and Moral Sensitivity." In *Women's Consciousness, Women's Conscience*. ed. Barbara Andolsen, Christine Gudorf, and Mary Pellauer. San Francisco: Harper and Row, pp. 33-51.

Pellauer, Mary D. (1987). "Violence Against Women: The Theological Dimension." In *Sexual Assault and Abuse*. ed. Mary Pellauer, Barbara Chester, and Jane Boyajian. San Francisco: Harper and Row, pp. 51-61.

Randall, Margaret (1992). "Doublespeak and Doublehear–Anita Hill in Our Lives." In *Sexual Harassment: Women Speak Out*, see Sumrall and Taylor, pp. 18-22.

Rapp, Ellen (1992). "Dangerous Liasons." *Working Woman* (February), pp. 56-61.

Reich, Sheryl E. (1993). "Crying Wolf in Albany." *The New York Times* (23 January), op.ed.p.

Richardson, John E., ed. (1990). *Business Ethics 90/91*. Guilford, Ct.: Dushkin Publ. Group, Inc.

Roiphe, Katie (1993). "Date Rape's Other Victim." *The New York Times Magazine* (13 June), pp. 26-30ff.

Sheffield, Carole J. (1989). "Sexual Terrorism." In *Woman: A Feminist Perspective*, see Freeman, pp. 3-19.

Smith, Christine C. (1992). *Preaching as Weeeping, Confession, and Resistance: Radical Responses to Radical Evil*. Louisville: Westminster/John Knox Press.

Sumrall, Amber Coverdale, and Dena Taylor, eds. (1992). *Sexual Harassment: Women Speak Out*. Freedom, Cal.: The Crossing Press.

Thistlethwaite, Susan Brooks (1991). "Sexual Harassment: To Protect, Empower." *Christianity and Crisis*, 51 (21 October), pp. 328-30.

Tong, Rosemarie (1986). "Sexual Harassment." In *Women and Values: Recent Readings in Feminist Philosophy*. ed. by Marilyn Pearsall. Belmont, Cal.: Wadsworth Publ. Co., pp. 148-66.

United Methodist Church (1991). "Sexual Harassment in Church and Society." *Christian Social Action*, 4 (July-August), p. 16.

Vaught, Carl G. (1986). *The Sermon on the Mount: A Theological Interpretation*. Albany: The State University of New York Press.

Wall, James M. (1991). "Sexual Harassment and Conflicting Perspectives." *Christian Century*, 108 (23 October), pp. 955-56.

SECTION II

Chapter Nine

WORK REWARDS: COMPLEMENTARY AND CONFLICTING DISTRIBUTIVE DEMANDS

Frank D. Tinari

1. Introduction

Work rewards include both intrinsic and extrinsic forms. Intrinsic rewards include job satisfaction as well as personal growth and fulfillment. In fact, because work comprises by far the dominant use of our waking hours, our self-image greatly depends upon the extent to which we receive intrinsic work rewards. Many thinkers would agree with the spirit of the idea expressed by John Ruskin: "Reward for work is not what we get paid for it but what we become through it."

The extrinsic rewards of work consist of wages (paid remuneration) and non-wage benefits.[1] In turn, the latter comprise two types: benefits in lieu of wages (generally called fringe benefits, such as health insurance, subsidized meals, use of an automobile, stock options, etc.) and benefits not in lieu of wages such as a favorable workplace environment, positive interpersonal relations on the job, etc.

When economists speak of the rewards of work, however, they almost always refer to paid remuneration. Moreover, many economists would broadly define remuneration to include the pecuniary value of fringe benefits. Unfortunately, the rich dimensions of non-pecuniary, intrinsic rewards for work typically are ignored by economists. Yet greater job security, less control by superiors, and greater flexibility in work schedules have value to employees. A recent study of the salaries of Ph.D.s found that those in academe have lower salaries than those in industry, even after controlling for several possible explanatory variables (such as age, quality of work, field, job mobility, etc.). The conclusion was that a great deal of the inequality of income between comparable academics and non-academics may be explained by the more favorable work environment enjoyed by academics.[2]

Fair rewards for human work is one of the two great themes addressed by economists over the past several hundred years. The other theme is increased efficiency. Classical "political economy," which contained within its scope all matters of social and political issues, dealt with both themes, but the discipline evolved gradually into what is allegedly the "science of economics." There were two driving forces behind this shift. The first was the desire by economists to make their craft more "scientific," more "objective." The distinction between normative and positive statements became the underpinning for this development. At bottom, of course, all analysis is normative, i.e., dependent on either explicit or unstated norms, but that did not stop the thrust towards scientism in the field of economics.[3]

The second reason for the shift away from political economy was the difficulty encountered in analyzing and measuring "fairness." Thus the concept of efficiency became and still is the dominant focus of most of economic analysis. Efficiency is clearly understood, is measured in a singular, unambiguous way, and is assigned prominence in setting economic standards by which policy may be evaluated. The reality, too, is that efficiency is easier to define and to measure than fairness, so it may be said that economics thus far has chosen the easier path. This is not to say that the focus upon efficiency is unimportant. Because it deals with the day-by-day living standards of people and, more importantly, how those living standards may be improved, efficiency improvement is a significant goal for which to strive.

Yet many revolutions and bloody wars–from the American and French revolutions to the guerrilla-led revolutions in China and elsewhere–have had their genesis in conflict over the sharing of income and wealth. To be sure, economists have not ignored the study of income and wealth, which may be viewed as the extrinsic, measurable rewards for work. After all, pecuniary compensation for work is not an unimportant aspect of work's rewards. In this chapter, however, we will not analyze how compensation is determined. Instead, our purpose is to examine widely-accepted standards or criteria by which the sharing of income may be judged "fair" or "unfair" from a social point of view. Before doing so, it is appropriate to briefly review global developments that have been responsible for a widening in wage differentials.

2. Recent Concerns over Rising Wage Inequality

Current research indicates a trend of rising wage inequality in recent decades that appears to characterize many developed nations. During the 1980s, comparable changes in the distribution of income occurred in most advanced nations including Australia, Canada, Germany, Japan, Sweden, the United States, and the United Kingdom. Research also reveals that the pay gap mirrors an educational gap that has worsened. In fact, the pattern of change in wage inequality by education group appears to be similar among developed countries.[4]

Between 1963 and 1987, greater demand for more highly-skilled workers was the primary determinant of the widening gap in pay among U.S.

workers.[5] For at least the past two decades, in Japan, the United States, the United Kingdom, and France, the demand for well-educated workers has been increasing more rapidly than the demand for other workers, thereby causing educated workers to receive a wage premium for their college degree.[6] Global economic changes that reward the skilled and penalize the unskilled account for more than half the trend towards income inequality in recent years.[7]

In the United States the widening income gap of the 1980s is portrayed by the data in Figure 1. As noted above, this trend is explained to a great extent by a widening gap in pay between college graduates and less-educated workers. (This is sometimes interpreted as being a racial gap, but the educational factor holds true both between and within racial groupings.) Both foreign competition and technological change are requiring more skilled and more capable workers. To close the gap, a revival is needed in educational attainment rates,[8] which have stagnated since 1975. The problem is especially acute among urban blacks. In the U.S., 68% of white adults read at the 11th grade level but only 31% of blacks do. Overall, 70% of young Americans do not attain a college degree.[9] Moreover, businesses are desirous of hiring not only workers who possess adequate skills but also those who are motivated, take pride in good work, and are able to learn and work effectively with others.[10] More companies are using pay-for-performance incentive schemes, which appear to improve productivity significantly. But such reward systems do not reach far enough down into an organization to cover a large enough number of employees.[11]

With these troubling developments as our backdrop, let us explore the concept of wage equity.

3. The Concept of Equity

We begin by defining distributional equity as *fairness in the way in which goods and services (income) are shared by (or distributed among) the members of society.* Inasmuch as it is quite difficult to measure the actual consumption of goods and services, the distribution of money income is generally used as a proxy, albeit imperfect. In addition, our definition uses the word "fairness" which requires further elaboration.

Fairness does not necessarily mean equality, although in most societies there is a strong predilection towards political equality. But in the economic sphere, trying to achieve complete equality of per capita income severely hampers the capability to produce goods and services.[12] Beyond some point, further attempts to redistribute income reduce incentives to be productive, to work hard, and to innovate, thereby penalizing efficiency and investment. The evidence regarding redistribution policies supports the notion of a tradeoff between efficiency and equality. While the short-term gains of greater sharing of national wealth have been recognized by their proponents, the longer-term effects upon continued improvement in living standards have not been so favorable. It may be said that nations with extensive redistribution policies exhibit a preference for equality over efficiency. Of course, economic analysis cannot determine the "best" position for any community; that depends on people's willingness to give up some efficiency for more equity, and vice versa. Yet, the poor economic performance of those nations over the long term indicates that greater equality comes at a high cost to their citizens.

As noted previously, equality before the law and, in general, within the political domain, has fueled the belief that, consequently, equality in the distribution of income should be the preferred outcome of economic activity. A number of people justify equality of outcomes as an extension of the humanistic and social bases for equal rights. Interestingly, from the late nineteenth through the early twentieth century, it was thought within the economics profession that the marginal utility concept could be used scientifically to justify taxing the rich (whose marginal dollars it was believed provided low levels of marginal benefits) and giving to the poor (who presumably look upon extra dollars as providing high marginal benefits). However, several twentieth century economists disproved this view by pointing out that since marginal utilities are subjectively determined by each individual, they cannot be compared from person to person.

Yet, when obvious extremes in the access to goods and services are encountered, most observers would view a change in that distribution as desirable or fair. Who in good conscious would justify the luxurious lifestyle enjoyed by kings, dictators, and a few who are very rich when, at the same time in those societies, the majority of the population suffers from a bare subsistence standard of living? Thus, the citizenry would desire changes in the economic system to reduce the extreme inequality and would consider the results a more equitable distribution. At the other extreme, however, complete wage equality is generally not viewed as a fair way of rewarding individuals who differ in motivation, willingness to work, energy, productivity, educational attainment, and so forth. But once we move away from conditions of extreme differences in living standards, it is more difficult to get agreement on the meaning of equity. That is why it is useful to explore alternative fairness criteria. First, however, let us examine the primary methods available for changing the income distribution.

4. Methods for Changing the Income Distribution

If people voluntarily choose to give some of their goods to others because they perceive their marginal benefits (of feeling good about helping) to be greater than their marginal costs (sacrifice of goods) from doing so, then both recipients and donors gain from such transfers.[13] This is essentially what occurs among members of the same family unit. In fact, the income transfers among family members, which have been estimated at almost one third of a output, far outweigh both government and private charities' income transfers combined.[14] Moreover, these transfers are voluntary, not coerced, which gives them a moral attractiveness not ascribed to government transfers, which are financed out of compulsory taxes.

Despite religion's appeal to "love thy neighbor as thyself," private voluntary transfers by persons to those outside one's family comprise a relatively small portion of the gross domestic product. In the United States, the Great Depression of the 1930s tested the limits of the voluntary means of improving equity. Private charity was found wanting because it was inadequate to help the millions in great need.

During this century, government efforts to "help the needy" have expanded steadily. Voluntary charitable donations in the form of money and labor time still comprise major activities in this country, but they are now overshadowed by the sheer volume of governmental programs. Government has absorbed many charitable services through social programs that now compete with private charities.

In the twentieth century, then, the major cause of changes in the income distribution has been the growth of governmental programs. Redistribution has been accomplished relatively peacefully in some nations–by legally legislating taxation and transfer programs–and not so peacefully in others–by armed revolution. But no matter what method is used, distributional changes enforced by government imply that some persons suffer economic losses, even in situations where the majority vote to tax themselves to help others. Thus, when we speak of improving equity, we are necessarily forced to talk about the effects upon most citizens or "society," knowing full well that some individuals will be worse off after any given change. We thus turn to a discussion of several widely-shared distributional criteria.

5. Work-Reward Criteria

Economists do not use a single, generally accepted criterion to guide their thinking regarding the presence or absence of "equity." This is in sharp contrast to the use of the concept of efficiency. Philosophers, theologians, social critics, economists, and many other people of good will hold different opinions about what constitutes a fair distribution of wages. This simply reflects the great extent to which the issue depends on value judgments about what is "good" or "just," and the extent of differences in views. To discuss these views, equity criteria are divided into distributional system criteria and distributional outcome criteria.

By a *distributional system* we mean *the customs, institutions, penalties and rewards that guide human behavior and which help determine the means by which income is distributed*. We can inquire into the system that helps shape the distribution of goods and services in any society. For example, are people who belong to certain religious, racial, or political groups given an extra advantage in obtaining jobs? Do all members of society have equal access to a good education?

In contrast, *a distributional outcome* refers to the *actual observed distribution of income resulting from the operations of a particular economic system*. Again, there are various possible alternatives. Equality is conceptually appealing, but is very difficult to define, and even more difficult to measure. Furthermore, as noted earlier, a high degree of equality leads to a significant loss of efficiency and dropping living standards. Another possible preferred outcome is to limit how much incomes are permitted to vary from person to person. Tax and transfer policies have been adopted by most nations in order to achieve what are considered socially acceptable income differences. A third outcome criterion is to ensure that no person falls below a certain minimum standard of living. The idea is to eliminate the possibility of anyone falling into absolute poverty.

These distributional criteria are examined next in some detail.

6. System Criteria

A. Equal Pay for Equal Work / Unequal Pay for Unequal Work

This criterion for rewarding work is almost universally utilized. However, there are various interpretations of the standard. It could mean higher rewards for (a) harder work; (b) more creative work; (c) more productive work; (d) more socially valuable work; and/or (e) more distasteful work (*i.e.*, socially shunned work). In market economies, higher rewards are received for these forms of work, but only if such work produces additional or more highly valued (by consumers) goods and services. Thus, more satisfying work or more interesting work may or may not be rewarded. Further, not all socially valuable work is accounted for in labor markets and, hence, not rewarded adequately. (This is an aspect of the public goods problem not discussed in this chapter.)

Rewarding work in this fashion promotes higher living standards in the form of additional and/or improved goods and services. Such a system provides direct income incentives as a way of rewarding efficiency and, as a result, tends to drive the economy towards greater and greater output levels over time. It is based, of course, on the implied value judgment in economics regarding the desire for improved efficiency, namely, that more goods are preferable to fewer goods.

However, this reward criterion is viewed as unfair whenever some individuals are restricted from participating on an equal footing in the life of the economy. If productive differentials are judged to be unfairly acquired (for example, if daughters of the rich have more opportunity to go to a good college than the daughters of the non-rich), then the system becomes suspect on equity grounds. To remedy this, a second equity criterion is invoked.

B. Equal Opportunity

Equal opportunity means *providing equal access to all income-earning opportunities*. Barriers to equal opportunity come in a variety of forms. But unfair methods of discrimination warrant special consideration. Equal opportunity requires society to take steps to raise the work capabilities of restricted individuals. Unfortunately, it is not easy to achieve complete equality of opportunity in practice. For example, it has been shown that children from families in which the parents have attained a high degree of education tend to attain higher levels of education that children whose parents have lower educational attainments. Should we, therefore, somehow try to limit how far some children may be allowed to progress in school in order to equalize the career opportunities of all? To what extent can governmental policies and programs change educational attainment levels? Family upbringing or status can give some a head start in the productive race. Genetic and biological differences also enable some to outperform others.

Knowing that different people's productivities lead to different incomes, however, modern societies take great pains to try to reduce unequal access to education, training, and other job-related opportunities. While progress has been made, there is still plenty of room for improvement in this regard. There is no guarantee, of course, that attaining perfect and complete equal opportunity will lead to outcomes that are judged equitable. But at least the discriminatory bases for some of the inequality can be reduced.

Moreover, more equal opportunities tend to reduce income differentials over time. And improved job opportunities can serve to break the cumulative cycle of inefficiency, low incomes, and despair.

Once implemented, this criterion allows for wider acceptance of the first criterion. As noted earlier, the major focus of the equal opportunity criterion is to improve education and educational access.

C. Reward According to Need

An economic system relying on this equity standard would suffer the same kinds of inefficiency that would befall an equal-pay economy. The reason is that work rewards would not be connected to work effort. Perhaps just as troubling is the loss of human liberty that would be consequent to someone else (a government committee, perhaps) determining what your "needs" are. In practice, distribution "according to need" turns out to be a policy favoring equal distribution because human beings are viewed as equal in a number of ways, and because it is difficult for an outside body or individual to determine each person's "needs."

Now that we have examined several distributional system criteria, it is time to focus on preferred distributional *outcomes*. For no matter what the system, extremes in *actual* income results are not likely to be tolerated for long.

7. Outcome Criteria

D. Equal Pay for All (Functional Egalitarianism)

Many religious orders of the Roman Catholic Church, some Israeli kibbutzim, as well as Buddhist monasteries use this distributional system or some close variation. In the words of St. Paul:

> The relief of others ought not to impoverish you; there should be a certain *equality*. Your plenty at the present time should supply their need so that their surplus may in turn one day supply your need, with *equality* as a result. It is written, "He who gathered much had no excess and he who gathered little had no lack." (2 Corinthians 8; emphasis added)

Communistic distribution works well in families and fairly well in religious settings because of the great personal commitment each member brings to the group as well as their shared beliefs in a simple unified set of moral and ethical principles.

However, when communistic distribution is adopted by less zealous and less religious communities, or by society at large, it doesn't operate successfully for more than a relatively short period. The chief reason for its failure as the basis for distributing income for whole societies is simply its *harmful effect upon economic incentives.* For example, a report on food production in Africa was issued in 1982 by the World Food Council of the United Nations. It was found that food production had declined substantially in countries that had adopted policies of (a) government ownership of important resources and industries, and (b) significant income redistribution. The general populace in these countries was not helped by the well-intentioned policy of *redistribution*, that is, *transferring income from upper-income persons to lower-income persons*. On the contrary, millions of people experienced declining living standards and, in some cases, life-threatening starvation.

In the same way, domestic public assistance programs face the problem of helping those in need while trying to minimize work disincentives. Speaking of U.S. welfare programs, Tom Corbett states: "Child poverty persists in large part because we have not honestly confronted the basic conflict between the two putative goals of welfare reform: to enhance the well-being of children and to discourage dependency on government handouts targeted primarily at poor women with children...."

> The essential conundrum of welfare is that several equally desirable program goals–adequacy, vertical equity, and target efficiency–cannot be satisfied simultaneously.[15]

In short, reduced individual incentives cause production to drop. A smaller output causes economic, social, and political disruption. In 1848 John Stuart Mill stated in his *Principles of Political Economy:* "Once the product is there, mankind–socially or individually–can do with it whatever it pleases." The error made by those who adopt this view is their belief that distribution can be separated from production.

But what is meant by "equality"? It turns out that the idea is quite difficult to pin down. For example, it probably doesn't mean equal incomes for all *family units*, since family size can vary substantially. Does it mean equality among *individual persons?* Since young children don't have the same impact as teenagers or adults on the cost of maintaining a household, then a person basis for equality would not make sense either. These and several other important definitional problems plague those who seek to achieve "equality" of outcomes.

In practice, few if any nations seriously attempt to achieve equal outcomes. In recent times, China has gone the farthest in this regard. After the communist takeover in 1949, leaders implemented a system of eight pay scales for all professions and jobs. Less than 30 years later, the country began a reversal of that policy as the inefficiencies created by the system became too burdensome to ignore.

As we have seen, complete equality undeniably leads to a significant loss of efficiency and a corresponding drop in the flow of goods and services. Another cost imposed on society of policies that redistribute goods from the "haves" to the "have-nots" consists of administrative and policing costs associated with such policies. Both the government and, in the private sector, charitable organizations use up scarce resources in the very act of redistribution. In positive economic terms, greater equality is achieved at a cost–reduced output. The members of each community must decide how much of this cost they are willing to incur. Complete equality, therefore, is not usually desirable. This is why another desired set of distributional outcomes is often preferred.

E. Acceptable Pay Differences

A commonly preferred outcome is to limit the extent to which incomes vary from person to person. Suppose a particular country contains thousands of families, with the lowest income of $1,000 annually, and the highest income $75,000 per year. This degree of disparity might lead people in that society to take steps to change the distribution such that the income differences would fall within a narrower range than seventy-five to one. Differences between poorest and richest in that country would be maintained as incentives for efficiency purposes, but perhaps not differences greater than, say, forty to one or twenty to one. Of course, there is no objective standard so the degree of difference that is tolerated depends on cultural, political, and other values held by the general population. For lower income persons, envy may be a motivating factor in wanting to narrow the income gap between high and low income persons. However, high incomes persons may support redistribution schemes to reduce income differentials as a sort of insurance policy against political and social upheaval.

As noted earlier, in recent years China has recognized the tradeoff between equality and efficiency: "A certain level of gap [in incomes] encourages people to work", said Zhu Zingfang of the Chinese Academy of Social Sciences. "But if the gap is too big, it makes people feel uneasy."[16] Similarly, most developed countries have determined that their economic systems result in excessively large income differences. Thus, tax and transfer policies have been adopted in order to change such outcomes.

The two outcomes that we have been discussing take as their focus *differences* among people's incomes. It is possible, however, to take another approach, one that ignores differences but instead focuses solely upon the lowest income receivers. Let us see how this approach works.

F. Minimum Wage for All Workers

In this case, goods and services may be said to be distributed fairly if *no person falls below a certain minimum standard of living.* The idea is to ensure that everybody in society achieves at least a minimal acceptable standard, measured in absolute terms. According to this view, people would have to agree to the meaning of an "absolute minimum" in terms of food, clothing, housing, and other goods and services. Typically, the government in many countries sets a minimum money income in lieu of an actual bundle of goods and services. In some countries, there are several minimal standards, depending upon a family's size, age distribution, geographic location, and other factors.

The concept of a minimally-acceptable living standard for all is embodied in the Catholic Church's concept of a "just wage." According to Pope John Paul II in his 1991 encyclical *On Human Work*, a just wage is a wage "sufficient to enable the earner to support himself, his spouse and children." Many nations have instituted legal minimum wages, but these may or may not meet the definition of a just wage. Moreover, they have found to have perverse effects in that the least skilled and least experienced workers tend to be pushed out of the labor market as a result of adjustments made by businesses to the legal minimum wage.

The minimal standard concept also has found practical expression in the U.S. in the form of the "poverty line" developed in the early 1960s by the federal government. Eating patterns of poor Americans were studied in order to identify a minimal food budget. Since, at that time, food expenditures constituted about one-third of average family expenditures, the food budget was multiplied by three to determine the poverty budget. Actually, several budgets were developed to account for differences in family size. Furthermore, these poverty lines have been increased over the years in an attempt to offset the impact of inflation.

Obviously, determination of the "minimally acceptable standard" is quite subjective. Some people today argue that the poverty line in the United States is outmoded primarily because the one-to-three ratio of food costs to total income is no longer valid. Studies indicate that the ratio should approximate one to four. This implies that the food budget should be multiplied by four to get a more representative poverty threshold. The "low-level budget" developed by the Bureau of Labor Statistics of the U.S. Labor Department is viewed by some as a more accurate determination of minimal standards. (They may take this position in part because the low-level budget is numerically almost twice as high as the poverty line.)

The economist Victor Fuchs suggests that the poverty line should not be measured in absolute terms but should be measured relative to the average American's income. Admitting that this standard is purely arbitrary, no better or worse than other standards, he places his poverty line at fifty percent of the nation's median family income, *i.e.,* of the income at the middle of the entire economy's income distribution.[17] It appears that, on the basis of one study, at least at one point in time the subjective attitudes of people in the U.S. corresponded to this view.[18]

8. Application of Distributional Equity Criteria to Public Policy

We now examine selected policies aimed at achieving particular equity goals. Two questions will guide the analysis. The first is: Does the policy achieve its intended equity goal? And the second is: Does the policy also meet other equity criteria? The criteria that have been discussed are summarized as follows:

Criterion #1 A policy is judged fair if it distributes more income to those who contribute more to production.

Criterion #2 A policy is judged fair if it helps promote equal opportunity to earn money income.

Criterion #3 A policy is judged fair if it helps make the income distribution more equal.

Criterion #4 A policy is judged fair if it ensures that people do not fall below a specified minimum income.

It should be noted that criterion #3 is based on two previously discussed distributional outcomes: equal incomes, and achieving acceptable income differences. Actually, equity criterion #3 does not judge policy in terms of *complete* equality. But, if continually applied to economic policy-making over time, it does lead the income distribution *toward* equality. When social critics, columnists, and many economists speak about equity matters, frequently the equity standard they use is criterion #3, which is more often implied than stated.

The policies selected for analysis have been chosen to correspond to each equity criterion. Criterion #1 aims at rewarding productivity; thus, the policy example selected is the lowering of marginal income tax rates. The second criterion targets equal opportunity; the corresponding policy selected here is investment in education. Since the third criterion aims at equalizing incomes, the policy chosen for analysis is income transfers to low-income families. Finally, corresponding to criterion #4 is minimum wage legislation. Obviously, full treatment of these policies cannot be given in this paper. But points of complementarity and conflict among equity criteria are highlighted.

A. Lower Marginal Tax Rates

The conservative political policies that swept many developed and developing nations alike during the 1980s included across-the-board income tax rate reductions as a means of spurring work effort and economic growth. Clearly, these rate reductions increase the take-home incomes of higher-income earners who, in market economies, are defined as most productive. (We recognize, of course, that high pay in the marketplace is not necessarily associated with high productivity, but the general rule does apply for the vast majority of high income workers who generally are higher skilled and better educated.) Income tax rate reductions also serve as an incentive to entrepreneurs and others who innovate and attempt to better meet consumer wants.

Though the policy passes the intended equity criterion #1, it may or may not be consonant with attainment of other equity criteria. As for equity criterion #2 (equal opportunity enhancement), on the one hand lower tax rates do not directly promote more equal opportunity to earn income. They do promote earning opportunities, but tend to favor the skilled, the educated and the economically astute. On the other hand, as the economy increases its growth rate subsequent to income tax rate reduction, more jobs are created and more earning opportunities occur. Thus, lower-income workers would be favorably affected by the brighter economic outlook. In addition, higher work rewards may stimulate some less-educated to acquire more skills in order to participate in the more favorable opportunities. But that effect is both diffuse and long-term.

Does the policy meet criterion #3, reducing income inequalities. On balance, the answer would have to be negative, especially in the near term. As for equity criterion #4, ensuring a minimum income for all, lower income tax rates certainly increase the after-tax income available to all workers. Hence, the policy does move the economy in the direction of satisfying this equity criterion. In summary:

Criterion	#1	#2	#3	#4
Lower Tax Rates	Passes	Mixed	Fails	Passes

Given these results, it may be safely stated that the vocal criticism of income tax rate cuts reflects an implicit or explicit use of equity criterion #3 as the sole yardstick of equity attainment. We have seen, however, that application of the other equity criteria lead to different conclusions about the distributional fairness of such a policy.

B. Investment in Education

One of the multiple purposes of educational investment is to provide greater access to job opportunities by all citizens by raising the skills and abilities of individuals. In this sense, therefore, and assuming that job markets are reasonably competitive, this policy directly passes equity criterion #2.

With respect to equity criterion #1 (higher pay for higher productivity), educational investment programs clearly meet this criterion because markets generally reward higher skills (and higher productivity) with higher wages, assuming that the education is effective in the sense that enhanced education improves job skills. Equity criterion #3 may or may not be attained, depending on which income groups benefit from such programs. However, inasmuch as higher income families generally provide their offspring with a social/ psychological/educational head start, educational investment programs would tend to have a more positive effect upon the opportunities of the offspring of lower-income families, *ceteris paribus*. Thus, on balance, this policy passes the test of criterion #3.

Finally, educational investment policies tend to be congruent with criterion #4, especially over the long term because better education is connected with higher work skills and, consequently, higher wages. In summary:

Criterion	#1	#2	#3	#4
Education Investment	Passes	Passes	Passes	Passes

C. Transfer Payments

Typically, government transfer schemes involve either direct monetary payments or benefits in kind (such as free medical care, food stamps, subsidized housing, etc.), or both. These generally are means-tested, i.e., provided to individuals who meet certain criteria of low income and/or disability. These programs, also referred to as government welfare or public assistance, may be viewed as attempts to raise the income of low-income persons, which is expressed as criterion #4. They also may be viewed as a way of closing the income distribution gap as expressed by criterion #3. Such programs, therefore, may be judged as passing both criteria.

With respect to criterion #1, welfare programs do not promote payment in response to productivity inasmuch as they are given as a result of a lack of employment or due to low-pay employment. Thus, these programs fail with respect to the first equity criterion. As for the second criterion, government transfers do not typically promote more equal opportunity to attain income. In fact, in a fair number of cases, transfers tend to create dependency that serves to reduce the ability and/or willingness to participate in the labor market. In summary, therefore, we find the following results:

Criterion	#1	#2	#3	#4
Transfer Payments	Fails	Fails	Passes	Passes

D. Legislated Minimum Wage

Minimum wage laws are intended to ensure that the lowest paid workers receive adequate income, as defined by each society. Clearly, legislated wages fail to meet criterion #1 (payment in accordance with productivity). For jobs that would otherwise be paid lower wages in a competitive market, minimum wage legislation reduces labor demanded and increases labor supplied, thereby causing a market surplus of labor which means unemployment. Those who experience such unemployment have been found to be the least skilled and least desirable workers. Thus, for example, in the United States, black workers who tend to dominate the ranks of the unskilled are especially penalized by minimum wage legislation. It provides some workers (who retain their jobs) the opportunity to earn a higher income, but reduces that opportunity for lower skilled workers. Criterion #2, therefore, may be said to have mixed results.

As for criterion #3, the minimum wage appears to lower the gap between higher and lower paid workers. However, for those earning in a range above the minimum, there is a tendency to raise their wages so that their pay may be differentiated from the minimum wage of beginners. Overall, however, the wage gap does tend to diminish somewhat. However, for the least-skilled workers who become unemployed, the gap between their income and other workers widens significantly. Thus, the minimum wage generates mixed results with respect to criterion #3. Minimum wage legislation does raise the pay and income of the lowest-paid workers, thereby meeting equity criterion #4 (ensure minimum income). Again, however, the least-skilled who become unemployed lose whatever income they might have earned. Thus, we conclude that there are also mixed results with respect to the last criterion. In summary:

Criterion	#1	#2	#3	#4
Minimum Wage	Fails	Mixed	Mixed	Mixed

9. Conclusion: Conflict and Reinforcement among Distributional Equity Criteria

In light of the previous discussion, it should be evident that simple allegations that some policy proposal is "fair" or "unfair" are clearly inadequate for describing distributional effects. A more systematic analysis is called for, as outlined in this chapter. Such analysis can enlighten the public policy debate by pointing out whether or not certain equity criteria are attained by the policy.

Perhaps more significant is the possibility that political leaders could make use of "equity analysis" in guiding their political positions. Consider the following proposition: policies garner greater public support when they pass multiple equity criteria. The proposition assumes that different constituencies support different equity criteria. Hence, a policy meeting the goals of different constituencies has a greater chance of obtaining public support. To demonstrate, let us reorder the findings from the previous section in decreasing order of the widest possible support, *i.e.*, passing the greatest number of equity criteria, as follows:

	Equity Criterion			
Policy	#1	#2	#3	#4
Education Investment	Passes	Passes	Passes	Passes
Lower Tax Rates	Passes	Mixed	Fails	Passes
Transfer Payments	Fails	Fails	Passes	Passes
Minimum Wage	Fails	Mixed	Mixed	Mixed

It is illuminating to observe that investment in education appears to be a policy that would be supported by a wide variety of citizens with differing equity perspectives. In contrast, transfer payment programs appear to be the most clearly divisive. More telling is the relatively weak showing, among the policies discussed, of minimum wage legislation. This would leave us to believe that such legislation would garner relatively weak public support. Yet, in most developed nations, minimum wages are commonly found in various forms with apparently broad public support. This may be explained, however, by the generally poor level of economic understanding by the public, even in nations with relatively high educational attainment levels. Numerous surveys and studies reveal how thin is the public's economic literacy. Thus, we hypothesize that a policy that would otherwise be given weak public support in terms of equity goals is, in practice, supported due to the public's misperception of the equity efficacy of the minimum wage. But such illiteracy is a topic for another chapter!

Notes

1. In the case of barter, *i.e.*, direct receipt of goods and/or services in exchange for work, such goods may be viewed as equivalent to the amount of money needed to purchase like goods.

2. Albert Rees, "The Salaries of Ph.D.s in Academe and Elsewhere," *Journal of Economic Perspectives*, 7:1 (Winter 1993), pp. 151-58.

3. For example, economists assume that it is "good" for an economy to produce more rather than fewer goods and services. This is such a widely shared value judgment that it often goes unstated. Because it is usually implied, however, it is forgotten that this important value judgment lies at the foundation of economics as a science. The same may be said of several other crucial value judgments. Many philosophers of science have concluded, therefore, that there is no such thing as a "value-free science."

4. Steven Davis, "Cross-Country Patterns of Change in Relative Wages," National Bureau of Economic Research, Working Paper No. 4085, 1993.

5. Lawrence Katz and Kevin M. Murphy, "Changes in Relative Wages, 1963-87: Supply and Demand Factors," National Bureau of Economic Research, Working Paper No. 3927, 1992.

6. Lawrence Katz, Gary Loveman and David Blanchflower, "A Comparison of Changes in the Structure of Wages in Four OECD Countries," National Bureau of Economic Research, Working Paper No. 4227, 1993.

7. Kevin Phillips, *Boiling Point*. New York: Random House, 1993.

8. Erica L. Groshen and Colin Drozdowski, "The Recent Rise in the Value of Education: Market Forces at Work," *Economic Commentary*, Federal Reserve Bank of Cleveland (15 August 1992).

9. Steven Greenhouse, "The Coming Crisis of the American Work Force," *The New York Times* (7 June 1992).

10. "Report Highlights Work Force Changes," *Deloitte & Touche Review* (30 November 1992).

11. "Mixed Reviews on 'Pay-for-Performance'," *Christian Science Monitor* (20 July 1993).

12. For an elaboration of this point, *i.e.*, the tradeoff between efficiency and equality, see F.D. Tinari, "Reducing Income Inequality is Not the Only 'Equitable' Fairness Criterion," *Review of Social Economy*, 45:1 (April 1987), pp. 77-91.

13. Economic analysis has become increasingly helpful in understanding altruistic and charitable behavior. The growing body of "grants economics" literature includes Kenneth E. Boulding, *The Economy of Love and Fear* (Belmont, Cal.: Wadsworth, 1973); F. Dickson, ed., *Philanthropy and Public Policy* (New York: National Bureau

of Economic Research, 1962); Edmund S. Phelps, ed., *Altruism, Morality, and Economic Theory* (New York: Russell Sage Foundation, 1975); and Janos Horvath, "Grants Economics: An Outline," in Douglas Greenwald, ed., *Encyclopedia of Economics* (New York: McGraw-Hill, 1980).

14. J.H. Lillydahl and L.D. Singell, "The Scope of the Grants Economy and Income Distribution: An Examination of Intergenerational Transfers of Income," *American Journal of Economics and Sociology*, 41:2 (April 1982), pp. 125-39.

15. Thomas Corbett, "Child Poverty and Welfare Reform: Progress or Paralysis?", *Focus*, University of Wisconsin-Madison, Institute for Research on Poverty, 15:1, (Spring 1993), 1-17, p. 7.

16. Sheryl WuDunn, "As China Leaps Ahead, The Poor Slip Behind," *The New York Times* (23 May 1993).

17. Victor Fuchs, "Toward A Theory of Poverty," in *The Concept of Poverty* (Washington: U.S. Chamber of Commerce, 1965).

18. Lee Rainwater, *What Money Buys: Inequality and the Social Meanings of Income* (New York: Basic Books, 1974).

References

Boulding, Kenneth E. *The Economy of Love and Fear*. Belmont, Cal.: Wadsworth, 1973.

Corbett, Thomas. "Child Poverty and Welfare Reform: Progress or Paralysis?," *Focus*, University of Wisconsin-Madison, Institute for Research on Poverty, 15:1, Spring 1993, 1-17, p. 7.

Davis, Steven. "Cross-Country Patterns of Change in Relative Wages," National Bureau of Economic Research, Working Paper No. 4085, 1993.

Dickson, F., ed. *Philanthropy and Public Policy* (New York: National Bureau of Economic Research, 1962).

Fuchs, Victor. "Toward a Theory of Poverty," in *The Concept of Poverty.* Washington: U.S. Chamber of Commerce, 1965.

Greenhouse, Steven. "The Coming Crisis of the American Work Force," *The New York Times*, 7 June 1992.

Groshen, Erica L. and Colin Drozdowski. "The Recent Rise in the Value of Education: Market Forces at Work," *Economic Commentary*, Federal Reserve Bank of Cleveland, 15 August 1992.

Horvath, Janos. "Grants Economics: An Outline," in Douglas Greenwald, ed., *Encyclopedia of Economics* New York: McGraw-Hill, 1980.

Katz, Lawrence and Kevin M. Murphy. "Changes in Relative Wages, 1963-87: Supply and Demand Factors," National Bureau of Economic Research, Working Paper No. 3927, 1992.

Katz, Lawrence, Gary Loveman and David Blanchflower. "A Comparison of Changes in the Structure of Wages in Four OECD Countries," National Bureau of Economic Research, Working Paper No. 4227, 1993.

Lillydahl, J.H. and L.D. Singell. "The Scope of the Grants Economy and Income Distribution: An Examination of Intergenerational Transfers of Income," *American Journal of Economics and Sociology*, 41:2 (April, 1982), pp. 125-39.

"Mixed Reviews on 'Pay-for-Performance'," *Christian Science Monitor*, 20 July 1993.

Phelps, Edmund S., ed. *Altruism, Morality, and Economic Theory,* New York: Russell Sage Foundation, 1975.

Phillips, Kevin. *Boiling Point*. New York: Random House, 1993.

Rainwater, Lee. *What Money Buys: Inequality and the Social Meanings of Income,* New York: Basic Books, 1974.

Rees, Albert. "The Salaries of Ph.D.s in Academe and Elsewhere," *Journal of Economic Perspectives*, 7:1 (Winter 1993), pp. 151-58.

"Report Highlights Work Force Changes," *Deloitte & Touche Review* (30 November 1992).

Tinari, F.D. "Reducing Income Inequality is Not the Only 'Equitable' Fairness Criterion," *Review of Social Economy*, 45:1 (April 1987) pp. 77-91.

WuDunn, Sheryl. "As China Leaps Ahead, The Poor Slip Behind," *The New York Times* (23 May 1993).

Chapter Ten

U.S.-JAPAN COMPARATIVE LABOR LAWS: THE QUESTION OF ETHICS

Hugh McCabe
Janine Prete

1. Introduction

The relationship between unions and management in the world's two largest economic powers is clearly defined by labor relations law. In fact, the United States and Japan have very similar labor relations laws, which serve to guide the behavior of both management and unions in the public and private sectors of both nations. This similarity is by no means the result of chance occurrences for, while United States labor relations law evolved over time, Japanese labor laws were imposed on Japanese management and unions by the Supreme Commander of the Allied Powers. Despite radical cultural and historical differences between the two nations, the occupying forces of the United States required the Japanese government to adopt a series of labor relations laws aimed at establishing equal relations between employers and employees as a means of achieving industrial democracy (Kodansha 351).

The purpose of this chapter is to trace the development of labor relations law in the United States and to compare that process with the history of labor relations legislation in pre-war and occupied Japan. The chapter will also study the issue of whether a model which is developed over two hundred years and which is deeply intertwined with a national culture can be successfully and ethically imposed upon the people of a dramatically different culture.

2. Labor Legislation in the United States

A. Conspiracy Doctrine

For the first seventy-five years of its existence, the United States was an agricultural society; industrial development was slow and labor unions were few and far between. American courts during this period uniformly accepted the Conspiracy Doctrine in ruling that labor organizations or any group of workers acting in concert to increase wages or improve working conditions constituted an illegal conspiracy against the public. The Conspiracy Doctrine, based on English common law, held that individuals acting in concert have power to injure; that even if the objective is lawful for an individual, the combination of individuals to achieve it in concert is unlawful (Kelly 93).

B. Doctrine of Legal Ends and Legal Means

In 1842 the Massachusetts Supreme court rejected the Conspiracy Doctrine in the case of Commonwealth v. Hunt and dismissed an indictment against a union of cordwainers (shoemakers). The court held that the formation of labor organizations for lawful purposes such as increasing wages, improving working conditions, or establishing a closed shop was legal as long as the means used to obtain the purposes was legal. This landmark case substituted the Doctrine of Legal Ends and Legal Means for the Conspiracy Doctrine and effectively established a legal ground for union activity (Kelly 94).

C. Post-Civil War Union Activism

In many ways, the Civil War was a second revolution. Not only was the Union preserved, but a "new America of big business, heavy industry, and capital-intensive agriculture was established" (McPherson 452). But this new economy, which would surpass Britain to become the world's foremost industrial nation by 1880 (McPherson 452) and would become the world's breadbasket for much of the twentieth century, also spawned a labor union movement.

"Wartime activism and strikes, combined with labor's pride in its contribution to northern victory, caused an increase of worker militancy and organization" (McPherson 450). The war helped drive union membership to its highest proportion of the industrial labor force in the nineteenth century and paved the way for the founding of the National Labor Union in 1866 and the Knights of Labor in 1869. The Knights reached their peak in 1886, a year in which 1,600 strikes occurred and when their membership reached 700,000; that was also the year of the Haymarket Square Riot, during which a bomb exploded killing a number of policemen and civilians. The explosion was blamed on the leaders of the Knights, four of whom were arrested, tried, convicted and executed for their supposed part in the deaths. Interest in the Knights waned after that, but 1886 also saw the birth of the American Federation of Labor founded by Samuel Gompers.

D. The Arbitration Act–The First Federal Labor Relations Law

In 1888 Congress passed the "Arbitration Act"–often cited as the first federal labor relations law. The law provided for voluntary arbitration and established a Board of Investigation. Unfortunately, during the ten years of the law's existence, labor unions and management never entered into the voluntary arbitration provided by the legislation and the Board of Investigation was appointed only once–after the Pullman strike had begun in 1894 (Kelly 95).

E. The Erdman Act

In 1898 the Erdman Act replaced the Arbitration Act. This law provided for specific mediation and conciliation as well as voluntary arbitration (Kelly 95). Temporary Ad Hoc mediation and conciliation boards were established in each railway labor dispute; arbitration was urged in situations where mediation and conciliation failed. In addition, Section 10 of the act declared "yellow-dog" contracts illegal, prohibited the "black-listing" of union activists and members, and prohibited discharge of employees for union activities.

F. Sherman Anti-Trust Act

The Sherman Anti-Trust Act of 1890, although not originally intended as a labor relations law, had a significant impact on union activity. In 1897 the Hatter's Union launched an organizing drive to enforce the closed shop throughout the industry. D. E. Loewe and Company of Danbury defeated an organization strike in 1902 and the United Hatter's of Danbury instituted a primary and secondary boycott. In a landmark case, Loewe v. Lawlor, the United States Supreme Court upheld a suit for $240,000 against the Hatter's Union for conspiracy under the Sherman Act and the use of an unlawful secondary boycott, which was deemed to interfere with interstate commerce. The Supreme Court also ruled that members of the Hatter's Union were individually liable for injuries to D. E. Loewe & Company (Kelly 103).

In a separate decision in 1908, Adair v. The United States, the Supreme Court ruled that workers could be discharged for membership in a union.

G. Newlands Act

The Newlands Act of 1913 succeeded the Erdman Act, the key provision of which was to replace the Ad Hoc boards by a full-time Board of Mediation and Conciliation. In addition the Board was given a role in the settlement of disputes during the lifetime of a contract (hereafter referred to as minor disputes as opposed to disputes between contracts which are referred to as major disputes).

H. Clayton Act

The Clayton Anti-trust Act of 1914 contained provisions specific to unions; unions were declared exempt from anti-trust legislation and the act removed indiscriminate use of injunctions to curtail union activity (Kelly 103). Originally hailed as a pro-union law, court decisions under the act frequently went against labor. Secondary boycotts were ruled illegal, injunctions were upheld, and in the 1917 case, Hitchman Coal v. Mitchell, the Supreme Court ruled that the "yellow-dog" contract was a legal condition of employment.

I. The 1920s

The 1920s were marked by the passage of two federal labor laws. The Transportation Act of 1920 assured labor that it had the right to organize without interference by management. It also provided for disputes to be settled by an equal-numbered labor-management Board of Adjustment with final authority in all grievance or rights disputes. The act, however, was rendered useless because no means existed for enforcement of decisions of the Railway Labor Board (Kelly 97).

In 1926 the Railway Labor Act, in many ways a precursor of the Wagner Act, was passed. Its many provisions included the following:

1. Protected the right of employees to unionize.
2. Set forth an enforceable dispute settlement machinery.
3. Outlawed company dominated unions.
4. Affirmed the right of labor to organize without coercion or interference.
5. Affirmed the right of employees to bargain collectively through representation of their own choosing. (This was the basis of the Wagner Act.)
6. Established the U. S. Board of Mediation. (Replaced by National Mediation Board in 1934.)
7. Established compulsory arbitration for minor disputes.
8. National Mediation Board dealt with representation disputes.
9. National Mediation Board provided mediation services in major disputes.
10. If impasse in negotiations is reached or a strike threatened, the NMB proposed voluntary arbitration. If arbitration is refused, parties are legally free to strike, lockout or change contracts after thirty days unless emergency dispute provisions are invoked. (Kelly 98)

J. The Influence of F.D.R.

While the Railway Labor Act had far-reaching influences, it took the Great Depression and the vision of Franklin D. Roosevelt to truly create a "bill of rights" for America's laborers. The Norris-LaGuardia Act (Federal Anti-Injunction Act of 1932) had curbed the widespread use of injunctions and the anti-trust provisions of the Sherman Act. It had also declared the "yellow-dog" contract "unlawful." During Roosevelt's administration, however, the face of America's economy was changed through legislation. The Securities Act of 1933 and the Securities Exchange Act of 1934 changed the way corporate stocks were traded and established the Security Exchange Commission to regulate the public markets. The Social Security Act guaranteed a pension for all workers; the National Industrial Recovery Act established the National Labor Board and gave employees the right to organize free from coercion or interference. In addition, the Fair Labor Standards Act (1938) established the 40-hour work week, a federal minimum wage, and time-and-a-half pay for overtime.

K. The Wagner Act

But, in the eyes of labor, none of these laws meant as much as The National Labor Relations Act, sponsored by Senator Robert Wagner of New York and passed in 1935. Often called labor's "Magna Carta," this law was designed to promote industrial peace by encouraging collective bargaining and establishing equality of power between corporate management and the labor unions. The key provisions of the act gave employees an absolute right to form or join unions without interference or coercion from management, and the National Labor Relations Board was established with the power to administer and enforce the act. Under the law management was obliged to engage in the process of collective bargaining with the representatives of recognized registered labor unions (Kelly 107).

What FDR's New Deal accomplished was to bind labor to a modified capitalist order through legislation and union-employer contracts. Unwittingly, this would serve as the central theme of labor relations law later imposed by the Supreme Commander of the Allied forces on the Japanese government after World War II.

L. The Taft-Hartley Act

With no limitations placed on boycotts, the closed shop attainable, and no provision for unfair labor practices by unions, the A.F.L. and its newly formed rival, The Congress of Industrial Organizations (C.I.O.), won many lucrative collective bargaining concessions. While union activity was largely curtailed during World War II, its post-war successes led to such a powerful lobbying effort by industrial management that an amendment, The Labor-Management Relations Act (better known as The Taft-Hartley Act), was passed over President Harry Truman's veto in 1947. This amendment was intended to curb labor excesses and return balance to the collective bargaining process. Under the law, closed shops, secondary boycotts, jurisdictional and sympathy strikes, and strikes by employees of the federal government were prohibited. In addition, while the union shop was permitted, the law allowed for individual states to pass "right to work laws," which effectively banned the union shop. (Twenty states, mostly in the south and midwest, have passed "right to work laws.")

Specifically, the Taft-Hartley Act identified "unfair" employer practices and "unfair" union practices. Under the law employers cannot interfere with, restrain, or coerce employees. Employers cannot seek to dominate a union or discriminate against union members; nor can employees be discharged for actions taken under the act.

Unions, meanwhile, were enjoined from coercing employees, causing employers to discriminate, refusing to bargain, promoting secondary boycotts, charging excessive initiation fees or dues or causing employers to pay for services not rendered (feather-bedding).

M. The 1950s

The 1950s saw the merger of the A.F.L. and the C.I.O., the McLelland Hearings and the subsequent jailing of Teamster President Jimmy Hoffa. In 1959, the Labor-Management Reporting and Disclosure Act (better known as The Landrum-Griffin Act) required the establishment of democratic practices within unions and public reporting and disclosure of union finances. The law regulates unions, their officers, and internal operations and protects individual union members from improper practices of the union officers.

N. Government Employees

In 1962, Executive Orders 10988 and 10987 gave federal employees the right to join or not join unions, but stipulated that such employees could not strike, advocate overthrow of the United States government, nor could they discriminate on the basis of race, color, creed, or nationality. Finally, in 1978, the Civil Service Reform Act (Title VII) gave civil servants the right to join or not join a union; such employees cannot strike and can only conduct informational picketing.

O. U. S. Labor Law Today

This is where Labor Relations law stands today in the United States. Industrial Management is required by law (The Wagner Act) to engage in the process of collective bargaining with the representatives of registered labor unions. Those same union representatives are required by law (The Taft-Hartley Act) to bargain with management. Coercion by either side is prohibited, strikes during the life of a contract (wildcat) are prohibited, and except in the case where a union shop requirement is in effect, employees have the right to join or not join a union. Management cannot interfere with the operations of the union, but those same unions must practice democratic procedures. Management cannot discriminate against union members, but unions cannot require management to pay for work not performed. Currently about 20 million members of the nation's workforce belong to unions and represent about 18% of the labor force.

3. Japanese Labor Relations Law

A. Pre-World War II

As one would expect, labor relations law was developing along entirely different lines in pre-war Japan. In the nineteenth century, the Meiji government left employment conditions to the employers, the result of which was something akin to a "benevolent master-servant" relationship. In the text Japanese Trade Unionism, labor specialist Kazuo Okochi is quoted: "There was the conception that the status of employers was higher than that of the workers. This feudalistic conception has been long entertained since the Meiji era. I think [this] conception still affects the current relations in Japan" (Cook 3). One exception was the Factory Law of 1911 which outlined work conditions for women and children but ignored adult men (Kodansha 351).

In 1919 Japan joined the International Labor Organization (ILO) in affiliation with its membership in the League of Nations. The Japanese government passed the Labor Dispute Mediation Law (Rodo Sogi Chotei Ho) in 1926. This compromise legislation established tripartite government, worker, and employer commissions for settling strikes and other conflicts between labor and management. While the law did not prohibit the existence of labor unions, it did not grant them the legal right to organize (Kodansha 351).

However, as part of the pre-war militarization movement, the government controlled "Sanpo" (Sangyo Hokoku Kai) labor front dissolved the few remaining labor unions and made the question of their legality moot (Kodansha 351).

B. Post-World War II

At the end of World War II the industrial and labor situation in Japan was understandably in chaos. Not only had the Japanese suffered a massive military defeat, two cities had been bombed with atomic bombs and the military-oriented industrial complex was in complete disarray (O'Neill 362). In fact, "more than 80 percent of the productive equipment in mining and manufacturing had been destroyed...with the result that four months after surrender, in January 1946, industrial production amounted to only 18.3 percent of the pre-war average (1932-38)" (Ayusawa 233).

In 1945 the Supreme Commander of the Allied Powers (SCAP) required the Japanese government to adopt the Labor Union Law (Rodo Kumiai Ho) and in 1946 the Labor Relations Adjustment Law (Rodo Kankei Chosei Ho). The intent of these two laws was to dissolve the "master-servant" relationship heretofore embraced in Japan and replace that relationship with reforms that would create equal relations between employers and employees as a means for achieving industrial democracy. Collectively the two laws approximated the Wagner Act with some wording in the laws almost exactly the same as the National Labor Relations Act of the United States (Kodansha 351).

Specifically, under the Labor Union Law, employees had the right to organize independently and could engage in collective bargaining on equal footing. In addition, they could carry on collective actions including strikes. (Firemen, police, and prison guards were excluded and a 30-day cooling-off period was established for strikes in public utilities) (Kodansha 351).

Under the Labor Relations Adjustment Law interference by employers in union activities was prohibited; and management could not refuse to bargain collectively. Like their cohorts in the United States, management could not discriminate against nor discharge workers for union activities.

For their part, unions were required to register with the government and establish bona fide democratic operations.

The government also established a tri-partite commission to settle disputes through conciliation (assen), mediation (chotei) and arbitration (chusai) on a voluntary basis (Kodansha 351).

C. The Public Sector

Since 1948 these two laws apply only to the private sector. After a threatened general strike in 1947, SCAP ordered the government to adopt a National Civil Service Law (Kokka Komuin Ho). Under this law, civil servants could form associations, but were denied other rights under the Labor Union Law. The National Personnel Authority (Jinjin) was established and serves to request wage and benefit adjustments from the government when the public sector lags behind the private sector (Kodansha 351).

D. The U.S. and Canada

The purpose of doing this comparison in such encyclopedic detail is to give a full picture of comparative labor relations law in the world's two economic superpowers. The fact is that current labor relations laws in the United States and Japan are very similar. While the same thing could be said about comparative labor relations laws of the United States and Canada, Canadian labor laws were composed by Canadians and responsive to and imitative of Canada's massive southern neighbor and trading partner. By necessity, Canada has adopted labor laws roughly equivalent to the National Labor Relations Act if for no other reason than that many of its industrial workers belong to international unions centered in the United States (*i.e.*, The United Auto Workers). In addition, Canada and the United States are the world's two largest trading partners and share an inter-connected national history and a similar culture. For those two nations to embrace labor laws that promote "equality and balance" in the relationship between employer and employee fits the non-class, democratic model prevalent in the North American society and culture shared by Canadians and Americans.

E. Counter-Cultural Model

When SCAP imposed this model on Japan, however, it was entirely counter-cultural; here was a society, formerly ruled by an emperor, which was both militaristic and feudal. "The Christian ethics and values that were the roots of many social reformist ideas in Western countries never were able to gain a foothold [in Japan]" (Shirai 339). It was also agricultural; in 1950 almost half of the work force was employed in either agriculture or fishing (Kodansha 353). Here was a society that had lived under the Peace Preservation Law (Chian Iji Ho), which effectively curbed union activity through government surveillance (Kodansha 351), and for whom a concept of equality between employer and employee fit no historical or cultural model. Here was an ancient homogeneous society in which one's place in the social order was clearly defined by tradition. "Isolationism goes very deep in national history. It was a matter of national policy for over two hundred years, and although westerners are apt to think of the Japanese as having copied or borrowed most of their cultural or technical heritage from other lands, the fact is that probably no country outside Tibet has lived longer in greater isolation from the rest of the world than Japan" (Cook 196). Unlike the United States, where wave upon wave of immigration forced a re-thinking of law and social order on a continual basis, Japan's laws were often based on tradition (Int. Encyc. 75). Labor disputes and strikes had always been relatively mild affairs by European or North American standards. True, military forces were called in at the Ashio Copper Mine labor dispute in 1907, and fairly large labor disputes had taken place at the Kawasaki and Mitsubishi shipyards in the summer of 1921 (Kodansha 350), but nothing rivaled the labor turmoil of the 1920s and 1930s in North America. In addition, over the centuries, the Japanese had imported Confucianism through their occupations of Korea and China; this is particularly important because of Confucianism's emphasis on respect for age and seniority and on education. This philosophy is partially responsible for Japan's lifetime employment systems and national commitment to education (O'Neill 362).

F. Japanese Respond

How, then, did the Japanese workers and the Japanese system respond to the new democratic equality imposed upon it by SCAP? At the end of the war, the leaders of big business and conservative party leaders sought to establish the old order of business in Japan. Under a guise of 1920s-style liberalism "taisho," they hoped to convince SCAP that they were democratizing business. The old order included "Kokutai," the family state with the emperor at its head, and "zaibatsu," great financial and industrial combines (Moore 3). In addition, the Higashikuni cabinet attempted to shift the blame of war upon the Japanese people. "Ichioku so zange" (collective confession of guilt of the 100 million) proposed that the war was not the result of the emperor or the military or the bureaucracy or the zaibatsu, but the people (Moore 7).

In September of 1945, employees at the Yomiuri Shinbum newspaper demanded improvements in economic conditions and internal democratization. The newspaper owner, Shoriki Matsutaro, refused and threatened to fire anyone who joined a union. Since SCAP had prohibited newspaper strikes, the workers moved to implement Seisan Kanri (production control). Shoriki only capitulated after his arrest by SCAP as a war criminal. Nine days later he signed an agreement to sell 30 percent of Yomiuri stock, reorganize the newspaper as a corporation, and establish a management council with equal representation of managers and employees. Under this new organization the Yomiuri became an advocate of and training ground for seisan kanri, a technique which quickly caught on in Japan's industries (O'Neill 366). As the technique of seisan kanri spread, the zaibatsu (big business) resisted by denying access to funds, supplies and markets. Workers became more radicalized and increasingly allied with the Japanese Communist Party. On the fifth of October, SCAP abolished the Tokko and Kempeitai (Police). On the fifteenth of October, SCAP abrogated the Public Peace Police Law and the Protection and Surveillance Law for Thought Offenses of 1936. These two laws had served as the bedrock of big business and government control of labor. In addition, on the tenth of October, three thousand political prisoners were freed by orders of SCAP; on the seventeenth of October, an additional 320,000 political prisoners were pardoned by imperial amnesty and 600,000 previously released political prisoners were restored their full civil rights. Many of these political prisoners had been imprisoned for their association with the labor movement or the Communist party. The conservatives and the big business leaders were horrified. They were convinced that the balance would be tipped against their interests and in favor of the radical Communists who had gained power within the union movement.

However, following a mass demonstration in Tokyo on 1 May 1946, SCAP officially denounced mass violence (O'Neill 365). This was interpreted by the government as a repudiation of the labor movement and endorsement of the laissez-faire labor policy advocated by the zaibatsu (O'Neill 367). When SCAP again intervened to prevent a general strike in 1947, the balance was tipped in favor of the right-wing within labor, breaking the industrial unions and creating the uniquely Japanese "enterprise union" (O'Neill 367). SCAP's prohibition of the strike (1 February 1947) turned the tide in favor of the essential moderation and conservatism of the Japanese people (Moore xiv). Just in case the Japanese had not gotten the message, General MacArthur himself called in the new head of Yomiuri and told him to "kick out the communists" (O'Neill 368). SCAP had decided that Japan was to have "balance," not between the zaibatsu and industrial unions dominated by the Japan Communist party, but rather between the management and unions of individual enterprises.

It should also be pointed out that in 1946 the Japanese government adopted a constitution largely influenced by SCAP; Articles 27 and 28 specifically dealt with the rights of workers. Combined with the aforementioned legislation and other interference from SCAP, Japan's direction can legitimately be described as having been set by the United States, SCAP, and General Douglas MacArthur (International Encyclopedia 67).

Some of the best insights to this period come from Alfred Oppler, a German jurist who emigrated to the United States to escape Hitler's anti-Semitic terrorism. Oppler was raised a Protestant, but was of Jewish ancestry and had been "deprived piecemeal of citizenship and all other rights, and finally reduced to the status of a dehumanized outcast" (Oppler 7). Assigned to the Government Section (GS) of SCAP he wrote:

> It so happened that my start in Government Section coincided with the most dramatic period of that institution when its members had just completed in strict seclusion and secrecy, the draft of a revised Japanese constitution after it had become evident that the Japanese government needed guidance and assistance to produce a document that would embody the essentials of democratic government... I made a few suggestions and offered some criticism, but that was my only contribution to the remarkable instrument of guidance that was adopted by the Japanese government, initiated as constitutional amendment by the Emperor, with few changes enacted by the Diet (the Japanese Parliament), and promulgated on November 3, 1946. It has survived until the present day. Not one change has been made, in spite of the criticism that was imposed by the foreign victor and that its Jeffersonian language and its individualistic as well as egalitarian principles were alien to the tradition of Japan and the mainstream of popular Japanese attitudes. (Oppler 20)

4. The Ethical Question: The Intent

To the question we have posed, "Is it ethical for an occupying force to impose laws upon another country and culture?" we might consider the ethics of SCAP's policies from both the point of view of intent and of results. Oppler writes of SCAP:

> ...its members' motivations for serving in Japan, as well as their attitudes toward the Japanese people varied considerably. In none have I discovered hatred, but with respect to the presence or absence of feelings of superiority or compassion there was a great deal of difference. Still, I would say that we had in common a belief in democratic institutions, interpreted within a wide range from strongly liberal to a cautiously conservative viewpoint, and in the possibility of influencing an alien and completely different civilization. There also was in some of us a good portion of idealism, a term I do not use in the meaning of aloofness from reality. (Oppler 33)

Clearly, the labor laws imposed by SCAP were well within the goals expressed in the Potsdam Declaration to "remove all obstacles to the revival and strengthening of democratic tendencies among the Japanese People" (O'Neill 376). The Potsdam Declaration of 26 July 1945, which was agreed to unconditionally as part of the Japanese surrender, specifically stated:

> Article 10–We do not intend that the Japanese shall be enslaved as a race or destroyed as a nation...The Japanese government shall remove all obstacles to the revival and strengthening of democratic tendencies among the Japanese people. Freedom of speech, of religion, and of thought, as well as respect for the fundamental human rights shall be established.
> Article 12–The occupying forces of the Allies shall be withdrawn from Japan as soon as these objectives have been accomplished.... (Ayusawa 235)

The Potsdam Declaration had a motive or objective to reform Japan and transform her into a democratic nation (Ayusawa 236).

MacArthur's policies were guided by the Potsdam Declaration and "The United States Initial Post-Surrender Policy for Japan" of 29 August 1945. This policy came to occupy the major attention of the occupying forces: that was, a program of political and economic reformation of Japan based on democratic principles (Ayusawa 240).

As to MacArthur's personal intent, Oppler repeats MacArthur's own words:

> ... the entire human race, irrespective of geographical limitations or cultural tradition is capable of absorbing, cherishing and defending liberty, tolerance, and justice and will find maximum strength when so blessed.
> The same announcement made it clear that the pattern of his course in the occupation of Japan lay deeply rooted in American history and that he had:
>
> merely sought to draw therefrom the political, economic, and social concepts which throughout our own past have worked and provided the American people with a spiritual and material strength never before equalled in human history.

This was the spirit in which the Supreme Commander interpreted his mission (Oppler 35).

Both laws sought to protect the rights of all parties involved in labor disputes and create a balance between employer and employee in collective bargaining negotiations; both laws promoted a more democratic method of solving labor disputes. Insofar as the new labor laws as well as the new constitution's provisions for workers' rights fit a broadly accepted concept of fairness and equality under law, the imposition of such laws can well be accepted as "ethical."

As to MacArthur's goal of checking radicalism among the unions and "kicking out the communists," it too fits the overall goal of instilling a sense of democratic values in the people of Japan, who were to live under a new system. Under Part IV, Economic Section 2: Promotion of Democratic Forces, it states, "...it shall be the policy of the Supreme Commander: (a)

To prohibit the retention in or selection for places of importance in the economic field of individuals who do not direct future Japanese economic effort solely towards peaceful ends" (Ayusawa 241). By 1947 the world had witnessed thirty years of communist rule in the Soviet Union and was well aware that any idealistic notions of a "people's democracy" under communist rule were not realistic. Knowing the staunch anti-communist position of the United States it was totally unrealistic to expect that SCAP would allow a radical communist element to control industrial unions in occupied Japan; too much radicalism in Japan did not fit the well orchestrated, well-defined goal of the United States for postwar Japan that was to be reconstructed as a stable, economically productive democracy (O'Neill 377).

Another reason MacArthur chose to ban the general strike of 1947 and insist on less disruptive means of settling labor disputes was financial. Japan was incapable of self-support and relied heavily on the United States for food and other aid. A general strike would have added to an already significant financial burden placed on SCAP (O'Neill 377). In this light, prevention of a general strike to reduce the misery already being shouldered by the Japanese people was not unethical, nor was it unethical for SCAP to impose its will for the purpose of facilitating an orderly rebuilding of the Japanese economy.

It appears, therefore, that neither the laws themselves nor the intent behind their imposition were unethical. The problem still remains, however, as to whether a set of laws which had evolved over two hundred years and which reflected and crystallized the ethical values of one people can serve as binding rules of conduct for people of a very different culture.

5. The Ethical Question: The Results

A second method of answering this complex question is to study current literature written by Japanese scholars in an attempt to determine their feelings about such an imposition of foreign ethics on their legal system. One might expect some indication of resentment or even a ground swell for change given the passage of close to fifty years since the initial labor laws and the constitution were passed. In fact, our study did not reveal any such resentment. One author states simply, "I received a humanistic and cosmoplitan education directed by the American occupational policy which tried to liberate many people from the militaristic and feudalistic systems which existed in Japan at that time" (Kuwahara 244). The author continues, "Japan public labor relations law was fundamentally transferred from American statutes during the occupation period. Even today it seems to me that it is in part affected by American trends in court decisions and arguments in the field of collective actions including strikes" (Kuwahara 244). Professor Kuwahara clearly accepts and applauds the role of SCAP and suggests that, even today, the U. S. continues to be a model for Japanese labor relations decisions.

Another author states simply, "Japan was fortunate that the Supreme Commander for the Allied Powers happened to be a man of high calibre...General MacArthur carried out his mission with dignity, authority, and high competence" (Ayusawa 237).

In a comprehensive, ten thousand word article on collective bargaining in Japan, Kiyohiko Hagizawa, Professor of Law at Seikei University, makes several references to the Japanese constitution and fifty-four specific references to labor laws in Japan. Not once does he mention the role played by SCAP or the United States in the development of those laws. The wording in his article is particularly interesting; for example he states, "Japan adopted collective bargaining, management consultation, and grievance machinery around 1947 as the forms of negotiation and the procedures to settle industrial disputes" (Hagizawa 280). In a separate statement Professor Hagizawa states, "Grievance machinery has been modeled after that of the United States" (Hagizawa 280). Of course it was modeled after procedures in the United States; it was essentially written by Americans. If one did not know that the Japanese Constitution and Japanese Labor Relations Laws were very much a product of SCAP, one would never glean that information from this article. There is absolutely no indication that Japan's labor laws and constitution were anything but the product of Japanese lawmakers. This unconditional acceptance suggests that, for at least one Japanese law professor, the ethics of the origin of such laws is not even an issue.

In another lengthly article Kazuo Sugero from the University of Tokyo and Kazutoshi Koshiro from Yokohama National University discuss the definition and scope of shop-floor disputes and the process for their resolution in Japan. Again, numerous references are made to the Trade Union Law and the Labor Standards Act without any indication that these laws are anything but wholly Japanese in origin and application. The only reference to the role played by SCAP is in a single paragraph dedicated to explaining the historical background of joint consultation schemes at the Yawhata Steel Mills as part of a case analysis. Here the authors write "... left-wing forces dominated the union leadership, and they conducted shop floor struggles against management...the communist elements were purged by the order of General MacArthur in 1950" (Sugero and Koshiro 158). There is no other reference to SCAP or the fact that grievance machinery as a method for settling shop floor disputes is anything other than a Japanese notion within the realm of Japanese law.

The context of these articles suggests that, for modern Japanese labor law scholars, the issue of the origin of Japanese labor law is moot. If there ever was a sense of dissatisfaction, it has been resolved and the only issues left include the successful resolution of specific disagreements between unions and employers. In other words, the "ethics" issue, if there ever was one, has either been resolved or is, at least, not a current topic of scholarly debate in Japan.

A third way to look at the issue is to examine how unions and management have fared under the set of laws imposed by SCAP. If unions are unfairly fettered or if managment is subjected to unusual levels of strike activity, it might be argued that the labor laws as applied to Japan created a situation of unfair imbalance and were defacto "unethical." While the issue may require a much larger study than this paper will attempt, several statistical comparisions suggest that labor laws have not created an imbalance in Japan and neither side has an unfair advantage in either the collective bargaining process or the grievance procedure.

For example, at the Yawhata Steel Mills, where MacArthur had ordered the purge of the communist union leaders, labor productivity as measured by ton of crude steel output per man per year increased by 950% between 1950 and 1985 (Sugero and Koshiro 160). Management was able to accomplish this increase with the cooperation of the enterprise union which approved an attrition policy and the transfer of some 7,000 workers to other plants over the years (Sugero and Koshiro 160). As a matter of fact, that type of joint consultation has almost completely replaced the shop floor struggles favored by the communist unions of the 1940s (Sugero and Koshiro 153). Management has little to complain about in regard to strike activity as the result of labor disputes. Between 1965 and 1975, for example, Japanese industries lost an average of 1.53 working days per 10 employees per year due to strike activity, and the average duration of days of a strike was 2.74 days. In comparison, working days lost in the United States during that period of time were at an average of 5.71 and in the United Kingdom, 4.19. In addition, the average duration of a strike in the United States was 16.48 days and in the United Kingdom, 6.58 days (International Encyclopedia 238).

It should be pointed out, however, that while strikes are short in duration, their frequency of occurrence is higher than in most European countries except Italy (Int. Encycl. 235). Many strikes are only for an hour or two and are designed to attract the employer's attention and to serve as a demonstration of feelings rather than a weapon to press management after negotiations have failed (Int. Encycl. 235). The fact is that labor unions have many ways to express dissatisfaction without resorting to long term strikes; but, true to the image of Japanese behavior, of the 1,113 labor disputes adjusted by Labor Relations Commissions in 1983, 95.4 per cent were handled by conciliation, 3.9 per cent by mediation and only .7 per cent by arbitration (Sugero and Koshiro 151). These authors further conclude that "in Japanese industrial relations, the parties exert their major efforts to prevent the dispute from occurring rather than to resolve in an orderly way disputes which have already occurred" (Sugero and Koshiro 153). At least in the eyes of professors of labor relations law in Japan, there is little to suggest that either unions or management feel unfairly or "unethically" treated by labor law in Japan.

6. Summary

Labor relations laws evolved over a two hundred year period in the United States from the Conspiracy Doctrine of colonial times to the combined Wagner and Taft-Hartley Acts, under which the process of collective bargaining between unions and industrial management is carried out today.

In Japan, labor laws almost identical to the Wagner Act were imposed on the Japanese people by the Supreme Commander of the Allied Powers. With minor amendments those laws guide Japanese labor relations to this day.

This chapter served not only to compare the labor laws of the United States and Japan, but also to pose the question: "Is it ethical to impose the laws which reflect the values of one culture upon the people of a country whose history and ideals are vastly different?" This question, as with any question addressing the ethical implications of a nation's actions (such as those of the United States), grows more complex when examined in a broader context. For instance, we believe that, in order to determine the ethicality of the United States's actions, it is necessary to focus on the intent of this action. However, the question remains: "Can or should a nation have the power to force its laws and values on another nation even if its intentions are benevolent?" Is it then reasonable to assume that, if a nation has a system of laws that it perceives will benefit other nations, can it simply impose its system on others without question? Where, then, is the line drawn as to whether a nation should or should not intervene in the evolution of another nation's culture, and, if so, what would determine the basis of such power? Clearly, this is a complex issue which offers no simple, clearly defined answers.

An issue of this nature also prompts the need for a distinction between ethics and legality, as it is possible for an action to be deemed ethical, yet found illegal within the confines of the law. International law plays a vital role in this case, as nations are no longer accountable to just their own domestic law but to global laws which are attempting to shape and govern relations of all nations. As modern international law expands in its scope and purpose, the issue of one nation dictating the laws of another becomes a question of legality as well as morality.

In trying to evaluate the actions of the United States within this broad scope, we made a determination with regard to circumstances, intent and consequences. Was it ethical for the United States to impose its laws on the Japanese people? The answer is "a qualified yes!" Yes, since, in this case, the laws themselves are just and promote fairness and democracy. Yes, because they were imposed for legitimate economic and humane reasons. And yes, if, in fact, activity within the law provides for justice and balance and economic benefit for all parties which come under the law. The United States believed that it could successfully implement its own system in Japan, a nation crippled by war, with the intention to resuscitate its people, its economy and its structure–both physical and cultural–in order to expand and strengthen democracy.[1]

Note

1. The authors of this chapter extend their thanks to Professor Una Shih for her assistance in providing resource materials. We also wish to recognize Mrs. Patricia Horton for her editorial assistance and manuscript preparation. Thirdly, we thank Mrs. Virginia Fastje for her assistance in manuscript preparation.

References

Ayusawa, Iwao F. A History of Labor in Modern Japan. Honolulu:East-West Center Press, 1966.

Cook, Alice H. Japanese Trade Unionism. New York: Harry Hoffman & Sons: 1966.

Hagizawa, Kiyokiko. "Procedures and Structures of Collective Bargaining at the Enterprise and Plant Levels in Japan." Comparative Labor Law Journal, 7, 1985-86, pp. 177-308.

International Encyclopedia for Labor Law and Industrial Relations. Vol. 7, 12.

Kelly, Matthew A. Labor and Industrial Relations: Terms, Laws, Court Decisions, and Arbitration Standards. Baltimore, 1987.

Kodansha Encyclopedia of Japan. Vol. 4, 1983.

Kuwahara, Masahiro. "Comparing American with Japanese Labor Law." Comparative Labor Law Journal.

McPherson, James M. Battle Cry of Freedom: The Civil War Era. New York:Ballantine Books, 1988.

Moore, Joe. Japanese Workers and the Struggle for Power 1945-1947. Madison: The University of Wisconsin Press. 1983.

O'Neill, Kathleen B. "Industrial Relations in Korea: Will Korea Become Another Japan." Comparative Labor Law Journal, 12, 1991, pp. 360-384.

Oppler, Alfred C. Legal Reform in Occupied Japan. Princeton: Princeton University Press, 1976.

Shirai, Taishiro, ed. "Japanese Labor Unions and Politics." Contemporary Industrial Relations in Japan. Madison: University of Wisconsin Press, 1983.

Sugero, Kazuo and Koshiro, Kazutoshi. "Japan." Comparative Labor Law Journal, 9, (1987-88), pp. 129-163.

Chapter Eleven

CORPORATE CONCERN FOR NON-EMPLOYEES: AN ETHICALLY CORRECT LABOR POLICY FOR MIGRANT WORKERS

Robert Strittmatter

1. Introduction

The relationship between employer and employee begins when one person undertakes to perform services or do work under the direction and control of another (Anderson, 1990, pp. 820-21). This relationship is created with the consent of both parties and is generally regarded as forming a contract between them. Historically wages constituted the sole reward of labor but today additional benefits are usually granted employees by virtue of an employment contract or as mandated by statutory provision. The legal and moral responsibilities of employers to pay just wages and provide reasonable benefits and safe working conditions are usually defined in relation to those employed. But are there any situations where businesses, especially large national and multinational corporations, have a responsibility for those who are not employees in the usual sense and may be far removed from corporate oversight? Is there a moral dimension to this question even though no legal responsibility exists? The legal counsel for an American jeans maker acknowledged such when responding last year to a government inquiry into his company's possible violation of labor laws (Silverstein, 1992). This chapter will examine and present a specific basis for this moral dimension as it relates to a particular group of non-employee workers whose efforts are essential to production of the end products of some of the world's largest corporations. These workers, both as individuals and within groups, have encountered adverse conditions and abusive situations for many years and in many lands. These workers have long been the subject of story and song–they are the migrants who harvest our crops and produce our industrial products.

The following sections of this chapter will present information about migrant workers in both America and Europe: their history, identity and work; illustrations of the many difficulties they continue to encounter; a review of efforts to provide assistance and protection for them. The final section focuses on the unique nature of migrancy in America with the proposition that the responsibility to formulate and implement an ethically correct labor policy for migrants, both from a practical and moral viewpoint, is that of the large American corporations that benefit from their labor.

2. Identity and Demography of Migrants in America and Europe

In his recent book *American Agricultural,* economist Philip Martin has identified migrant farmworkers as crews of 20 to 30 immigrant men assembled and transported from farm to farm; as the stereotypical migrant families, memorialized in John Steinbeck's *The Grapes of Wrath*, who follow ripening crops from south to north, and as the lesser known but more skilled and better-paid workers who operate equipment and apply agricultural chemicals (Martin, 1988, pp. 1-2). Migrant farmworkers are not easily identified, counted, and classified since stereotypical descriptions and technical definitions are often contradictory and exclusionary. American government and academic research efforts produce varying data about the demographics, numbers, locations and activities of American's migrants.

Definitional and descriptive efforts to identify migrant farmworkers must begin with determination of what constitutes a farm and a farm worker (Martin, 1988, p. 9). Migrants are a subset of farm workers. Most of the farm work in the U.S. is done by farm operators and their families. The Census of Agriculture (COA) describes a farm as any place which sold or normally sells $1,000 of farm products during the year. Farm employers are classified as crop farms, livestock ranches, and agricultural service firms. The COA includes a variety of employment and wage data from crop farms but there is much less data from agricultural service firms which include farm labor contractors and processors and packagers of farm commodities. The latter employ migrant-type workers and it is estimated that all agricultural service firms employ perhaps half of all migrant farm workers (Martin, 1988, p. 12).

Farm workers must cross regional boundaries to be considered migrants, but which boundaries? How far must they travel? What portion of their earnings must come from migratory farm work? The U.S. Department of Agriculture has developed an approach to analyze farm worker data but alternative approaches have been developed by migrant assistance programs (Martin, 1988, p. 5). Differences in definitions and ambiguity in terms mean there is no straightforward or exacting way to accurately enumerate or describe migrant agricultural workers. Many studies of migrants have derived information by stating an exclusive definition and then proceeding to adjust available statistical and descriptive data to estimate the number and characteristics of migrants.

Concentration is a distinguishing characteristic of American agriculture: the largest 10 percent of all farms produce about two-thirds of all farm products. Farm employment is similarly concentrated: by size on large farms, by commodity on fruit and vegetable farms, and by geography in California and Florida. By deduction migrant farm workers may be similarly concentrated (Martin, 1988, p. 14). What is continually debatable is the exact number of migrants living and working in each state. Martin in his book *Harvest of Confusion* describes a number of specific approaches used in migrant studies to estimate the distribution of migrants (Martin, 1988, pp. 14-18). A reasonably credible approach to count and distribute migrants is based on a top-down methodology using a two-part formula which tracks workers using unemployment insurance definitions and data to estimate the number of migrants and then distributes migrants across states using state-by-state labor expenditure and other data. Analyzing data thus derived which is based on a definition of a migrant as a person with at least one farm job outside the county in which he or she had their maximum earnings from all farm and non-farm jobs, the following results are available for 1982: California has 23 percent of migrant activity, Florida 10 percent, Washington and Texas 5 percent each, with California's share implying that there are 1 million migrant agricultural workers in the U.S. (Martin, 1988, pp. 99-109).

Recent information on the characteristics and work patterns of U.S. workers performing seasonal agricultural services (SAS) during the period 1 October 1989 through 30 September 1990 is obtained from the National Agricultural Workers Survey (NAWS) (Mines, 1990). The Secretaries of Agriculture and Labor are charged with determining if there is a shortage of SAS workers; this requirement exists as a provision of the Immigration Reform and Control Act of 1986. The NAWS of 1990 was conducted to collect comprehensive job history information on SAS workers and is based on 2,115 interviews of randomly selected SAS workers in various regions and at various times during the year. NAWS findings are reported in three sections covering characteristics of SAS workers, their patterns of employment, and regional differences among the workers and their work.

Significant findings include but are not limited to the following:

1. The SAS labor force includes mainly young workers, men, Hispanics, and immigrants;
2. Most SAS workers have low levels of education and do not read or speak English with Spanish being the primary language for two of three;
3. The majority are married and/or have children with two of five living away from their families while performing SAS work;
4. One-half of worker families have incomes below the poverty level despite the prevalence of families with two wage-earners;
5. Only one-fifth of SAS workers are recipients of needs-based social services;
6. Three-fourths work in fruits, nuts or vegetables with one-half engaged in harvesting, over three-fourths employed directly by the producer with farm labor contractors employing most of the remainder;
7. Most SAS jobs pay relatively low wages, have relatively few fringe benefits with less than one-half covered by unemployment insurance and less than one-fourth covered by health insurance;
8. Substandard working conditions such as lack of access to basic sanitary facilities continue to prevail in some farm work sectors;
9. The Southeast U.S. has the highest proportion of unauthorized workers and poor workers, the highest concentration of hand-harvesting jobs, and the highest concentration employed by farm labor contractors;

10. Employers in the Southeast rarely offer workers' compensation or unemployment insurance.

Migrants were not supposed to be a continuing part of America's family farm system which was expected to supply most of its own labor and capital. A distinct class of migrant farmworkers emerged in the 1850s when midwestern farmers began to specialize in wheat farming which required itinerant workers for harvesting. As these systems of large and specialized farms moved westward the need for migrant farmworkers increased. California farmers hired successive waves of immigrants from China, Japan, Mexico, and the Philippines. White Americans and European immigrants were also migrant farmworkers but most of them or their children escaped to other occupations. It should be noted though that the Great Depression of the 1930s forced many Americans to become migrants (Martin, 1988, pp. 4-5). Black Americans harvested sugar in the south in the 1930s and early 1940s until many moved north or entered World War II. Their places in the cane fields were taken by West Indians, most often from Jamaica (Wilkinson, 1989, p. 4). The U.S. government has supported programs to increase the number of migrants available for agricultural work. The bracero program began in 1942 and, lasting until 1964, authorized the importation of several hundred thousand Mexican workers into the farm labor market. The H-2 program begun in 1982 and the succeeding H-2A program of 1986 were enacted to bring foreigners to the United States to help plant and harvest apples, sugar cane and tobacco. Under this program sugar companies have brought in more than 8,000 cane cutters each year.

Various guestworker programs have been the basis for extensive worker migration in Europe since the end of World War II. In Britain during the late 1940s and early 1950s volunteer workers included many Indians, Pakistanis, and West Indians and others recruited from displaced persons camps in Germany. The Ministry of Labor admitted them into the UK on condition that they took the employment assigned them and did not change jobs without official permission. These workers could be directed by the government to what were considered essential industries. This program was similar to those developed in France and Germany. For the 35-year period ending in 1980, Europe has admitted for temporary employment more than 30 million workers outside permanent immigration channels (Martin, 1981). During this period France and Germany recruited about 70 percent of all guestworkers but their greatest impact was in Switzerland where in 1975 almost 35 percent of the workforce was foreign. As guestworker programs were being abandoned in the mid-1970s there were an estimated 6.5 million guestworkers in Europe with 1 million of them from Italy. Countries with the largest guestworker populations were Germany, 2.3 million; France, 1.9 million; and England, 775,000.

The energy crisis of 1973-74, related economic recession and various political and social factors were among the causes that turned the tide against immigrant workers in Europe. Even before this time several countries debated proposals to limit the number of foreign workers. Despite work permits limited to one year and attempts to rotate the foreign workforce many temporary workers became permanent residents. The menial jobs foreigners were imported to fill did not disappear and the activities of humanitarian religious groups added to pressures from labor-sending governments to extend civil and political rights to guestworkers. Also many guestworkers found employment in construction, mining and auto assembly, relatively well-paid unionized jobs shunned by some Europeans, although not by American workers (Martin, 1981). Guestworkers also found employment in fields as diverse as civil engineering and agriculture but large numbers were qualified only for service-type jobs in such places as hotels and restaurants.

In a sharp shift from the era beginning after World War II and ending in the 1970s, the industrialized countries of Europe, which had extensively recruited guestworkers to ease labor shortages and reduce wage and price pressures for competitive purposes, now changed course. Western Europe's economies were now slumping and unemployment among local workers was increasing (*U.S. News & World Report*, 1979). Millions of guestworkers headed home, some voluntarily but most encouraged or forced out by countries that once eagerly sought their services. Commonly held work permits were not renewed and workers were expelled from the host country but many governments offered monetary grants as incentives for workers to leave. Important to consider in the reverse migration of many guestworkers were the social and racial tensions between immigrants and native populations: Arabs were unwelcome in France, Turks in Germany, Africans in Italy, and West Indians in Britain.

Immigrants still play a vital role in western Europe's economies. In 1988, in France immigrants were 25 percent of the construction and public works labor force, 18 percent in service and commerce, 15 percent in mining and materials, and 13 percent in the auto industry (Parry, 1991). Many migrant workers in France are North Africans, reflecting the use by countries such as Britain, France, and Italy of labor from their former colonies. Imported labor also bolsters the Austrian and Swiss economies, and 4.5 million mostly Turkish, Yugoslav, and Bulgarian migrant workers work in engineering and the auto industry in Germany. The unification of Germany, however, has added 8.9 million eastern workers to the existing labor force of 28.8 million. As unemployment rises competition in certain industries is developing between east Germans now with full citizenship and immigrants. Mercedes-Benz employs more than 15,000 mainly Turkish and Yugoslav guestworkers within its German workforce of 170,000. The company provides pay and opportunity equal to its permanent workforce but many guestworkers have short-term employment contracts.

Trained east Europeans could replace some of the existing migrant workforce throughout western Europe both in professional positions such as engineering and teaching and in low-skill service jobs (Parry, 1991). Eastern European economies are collapsing as they adjust to the pressures of market forces and "economic migrants" are heading west. But western Europe is in recession and the social and racial tensions that erupted in the 1970s are catching fire again. Some immigrant welfare groups fear that the influx from the east has incited in employers a latent racial prejudice against minorities, even those with citizenship within the European Community.

Even as polls show that many Europeans believe there are too many immigrants in their countries and as right-wing extremists espouse anti-immigration rhetoric some economists are suggesting that Europe faces an acute shortage of certain kinds of workers (LaFranchi, 1991). An idea gaining increasing attention is a return to guestworker programs. Countries such as Austria, Belgium, and Spain face population declines and Italy's fertility rate of 1.7 is below the replacement level of 2.1 children per woman. France's population would be nearing decline if not for the high birth rate among its immigrants. Some of Europe's current labor needs are being filled by illegal immigrants and political refugees.

3. Continuing Adversity for Migrant Workers

In 1942 the U.S. Senate Committee on Education and Labor, popularly known as the LaFollette Committee, reviewed a wealth of materials on migrant farmworkers in California from the 1880s to the 1930s. The committee concluded that "the economic and social plight of California's agricultural labor is miserable beyond belief" due to low annual earnings, poor housing and lack of job security (Martin, 1988, p. 5). Much of the committee's criticism was directed against the organizations created by farmers, food processors and bankers "to preserve in themselves an unfettered control of labor and the labor market" (Martin, 1988, p. 6). Employer-oriented organizations were charged with encouraging an oversupply of workers to hold down wages, mounting campaigns to prevent workers from organizing unions, acting to exclude farmworkers from the protection of the National Labor Relations Act of 1935, and working with local law enforcement agencies to frustrate strikes and picketing activities.

The plight of migrants became a national concern during the 1960s. CBS television aired "Harvest of Shame," a striking exposé of migrant farmworker conditions (Martin, 1988, p. 7). The platforms of both the Democratic and Republican parties included statements on migrants and both houses of Congress created subcommittees on migratory labor. Federal assistance programs to benefit migrants were begun and as these programs continued into the 1970s the number of family migrants began to decrease, a tribute to the success of assistance programs giving migrants and their children the option of nonfarm jobs (Martin, 1988, p. 9). The plight of migrants became a lower profile issue in the 1980s. Despite previous recurrent and sympathetic attention migrant farmworkers in America still seem invisible to us, they continue to remain ciphers, generic "stoop labor," fruit tramps as they often refer to themselves, with their existence assumed but unquestioned (Emmet, 1989, p. xi).

In 1991 the U.S. House of Representatives Select Committee on Aging held its second hearing on the conditions of migrant and seasonal workers in the U.S. The hearing focused on the lack of federal protection and oversight regarding the working conditions of this population; a lack of leadership and action on the part of Congress was also mentioned (Select Committee on Aging, 1991). The hearing included testimony from a General Accounting Office (GAO) director citing an investigation indicating that federal laws and regulations provide less protection to farmworkers exposed to pesticides while allowing children to work at a younger age in agriculture than in other industries. In addition the GAO investigation documented additional findings: federal agencies responsible for regulating pesticide use and field sanitation could better enforce applicable laws and regulations, existing barriers to farm workers' access to the Medicaid and Social Security programs could be reduced, and reliable and comprehensive data on farm workers could be compiled to determine the best course of action to improve their quality of life. An appendix to the select committee's hearing report prepared as testimony by the Association of Farm Worker Opportunity Programs referred to a recent *Washington Post* survey citing migrant farmwork as "the worst job in America."

So much more than the above can be explored to document the changing and continuing plight of America's migrants. The harvesting by hand of sugar cane in southern Florida is performed by men from the West Indies, primarily from Jamaica, who live in camps and barracks on sugar plantations and are paid using a piece-rate calculation assuming each will cut at least a ton of cane an hour. They are the largest group of foreign workers admitted each year to the U.S. (Wilkinson, 1989, p. 3). Their quarters are cheerless and lack privacy, they are often cheated by their employers and they are tormented by separation from family and friends. In the fields they wear aluminum guards on their hands and legs, heavy boots on their feet. They are cut by their own or another's knife, they are bitten by fire ants, or have their eyes pierced by sharp cane leaf (Wilkinson, 1989, p. 4).

Looking toward California the Salinas Valley has changed little since John Steinbeck's day. California continues to rely on migrant labor from Mexico and today many are illegal. Some migrants live in shacks in labor camps but such housing is becoming increasingly expensive and scarce with only 7 percent of workers housed by their employers.

Tighter regulations have persuaded growers to shift employee responsibilities to farm labor contractors to avoid administrative requirements and legal liability (*Economist*, 1993). By 1992 contractors employed over half the migrant workforce with some contractors reportedly enhancing their profits by deducting charges for items such as drinking water from workers' wages. But the increasingly competitive labor market is providing an incentive for more growers to change to labor-intensive crops such as strawberries. Even in parts of the Silicon Valley the same kind of migrant workforce that picks strawberries can be found assembling computer circuit-boards. While many migrant workers in America live in an environment of impoverishment and neglect, Europe's migrants exist amid fear and uncertainty. Economic recession, the availability of thousands of skilled and willing workers from eastern Europe, and the ability of employers and governments to terminate work and immigration agreements have created great doubt among migrants and their families about their future in host countries. But fears for the safety of their lives and property have dominated the thoughts of immigrants in recent months. The neo-Nazi firebombing in November near Hamburg, Germany, which killed a longtime Turkish resident of Germany, her granddaughter, and another girl was the deadliest assault to date in the current wave of right-wing violence and the first attack directed against Turks who have lived most or all of their lives in Germany (Fisher, 1993). Although never assimilating totally into German society and remaining guestworkers rather than citizens, many Turks had come to believe that they were at least tolerated.

The resentment against immigrants predates recent incidents. In the 1980s racial and social unrest erupted in violent clashes in Britain between whites and Asians and West Indians (*U.S. News & World Report*, 1982). Many migrants with low-paying jobs were not able to afford houses in towns and suburbs, living in older inner-city ghetto areas such as London's Brixton and Berlin's Kreunberg and facing increasing resentment from remaining natives. Laws banning outright discrimination were enacted but racial incidents involving stone throwing, slashing of auto tires and shouted insults continued to increase. Poor housing, inadequate education, and social ostracism remain common complaints among guestworkers. Many still find themselves regarded as troublemakers and undesirables, but more importantly, as competitors for hard-to-find jobs in difficult economic times.

4. Assistance for Migrants in America and Europe

Efforts to improve the status of migrants have evolved from many and varied sources: from the work of charitable, education, health, and religious organizations; through the advocacy of labor organizers and legal-aid lawyers; from government in the form of assistance programs, investigative hearings and protective legislation; and through the cooperation and contributions of many businesses, large and small.

In 1989 the Catholic archbishop of Venice, Florida, John Nevins, a graduate of Iona College, requested assistance for Hispanic migrants in his diocese from the Congregation of Christian Brothers at Iona. Two brothers, later joined by others, established a small community in Bonita Springs. The brothers began by teaching English and civics to native Spanish-speaking migrants as a means of helping them and their families survive amid many difficulties (Becker, 1990). The members of Los Hermanos, now including student and adult volunteers, expanded their efforts and conduct a variety of outreach programs: english tutoring, immigration counseling, home health care visits, housing renovation, food and clothing distribution, Bible study and choir. The efforts of the brothers have been directed toward education which is their primary focus but they also emphasize their availability to address the personal concerns of the people they serve. Los Hermanos has created a far-reaching awareness of the needs of the poor and the level of assistance and involvement of the native people of the surrounding area has increased dramatically.

The most famous labor advocate for the cause of migrant farm workers in the U.S. was Cesar Chavez. His recent death on 29 April 1993 provokes a recall of the efforts and successes he guided as organizer of the United Farm Workers of America. Chavez and his family were migrant farmworkers and though he was not highly educated he was deeply influenced by Catholic social teaching and the growing knowledge that California's huge farming businesses were exploiting their migrant workers (Filteau, 1993). Chavez's union called a strike against table grape growers in the San Joaquin Valley of California in 1965. The union achieved some initial successes but its existence since has been marked by additional progress mixed with internal strife, disputes with other unions and the effects of mechanization in agriculture and depressed produce prices. Cesar Chavez came to personify not only the union he founded but the farmworker rights movement itself.

Legislative efforts of the federal government to protect migrant farmworkers are embodied in the Migrant and Seasonal Agricultural Worker Protection Act passed in 1983 and amended in 1986. The law provides for registration of farm labor contractors with specific protections for migrant and seasonal agricultural workers in the following areas: information and recordkeeping; wages, supplies and other working conditions; health and safety of housing; and safety of motor vehicles. Additional sections of the law include administrative regulations and enforcement provisions. Departments and agencies of the federal government have numerous programs that provide services to migrant farmworkers and their families. The Office of Migrant Education of the U.S. Department of Education has published the Directory of Services for Migrant and Seasonal Farmworkers and Their Families. The directory is designed to improve the coordination efforts of the agencies providing these services and promote a greater knowledge of the breadth and scope of the national migrant effort (Office of Migrant Education, 1992).

In Germany, after the tragic deaths of three Turkish residents mentioned earlier, efforts to express concern for and assist immigrants were initiated. Germans shocked by the mounting violence sought ways to show that right-wing extremists are a distinct minority (Fisher, 1992). A committee of emergency-care physicians announced it will form a group to rebuild the houses of homeless Turkish-Germans in the area. In Bonn the parliament stood in silent memorial to the victims of the bombing and issued a statement expressing shame and rage over the height of violence. The German subsidiary of General Motors, Adam Opel which employs thousands of Turkish workers, offered a reward for the arrest and conviction of those responsible for the bombing.

Title III, "Free movement of persons, services and capital," of the treaty establishing the European Economic Community (EEC) signed in Rome on 25 March 1957, provides for freedom of movement for workers within the Community. Such freedom shall entail the abolition of discrimination based on nationality between workers of the member states and the rights to accept offers of employment, move freely within the territory of member states, stay for the purpose of employment and remain after having been employed. Article 49 of Title III directs the Council of the EEC to issue directives or make regulations setting the measures required to bring about progressively the freedom of movement previously defined. Article 51 includes a reference to migrant workers in directing the EEC Council to adopt measures to secure for migrants and their dependents the aggregation and payment of social security benefits (Treaties Establishing the European Communities, 1987, pp. 167-69). Specific rights granted by Title III, however, may be subject to limitations justified on grounds of public policy, health or security. At a meeting of the European Council in Strasbourg, in December 1989, the heads of state of the European Community member states adopted the Community Charter of Fundamental Social Rights of Workers. The document was intended to be a statement of progress in the field and a preparation for new advances. The document specified among the fundamental rights of workers the rights to freedom of movement and social protection previously established by treaty. Thus, the European Community and its member states have acted to establish the rights of all workers including migrants.

In 1968, Auburndale in central Florida was the headquarters of Coca-Cola's Minute Maid operation. The existing conditions were typical of those which many migrant farm workers had to endure. In succeeding years dramatic change was to occur, approved and sponsored by the parent company. The improvements that developed were the result of a unique partnership which included Coca-Cola, management consultants from the SRI-Human Resources Institute, and the migrant workers themselves (Harris, 1978, pp. xii-xvi). An important element in the plan for improvement was worker involvement. The goal was to alter and enrich the quality of life for the workers and their families and the results achieved were evidenced by the beginning of a child development program, the opening of a health center and a library, construction of low-income housing, and most notably, a decrease in migrancy with many workers becoming regular employees with seniority rights and fringe benefits. Executives, managers, and employees of the Coca-Cola Company who committed to and worked for the improvements that occurred exhibited the highest levels of corporate awareness and concern.

A unique relationship has developed among the H.J. Heinz Company, its cucumber growers in northwestern Ohio and the Farm Labor Organizing Committee, a union representing migrant farmworkers in the area (Select

Committee on Aging, 1991). As a result of research and negotiation the three parties agreed to measures to ensure the future of the local cucumber industry, thus preserving jobs for the migrants while at the same time working for improvements in migrants' housing, health care, education, pesticide protection and worker status. The long-standing practice in Ohio of considering migrant farmworkers independent contractors, making them ineligible for workers' compensation and unemployment insurance and requiring them to bear the full cost of social security payments, will be changed. They will become employees of the cucumber growers, thus enjoying the benefits of employee status.

Every business developing a concern for migrant workers is not a multinational like Coca-Cola or H. J. Heinz. In Florida, A. Duda & Sons, a major producer of fruits and vegetables, is one of an increasing number of growers that is taking its investment in migrant workers seriously and reporting surprising benefits (Stuart, 1992). As early as 1960 Duda began providing housing for some of its migrant workers; in 1991 the company spent more than $1,000,000 to expand its existing housing in La Belle. The company works with several federally funded providers of day care to furnish this benefit to the children of its workers; it hires no one younger than 18 years of age and encourages its workers to complete their education. Lack of education is believed to be the most serious problem for migrant workers and their families. Duda also provides eligible employees with vacation pay, paid holidays, basic group medical coverage, and vesting in a retirement plan. In addition the company seeks off-season employment opportunities for its workers with other reputable growers. The benefits of these initiatives to Duda include the following: using the same migrant workers each season reduces recruitment and training costs, increases productivity, and requires less supervision; trained workers are involved in fewer accidents especially those involving misuse of pesticides; the work force has become dependable and quality-minded. Progressive growers like Duda have been sharing their knowledge and experience with one another, and combined with a new generation of educated and concerned managers, these efforts will move the industry to a greater level of awareness and accomplishment on behalf of America's migrants.

5. Corporate Responsibility for America's Migrant Workers

The existence of migrants' living and working conditions in America can be attributed to many factors: general apathy among the public, ineffective writing and enforcement of protective legislation, the unscrupulous and often illegal activity of farm labor contractors, the lack of concern and resources of small farmers and growers, and the indifferent and sometimes confrontational attitudes of large businesses. Some of these factors are illustrated by the continuing plight of Florida's West Indian sugar cane cutters. Brought to the U.S. under the controversial H-2 and H-2A programs, these men and their public-interest attorneys have been pursuing continuous litigation in an attempt to force Florida's sugar companies to correct abuses, many relating to failures to pay the migrants the wages promised (Resnick, 1991). But attorneys from Florida Rural Legal Services can claim only limited success citing use of high-priced defense attorneys by the sugar industry, lax enforcement policies of the U.S. Department of Labor and reluctance of West Indian governments to disrupt the flow of money workers send home. Florida sugar companies such as Okeelanta and U.S. Sugar maintain that they follow the law and pay the wages required, and wary of continuing and costly litigation are moving toward mechanical harvesting. In 1983 the Subcommittee on Labor Standards, part of the House of Representatives Committee on Education and Labor, conducted an investigation of domestic workers in the Florida sugar cane industry and presented the following among its findings: piece-rate productivity standards used by the industry are unreasonable; there is a preference for foreign workers who can be summarily dismissed, blacklisted, and sent home; the H-2 program by providing an endless supply of West Indian cutters protects the industry from labor competition which might cause it to raise wages, improve working conditions, and adopt attainable standards of production. The subcommittee viewed the H-2 program as a subsidy of considerable magnitude to the industry (Wilkinson, 1989, pp. 241-43). In addition to the cost subsidy accruing to sugar growers because of the H-2 program, the price they receive for their sugar is protected by import quotas, denying access to the American market to growers from the Caribbean, Central America, and the Philippines.

A frequently abusive situation is the use of independent farm labor contractors, sometimes called crew leaders or crew chiefs, to supply seasonal workers. This practice has tended to relieve growers of responsibility for the welfare of people working in their fields. The contractors recruit, hire, transport, and supervise farm laborers for growers. Many of the most publicized and flagrant abuses of migrant farmworkers have been attributed to farm labor contractors who have gone to great lengths to avoid compliance with laws and regulations and line their own pockets at the expense of victimized farmworkers. Enforcement of the Migrant and Seasonal Agricultural Worker Protection Act is the responsibility of the Department of Labor, but its enforcement efforts are largely ineffectual (Stuart, 1992).

An additional difficulty rests with the laws and regulations designed to protect migrant farm workers. These laws regulate housing, minimum wage, and health and environmental standards, but they have done little to raise migrant farmworkers from poverty or alleviate poor working and living conditions (Grace, 1992). Testimony before the U.S. Commission on Security and Cooperation in Europe indicated that only one-third of all farm workers are covered by federal minimum wage and child labor laws with none entitled to overtime pay; 80 percent are exempt from requirements for field toilets and drinking water. Exemptions are often based on size of work crews and number of hours worked. A review of Section 4 of the Migrant and Seasonal Agricultural Worker Protection Act provides numerous exemptions from act requirements such as those for farm labor contractors in the employ of family businesses or agricultural associations.

Migrants, farm workers primarily and others, are voiceless victims of injustice. Who should step forward and accept the immediate and final responsibility for providing education for them, improving their living and working conditions, and establishing their dignity as human beings? It will not be small and midsize farmers and growers. These businesses do not have the financial resources to provide necessary housing for the large numbers of migrants with their families who plant and harvest for a few weeks or months and then move on. This process is the reality of single-crop farming and migrancy itself. It may be unrealistic to ask small businesses to provide that which is beyond their means and greater than required by law. Can labor unions and legal-aid associations help? Yes, but these advocates of migrant worker causes often encounter public apathy and corporate opposition and the success they have achieved has been gradual and inconsistent. Charitable, public service, and religious organizations have limited financial resources and innumerable worthy causes toward which they must direct their efforts. Federal, state, and local governments have passed laws, crafted regulations, collected data, sent investigators, held hearings, written reports, assessed penalties, developed programs, appointed coordinators, and provided services---all on behalf of migrant workers. Government has helped, but with less than total effectiveness and maximum efficiency.

Almost one year ago the U.S. Department of Labor and jeansmaker *Guess?*, Inc. reached a landmark agreement to eliminate possible violations of the Fair Labor Standards Act by the company's estimated 100 contractors in southern California (Silverstein, 1992). This marks the first time a major manufacturer will be held directly responsible for the wages and working conditions under which its brand-name products are made, in spite of the fact that the garments were sewn by independent contractors, not employees. The agreement with the government is intended to force the small sweatshops and other contractors sewing for *Guess?* to pay minimum wages and overtime and to stop using child labor. Under the agreement *Guess?* will regularly inspect its contractors' workshops, review their payroll records and interview employees to ensure there have been no labor law violations. In addition *Guess?* pledged to compensate workers who in the future may be illegally underpaid by contractors. In the past federal and state labor officials had been frustrated in efforts to curb sweatshop abuses by the elusive nature of the apparel manufacturing business. Stanley Levy, general counsel for *Guess?*, acknowledged that the government had approached the company about possible labor law violations but the company responded by developing a voluntary compliance program more extensive than any measures the government could have imposed. Quoting Mr. Levy: "We have no legal responsibility toward these employees; these are employees of independent contractors. But we believe we have a moral responsibility, a social responsibility...we were interested in coming forward to do what responsible corporate America is supposed to do."

The comparisons to be made between the situation just described and the relationship between migrant farmworkers and giant American food processors and marketers is interesting. Most migrants work as independent contractors or transient employees of farmers and growers and are not eligible for the wages, benefits, assistance and protection provided by business and government for full-time employees. The labor of migrants is essential since it provides the raw agricultural products which will be processed into the end products sold by many of America's well-known corporate enterprises–*Campbell's Tomato Soup, Heinz' Pickles, Tropicana Orange Juice*. These companies have no legal responsibility for migrant farm workers and their families. But Mr. Levy of *Guess?* Jeans mentions a moral responsibility although he does not elaborate further. What may serve as a source and inspiration for this responsibility?

> Work is a good thing for man–a good thing for his humanity–because through work man *not only transforms nature*, adapting it to his own needs, but he also *achieves fulfillment* as a human being and indeed, in a sense, becomes more a human being....However true it may be that man is destined for work and called to it, in the first place work is "for man" and not man "for work."...In the final analysis it is always man who is *the purpose of the work,* whatever work it is that is done by man–even if the common scale of values rates it as the merest "service," as the most monotonous, even the most alienating work. (John Paul II, 1981, pp. 17, 23)

The words of Pope John Paul II from his encyclical letter *On Human Work* form a moral basis for the extraordinary commitment needed to help migrant workers and their families achieve fulfillment as human beings through the dignity of their work. Man/woman is to be seen primarily as the subject of work, not as a mere object or solely as an instrument of production. As a person in the image of God, man/woman is a subjective being, capable of planned and rational action and capable of deciding about himself/herself with a tendency to self-realization. As a person who works, man/woman performs various work actions which must all serve to help him/her realize his/her humanity. The ethical nature of work is thereby conditioned by its subjective dimension, a realization that the one who works is a person.

In work man/woman should not experience a lowering of his/her dignity, and his/her rights as a worker, corresponding to his/her moral obligation as a worker, must be respected. This is first seen in the context of the relationship between the worker and the employer, direct or indirect (John Paul II, 1981, p. 40). The direct employer is the person or institution with whom the worker enters directly into a work contract. For migrant farm workers the direct employer may be a grower or farm labor contractor. The concept of indirect employer includes persons and institutions of various kinds and their labor contracts and principles of conduct, which determine the whole socioeconomic system or are its result. Indirect employer includes many elements and the responsibility differs from that of a direct employer but remains a true responsibility: the indirect employer substantially determines facets of a labor relationship thus conditioning the conduct of the direct employer. The encyclical states that the concept of indirect employer is applicable to every society and in the first place to the state. But try to apply the concept to the large companies who are the final beneficiaries of migrant farm workers' labor and it suits them. The socioeconomic system in which migrant farmworkers and their families find themselves has been determined by many indirect employers including America's largest corporations. These are the only organizations with the financial and managerial resources required to make the extraordinary commitment needed to help migrant workers. As the "indirect employers of last resort" these companies have a moral responsibility to reform the socioeconomic systems which they have helped to establish by developing an ethically correct labor policy for the migrant workers who contribute to their success.

References

Anderson, R., Fox, I. and D. Twomey, (1990). *Business Law and the Legal Environment,* 14th Ed. Cincinnati, Ohio: South-Western Publishing Company.

Becker, K. (1990). "Los Hermanos Brothers: A Source of Hope." *Fort Myers News-Press* (1 October), pp. 1-2, pt. E.

Economist. (1993). "Strawberries and Circuit Boards." (27 March), 30.

Emmet, H. (1989). *Fruit Tramps: A Family of Migrant Farmworkers*. Albuquerque: University of New Mexico Press.

Filteau, J. (1993). "Cesar Chavez: Farmworker's Leader Dies Unexpectedly at 66." *Catholic New York* (29 April), p. 37, col. 3.

Fisher, M. (1992). "Arson Attack Demoralizes Germany's Turks." *Washington Post* (25 November), Final edition, p. A11, col. 5.

Grace, S. (1992). "Laws to Aid Farmworkers Ineffective, U.S. Panel Told." *Los Angeles Times* (21 July), Home edition, p. 12, col. 2, pt. A.

Harris, S. and R. Allen. (1978). *The Quiet Revolution*. New York: Rawson Associates Publishers.

LaFranchi, Henri. (1991). "Europe's Demographics Signal New Need for Migrant Labor." *Christian Science Monitor* (7 August), Special report, p. 13, col. 2.

Martin, P. (1988). *Harvest of Confusion: Migrant Workers in U.S. Agriculture*. Boulder, Colo.: Westview Press.

Martin, P. (1981). "The European Guestworker Program and Why It Failed." *AFL-CIO American Federationist.* 88 (February), 4-5.

Mines, Robert. (1990). *Findings from the National Agricultural Workers Survey: A Demographic and Employment Profile of Perishable Crop Farm Workers*. Washington: U.S. Department of Labor, Office of Program Economics.

Office of Migrant Education, U.S. Department of Education. (1992). *Directory of Services for Migrant and Seasonal Farmworkers and Their Families*. (September), Washington.

Parry, J. (1991). "Paying Guests." *International Management*. 46 (February), 39-41.

Pope John Paul II. (1981). *On Human Work.* Boston: St. Paul Editions.

Resnick, R. (1991). "Raising Cane." *National Law Journal* (1 April), 24-28.

Select Committee on Aging, U.S. House of Representatives. (1991). *Farmworkers High Mortality: Government Neglect?* Hearing (17 July), Washington.

Silverstein, S. and S. Efron. (1992). "*Guess?* Accepts Pact to Curb Labor Violations." *Los Angeles Times* (5 August), Home edition, p. 1, col. 2, pt. A.

Stuart, P. (1992). "A Better Future for Migrant Workers." *Personnel Journal*. 71 (December), 65-74.

Treaties Establishing the European Communities. (1987). Abridged edition. Luxembourg: Office of Official Publications of the European Communities.

U.S. News & World Report. (1982). "Europe's Growing Problem with Migrants." (15 February), 41-42.

U.S. News & World Report. (1979). Europe Turns Its Back on Migrant Workers." (29 October), 74-77.

Wilkinson, A. (1989). *Big Sugar: Seasons in the Cane Fields of Florida*. New York: Alfred A. Knopf.

Chapter Twelve

THE COOPERATIVE ASSOCIATION AND THE COMMUNITY OF WORK

Peter Davis

1. Introduction

Some starting points on work from a Christian perspective. Human labor or work is summed up in Catholic social teaching as being any activity that leads to human subsistence, personal growth and social and technological development.[1] Both work and rest are seen as part of God's plan for humankind and provide the opportunity for our participation in God's act of Creation.[2] The value of work, however, lies in what it does for humankind. "Work is for man not man for work."[3] These three aspects of human labor underline the Catholic principle that humankind is the *subject* of work. Thus, all work that has people as its subject has dignity and meaning no matter how humble and mundane may be the tasks carried out. Such work gives concrete expression at its very heart to the values of the person carrying it out.[4] Capital is the fruits of past accumulations of labor and the instrument that enhances the effectiveness of labor.[5] Labor's priority over capital is a key principle of Catholic social teaching that follows from this understanding of work as provided by the Bible and as it has been understood and interpreted by the Church over the centuries. While not precluding the necessity under some circumstances of collective and bureaucratic ownership, whether in joint stock companies and other institutions like Building Societies, Insurance Companies and Banks, etc. or by the State, Catholic teaching emphasizes the importance of involvement of the person through their individual or personal ownership of "private" property.[6] The principle of private ownership, however, is itself qualified by the need to recognize the primacy of *"...the first principle of the whole ethical and social order namely: the principle of the common use of goods."*[7] In essence, the practical consequence of this principle for Christians is that they may not use their personal ownership of the means of subsistence to exclude others whose need for subsistence and growth require that they should have access to those means. Finally, work is important for determining personal spiritual growth.[8] The absence of work whether through personal choice or due to circumstances beyond one's control we can assume will lead, as St. Paul (2 Thessalonians 3:15) implies, to a misdirection of our energies and powers into evil.

This brief summary of what I take to be the core of Catholic teaching on work constitutes my starting point. What follows will not attempt to defend or elaborate these teachings but accepting them as true, I will go on to explore what may be done to facilitate opportunities for work that does have the person of the worker as its subject.

Such a program itself implies that there are obstacles to the realization of Catholic teaching on the meaning and practice of Christian concept of work and I shall attempt to identify these in the next section. I will then go on to explore how an appreciation of the concepts of the Association of Labor and its goal in Community may give expression to Catholic social teaching on work and overcome the problems previously identified. I will suggest that the significance of these concepts lies in their ability to respond flexibly to people's needs in a form that can best overcome the two principle social divisions (imbalances in power) in the modern age; that between labor and capital and that from within labor itself between waged work and domestic (unwaged) work. This later division has itself become exacerbated by the growing dependence of Labor on Capital. That the structure of work and work relations are central from the stand-point of Catholic social teaching to the resolution of these two great social divisions can be demonstrated from two references to *Laborem exercens*:

Firstly,

> A labor system can be right...in the sense of being intrinsically true and also morally legitimate, if in its very basis it overcomes the opposition between capital and labor through an effort at being shaped in accordance with...the principle of the substantial and real priority of Labor....[9]

And secondly,

> The true advancement of women requires that labor should be structured in such a way that women do not have to pay for their advancement by abandoning what is specific to them and at the expense of the family, in which women have an irreplaceable role.[10]

Work (waged and domestic) is at the foundation of the material conditions for family life. The *economy* of the family lies at the heart of the labor issue and the gender issue just as the *spiritual* condition of family life lies at the heart of the health of society in general. The Association of Labor has failed to organize effectively around domestic and wage labor up to now. Capital-based business organizations have, however, failed to develop social relations beyond those creating dependency on the wage economy and the state. At the heart of this dependency lies the shrinking of the domestic economy and its replacement by the commodity economy.[11]

If this analysis has any proximity to the truth, it suggests that the organization and past practice of the Associations of Labor has been fatally one-sided and flawed in their focus on the relationship between capital and waged labor and by their failure to recognize and organize around domestic labor. It also suggests that we might usefully search for an organizational basis to help us resolve the divisions between waged and domestic labor in adaptations and developments in the current organizational forms and principles found within the association of labor. To overcome the division between waged and domestic labor will not only overcome one major economic factor behind labor's growing dependence on capital, it will also contribute to the resolution of the key economic factor behind inequality between genders.

Some may see the above quotation on women's role in the family as merely seeking to "confine" women to the domestic terrain and hence to an implicit subordination to men. This reading is in my view mistaken. Istead, the quotation suggests seeking to *raise* the status and influence of domestic work to that of equality with waged work in order that women who *choose* not to undertake waged work may not face being marginalized and subordinated within both the economy of the family (and their relations to their husbands) as well as within society at large.

By emphasizing the employment field the women's movement has been led into the same one sided strategy as has the traditional labor movement's emphasis on collective bargaining. This is easy enough to say in itself. *The difficult question is how to constitute an economic organization of labor that facilitates the re-establishment of domestic labor as a center for the production of goods and services and enables the realization of the value of domestic labor in the money economy?* The need for such a realization is no more than the recognition that unless domestic labor can be translated into money its value cannot be related or equated with values established in the modern capital-dominated economy.

If this translation were to be achievable then the subordination of waged labor to capital will itself become problematic. Labor will have regained the power to generate independent domestic means of production and hence lessened the dependence of the family on employment by investment-based capital for the means of subsistence and well-being. At the same time women at home will be at the center of a real alternative base of economic independence and social influence based not within the impersonal world of the capitalist market place (whose power and importance will have shrunk) but at the heart of a community of love–the family. Such a possibility opens up the prospect of enhancement in social status and influence for *all* those excluded for various reasons from the wage economy, or for whom the wage economy provides little material and spiritual reward.

2. The Problem: Labor as the Dependent Object of Capital

The concept of work does not of itself help us to bring out the key distinction between waged and unwaged (or domestic) work until we first recognize the reality that waged work arises as a result of a contract of employment between an individual and a person(s) or institution who can advance wages in exchange for services rendered. Such employment is a priority for all people without independent means. For most people work outside the employment relationship has its highest expression–is at its most significant and meaningful–in the work of parenting. Yet even this cannot be successfully pursued without the support of a community, ideally in the form of a family unit, and without some member(s) of that community being in employment.

Yet employment within the labor market is becoming increasingly problematic for a substantial minority of people due to slower levels of economic growth and the displacement of labor by capital. Growing segments of the labor market are characterized by employment that has become degraded in terms both of the security offered by the contract and in the scope for human self development and self-realization intrinsic to the tasks required by the contract.

We have witnessed the growing realization that the labor market has become divided between those jobs with relative security and continuity (sometimes referred to as core jobs) and a growing number of jobs where the relationship between employer and employed is more tenuous (sometimes referred to in the literature as peripheral jobs). The concept of the increasingly "flexible" use of labor by organizations has been the principal subject of discussion in the literature dealing with the restructuring of the labor market for the past decade.[12]

Whilst the extent and direction of managerial policy is still contested, the growth in what has been referred to as "atypical employment" continues.[13] The particular form the atypical employment takes may vary but is generally identified by being in one of the following categories: part-time, temporary, seasonal, agency, subcontracted, self employed, fixed term, and various forms of outworking. Some have argued that there is an increasing supply side demand for such work.[14] The evidence for this is far from conclusive. The background to the growth of these forms of employment, however, is of high levels of widespread and continuing unemployment, the absence of substantial employment protection legislation, and a reduction in minimum wage protection. Given the increasing market pressures to reduce costs, all these factors point in the direction of low pay and limited job security for the average atypical employee.

A further tendency toward deskilling in the tasks of employment, whilst separate from the issue of the nature of the contractual relationship and employment security, may well be adding to the pressures in these areas.[15] There is a growing emphasis on training and vocational qualification which leads some to deny the overall validity of the deskilling hypothesis.[16] The overall impression, however, is that the learning time and the technical level required for many of the "skills" required by the jobs available to the non-academically oriented young person is falling.[17] To some extent this is a result of the decline in employment opportunities in manufacturing and the shift towards service sector employment.[18] It may be that while for some segments of the labor market increased educations is required within the semi-skilled and manual segments there is a convergence of market forces, managerial practices and technological innovations that have had a detrimental impact on the quality of and availability of such employment. That much of this type of employment is occupied by immigrants/migrants and women is well understood. The main burden of unemployment and forced early retirement, on the other hand, has fallen on men under 25 and over 50 years of age. Again this has resulted from the shifts in the structure of the economy away from industries formally predominantly employing men.[19]

The confinement of families in small spaces with little or no capital is not a recent development but was in a sense the necessary precondition for the growth of a wage economy without which industrialization could not have occurred as it did. The work available to domestic labor continues to be restricted. It is further degraded in that what is left is dependent for its own functioning on wage labor and apart from free child-minding/rearing and some personnel services domestic labor creates little of commercial value. Please note I am not referring here to the intrinsic values of family relationships and family life but to the relative economic importance of what is left of domestic labor today. This is largely because nearly everything that is consumed within the family has first to be purchased for money normally acquired as wages or social security benefit. The average family home lacks the space or the facilities any longer to create for itself many of the primary items of consumption. The rising tide of domestic appliances are in the main labor–saving not product–creating items of domestic capital, or else they are designed to enhance leisure and recreation (often by requiring the family members to purchase more goods and services requiring more wage income rather than less).

The increasing dependency on employment at a time of decreasing opportunities both for and within employment suggests that we should take a fresh look at how society might resolve the problems of meaning, status and income associated with work outside the employment relationship. To downgrade the importance of the employment relationship and resolve the division between domestic and wage labor in the form of a new community of work requires the re-introduction of high value added tasks within the domestic sphere. Such a transformation is clearly not a practical proposition from within the slender resources of those families whose members (both men and women) occupy the most depressed and insecure segments of the labor market. This is also true for a larger segment of people in the lower to middle income brackets.

I will argue below that an exploration of possible adaptations to the Cooperative ideal, and in particular the Consumer Society expression of the Association of Labor, provides some interesting possibilities for the reinstatement and development of domestic work and the enhancement of the cultural and educational level of lower and middle income families.

3. The Association of Labor

Let us return to our starting point of the three key Catholic principles as developed in *Laborem exercens* in the context of the question "what form or type of commercial or business organization best enables the realization of all three of the above principles?", namely,

(a) Labor's priority over capital

(b) Private ownership of property, and,

(c) The right of all human beings to access to the means of subsistence and welfare to which both (a) and (b) above are subordinate.

If we were just interested in (a) and (b) we could unhesitatingly opt for the self-employed, sole proprietor or family business forms of employment. Clearly access to the property of those whose ownership was under these forms of enterprise depends on the need to employ outsiders or the charity of the persons concerned. In reality, of course, these small businesses are far from powerful and may well have their own access to resources to grow and develop hindered by yet larger institutions (such as banks) and competitors or monopolistic suppliers and customers. Market forces can and do create bankruptcy or unjust terms of trade just as they create redundancy and unjust terms of employment. Thus, small proprietors, farmers, manufacturers, the self-employed, wage workers, and consumers all need to associate to counter balance unfavorable market forces.

By an Association of Labor I mean a membership-based association in which membership is open, voluntary, and based on the perception of a community of interest or common bond.[20] The principle of open membership comes closer than any other form of business in meeting the central and overriding Catholic principle of open access to the means of subsistence for those who need them. The management of the association is either directly conducted by its members or is governed and answerable to the membership in general meeting on the basis of one member one vote. The association hires capital to support the members in the provision of employment, goods or services, or all three, meeting the principle of labor's priority over capital. Individual members own a share in the business and are able to accumulate savings as a result of their transactions or employment with the Association in accordance with the surpluses generated by the Association's business.[21] As such the Catholic principle of the right to private ownership of property and the sense of working for oneself is also enshrined in these Association's practice.

Of course, such Associations exist and have existed for over one hundred and fifty years all over the world providing almost every kind of service and employment. They enable the poor in every society to organize around their community of need. They have provided employment. They have provided the channel for philanthropic deeds and they have encouraged thrift and education and a greater sense of community.[22] The roots of the cooperative movement are to be found primarily in the last century within the traditions of four European countries: England, France, Ireland, and Germany.

The English produced perhaps the richest variety of cooperatives, although the earliest Owenite forms spread beyond its frontiers into Ireland and North America. These *Community Cooperatives* originated by Robert Owen tried to establish economically self-sufficient communities. Support by the rich was central to Owen's political program. Philanthropic support by the rich was crucial in view of the large amounts of capital needed to fund the projects.

The modern Consumer Cooperatives adopted narrower goals based upon the idea of the primacy of cooperative consumption. They grew out of an alternative approach to Owenism that continued with Owen's objectives but followed a strategy based upon the *Incremental Accumulation of Capital* through small business ventures–often commencing in retailing. Pioneers like William King, William Thompson, William Pare, John Francis Bray, and Thomas Hole tried to encourage working people to participate in smaller-scale local initiatives that would build gradually towards the aim of economic independence. The Rochdale Society of 1844, seen as the birthplace of the modern day *Consumer Cooperative* movement, started out in fact attempting to implement Owenite goals of member employment, education and community. There were also other cooperative community ventures sponsored by the northern Redemption Societies as late as 1856.[23] The London-based Christian Socialists led by Vansitate Neale, Ludlow and Abraham Greenwood were also part of this more gradualist movement for the association of labor and sponsored producer-based *Cooperative Workshops*.[24] These owed much of their inspiration, however, to the French worker cooperative movement influenced by Saint-Simon and Philippe Buchez that had inspired Ludlow during his stay in France.

The *Consumer Cooperative Movement* sprang out of the post–Owenite attempts at *Incremental Capital Accumulation* largely because of the success of dividend on purchase–a relatively insignificant rule in the early Rochdale Society's rule book (Rule 22).[25] It had become a clearly articulated ideology by Beatrice Potter (later Webb) and J.T.W. Mitchell by the 1860s. The producer strand of Cooperation became eclipsed within the Cooperative Union despite Neale's later efforts to encourage labor owned cooperative production. The CWS Ltd. abandoned profit sharing–with the workers as the terms of the debate were conducted whether workers or consumers should be most entitled to share the surpluses.

Thus, the early Owenite principle that none of the surplus be distributed (1832 Congress) dropped out of sight within the main stream UK Cooperative Movement along with other Owenite goals of community and the independence and priority of labor over capital that community represented. However, some consumer cooperative societies continued to support cooperative employment in worker cooperatives formed under the auspices of the Cooperative Productive Federation founded by Thomas Blandford. These *Cooperative Co-Partnerships* flowered in the 1880s and some are still trading more than a century later. By the 1960s, the Industrial Common Ownership Movement had become the leading promoter of worker cooperatives in the UK. The CPF had by the 1970s been wound up and its affairs transferred to the Cooperative Union Ltd. It is in southern Europe, however, in the Basque's Catholic-led Mondragon Cooperative in northern Spain and the Italian worker cooperatives that the most successful instances of worker cooperation are to be found in the post-war period.

The first *Credit Unions* were established in Germany by Frederich Rafiffeisen in 1849 to prevent low income farmers from being enslaved by debt. The idea spread rapidly arriving in North America by 1900. In Ireland *Agricultural Cooperation* under the leadership of Horace Plunkett became firmly established and quickly spread to North America and the United Kingdom. Agricultural cooperation predominates in some sectors of the Mediterranean economy.

Perhaps the earliest attempt at *Cooperative Housing* can be traced back to the London Economical Society that in 1821 attempted to establish an urban version of an Owenite Community. A century later the English *Cooperative Tenants Societies* were established in the inter-war years and there were similar efforts in other European countries. It was in this period that the British Cooperative Women's Guild was most active and the Guild placed a considerable focus on the issues of housing and house work. The debate at that time was understandably concerned with the issues of the drudgery and lack of recognition for the work women undertook.[26] Nevertheless, echoes of the earlier Owenite search for a new independent community of labor informed the idealism of the Guilds leadership far more than was apparent in the rest of the movement at that time.[27] The Guild helped to prompt the consumer movement into opening cooperative laundries and agitated for better designed *Cooperative Housing.* The further question raised by some contemporary feminists of the right to wages for housework misses the point that wages come out of the employment relationship between labor and capital. Wages arise not out of the conduct of work as such, but out of the contract of employment. The potential power of domestic labor lies in its ability, firstly, to dispense with outside investment capital in the creation of value, and secondly, in its ability to retain the whole value of its product. *Cooperative Housing* received special attention by the International Cooperative Alliance and Dr. E. Bodien of Germany drew up model rules. The United States and Canada have large and successful *Housing Cooperatives, Credit Unions, Agricultural Cooperatives and Rural Electric Cooperatives.*[28] Today most cooperative members are to be found in Asia where the world's largest cooperative is the Anand Dairy Cooperative in India.[29]

Given the emphasis of Catholic social teaching and given that these associations can and do work over such a diverse range of cultures, types of economic activity and historical and political context, it is perhaps surprising that there has not been a deeper and more concentrated analysis of the possibility of their further adaptation to meet modern needs. Of course there are a number of explanations of which not the least is the undoubted fact that not everything is perfection in the real performance of these association. I shall leave discussion of the problems inherent in the successful development of these associations and their possible solution until the subsequent section.

The immediate question now becomes what adaptations/developments of existing cooperative and other frameworks broadly found under the banner of the Association of Labor can be utilized to provide for the fundamental needs of people in the modern urban environment in both material and spiritual terms?

The needs are:

1. The reinstatement and empowerment of domestic labor.

2. Access to the means of subsistence and personal development.

3. Reduction in the dependency upon wage labor.

The goals are:

1. Equality between individual men and women.

2. The enhancement in the status and dignity of the individual as a member of an established and defined community.

3. The strengthening in solidarity and fraternity within families and communities.

4. The increased opportunity for meaningful and rewarding work leading to material welfare and the development of the whole person.

This could be achieved by the use of a New Model Consumer Cooperative Association. These associations have the same rule-book as existing Consumer Cooperatives but they define themselves as alliances between waged and the unwaged people for the production and distribution of goods and services. The alliance is given expression through a dual strand economic strategy. One strand based as with existing mainstream societies on commerce: through retailing, distribution and/or production of goods and services between members. Surpluses of high quality and high value added goods produced in the barter strand would be available for transfer into the commercial strand of the associations business when appropriate.

The barter strand would need to be as well managed as the commercial strand and to be built up gradually. The initial facilities, training and material could be gradually financed out of the surpluses generated by the commercial strand of the associations activities. Members would trade freely with each other through the barter strand and with the association with what disposable cash income they had available. By seeking to trade in the barter strand as much as possible those members with limited disposable income could conserve their cash for those items not available to them through the barter system. Some objects of unique artistic or intrinsic value could be offered for cash sale by members when it was not possible to find an appropriate object or service with which to barter. But with the barter strand the emphasis would be on non-cash transactions.

That barter strands facilities would enable members to effectively enhance their income and would encourage the growth in membership of the association as a whole. Increased recognition of the social purpose of the association would give its commercial strand added legitimacy as a socially responsible business supporting local families and the local community. The traditional ethical differentiation of Cooperative Business would be re-established. As the barter strand would be quite separately managed from the commercial strand the basic commercial viability of the association would not be threatened.

How would the barter strand operate? The barter strand as a whole would be run on the voluntary/charity sector model of leadership by professional but most of the work being undertaken by volunteers and management policy decided by a committee elected by the members and reporting to the general meeting of members. The over-riding principle governing the management of the barter strand would be *collective support for individual and family autonomy of production.* Otherwise there would be a danger of degenerating into a means to create a huge outworking system run by the association.

The first stage would be to encourage people to identify skills, interests and previous experience that could be developed for their personal development; to satisfy their family or other families' needs or that could become a means to generate cash income from home based production of goods or services. The focus would be on the production of items for domestic consumption, *i.e.*, food, furniture, clothing, soft furnishings, carpets, games, toys, musical instruments, pottery, jewelry, utensils, ornaments, paintings, fabrics, and on services such as repairs, renovation, maintenance, gardening, decorating. A thriving second-hand market might also be a possibility amongst members.

Members' social, cultural, and leisure activities would be run separately from both the commercial and barter strands of the Association but in close cooperation with them and receiving from each support for these activities commensurate with their respective resources.

The second stage would be to provide the training, equipment, materials, and facilities to re-establish domestic based production of goods and services. Links with the local authorities, churches, and other community associations and the mainstream commercial strand itself would help identify managerial and technical know-how, premises and equipment. Self-help to organize these training and production programs involving women's groups, youth groups, unemployed people, and people in enforced early retirement would be the emphasis.

The third stage would be for the association to provide the marketing and the market place for the domestic labor. Products could be exchanged via members advertising boards, craft fairs, car boot sales, member market stalls, a free barter strand trade paper with special offer and other commercial advertising revenue used to pay for its production and distribution to all members.

The medium of exchange could be direct barter by individual agreement, cash payments or a mixture of cash plus goods/services. Items for sale could be deposited at a barter shop separate from the commercial premises but not necessarily far apart from them, with a price or exchange item(s) request slip. The price could be subject to a small percentage towards the cost of heating and lighting but volunteers would operate the premises from among the members.

Membership would be open to all partners of employees, and all people living within the Association's catchment area and/or the local community in which the business is situated. Although some production equipment and other facilities might be provided for collective use like garages, work benches and facilities for dyeing and bleaching, etc., the main objective would be for production that could be carried out in the home for the home and family to be the priority. If viable commercial businesses that could supply the commercial strand of the Association did develop that would be a bonus but is not the objective of the exercise. Sales of goods of charity or to raise funds for further member-based leisure or education/training projects would also be a possibility.

Promotion of participation in the training and development programs to assist members involvement in the barter strand would aim at encouraging all unemployed persons, women at home, and children and young adults as well as the elderly. Key skills might include building trade skills, tailoring, shoe-making and repairing, furniture making, soft furnishings, knitting, pottery, cooking, jewelry, some metal working, and a wide range of repair and renovation skills. Courses on decoration and design would also contribute to the development of the individual's craft skills both enriching the home and providing opportunities for the generation of income from surplus production of high value added craft work.

A training and skills register of members who could assist in the sharing of skills and knowledge with other members could help the development program. Surpluses generated by the commercial strand (after the needs for re-investment and development had been met) would be just one means of funding these developments. Member's fund-raising activities, using own produce, the possibility of public sector grants in areas of acute social deprivation, and the support of registered charities are all possible sources for initial funding.

Cooperation works most effectively when it is addressing a real need. Unemployed people, including women at home, have a real need for autonomy and a sense of worth that the development of the barter strand could provide. The advantages of participation would be in the enhanced quality of life in the home and the meaning that working to produce items for the home and for self and family members would provide. The economic consequences would be to reduce the dependence on the labor market as the sole means of subsistence and to enable low income households to make their money stretch that bit farther. The self-confidence and strengthened self image that comes from being able to practice a socially useful skill and the reduced sense of economic dependence would itself do much to break the sense of apathy and isolation felt by many people in today's urban environment. For young people it would be an important outlet for creativity and energy and possibly a preparation for employment or self-employment.

The recognition of the importance of the success of the commercial strand of the Association to the overall support given to the barter strand would help to cement customer loyalty and the sense of purpose and commitment of staff and management running the commercial strand. Keeping staff and customers informed and encouraging them and their families involvement would also be important to the overall sense of unity and community of purpose by the Association's members, employees and customers. There is the possibility that later, as skills develop, the sale of some unique items of local domestic production in the commercial strand might itself create added interest and enjoyment for customers during their visit to the commercial retail outlets. Space near cafes, foyers, and in car parks might be suitable for certain "domestic goods" that had been vetted for quality and safety by commercial management.

For the home to become once again a value creating rather than just value consuming center would do much for enriching the experience of family members and to increase the status of its unwaged or low income members who would no longer be simply "dependents" on a "bread-winner."

Domestic based production has other advantages for those engaged in it. Firstly, its subject is the people who are immediately known to the domestic worker. Secondly, being craft based the domestic worker is in control of the pace and the quality of the production and sees it as a whole rather than in its fragmented aspect experienced in almost all distributive and productive processes today. Thirdly, the practice develops, enriches and empowers the person undertaking the work. Fourthly, all members are equally involved in the governance and ownership of the wider association that provides the inputs and resources to enable the re-establishment of domestic production. Women at home and the unemployed thereby gain access and involvement in decision-making in the wider socioeconomic infrastructure of their association and through their involvement in its barter strand perhaps a greater interest in its wider functioning and commercial performance. From being isolated, dependent, unproductive, powerless and unskilled they become equal, empowered, integrated, productive and skilled members of a community of labor.

The encouragement of domestic production for the reduction in reliance and importance of wage income could have important consequences in reducing the labor supply, cutting unemployment and dependence on the state on the one hand and improving the leverage in the labor market for trade unions on the other. Employers having to compete with alternative means of subsistence above and beyond the minimalist provisions of the state would be forced to raise the quality of their offers of employment. Domestic labor organized through cooperative associations could be seen as part of a parallel strategy with that of conventional worker cooperatives to take up some of the slack in the labor supply. I have argued elsewhere that the Trade Unions, as another expression of the Association of Labor, should recognize and support such developments amongst their own unemployed members.[30] These developments might also have the effect of creating a greater impetus towards the widespread use of collective employee shareholding. The developing culture of domestic and self-employment, employee shareholding and association could generate a culture that was both welfare and enterprise orientated and in which the distinctions between capitalism and socialism would become distinctly blurred.

4. Causes for the Past and Present Difficulties Facing Labor Associations

Despite the widespread practical success and flexible application of Cooperative Associations one is forced to recognize that the record is patchy and their potential is far from always apparent even to those directly involved. Where they are seen as being successful they provide very specific services with all community and social functions seen as auxiliary to the main business. This is of course quite the reverse of the original intention of the Association of Labor in which the business activities were seen as instrumental in developing the associations, long term socioeconomic goals; namely of achieving the priority of labor over capital, the strengthening of community, and the growth and education of the whole person.

Although Robert Owen's ambitious projects came to nothing, his objectives remained valid in the eyes of many of those that came after him in the early stages of the development of the Association of Labor. Today Owen's emphasis on the importance of character building may yet prove to be his abiding legacy to the Association of Labor.[31]

Secondly, not all Cooperative and other Associations of Labor have a very positive public image. In the United Kingdom the popular perception of the Cooperative Movement is of a dying edifice whose day has passed. Associations have also failed many times through corruption, nepotism, lack of skill, lack of entrepreneurial drive, government interference and the apathy and lack of vision and commitment of their managements and members. Despite having blazed trails in retailing, whole-foods, employment and financial and rural services, they have found themselves overtaken and left standing only a decade or sometimes a generation latter. The British consumer movement has today has shown renewed managerial vigor and some commercial viability.[32]

The community of interest has, however, been diluted to the vanishing point and it remains not so much a social movement as a benign oligarchy of management and lay directors elected from a tiny fragment of members and staff. They do offer some more or less creative social activities from limited and begrudged resources. These, one suspects, are maintained more for appearances sake than from a real sense of purpose on the part of senior management. The history of the Association of Labor is full of cases of organizations seeking to change the basis of society or economy that end up mirroring the very set of relations they were bent on removing. Why does such a good and worthy idea as often as not fail in its limited immediate goals and rarely gets close to its more ambitious long term social goals?

Any reviewer of Cooperative Association's growth and development over the last century and a half must be struck by the fact that, popular and democratic as they are in form, their development and growth owed so much to charismatic vision and leadership combined to high levels of managerial ability. The vision and professionalism of the founders, promoters and activists when linked to the self-interest of the followers or rank and file members was able to create a cooperative culture and sense of community.

But the Association of Labor (like the Church) needs periods of spiritual renewal. It falls into complacency and its leadership's vision narrows and falters. The increase in success brings with it increased size and complexity of operation and a widening gap of knowledge and power between the management and the membership. Soon leaders who were once persons dedicated to the service and improvement of their association's membership become a privileged oligarchy bent on excluding members from interference that might endanger their position. Excluded and outmaneuvered members drift into apathy and indifference and the unity and cohesion of the association and its social purpose evaporates. With the loss of purpose comes a loss of direction and eventual failure. Robert Michels writing in 1915[33] noted the progress of bureaucracy in the Labor Movement of his day and much of the history of the Association of Labor supports the growing pessimism which led Michels toward the end of his life to support Italian fascism.[34]

The root of this failure lies not in structures as in the fallibility of people. Structures are important for the opportunities they offer for good and for ill, but it is the people themselves who determine the outcome within those structural boundaries. Their greed for power, their pride, and particularly intellectual pride in the case of the Labor Movement, selfishness lack of compassion and apathy towards others are spiritual problems that education in terms of factual knowledge does not touch. Such problems are to be found amongst people with plenty and people with very little in material terms. The provision of material goods and services were means not ends .

Sadly secularism, materialism, and the enormous and tragic *cul de sac* of historical materialism meant that most of the leadership of organized labor when it had vision was inspired by a false prophet whilst a few were cynically seeking self advancement rather than social reform. You cannot expect to build the new Jerusalem without acknowledging the one who was crucified in the old Jerusalem.

Renewal of the person and the community in which the person functions, and hopefully serves, is a matter requiring prayer, openness to the Holy Spirit, and ultimately openness to the grace of our Creator. The struggle for the Community of Labor is a spiritual struggle that must be conducted within the structures and amongst the members of those Associations. In order to establish the Community of Labor as a united and fraternal expression of brotherhood and sisterhood and to protect it from the threat Michels identified as an "iron law of oligarchy" such Associations must have Christ at their head and acknowledge Him in all they do. The Church empowered by the Holy Spirit can address the Labor Movement concerning the nature of human work with confidence and purpose basing its program for labor squarely on the principles of *Laborem exercens.*

But the Church needs deeds as well as words. Community is at the very center of the life and teaching of the Church. By adapting the tried and tested frameworks for associations of labor, the Church can give practical expression to the teaching of *Laborem exercens.*[35] To minister to both the material and spiritual needs of the poor and dispossessed has always been the mission of the Church. Thus, the Church needs the concept and organizational framework of the Association of Labor to conduct this ministry as effectively as possible in the modern age. In helping to address the problems of work through the community of labor we see that the Church is also able to strengthen the family and give substance to the recognition of the equal share in His creation God has planned for men and women. To succeed in the development of the whole person the members of these associations need to be evangelized and galvanized by the Gospels.

Many, perhaps most, people will ignore the opportunity for autonomy and self development that a program such as I have outlined above offers. It is not for the first time that the Body of Christ on earth has found itself challenged by materialism and cynicism. At the very birth of Capitalism in the Italian city-states of the middle ages the church faced just such a challenge and found a champion and a community of saints in St. Francis and the Franciscans who responded to that challenge.[36] Today the analysis of *Laborem exercens* calls Christians to respond to the instrumental use of people in employment and the denial of access to adequate means for subsistence and welfare to millions of people in our own times.

Notes

1. John Paul II, *Laborem exercens* (London: Catholic Truth Society, 1981), pp. 1-5.

2. *Ibid.*, p.3.

3. *Ibid.*, p.22.

4. *Ibid.*, p.56.

5. *Ibid.*, p.46.

6. *Ibid.*, pp.50-51.

7. *Ibid.*, p.51.

8. *Ibid.*, pp.84-85.

9. *Ibid.* p.45.

10. *Ibid*. p.71.

11. Harry Braverman, "The Universal Market," *Labor and Monopoly Capital*, *The Monthly Review Press*, 1974, ch.13 pp. 271-283.

12. John Atkinson, Institute of Manpower Studies, University of Sussex, on the flexible use of labor in *Industrial Relations Review and Report*, 7:8 (1984): *Personnel Management*, August 1984: *New Society*, August 1985. For a critical appraisal see A. Pollert, *The Flexible Firm a Model in Search of Reality*, Warwick Papers in Industrial Relations, no. 19, December 1987. Industrial Relations Unit, University of Warwick.

13. See Catherine Hakim, "Trends in the Flexible Workforce," *Employment Gazette*, November 1987, pp. 549-560 and "Workforce Restructuring in Europe in the 1980s," *International Journal of Labor Law and Industrial Relations*, University of Leicester, 1989, pp.167-203, and M.J. MaGiure and D. N. Ashton, *British Labor Market Trends*, Center for Labor Market Studies, University of Leicester, 1988.

14. Alan Neal, "Atypical Workforms and European Labor Law," in 45 *Recht der Arbeit*, 1992, pp. 115-119.

15. For a discussion of the various definitions and approaches to the concept of Skill, see C.R. Littler, *The Developments of the Labor Process Capitalist Societies,* (Heinemann, 1982), pp. 7-14.

16. H. Braverman, *Labor and Monopoly Capital*, pp. 251-267.

17. S. Gordon, "Clearing the Qualifications Jungle," *Employment Gazette* (1992), pp. 27-32.

18. MaGiure and Ashton, *British Labor Market Trends*, pp. 4-5.

19. *Ibid*., pp. 1-2.

20. See W. P. Watkins, *Cooperative Principles Today and Tomorrow* (Manchester: Holyoake Books, 1986.)

21. John Nelson-Jones and Graham Nuttal, *Employee Ownership: Legal and Tax Aspects* (London: Format Publishing, 1987), pp. 8-9.

22. For an up-to-date review of the breadth and scale of cooperative enterprise worldwide see, *The Yearbook of Cooperative Enterprise* (Oxford: The Plunkett Foundation for Cooperative Studies, 1993) published annually, and the *Review of International Cooperation*, (Geneva: ICA).

23. For a series of brief extracts from the key texts of this time, see Cole and Filson, *British Working Class Movements* (London: Macmillan, 1965.)

24. The work of Phillip Backstrom, *Christian Socialism and Cooperation in Victorian England* (London: Croom Helm, 1974) provides a comprehensive description of the divisions and debates that arose with the emergence of the philosophy of Consumer Cooperation. Also see Paul Lambert, *Studies in the Social Philosophy of Cooperation* (Manchester: Cooperative Union Ltd., 1963), p.94, who also argues that the crucial element in the Rochdale legacy was not the idea of the supremacy of the consumer.

25. Arnold Bonner, *British Cooperation* (Manchester: Cooperative Union Ltd., 1961), p.46.

26. Alistair Thompson, "Domestic Drudgery Will Be a Thing of the Past." Cooperative Women and the Reform of Housework, ch.7 in *New Views of Cooperation*, ed. Stephen Yeo (London: Routledge, 1988), pp.114-115.

27. Richard A. Pence, ed. *The Next Greatest Thing* (Washington: The National Rural Electric Cooperative Association, 1984).

28. A feel for the relative balance of Cooperative activity (not simply numbers of members) can be seen by a reference to the cumulative index of articles by country going back to 1927 in the *Year Book of the Agricultual Cooperation* (Oxford: published jointly by The Plunkett Foundation and the ICA).

29. Peter Davis, "Cooperation and the Labor Movement," *Review of International Cooperation*, 82:1 (1989), (Geneva), pp. 60-66.

30. Dame Margaret Cole, "Robert Owen Until after New Lanark," ch. 1 in *Robert Owen* (Robert Owen Bicentenary Association, 1971), p. 9.

31. P.H.J.H. Gosden, *Self-Help Voluntary Associations in the 19th Century*, (London: BT Batsford Ltd., 1973), pp.126-127.

32. See the annual analysis of consumer cooperative statistics produced and published by the Cooperative Union Ltd. Some more recent statistics have been

reviewed by Prof. N. Branton *et al*. as "Cooperative Trade 1991: Reflections and Projections," *Journal of Cooperative Studies*, Supplement to No. 74 (June 1992).

33. Robert Michels, *Political Parties* (New York: The Free Press, 1962).

34. *Ibid*. Introduction by Seymour Martin Lipset, p.33.

35. Peter Davis, *Christian Cooperation: St. Paul Solidarity and Community* Northampton, England: Disciples Press, The Daily Bread Cooperative Society, 1988), Part 3. "St Paul's Concept of the Christian Community."

36. Rev. Theodore A. Zarembra, *Franciscan Social Reform: A Study of the Third Order Secular of St. Francis* (Washington: The Catholic University of America, Studies in Sociology, Vol. 26, Catholic University of America Press, 1947), p.78. Pope Leo XIII saw in many of the social attitudes and values emerging in the modern world parallels with those in the thirteenth century that were hostile to the Church and its teaching. Zarembra goes on (p.132) to note "...the faithful of various places gathered together into lay communities in order to serve God more perfectly and at the same time to provide a better livelihood...lay associations which had in no way been connected with the Franciscan movement affiliated themselves with the Third Order. Such was the case with the Begard weavers of the Netherlands who one by one adopted the rule of the Third Order."

SECTION III

Chapter Thirteen

QUALITY AS A PERMEATING ETHIC

Sebastian A. Sora
Samuel M. Natale
Joseph W. Sora

This chapter, based on a study of twenty-four (24) executives, was undertaken to understand the attitudes and feelings of executives in American corporations as they related to the commitment that such companies are making to achieve quality in their products and services. Corporate America is committing itself to achieve quality in all aspects of its products and services as well as its work-place employee activities. Terms like "Quality Management," "Quality is Free," "The Cost of Quality," "The Ethic of the Work Force," and "Six Sigma," have become the shorthand that is used to encourage a transition aimed at familiarizing the worker with the concept of quality. In fact, the terms are lead-ins to the issue that quality has been missing in American products and this absence translates into a competitive disadvantage for American corporations world wide.

If quality is to go beyond concept into actualization, then it must become a permeating ethic. It must pervade the entire organization in the form of an embodying, encompassing organizational ethic. In turn, however, this requires a commitment from the executive ranks of the American corporation as well as a sense of commitment to the ethic, that goes beyond the immediate bottom line. Without this awareness, quality will become a sales gimmick not a behavior. If workers understand this as a mere gimmick, then quality dies, and what is being achieved is nothing more than sloganism. This study provided significant information about the present executive awareness of the what quality is all about from their job-perspective.

Because a product is essentially made of a variety of parts or components, the overall amount of quality that a product possesses depends on the amount of quality that resides in each of those constitutive parts or components. These components depend on a variety of different processes and it is essential that each component of that process be characterized by the assurance of quality. In short, our study established that quality, like ethics, must be systemic rather than discreet.

With the above in mind, it then follows that a successful quality thrust must pervade the entire organizational structure that is involved with the processes that constitute the creation and maintenance of each and every part of the product. Quality obtains the characteristics of the organizational ethic, which is described by Larry L. Axline as "pervasive...the way an organization decides and acts" (Axline, p. 64). In this light, quality becomes a part of the organization's belief system and subsequently a part of the organization's culture. This is evident from the observation that, employees, whether administrative, research or manufacturing, make decisions affecting the creation of the product or service according to an operating and governing belief system that their organization values and affirms. As Axline states, the method by which an organization makes decisions and acts, reflects its underlying belief system or governing ethic. In short, quality is "exteriorized interiority."

Quality within the organization is living, developmental and synergistic, if it is believed, applied, and internalized in worker and management activities. If this does not happen, it remains simply a variant set of standards as would be found in a quality control manual. David A. Garvin outlines various components of quality as they relate to a product. He describes quality as a composite term that relates to each and every aspect of a product (Garvin 26). If any one aspect of the product is quality deficient, then in the view of the user, the entire product will be perceived as lacking quality. It would appear that, at least in terms of our research, the executive ranks only partially understand this fact.

In arguing that the concept of quality must operate systemically, we are really stating that quality, if it is to become a reality, must be taught, valued, and monitored by each and every individual that is part of the process. This process is essentially an educational and an empowering task which requires ongoing instruction, motivation and control to assure continuance with the corporate environment. With the empowering aspect, both management and the worker enter into teaming to achieve an end. This teaming, although conceptually appealing is difficult for management to accept since it requires a sharing of the traditional power of managers. Even within the management layers, power is transferred, such that less direct management is needed. While less direct management is needed, more skilled management is required. This skill must go beyond the management skill, but be technical, developmental, and/or administrative.

Webster defines an organization as an entity that, "comprises elements with varied functions that contribute to the whole and collective functions." The often overlooked word in this definition is "varied." "Varied" suggests that a level of individuality exists within the organization. This individuality does not transform into a faceless mass of people upon the placing of a corporate logo above them. In fact, it is the synergistic quality of the search for and maintenance of quality that brings the individual to the fore. This theory would argue that the individual, who is empowered, achieves better levels of quality and higher levels of motivation.

O'Donnell and Paderon, in their article entitled, "The Individual as the Ground for Organizational Ethics," state that, "it is easy to forget the individual person who ultimately constitutes the collective whole"

(O'Donnell, Paderon 1). Clearly they are assuming Webster's definition of the organization and accenting the word "varied." Each different from the other, each empowered to achieve quality, but interlinked by dependencies and connectedness which transcends the actual day to day encounters. When each individual achieves this level of product connectedness, and responsibility, a successful quality ethic has been instilled. Given that instillation we come to the concept of Total Quality Management (TQM).

TQM refers to an organization wide performance management system that emphasizes continuous improvement in processes and services. In its most pervasive form, it escorts people, products and services from the organizational cradle to the grave, providing attentive leaders, trained workers, service providers, data and measurement, a guiding vision and operating values (Holpp, 72). TQM enforces the permeating ethical value of quality and each worker or manager is seen as an agent of "continuous improvement."

TQM recognizes that customers operate in a state of flux. Their specifications and requirements for products and services are always changing. As a result processes must exist that translate these requirements and specifications into a suitable product or service. These processes must remain sensitive to the changing state of initial requirements and operate under a system dedicated to "continuous improvement." Such processes are open, modular and flexible. Data gather in this study seem to indicate that executives are not always aware that a gulf exists between what has been designed and what is currently needed.

Reality dictates, however, that even with "perfect specifications," translation into a product design or a service is neither easy nor necessarily free of deficiencies. These deficiencies can be caused by perceptual model differences, miscommunication, or the technology itself. Whatever the cause, the effect is a decreased level of product quality. This argues for a careful process that involves continual consultation, scanning, control and energy that will translate the dynamic and changing needs of the customer into a product or a service. If this process does not exist, then the level of quality is diminished or destroyed. Again, the necessary facilitation process here requires educational intervention. Data gathered in this study indicates that the issue of education can be compromised.

One of the aims of TQM is the provision of an "attentive leader" or "owner" to the process. The responsibility of the owner is to maintain a relationship with the end user to insure that the overall process is producing a product that meets the changing requirements of that end user. This maintenance of relationship is a function of management. However, data gathered in this study seems to indicate that executives do not understand the concept of a relationship based on equitable communication. The relationship management duty must engender trust; without trust no relationship can exist. This underpinning to quality is understood to be important but not necessary. The relationship process is one of many processes that must be owned by "someone." It is only in this way that a process can improve and change. But who chooses the process owners? Clearly this is a function of management; but on what criteria is this done? Owners have strengths and weaknesses and what is clear is that processes must be owned by individuals and not simply because these individuals hold specific jobs. Instead, it requires individuals that can insure the health of the process because of what they bring to that ownership. This matching of the "right" owner to the process is the fundamental requirement of instilling quality into any process. It becomes a fundamental issue of quality control.

Logic would dictate that the owner who has the greatest potential to be an expert in a process, as measured by matching personal strengths to the demands of the process, is the correct owner for the process. The only possible way to place the "right" owner comes to the correct process is by achieving an understanding of the nature of the process and an understanding of the individual who has the appropriate skills to govern such a process and communicate across processes. Once having achieved this, what follows is the establishing of sub-process owners to the overall quality process. The responsibility of the owner now goes beyond simply understanding the needs of the end-user and assumes an educational dimension. It now includes working with the sub-process and "other" process owners to insure constant validation of all processes against end-user requirements.

Our analysis of quality has, thus far, led us to the understanding that quality must pervade and permeate the entire organization. In stating that a product has a high level of quality, we are saying that each part of the product or service also possesses a high degree of quality. It therefore seems that all aspects of the organization, *i.e.*, those involved with production, design, use form, materials, etc., must all act to increase the quality of the product. Competition to succeed must encompass competition to achieve from a systems perspective. Quality cannot be controlled by a "department of quality" or as Dr. J. M. Juran states, "If the quality council is at the middle of the organization, that a signal to the rest of the organization that quality does not have a high priority" (Retkwa 9).

To be successful quality is the governing guideline that directs organizational decision making as it relates to the product and to its conception of the "varied" strengths and weaknesses that constitute organizational membership. This systemic view of quality then effects the understandings, decision making processes and actions of the organization. Processes are born; processes are owned; processes are replaced, and the road to continuous improvement realized.

The internalization of the quality process and the establishment of the process owners in constant validation, rides on the wings of education and communication. At all times the process owner must see themselves as managing ethical demands against "their" expertise in the following areas:

Process components
Process contributions
Process relationships
Process change issues
Process efficiencies
Process control
Process development
Meta-process management

Our study was concerned with understanding applied criteria that business people involved with quality actually used and were concerned about. In order to survey this, written and oral interviews were held with twenty-four individuals involved in achieving quality organizations. These interviews were coded and factor analyzed. They generated three (3) recurrent themes and values which we refer to as: Dependency, Connectedness, and Particularity.

Dependency: is defined to be a product of utility which matches specification. This is essential, ethically, because it reflects the fact that the end user requirements have been built into the product. Directly related to dependency is the essential link to Interdependency which states that the relationship between supplier and user is interdependent in nature.

Connectedness: as it relates to quality control requires that the provider assumes the responsibility to provide a product which is of high quality within the constraints that the end user sets. This creates a relationship of mutual and accepted accountability between producer and end user. The product provider must assure himself/herself *as experts* that they are providing the best from a quality perspective and are not providing a substandard item. That in fact, what they are providing can be "best of breed." The very nature of expertise demands higher responsibility and accountability in the process.

Particularity: asks the question: In providing a product where does the process become compromised? That is to say, where does the product development process yield to economic, environment (i.e., the choice of virtual slave labor to produce), production realities and financial concerns and possible uses.

We followed up the interviews with written interviews and coded grids to clarify our initial observations. What follows is a description of that research.

In order to understand or assess whether executives who are directly concerned with quality understand their ethical responsibility, we interviewed 24 executives who responded to the following questionnaires.

1. Question Format

The purpose of the form is to measure the executive's awareness of the ethical components present in the issue of quality management. To that end, the following interview protocols were implemented.

The format was open-ended and questions were framed as follows:

1. Concretely, how did the executive understand, specify and implement the relationship between the product, service and end user requirements.
2. How did the executive educate the end user in developing specifications.
3. Did the executive tell the end user when and what aspects of the ideal specification could not be honored for competitive reasons.
4. Did the executive tell the end user when and what aspects of the ideal specification could not be honored for economic reasons.
5. Did the executive tell the end user when and what aspects or ideal specifications could not be honored for financial reasons.
6. Did the executive feel he actually controls the quality process.
7. How does the executive respond when he understands that layers of the corporation impede the relationship with the end user.
8. Does the executive tell the end user when corporate constraints are in fact impeding quality delivery.
9. What does the executive believe to be the greatest impediment to quality.

Finally the respondent was asked to define the relevancy of dependency, connectedness, and particularity to process.

2. Data Analysis

To each of the aforementioned questions, a total of 24 answers were given. The answers were tabulated as follows:

OUESTION	SUM		% OF TOTAL	% OF REMAINDER
RELATIONSHIP	51	72	70.8	29.2
EDUCATION	52	72	72.2	27.8
COMPETITION	43	72	59.7	40.3
ECONOMIC	48	72	66.7	33.3
FINANCIAL	43	72	59.7	40.3
CONTROL	42	72	58.3	41.7
IMPEDE	40	72	55.6	44.4
CONSTRAINTS	29	72	40.3	59.7
IMPEDIMENTS	21	72	29.2	70.8
DEPENDENCY	45	72	62.5	37.5
CONNECTIVITY	43	72	59.7	40.3
PARTICULARITY	42	72	58.3	41.7
TOTAL VALUES	500	864	57.9	42.1

Maximum score for each answer is 3, yielding a max value for the question of 72, i.e., 3 x 24.

Intent of Question 1: Quality Theory is predicated on establishing an understanding with the customer as to his/her requirements and building a relationship of trust. The answers received show significance in that of the executives responding almost 30% do not understand this as a pre-requisite to any aspect of quality.

Possible explanations for the above can be rooted in the issue of expert power. So often end users do not understand their needs, while solutions are given by corporations which are general in nature. These general solutions are sufficient but not satisfying to the end users. The executive, on the other hand, is tied to financial issues which govern what can and can not be done at a certain cost level. Hence, while 70% of the executives understand the need for relationship, the relationship is tempered. From a quality perspective it is clear, that without a reasonable relationship with the end user, quality will not be realized.

Intent of Question 2: If the consumers or end users are to understand their needs and requirements, they must be educated in the realities of solutions. The intent of this question is to understand the commitment that executives have toward supplying this education.

The answers received was statistically equivalent to question 1. Education is absolutely required for the end user to be able to define their needs, otherwise they are poorly expressed and the executive trying to generate a solution is viewing a moving target.

Question 1 and Question 2 are reciprocals. If the executive takes the time to educate the end user, s/he is building a relationship. How well s/he does this education can be a measure of the strength of the relationship. However, this activity (education) involves a commitment by the executive of corporate resources. It becomes an investment in the future and can be risky. It is unclear if an informed consumer is a better customer than one less informed. Further, if products or services are not tailored or of sufficient quality, the informed consumer could be a difficult challenge. However, from a quality perspective, an informed consumer increases the quality level of products and services and in the long run is best for the product and service dynamic. It creates a tension between the expert and the user which can be highly productive if managed.

Intent of Question 3: When an end user develops a specification that specification must be tested or modelled to assure that it solves the perceived problem. The intent of this question was to understand whether the executive is willing to look at the specifications from the competitive perspective.

Does the executive look for competitive advantage or disadvantage when studying an end users specifications? Forty percent of the executives do not tell the end users the competitive advantage or disadvantage of the specification. Thus, the end user is not made aware of whether the executives' product or service is the best of breed. Best of breed clearly is a function of meeting or exceeding the end users' specification. If the specification cannot be met, the executive does not state that their company's product is lacking or a competitor's product has advantages.

The issue here is one of trust in the quality equation. It would seem that while education is believed in, directed eduction is what is given. Its effect on quality is obvious but the end user must be wary of the education received and must clearly understand the deficiencies in the educational process if he/she is to achieve best of breed in satisfying the requirements.

Intent of Question 4: This question was asked to see if the executive would instruct the end user in balanced requirements. Requirements which could be weighted as to the value of each to the customer, when compared with the cost, the environmental effect, the human effect and finally its ultimate value to society. Interestingly 66% answered affirmatively, while 33%, thought it was not required. The higher mean value for this score is clear. Ranking the end users requirements does not effect the product offered directly nor does it effect the product of competitors. In fact in this activity the executive can be seen as mentoring the end user. The data indicates that this is tied to the concept of relationship and education and ranked third in overall mean.

Intent of Question 5: This question becomes the flip side of question 4. Would the executive tell the end user why his or her requirements could not financially met by the executive as would be expected, and as indicated in Question 3, the answers had a low mean. Fully 40% said no; the same as in Question 3.

Thus, we see corroborating evidence that quality suffers when the issue is financial and could effect the user view of best of breed. It would appear that the executive sees quality as an objective to be achieved but the road to achievement is fraught with ethical issues. The key issue is the shaping of truth.

Intent of Question 6: A fundamental underpinning of a quality process is process responsibility and ownership. Would the executive take such responsibility. Oddly, the data indicates a very low mean, with 44% of the respondents blaming others for responsibility not taken. Without executive ownership there can not be a quality process. Without an executive using such a process and continuously improving it as the owner, others will not follow it and the entire quality process is in jeopardy. The answer to this question is an indicator of how well quality will flourish within an organization.

Intent of Question 7: When an executive cannot do his/her job or manage a quality process because of the corporation/firm, what do they do? The correct answer of course is to change that which impedes and work on that until it does not effect quality. Fully 44% of the executives would do little.

Thus it is apparent that executives may not be agents of change. To be a quality process owner requires continuous improvement management, and continuous monitoring to assure that processesare in step with the environment. Data seems to indicate (Sora, Natale, 1993) that executives are by nature there to preserve the *status quo* and that change must be gradual. The nature of quality is more dynamic since it is based on the relationship concept with customers and it may be that the executive may not be the right person to manage in this sphere.

Intent of Question 8: Question 7 tested the executive's ability to be an agent of change, Question 8 asks whether the executive would tell the customer when the corporation or firm is impeding quality. Overwhelmingly the answer is "No." 60% of the executives would not inform the end user. Linking this to Question 7, we know that 44% would *not* act to make changes.

The conclusion is obvious: at some level the executive feels that opening this issue to the end user in some way involves loyalty. However, it could be conjectured that by opening this up, the end user can help the executive be an agent of change and both the customer and the corporation would benefit.

Intent of Question 9: The achievement of quality is ultimately the responsibility of each individual. This is what "empowerment" is all about. This question was to understand, if the executive saw it this way; *i.e.*, personal responsibility. Sadly, 70% said "No." If it is not the executive's responsibility, then whose responsiblity is it? The answers to the above question lend some support to why those executives did not feel they could be agents of change. The answers were always directed to others as responsible, *e.g.*, management, people, politics.... It would appear that the executives did not feel they had control over why processes do not work, what processes there were, and finally who is responsible. Has the work environment become so complex that no one person can be responsible for anything? If this is so, the issue of quality is mute. It will degenerate from a philosophy or ethic to a sales gimmick.

The last part of the questionnaire centered on the concepts of *particularity*, *connectedness*, and *dependency*. Connectedness and Particularity received low scores that were not significantly different. In the case of connectedness, the mean was 1.89, and the mean for particularity was 1.84. Connectedness is a measure of executive responsibility for high quality as measured by the end user. Fully 40% of the respondents did not answer positively, while with particularity, which is a measure of executive trading off the economic, financial or other realities, we see the respondents refusing responsibility for the activity. These questions were asked in a different manner than the nine questions of the survey but reflect the same reality with this sample.

Dependency has a mean of 1.98, significantly different than connectedness and particularity. This is indicative of the desire of the executive to satisfy the wants of the end user but with the lower scores in connectedness and particularity, the goal is not actualized in this sample of executives.

3. Summary and Conclusions

It is difficult to extend the results of this random sample to the population at large. However, if the attitudes evident in this study are extendable to the general, then there is considerable concern. The concern is real because we have shown that quality must be an ethic, if it is to have any real effect on American business. The ethic must be pervasive and the executive ranks of the American corporation must understand it as the ultimate competitive advantage. To that end, it must be used, believed in, and rewarded at all levels. Clearly, the evaluation/assessment system for executive and managers must be challenged to realize the systemic requirements that quality demands. Competition and its rewards are no longer how well I did, but how well we did. Leadership comes in managing a process for continuous improvement and success comes when best of breed is realized.

Three immediate areas of concern that are indicated by this research are:

1. Lack of process ownership and control
2. Executive short sightedness as it relates to user specifications and product formulation
3. The use of education to foster corporate goals as opposed to quality goals.

Without process ownership (as defined in this chapter) and education, quality will be nothing more than a corporate slogan. Users and customers must understand that corporate power is shared and that the definition for products and services come from the user of such products and services. This does not mean that corporate America cannot favor research and development, for it is here that the technological advancement of society comes. All development must be understood in terms of how it benefits users and society as a whole.

We believe that a key result of this study is that the concept of quality can be centered in the concept of relationship. The data indicated that 30% of the executives surveyed did not understand this. They see themselves solely as product and service managers; this perspective must be expanded to include relationship management as well. Executives must be rewarded on how well these relationships are managed.

It is understood that the day of the executive is filled with immediate things to do but relationships usually wane slowly and its immediacy is not visible from a quarter to quarter economic perspective. Managing the long term is what relationship management is all about. The corporate ethic of quality demands this long term commitment.

The research confirms the centrality of systemic and continuous value-based decision making and requires ongoing monitoring. An adequate corporate strategy must include non-economic goals. An economic strategy is the optimal match of a company's product and market opportunities with its resources and distinctive competence. But economic strategy is humanized and made attainable by deciding what kind of organization the company will be–its character, the values it espouses, its relationship to customers, employees, communities, and shareholders. The personal values and ethical aspirations of the company's leaders, though probably not specifically stated, are implicit in all strategic decisions. They show through the choices management makes and reveal themselves as the company goes about its business. "That is why this communication should be deliberate and purposeful rather than random.... [Further] Defining the purpose of the corporation as exclusively economic is a deadly oversimplification, which allows overemphasis on self-interest at the expense of consideration of others." (Andrews, 1989)

While these choices are clearly difficult and often have no completely satisfactory solution, it is clear that no progress can be made until and unless individuals accept "ownership" (accountability) for their actions. The projection of responsiblity is a deadly ethically as it is psychologically.

Finally, the ethical-educational component required in assuring ownership and integrity in the quality process demands an education that is aimed at affect, behavior and cognition *simultaneously* to guarantee internalization and implementation. The ultimate goal is a reorientation of awareness from individual self-concern to a more corporate vision which includes the fact that:

> The primary ethical question...is not what is predictable. Nor is it what is possible. Nor is it what will enable the human species merely to survive. It is rather what will conduce to the common good. Human life is intrinsically relational. It is lived in a set of contexts...a biosphere...a sociosphere...and a psychosphere.... The common good is that texture of relationships in which the life of all is enhanced by the actions and dispositions of each one. Its common name is sympathy.... Its ordinary, everyday demand is justice. Its grounding is ultimately ontological. That is, the common good is not an abstract principle imposed upon the reality of the world. It is a quality that derives from the structure of experience. It is the deepest impulse and profoundest need of all being. The suffering and misery that result from its violation are themselves witness to its presence. (Sturm, p. 153)

References

Andrews, Kenneth R. *Ethics in Practice: Managing the Moral Corporation* (Cambridge, Mass.: Harvard Business School Press, 1989).

Axline, Larry L. "TQM: A Look in the Mirror," *Management Review*, 64 (November 1991).

Batten, Joe. "A Total Quality Culture," *Executive Excellence* (May 1991), pp. 1-3.

Behrman, Jack N. *Essays on Ethics in Business and the Professions* (Englewood Cliffs, N.J.: Prentice Hall, 1987).

Garvin, David A. "What Does Product Quality Really Mean?", *Sloan Management Review* (Fall 1984), pp.25-28.

Greenwood, Frank. "Continuous Improvements to Meet Customer Expectations," *Journal of Systems Management* (February 1992), pp. 13-15.

Holpp, Lawrence. "Making Choices: Self Directed Teams or Total Quality Management," *Management Review* (April 1992), pp. 42-47.

Ishikawa, Kaoru. *What Is Total Quality Control?* (London: Prentice-Hall, Inc., 1985).

Natale, Samuel M., Sebastian A. Sora. "Quality as an Ethic," *Proceedings*, Second International Conference on Social Values (Oxford: 1993).

Paderon, Eduardo S., Charles F. O'Donnell. "The Individual as the Ground of Organizational Ethics," *Proceedings*, Second International Conference on Social Values (Oxford: 1993).

Paquette, Joseph F. "Total Quality Management," *Public Utilities Fortnightly* (May 1992), pp. 67-75.

Perkins, Charles A., and James H. Perry. "Operationalizing Quality Considerations in the Purchasing Process," *HR Focus* (January 1992), pp. 10-14.

Peters, Thomas J. and Robert H. Waterman. *In Search of Excellence* (New York: Harper & Row, 1981).

Retkwa, Rosalyn. "Quality Management, Not Just Quality Control, Should Be the Corporate Ideal," *Business Marketing* (April 1992), p. 9.

Sora, Sebastian A., Samuel M. Natale. "Quality: A Prerequisite View," *Proceedings*, Chicago: (TIMS/ORSA Conference, 1993).

Steiner, G., and J. Steine., *Business, Government, and Society* New York: McGraw Hill, 1991).

Sturm, Douglas, "Corporate Culture and the Common Good: The Need for Thick Description and Critical Interpretation," *Thought*, 40:237 (1985), pp. 141-160.

Chapter Fourteen

VALUES AT WORK: A CASE STUDY IN BUSINESS

William J. Heisler
J. Wayne Brockbank

For many years, the expression of shared values within business organizations has often been viewed as interesting and charming, but as generally unnecessary (Deal and Kennedy, 1982). During the past decade, however, shared work values have been reframed as an important source of competitive advantage (Tichy, 1993). With an increasingly global business world, international competition has intensified. Having world-class quality and on-time delivery are prerequisites for joining the competitive arena, but they are no longer primary predictors of success. Quality and delivery standards are now assumed; low price and innovation have become the differentiating factors of success or failure (Prahalad and Doz, 1987).

Cost competitiveness requires that companies reduce the number of management layers along with the number of employees in staff functions. The evidence of this trend has been well documented in the popular press. The traditional functions of management and staff have been bureaucratic control and coordination. As a result of de-layering, the span of control increases and lower level employees become responsible for a broader range of tasks. As these changes unfold, two problems may occur. With the traditional institutional control mechanisms reduced, the possibility of institutional spin-out increases. Traditional bureaucratic control and coordination must be replaced by other forms of control. In addition, individuals who have traditionally been the recipients of managerial decisions are now expected to take on more responsibility for intellectual value-added. The challenge is intensified by traditional employees having been buffered from institutional decision-criteria by multiple-layered hierarchies. As employees become more involved in decision-making, they need to understand the broader direction and strategies of the firm. The social control achieved by shared values provides the cognitive parameters within which employees function while concurrently providing the decision criteria which newly "empowered" employees must apply in decision-making roles.

Innovation becomes increasingly important as firms seek for the advantages of captured markets in business environments of immediate imitation. Innovative companies have financial advantages over the less innovative. However, innovation requires greater mental involvement of employees. But mental commitment of employees cannot be dictated through hierarchical edicts. With fewer financial resources available, the costs of purchasing mental commitment on a piece-rate basis become prohibitive; instead, employees must find personal value in engaging their minds. Shared work values provide broad guidelines within which innovation can occur and encourage innovative contributions from employees. For employees such as research scientists, whose jobs specifically demand innovation, another challenge emerges. Such individuals are specialists by definition. As they function within increasingly specialized niches, the danger of interdisciplinary walls grows. A major vehicle for breaking down such barriers is a sense of shared values among departments.

As shared work values become a source of competitive advantage, it is useful to consider the following questions. What are they? What purposes do they accomplish? How can they be created in the hearts and minds of employees?

1. Shared Work Values: Conceptual Underpinnings

Work values can be conceptualized in a number of ways. For our current purposes, work values are viewed as the deepest level of cognition which is directly accessible to self examination and which is relevant to the work place. This definition is based on previous work by Taylor and Crocker (1981) and Schein (1985). Work values differ from other cognitive constructs in several ways. First, values differ from assumptions in that values are accessible to self examination whereas assumptions, by definition, are not. Assumptions are pre-conscious molders of thought and behavior. Second, values differ from attitudes in that values are conceptually broader, more deeply felt, and less transitory. Third, intentions are even more immediate and specific than attitudes. Intentions are cognitive states which result most directly in consciously directed specific behaviors. Fourth, work values differ from non-work values in that they are relevant to feelings, thoughts, objects, and people which are associated with the work place. Shared work values are those values within the work place which are shared, to a greater or lesser extent, among employees. They may be shared along horizontal (*i.e.*, between departments) or vertical (*i.e.*, between levels) axes, or they may be shared between the inside and the outside of the organization (*e.g.*, between employees and customers). The intensity with which they are shared may be measured along each of these three axes.

A. Categories

Three general categories of shared work values may be distinguished: ethical values, strategic values, and job values. Ethical values define the moral parameters in which employees are expected to work. Ethical values may be isomorphic with legal constraints; however, they may also be more rigid or less rigid than legal constraints. Ethical values are often embodied in words such as integrity, respect for the environment, honesty, mutual respect or safety. Values which fall under the ethical umbrella may vary substantially across companies. Employees whose behaviors fail to reflect these specific guidelines are often terminated or severely sanctioned.

Strategic values are targeted corporate outcomes. They reflect the strategic direction of the company and the metrics which indicate performance in the desired directions. Strategic values may be communicated in market share, ROI, globalization, portfolio decisions, growth rates, new product introduction, or return on shareholder value.

Job values are work values which focus on how work is to be accomplished. Job values tend to provide cognitive criteria about throughput processes. They communicate priorities which members need to have in their work life if the company is to be successful. Examples of such values include teamwork, speed, disciplined creativity, customer responsiveness, aggressive achievement, or involved commitment.

It is further possible to distinguish ideal shared work values from realized shared work values. Ideal values are values which individual organizations must have in order to survive and prosper. Ideal values must be conceptualized so as to be consistent with the organization's external, internal, and technological demands. External demands include customer needs, competitors' capabilities, market structure, regulatory directives, owners' expectations and the community at large. When fully realized among organization members, ideal values should create a collective human organization which is capable of meeting key stakeholders' needs. Internal demands are the demands of employees, including both salaried and hourly categories. Technological demands are the operational or working requirements of the firm's core technology. Realized work values are work values which are shared at any given point in time among organization members. If the realized internal values are inconsistent with the ideal values, the challenge is generally to change the internal values.

B. Purposes

Shared work values serve four important purposes relative to organizational success. First, they determine which external events merit attention. With virtually unlimited events and information, organizations apply shared work values to order the saliency of external information and events. They focus attention on and prioritize selected environmental stakeholders and events. Members select niches, markets, customers, suppliers and financiers from an almost unlimited variety of information sources. Second, shared work values determine the meanings which are attributed to environmental events. Similar environmental events can be viewed differently. Shared work values assist organization members in achieving consensus in the interpretation of environmental events. While consensus can lead to serendipitous group think, it also facilitates speed of decision making and execution. Third, shared work values provide the basis for evaluating the appropriateness of collective action relative to environmental options and targeted priorities. Some organizational activities may be less appropriate than others given collective work values. Work values determine what behaviors ought to be evidenced and how they ought to carried out. Fourth, shared work values provide the criteria against which individual and collective effectiveness can be measured.

C. Influences

Three factors influence the construction of shared work values: information, behavior, and reinforcement. Shared work values evolve as the collective organizational members systematically process information, act out common behaviors, and perceive that interlocked behaviors preserve self-interest. Exposure to information plays a central role in creating and maintaining shared work values (Salancik and Pfeffer, 1978; Schwenk, 1986). The quantity and consistency of information signal its saliency and encourage the internalization of entailed messages into the collective cognitive structure. Such information can come from formal and informal statements by management, the symbolic content of the appraisal, reward, and development systems, and interaction with internal and external stakeholders.

While the debate over the causal relationship between behavior and cognition continues (Staw and Ross, 1987), it appears that, in addition to information, behavior also influences the creation and maintenance of shared values in several ways. As individuals observe regularity in their behaviors, they receive immediate, clear and credible information which then encourages the creation and maintenance of values which are consistent with their behaviors (Salancik and Pfeffer, 1977). Also, even if individuals behave with rational intentionality, they tend to reconstruct their behaviors in cognitive terms that are consistent with each other and with the original behaviors. Finally, individuals tend to prefer consistency between the private and public self (Staw, 1980). When individuals voluntarily undertake public action, they tend to reconstruct their values to be consistent with their behaviors. The collective occurrence of such behaviors can be orchestrated through on-the-job training, selection practices, performance management systems, and job design.

Preservation of self interest is the third factor that influences the construction of shared work values. Recent theoretical work in individual cognition suggests self-preservation as the ultimate driving force behind the structure of cognitive patterns (Guidano, 1987). From an early age and through maturation, individuals create cognitive patterns that intertwine and protect the physical and psychological self. The process has two implications for the creation of work values. First, to maintain the integrity of one's identity, individuals tend to focus attention on and accept information which reconfirms realized work values. Second, as contextual conditions change, individuals will tend to modify realized work values into ideal work values to the extent that ideal work values ensure individual self-interest. Preservation of self interest is most clearly found in compliance with utility optimization as dictated by formal and informal reward systems. It is also found in the acceptance of those ideal values which are rationalized as necessary to ensure organizational viability which, in most cases, enhances self-interest achievement.

These linkages can be conceptualized in the following chart:

LINKAGES BETWEEN STRATEGY
AND
HUMAN RESOURCE MANAGEMENT
↓
BUSINESS STRATEGY

IMPLEMENT CRITERIA
↓ ↓
SHARED WORK VALUES
↓ ↓
CREATE CRITERIA
↓ ↓
INSTITUTIONAL STRATEGIES
AND PRACTICES

This chart provides the conceptual linkage among strategic challenges, shared work values, and the institutional practices which create shared work values. A firm's strategic challenges sets the criteria for the identification of the ideal shared work values. Shared work values then embody the criteria for the design and delivery of institutional strategies and practices. As alignment occurs among strategy, shared work values, and institutional practices, the institutional practices help create the shared work values which then implement the firm's strategy.

2. Case Application

The following case study discusses how one organization, Newport News Shipbuilding, a Tenneco company, went about creating a set of shared work values in its Human Resources division. Newport News Shipbuilding is a 25,000-employee ship construction and repair organization. For the past several decades, its primary customer has been the U.S. Navy and its principal products are aircraft carriers and submarines. Because of its lengthy history and close association with the U.S. Navy, its primary culture has been based in the characteristics of a large, bureaucratic organization.

In 1989, the Vice President of Human Resources, and his staff foresaw that change was needed in the organization's culture to meet the competitive challenges facing the shipbuilding industry. However, the prospect for changing the culture of the entire company appeared out of reach. Therefore, he and his staff determined to focus their change efforts upon the Human Resources (HR) function. If, and when, the efforts were successful, they would serve as a catalyst for fostering similar change in the remainder of the company.

A. Initial Workshop

In the fall of 1989, an external consultant was retained to frame and facilitate the culture change process. During this process he worked closely with the manager of Management Development and Salaried Employee Training. They conducted a series of interviews with the HR staff and their primary clients within the company. The perceptions of the HR function gathered from these interviews served as the information base for future planning activities.

In November 1989, the senior HR executives with the external consultant held a two-day planning retreat. They reviewed the perceived strengths and weaknesses of the HR function as revealed through the earlier customer interviews. After discussing the positive and negative attributes, the staff developed a list of desired improvements (e.g., establish a two-year manpower planning horizon, align the company's labor relations function to better service the company's product lines). They drafted a list of ideal work values for the company's HR function. The initial list contained the following eight values: business-directed, responsiveness, effectiveness, proactive, leadership, equality, committed and involved employees, and professional integrity. They then reviewed the research from the Michigan Business School which identified the competencies that business executives wanted in their HR functions. These competencies included the ability to manage and facilitate change, knowledge of the business, and the provision of world-class HR practices. With these findings in mind, the staff reviewed their previous work and developed consensus about the type of changes they desired to undertake. Following the workshop, the external consultant analyzed the staff's initial set of values and comments and provided a refined set of values for the staff's consideration.

B. Workshop Follow-Up

With the consultant's input, the HR managers held a series of meetings to review and further refine the function's value statements and to develop a mission statement. The mission statement reflected the department's goals and primary direction (strategic values); the values statements reflected organizational values which would guide the behaviors and priorities of HR department employees as they carried out the function's mission. By the end of March 1990, the staff had reached consensus on both the mission statement and the values statements.

To inform and involve others within the HR function in this process, an off-site meeting was held in April 1990. The meeting involved the HR staff and about twenty-five of their direct reports. The meeting began with an overview of the changing nature of the business environment and the company. Emphasis was placed on the need for change in order to achieve strategic advantage. The work of the staff to date was reviewed. After some clarifying questions, the group suggested a somewhat broader mission for the function, and proposed that the values reflect a higher level of proactivity (*e.g.*, "share in..." v. "support..."), and recommended that the meanings of the some of the values be made more explicit to avoid misunderstanding.

The input from the group was used to modify the existing mission and values statements. Revisions were drafted and sent to all meeting participants for comment in May 1990. Feedback from the revised drafts indicated that the mission and value statements now reflected the desires of the group.

C. The PEOPLE Program

Despite agreement on the statement of basic mission and values of the HR department, the values as stated were cumbersome and difficult to recall. Considerable time was spent during the remainder of 1990 to consolidate the values and develop an acronym that would reflect the basic intent of the program and facilitate recall. After several iterations, the acronym "PEOPLE" was suggested. It was felt that this acronym would be effective in reflecting the intent of our values thrust. Since people were the key to achieving our business objectives, we wanted to reflect their centrality to the department in the statement of the departments basic values.

Recognizing also that a measure was needed to effectively assess the division's effectiveness in achieving its espoused values, an HR Values Survey was developed. The survey contained 28 items asking respondents to indicate on a scale of 1 to 5 the degree to which they agreed that values statements related to the six primary PEOPLE values were reflected in our daily operations. The survey was circulated to the HR senior staff and to their direct reports for comment.

D. Program Introduction

In December 1990, the PEOPLE program was introduced within the HR function via a personal letter from the V.P., Human Resources to each HR associate. A cover letter explained the need for the program and described the programs development. Each employee was asked to make a personal commitment to exhibit these values in daily work behavior. To obtain a baseline for future assessment, the HR Values Survey was administered throughout the department in February 1991. The survey was administered during work hours in group sessions to demonstrate to employees that the survey and the program were important to the HR function. Ninety-five percent of all HR associates participated.

E. Initial Survey Results

The results of the first survey indicated that people in the HR division saw themselves as qualified individuals who were very effective in daily task accomplishment. However, they also tended to minimally share information, to work as individual contributors rather than as team members, and to be responsive rather than proactive in meeting company needs. Overall, the results of the 28-item survey averaged 3.6 on a 5-point scale.

The six individual work values were rated in the following manner:

Performance	3.65
Effectiveness	3.92
Openness	3.22
Professionalism	3.66
Leadership	3.42
Equality	3.62

The results were reviewed at a meeting of the HR staff, and departmental results were shared with each department head with instructions to conduct review sessions with their employees and to develop improvement plans. Copies of the improvement plans were forwarded to the V.P., Human Resources for review. In addition, a brief summary of the survey results was sent to each HR associate.

F. Follow-Up Meeting

In August 1991, a follow-up meeting was held with members of the senior HR staff and their direct reports, the same group that participated in finalizing the original mission and values statements. The purpose of this meeting was to evaluate program effectiveness and to make adjustments as necessary. At the meeting, members of the HR staff shared the improvement actions being undertaken within their respective departments. Structured, concurrent small group sessions were held to provide the opportunity to share feelings and express concerns about the program. Several positive changes were noted but a number of areas of concern were also raised. All items were recorded for further investigation and review. Concerns appeared to fall within four basic areas:

1. We have done a good job increasing downward communication, but how do we create better upward communication?

2. We understand the values, but how do they apply as we face the possibility of downsizing in the future?
3. We are off to a good start, but how do we sustain our efforts on a daily basis? How do we make our values a "way of life?"
4. We support our values, but they do not appear to be widely shared within the rest of the company. How do we address this divergence and what impact might it have on how we are seen within the rest of the company?

To address these issues, four task teams were established with representatives drawn from each HR department. This approach was selected to enhance the spirit of openness and participation within the division. Task team members were selected from all HR levels except for the senior HR staff. The four teams were titled Communications, Downsizing, Assimilation, and Company Interface.

G. Second Values Survey

Although a full year had not elapsed since the administration of the first survey, a second survey was scheduled for the beginning of December 1991. This time period was selected so that survey administration could be conducted at the end of each year. Ninety-three percent of all HR employees participated.

The survey results indicated no statistically significant gains, but all of the trends were in the desired direction. Some departments reflected gains across all values, while other departments experienced inconsistent improvements. The most meaningful finding was that while supervisory personnel continued to report more favorable perceptions of value expression than non-supervisory personnel, the gap between the two decreased substantially. As with the previous survey, the results were discussed and provided to each member of the HR staff who, in turn, conducted departmental meetings to review the results and solicit ideas for improvement. A summary was again provided to all HR employees.

Having completed about four months of deliberation, each of the four values task teams presented its recommendations to the senior HR staff in April 1992. Each team made from seven to twelve recommendations on its assigned topic.

After a period of review, the HR staff met and acted upon each of the task teams' proposals. In general, most of the recommendations were accepted with little or no change. A subsequent meeting was held with each task team to inform them of the staff's decisions or recommendations regarding their proposals.

One major outcome of the task team proposals was the establishment of a standing HR Values Committee to oversee the Values program. A second was the establishment of a Communications Committee to enhance communications within the HR division. Through these actions, responsibility for program management was shared with a broader range of HR employees, thereby reinforcing the value of employee participation/ involvement.

I. Third Values Survey

In December 1992, a third Values Survey was conducted. Overall, the results of the survey were favorable, with every value showing improvement over the previous year. However, several opportunities for improvement remained. As before, the gap between supervisory and non-supervisory responses continued to decrease. Supervisory responses improved significantly in Openness and remained about the same for other values. Non-supervisory responses improved significantly in every area except Effectiveness which remained constant. Results were communicated to all employees using the same procedures discussed previously.

J. Current Status

Although continuing improvements have been attained since the program was established, the rate of improvement has been small and the level of investment required to sustain movement appears to be increasing. Several contextual factors also appear to be affecting the results.

First, the end of the Cold War has had a major impact on the business outlook for the company. With significant cuts in the Navy's budget, the company has undergone three reductions in force within the past two years. The Human Resources division was hit particularly hard by these cuts. Although the values espoused by the PEOPLE program are especially needed at this time, the increase in work load and anxiety about the future is having a disquieting effect on employees. Within this context, the PEOPLE Program may be considered a substantial success because the survey results failed to reveal decrease in the PEOPLE values. A related effect of downsizing is that employees are reporting increased difficulty in making the time commitments necessary to participate in values committee activities, sustain ongoing programs, and develop new ones.

Another event which has influenced the HR division since the program's inception is the addition of a new function to the division. About one year ago, a large function was transferred from the Finance division to the HR division. The addition of this new function almost doubled the HR division roll. None of the employees of this new function were part of the original development and implementation of the PEOPLE program. Therefore, they have less understanding of the program and less commitment to its success. Also, in contrast to the salaried status of the initial HR division members, most of the members of the new function are unionized, hourly employees.

A third factor affecting the status of the PEOPLE program is a newly introduced culture change initiative by Newport News's parent company, Tenneco. While Tenneco's efforts parallel and reinforce the HR program at

Newport News, the question of the need for a separate, distinct values program within the Human Resources division has been raised. As a result of these events and trends, the current outlook for the PEOPLE program remains uncertain.

3. Summary and Conclusions

Shared work values can be an important mobilizing force in the achievement of company or divisional objectives. The experiences described in this case application show that an organizational change approach focused on shared work values can be effective, but that desired results are difficult to obtain. Several learnings are evident. First, continuing attention is necessary necessity. We found that continuing attention is best obtained with a committed program champion. Although it is desirable to involve as many others as possible in the effort, a central motivating force is necessary in keeping the effort focused and vibrant.

Second, while fewer difficulties would be experienced if the local change effort were part of a larger organizational initiative, our experience suggests that values-focused change efforts can work within individual operating units if the unit manager is supportive. In this case, the effort indicated weak but consistently positive progress within a limited corporate sub-sample. We suggest that the program may yet achieve its goal of providing a base from which to transform the larger institution. With a two-year head start, the local initiative gave the division a distinct advantage in leading the change effort in other sectors of the company.

Finally, values-focused change efforts are affected by external influences over which the change agent has little control. These changes are often unpredictable and require continuing diligence and adjustments if progress in the change effort is to be sustained.

References

Deal, T.E. and A.A. Kennedy. (1982). *Corporate Cultures*. Reading, Mass.: Addison-Wesley Publishing Company.

Guidano, V.F. (1987). *Complexity of the Self*. New York: Guilford Press.

Prahalad, C.K. and Doz, Y.L. (1987). *The Multi-National Mission*. New York: The Free Press.

Salancik, G.R. and J. Pfeffer. 1978. "A Social Information Processing Approach to Job Attitudes and Task Design," *Administrative Science Quarterly*, 23, pp.224-252.

Schein, E.H. (1985). *Organizational Culture and Leadership*. New York: Jossey-Bass.

Schwenk, C.R. (1986). "Information, Cognitive Biases, and Commitment to Course of Action," *Academy of Management Review*, 2, pp. 298-310.

Staw, B.M. (1980). "Rationality and Justification in Organizational Life," *Research in Organizations*, eds. B.M. Staw and L.L. Cummings, 2, 45-80, Greenwich, Conn.: JAI Press.

Staw, B.M. and J. Ross. (1987). "Understanding Escalation Situations: Antecedents, Prototypes, and Solutions," *Research in Organizational Behavior*, eds. B.M. Staw and L.L. Cummings, Greenwich, Conn.: JAI Press, pp. 39-78..

Taylor, C.E. and J. Crocker. (1981). "Schematic Bases of Social Information Processing," *Social Cognition*, eds. E.T. Higgins. C.P. Herman, and M.P. Zanna, Hillsdale, N.J.: Erlbaum, pp.89-134.

Tichy, N.M. and S. Sherman. (1993). *Control Your Destiny or Someone Else Will*. New York: Doubleday.

Chapter Fifteen

WORK WITHOUT WORKERS: VALUE ISSÙES AND COMPUTER-BASED DECISION-MAKING

Kurt J. Engemann
Holmes E. Miller

1. Introduction

Businesses today are under increased pressure to boost the bottom line. In many industries there is a growing trend toward demanding the same sort of productivity improvements from white-collar workers that in the past have been demanded from the blue-collar work force. Information technology is playing a central role in this effort, even though in many companies the older generation of top management has a relatively low level of computer literacy. However, market forces have caused changes in corporate cultures. For many companies, individual capability has replaced longevity as a prerequisite for senior management, and technologically proficient people have taken the corporate helm.

This new generation of computer literate executives, coupled with continual advances in information technology, has squeezed middle management as never before, causing many middle managers to become superfluous. This current work force trend toward flatter organizations with fewer middle managers depends on information technology to link senior management with the rest of the organization. Improved communications and computer networks allow senior decision-makers to communicate with operational personnel without going through intermediaries. Offices are being transformed by office automation; e-mail, voice-mail, lap-top computers, and project management software have become staples. Technology's impact can be seen across the spectrum of industries: In retailing, expert systems pass top management's wisdom directly to store managers; in manufacturing, automated systems now schedule production and manage inventories; in financial services, decision support systems screen job applicants, manage receivables, and help determine payrolls.

Information technology can free people from mundane tasks, allowing them the opportunity to explore new ways of doing things. Without computers, decision-making is based primarily on judgment, intuition, and experience; with computers, decision-making is augmented by powerful decision aids such as simulation and modeling. Needless to say, information technology profoundly affects the decision process and the values which support it. In this chapter we will explore these issues, and focus on the impact of computers on value issues associated with decision-making in business organizations.

2. The Decision Process

Rational decision-making is a process in which a decision maker follows a series of steps that begin with defining the problem and end with implementing the preferred alternative. Rational decision-making processes can be contrasted with less structured and more flexible processes that perhaps are more representative of decision-making as it occurs in many organizational settings. Nevertheless, rational decision-making and support models are widely used by many organizations, particularly for high impact decision problems. Moreover, advances in decision theory and information technology may enable decision-makers to use rational based models more, rather than less.

The decision process can be viewed as consisting of six stages: defining the problem *frame*, defining the *objectives*, identifying the *alternatives*, developing a *decision model*, collecting and processing *information*, and *implementing* the solution (Strategic Decisions Group 1992).

The decision-maker's view of the problem defines its *frame*. A visual analogy can be used to discuss a decision's frame, for what is seen is what is generally acted on, and what is unseen is generally ignored. A decision frame is similar to a photographer's view of a scene to be photographed; what appears in the lens depends upon one's perspective. The decision frame determines how the decision is defined and perceived by the decision-maker and has significant implications regarding preferred solutions.

Objectives are statements about something one wishes to achieve (Keeney 1992); they make explicit the decision-maker's values. Objectives reflect outcomes and the tactical means to achieve those ends. As such, objectives form a hierarchy. One common shortcoming in many decision situations are ill-defined objectives, even for well-framed problems. This can result in solutions that ultimately do not represent the fundamental values of the decision-maker as related to the decision problem.

Decision-making involves selecting the best *alternative*. The set of alternatives must be properly aligned with the objective in order to arrive at a solution that satisfies the decision-maker's underlying values. Specifying alternatives is a creative process; alternatives often are not readily apparent. The alternative's scope and structure often say much about the decision-maker's values and ethical principles.

Decision models are logical or mathematical representations of the decision problem which facilitate evaluation of decision alternatives according to the decision objectives (Engemann and Moscato 1988). Key attributes of good models are that they reflect the problem objectives and that they accurately represent the underlying problem to the degree of detail appropriate in the problem.

Decision-makers use information to evaluate decision alternatives. Information must satisfy various quality attributes including relevance, scope, accuracy, and timeliness. In the decision process, information is processed in conjunction with a decision model. Thus the degree of detail and precision of the information must match its processing model. Proper linkage between model and information is necessary to ensure that the selection of alternatives reflect the decision-maker's values as stated in the decision objectives. When this linkage is missing or incomplete, decisions can be problematic and leave the decision maker with a false sense of security resulting from the misapplication of reams of information of dubious quality.

The final step in the decision process is *implementation*. Though implementation is presented here as a final step, in fact implementation must be considered throughout the decision process to ensure that an unimplementable alternative is not selected. Implementing a solution requires an understanding of the culture of the organization, a commitment to action on the part of the stakeholders in the decision, and a commitment of resources necessary to implement the decision.

The above steps define the decision process. Each step is affected by the values of the decision-maker and the values of the broader community in which the decision problem is defined.

3. Values and the Decision Process

In this section, we will discuss the relationship of values and the decision process in environments where the decision-maker is essentially unaided by computer support. Later in the chapter, we will discuss values issues in computer mediated and completely automated decision-making environments.

The decision-maker's values exert their initial influence in defining the decision's frame. An optimist may view a decision in terms of gains whereas a pessimist may view the same decision in terms of losses. Kahneman and Tversky (1979 and 1981) highlight the importance of the decision-maker's reference point (*e.g.* in a "losing" or "winning" monetary position) and perspective of the problem as a "loss" problem or a "gain" problem. They suggest how, relative to their reference point, individuals can be risk averse with respect to gains, and risk accepting with respect to losses. Another example of framing occurs in medical decisions where the problem can be framed in terms of being cured or dying (McNeil, Pauker, Sox, and Tversky 1982). The process has also been extended into political decisions (Levy 1992 and Shafir 1992). Many of the disagreements that we witness concerning issues facing society ultimately can be traced back to how the problems are framed. For example, the U.S. welfare system can be viewed from a purely economic frame, a sociological frame, a cultural frame or a combination of the three. Depending on the stakeholder group, values involving the siting of power plants depend on the stakeholder group and can be viewed from economic, environmental, or political frames (Edwards and von Winterfeldt 1987).

Establishing the proper frame is a challenge, particularly when the decision's scope affects an organization or community. Then the decision-maker's values must reflect the values of other stakeholders in the decision. This requires understanding the underlying problem, knowing the values of others, and having the ability to identify the values relevant to the decision process.

Even with an appropriate frame, decision problems must have objectives and alternatives which reflect the decision-maker's values. Keeney and McDaniels (1992) discuss how defining the fundamental objectives of a decision problem clarify the values of interest and provide a structure for evaluating alternatives. When a decision's fundamental objectives do not fully reflect the values of the decision-maker, certain values inherent in the decision situation may remain unaddressed, even if the objectives are satisfied. Keeney (1992) discusses how organizations often engage in alternative-based thinking where the focus of the problem is in selecting one of a set of predefined alternatives. Often these alternatives either ignore the decision-maker's values or consider them in perfunctory fashion. To illustrate this, think of the fundamental objectives as being at the top of a hierarchy which also includes tactical objectives and attributes used to measure each objective's degree of attainment, as well as the related alternatives. Developing a solution involves selecting an alternative and making tradeoffs between objectives and thus, values. Failure to fully incorporate all the decision-makers values results in tradeoffs that may ignore key values.

"Value gaps" manifest themselves in unforeseen results and implicit value judgments. For an example of the former, many corporations are moving their manufacturing operations offshore to reduce manufacturing costs. In addition, they have increasingly been outsourcing other functions such as product design and engineering. Often, cost minimization also drives these decisions. However, this may result in loss of in house expertise which can place the company at risk (Bettis, Bradley, and Hamel 1992).

Implicit value judgments often occur in ill-defined health care system decisions. For example, if cost and universal coverage for the young are the sole attributes which drive health care system design, patients may experience long waiting times for service and some (the elderly) may be shut out entirely. Failure to explicitly consider values such as patient inconvenience and age equity in effect, is equivalent to deciding that long waiting times are acceptable and service to the elderly is less desirable than service to the young.

After the objectives and alternatives have been defined, decision models and information are used to select a preferred alternative. The values inherent in the decision-maker's objectives must be present in the decision model, which should also facilitate weighing tradeoffs among these values.

An obvious flaw in the process is when the model does not reflect underlying values.

Implicit models, where the decision-maker often is guided by a set of ill-defined decision rules, are particularly susceptible to arriving at solutions which overlook underlying values. For example, suppose a manager is selecting one from among many job applicants. Often decisions of this sort are based on the decision-maker's perceptions filtered through an implicit model of the relative importance of attributes, such as experience, technical skill, attitude, and interpersonal skills, and perhaps other personal attributes such as appearance, age and gender. Attributes such as these can in two ways reflect a decision-maker's values, including prejudices. First, the observed information is filtered through the decision-maker's value window. For example, does the applicant's seasoning his meat before tasting reflect narrow-mindedness? Do extroverts have better attitudes than introverts? Second, the model and how it weighs the various attributes and makes tradeoffs, illustrates the relative importance the decision-maker places upon his or her values. Because the decision model is implicit, decisions often are made according to the value systems that are often unexamined.

Explicit models, though more straightforward, also illustrate many of the value issues mentioned above. Often the model does not adequately represent a complex underlying decision problem. Thus, the decision-maker resorts to picking and choosing which elements of the real problem should appear in the model; often the criteria reflect his or her values. Interpreting the output from explicit models, also can reflect the values of the interpreter. For example, economics is a social science with laws that are generally accepted by its practitioners. However, we are all aware of instances where the same set of economic statistics lead to diverse conclusions, which often result from different interpretations of economists from disparate schools of thought. Again, values affect the information and the model with which that information is interpreted.

Implementation is the final step in the decision-making process and involves some degree of change. In organizations, implementation is a two way process involving the implementor of a decision as well as the individuals and processes comprising the organization. Both the values of the implementor and the values inherent in the organization's culture are important. When the decision-maker's values reflect those of the underlying corporate culture, implementation problems due to issues other than a mismatch of values may arise. One example would be technical or resource availability problems. A new dimension is added when the decision-maker's values conflict with those of the organization. Examples include cases where a member of the culture seeks to change it or someone from outside is brought into the organization. In these situations implementation difficulties can occur that are distinct from issues that arise out of the decision itself.

4. Decision Models

Effective decision-making is critical to a firm's survival and today's managers need to be familiar with the available tools to enhance their capabilities. Continuous development of quantitative methodologies and rapidly developing technology offer many opportunities for benefiting from the use of decision models.

Business decisions can be classified by functional area, by time horizon, and by number of decision-makers. The functions of marketing, finance, production, and human resources form the nucleus of a business enterprise. A further method of viewing the business decision is from the degree of structure present in the environment. Structured decisions involve well-defined objectives, measurable inputs and outcomes, and are usually repetitive in nature. These decisions are amenable to modeling and are often tied to routine reporting from a management information system. At the other end of the spectrum are unstructured decisions. These decisions are characterized by ill-defined objectives, uncertain problem definitions, and unfocused data requirements.

A decision model is a quantitative or logical abstraction of reality which contains sufficient detail to be useful to the decision-maker. The transition from a verbal problem, which rests in the mind of the decision-maker, to a computer-resident model is known as model formulation. A major benefit of modeling is that the complexity of the environment can be analyzed in a rational framework. Decision-makers must identify which assumptions are to be explicitly represented in the model. Modeling discourages vague descriptions of reality that often permeate the decision-making environment. Managers quickly come to realize how much or how little they actually understand the situation being studied. The presence of a computer model allows for more scenarios to be reviewed in a short time. Another benefit is the value gained as a result of using the model as both a vehicle for training and communication within an organization.

The first step in modeling is to understand the decision that is to be made. In decision modeling it is necessary to state clearly what decisions are to be made and how those decisions are related. Determining the objectives to be achieved in decision-making is not always obvious. Model building is a creative process which is usually done non-procedurally. The variables to be used in the model must be specified, along with the decision-maker's preference of alternative outcomes. The new generation of modeling systems should have a rigorous conceptual framework for modeling and a representation format simultaneously suitable for managerial communication, mathematical use, and direct computer execution. A modeler must be able to communicate with the computer that runs the model as well as with decision-makers.

An integral step in the modeling process is model validation to ensure that the model is an accurate depiction of the actual situation. Problems may exist with a model with respect to data integrity, model completeness, hypothesis authenticity, predictive validity, and internal logic. These are difficult problems and even with conscientious effort they may not be overcome.

While much attention has focused on the solution to formulated models, a generalized approach to modeling is not currently in practice. The discipline of modeling has advanced slowly compared to disciplines concerned with analyzing and solving models once they are brought into being. A good modeling discipline would facilitate the building of reliable models that accurately reflect the assumptions of the decision-makers. Models should be extendable, yet kept as simple as possible.

5. Managers and Decision Models

Models have long been used by managers to aid in decision-making. Originally computer-based modeling was done solely by technically trained staff who supported the needs of the line manager. Their primary focus was to determine model specifications from high-level managers and develop the underlying logic and computer implementation. Acting in this capacity the model builder did not have decision-making responsibility.

Recent developments in software for model building have enabled the line manager to become more actively involved in the development of decision models. However, it is rare for a senior-level manager to get directly involved in building a model without the aid of an analyst. S/he usually limits his activity to setting the overall objectives and requesting specific scenarios be analyzed.

Every manager approaches a business decision from his unique perspective. Some combination of intuitive and analytical thought process is used based upon individual preference. Models can be constructed which closely correspond to the way the decision-maker appears to operate, regardless of his/her attitude.

The manner of incorporating the manager's attitude toward risk into the decision-making process is a central concern of model builders. Decision-making involves making choices in environments which may be characterized as being either deterministic or uncertain. In a totally deterministic environment every variable and relationship is known with certainty. Problems involving deciding upon appropriate alternatives in the face of uncertainty with respect to the environment arise often. Uncertainty manifests itself when different payoffs are obtained for different events, and we do not know which event will occur or their likelihood. Engemann, Miller, and Yager (1993) provide a general formulation for decision-making in this situation. The role of the decision-maker's attitude or level of optimism plays a central role in the selection of the optimal alternative in situations in which knowledge about the environment is characterized as uncertain.

Sulek and Marucheck (1992) examined the impact of the implementation of an integrated information technology on the time utilization of information workers and report that higher level knowledge workers reallocated work time to important relatively unstructured tasks.

While computer models are in widespread use in some areas of business decision-making, unstructured situations remain the domain of human decision-makers, generally unaided by computer models. Miller and Engemann (1992) observed the individual and organizational values brought to the decision process in an unstructured situation, namely, a war game which was developed for the senior management of a large money center bank to simulate a time constrained decision involving events that could have led to a financial crisis. The game scenario involved tradeoffs between the interests of the bank and the banking system. Although computers were not used to formulate alternatives nor to make decisions, computers were used to deliver information to the decision-makers. The game exercise introduced elements of how management weighs value issues in a crisis. In addition to drawing conclusions regarding information and the actual decision process, Miller and Engemann also concluded that core values manifest themselves in crisis decisions, and that crises lend themselves to systemic solutions. The complexity of the decision process and the nature of the value issues encountered in the game are examples of how difficult it is for computer models to completely take over the role of human decision-makers in unstructured situations.

6. Automated Decision-Making

Computer models initially were adjuncts to the decision making process. As technology evolved, computer models became more intertwined with the process until today they exist in computer mediated environments, where the decision maker and the model form a symbiotic relationship, and in completely automated environments, where the model often replaces the decision-maker. The following discusses several types of computer systems used for computer mediated and completely automated decision-making: Decision Support Systems, Group Decision Support Systems, and Expert Systems.

A. Decision Support Systems

Decision Support Systems (DSS) can be defined as interactive computer systems that support decision-making, in semi-structured and unstructured decision situations, by providing easy access to models and data (Kroeber and Watson 1987). DSS are usually aimed at the underspecified problems that upper-level managers typically face. They possess features that make them easy to use by noncomputer people and should be flexible enough to accommodate changes in the environment and the decision-making approach. DSS do not make decisions for managers. The systems use is controlled by the decision-maker, who has easy access to the models and data provided by the computer. The models are customized for the specific decision-making tasks being supported, and typically, the decision-making tasks require managerial judgment in addition to analytic aids.

Sprague (1987) explored an intuitive dichotomy of work labeled Type I and Type II information activity. Type I work involves large volume-low value transactions, well defined procedures, and well structured data. Type II work involves low volume-large value transactions, ill-defined procedures, less structured data where the output is not easily measured. Type II work consists of problem solving and goal attainment, and determining the necessary steps is part of the job, and may be significantly different for different people. The DSS movement has become one of the most substantive on-going efforts to deal with support for Type II activities.

A DSS is the vehicle for creating, modifying, validating, and using a decision model. A useful way of thinking about the component parts of a DSS is to use the dialog, data, and models paradigm (Watson and Sprague 1993). From the user's perspective, the dialog is the system. What the user has to know in order to use the system, the options for directing the system's actions, and the alternative system's responses are what is important. Accommodating the cognitive style of the user can be done through the design of the dialog. The dialog can be written in terms of action language and presentation language. Through action language the user directs the system, and through presentation language, the system provides output to the user. DSS seeks to establish a high degree of human-computer interaction and allows the user to maintain direct control over the computer's tasks and outcomes. Many aspects of the decision-making process are unstructured and involve judgment, creativity, and some ambiguity. The human-computer interaction in the DSS approach supports these more intuitive and less structured aspects of decision-making.

In the early stages of DSS, methods for handling data were advanced relative to methods for managing models. The situation is changing as conceptual breakthroughs are taking place in how models can be stored, used, and managed. These systems are commonly referred to as model management systems. The purpose of a model management system is analogous to that of a data management system, in that both insulate their users from the physical aspects of data organization and processing. Model management systems do this by specifying the relationships between models, documenting the models, integrating them in response to a user query, integrating them with data files, and specifying inputs and output formats for the models.

DSS require a form of development that allows them to evolve and change as the situation changes. A DSS needs to be built with frequent feedback from users to ensure that development is proceeding correctly. The system development activities of analysis, design, development, and implementation are combined into a single phase, which is iteratively repeated in a relatively short time. Hogue (1987) identified the manager's role in the phases of DSS implementation as administrator, developer, operator, and user.

Different types of DSS are appropriate for various managerial activities. DSS can be divided into two categories: institutional DSS which deals with decisions of a recurring nature and ad hoc DSS which deals with specific decisions which are not usually anticipated or recurring (Garnto and Watson 1985). Executive Information Systems are computer-based systems specifically designed to meet the needs of top executives without the use of intermediaries and are tailored to the individual executives decision making style. Timely information is a critical attribute of Executive Information Systems. They are designed to fit the corporate culture and decision-making orientation. Executive Information Systems possess a broader set of capabilities to include support of electronic communications, data analysis capabilities, and organizing tools.

B. Group Decision Support Systems

Group decision-making is an integral part of most organizations. Some critical decisions are too important to leave to one person, especially when the knowledge needed does not reside with one individual. Technology is assisting group decision making through the use of decision rooms which provide individuals with computers and public displays that can be seen by everyone. Participants can do private work at their individual stations and a facilitator operates software which presents group responses on the public displays. This environment is characterized by factors such as speed, anonymity, voting, and recording of group processes. Anonymity encourages broad-based participation. Although most group decision meetings are face-to-face, technology makes it possible for participants to be separated.

Some organizations are making use of Group Decision Support Systems (GDSS). The success of GDSS depend on the capabilities of the participants in managing a decision group and drawing appropriately on technology. Group activities typically require more textual and relational information than do individual DSS, most of which deal largely with numeric information. A GDSS consists of a set of software, hardware, language components, and procedures that support a group of decision-makers in a meeting. The purpose of GDSS is to increase the effectiveness of group decisions by facilitating the sharing of information among group members and also between the group and the computer. A comprehensive GDSS is a network incorporating individual DSS with the GDSS components. In such networks individuals act as decision makers themselves, and these decisions interface with the GDSS to reach consensus (Bui and Jarke 1986).

C. Expert Systems

Expert systems are computer applications that contain the knowledge, experience, and judgment of skilled professionals. An expert's knowledge comes from years of experience and often formal education. Experts know many tricks of the trade that are not in books. They are proficient at forming, testing, and eliminating hypotheses. They make judgments and evaluations and arrive at conclusions. Their intuition allows them to make educated guesses that often cut right through to the solution. An expert system attempts to emulate the problem-solving skills of human experts and are built from their knowledge. They offer decisions and the reasoning behind their recommendations. Expert systems use specialized knowledge about a particular problem rather than general purpose knowledge that would apply to many problems.

To create an expert system, model builders interview experts and elicit the relevant expertise in a form that can be programmed. Experts may have difficulty in explaining how they solve problems. In many situations several experts may hold conflicting views. The model builder usually asks the expert to describe many cases and then derives the rules that are being used. Specialized tools are available to build expert systems which provide convenient ways to represent knowledge and complex concepts. Current techniques of knowledge representation have considerable power in that they capture knowledge so that it can be utilized by the "inference engine" which contains the reasoning methods used by the human problem solvers. After these rules are programmed into the computer, they are tested against known cases. The model builder and the expert continue to refine and expand the set of rules until it is possible to construct a prototype. The accuracy and consistency of the rules are then checked with other experts.

There are several reasons why it may be worth the effort to construct an expert system. One reason is that the knowledge contained in an expert system is permanent compared to that of a human expert. Another advantage is the ease with which it can be reproduced. Also, once developed, expert-system knowledge is relatively easy to document and produces more consistent results than does human expertise.

7. Values and Computer Mediated Decision-Making

In this section we will discuss the values issues that occur when the decision-maker is supported by computer-based decision models such as the decision models, decision support systems, group decision support systems and expert systems discussed above. We define three stereotypical decision makers in the computer mediated environment as *visionaries*, *conformists*, and *captains*.

Visionaries are decision-makers who follow an internal vision which itself is a product of their values. In the traditional environment, visionaries often make decisions based on intuition, perhaps supplemented by a crude model, rather than by using a logical process guided by information. For a visionary in a computer mediated environment, access to information opens new windows. Now the potential exists for an interplay between their vision and evolving levels of information which can lead to a redefinition of where the decision-maker wants to go. In the process, hidden values may surface, be clarified, and even be redefined. Properly utilized, computer mediated environments facilitate more introspection and as a result, clearer values to support the decision-making process. However, computer-mediated environments also may constrain the visionary resulting in decisions, which though more rationally determined, are no better than the old.

Conformists are the decision-makers who "follow all of the rules." The risk is that a computerized decision support system may not contain all of the important information. The conformist, following the rules, may not question the information's absence and may hence ignore the values associated with it. For example, a corporation seeking to relocate a manufacturing facility may not have information concerning political risk for the country in question. A visionary may intuitively introduce a non-quantified value into the decision matrix, but the conformist may equate the lack of information with a value that political risk is not an issue in the decision and hence ignore it. Conversely, for conformists, well designed computer mediated decision systems which incorporate prevailing values into the decision process, can facilitate more uniform and often better decisions. This is particularly true for more structured decisions such as personnel or hiring, where the relationship between values and information are often well defined.

Captains fit the stereotype of the rational decision-maker in large organizations. Captains manage decision teams which collect and analyze information and then present options which the captain mulls over before making a final decision. In computer-mediated decision environments, captains are more involved in the entire decision-making process. Moreover, because the process itself is more flexible and less structured, the "staff filter" present in the traditional environments is missing. This allows the captain to directly apply his or her values to various stages in the decision process. Benefits include less frequent misinterpretation of values and increased flexibility in reacting to the changing landscape of available information, and can lead to a more profound definition of decision frames and objectives that more accurately reflect the values of the decision-maker. However, direct involvement has several difficulties. First, the captain may confound his or her personal values with organizational values, and values of other stakeholders in the decision may be ignored. Unchecked biases that previously would have been filtered out by third-party involvement can also be introduced into the decision process. Also captains may incorrectly operationalize correctly realized values. For example, employee satisfaction may be a value associated with a decision but the captain may interpret this to include a preference for bonuses and merit increases in an environment where employees prefer equal percentage pay increases.

The above discussion focuses on the decision-maker's values. However, the modelers' values also affect the computer mediated decision-making process via the decision model, the information that is collected, and the ways in which it is interpreted. Builders of decision support models usually follow methodologies based on eliciting the values and the behaviors of decision-makers and incorporating them into the design and application of the decision model. Builders often view their methods and models as being value neutral. For example, Howard (1980) claims that the formalism of decision analysis is amoral and what moral considerations are applied, come from the people involved in the applications. Keeney (1984) discusses decision analysis and how its methodology can be used under various ethical systems. The information used by decision models is, in pure form, is often taken to be value free (see Edwards and von Winterfeldt 1987, Rockart and Crescenzi 1984, and Rockart 1979).

Despite the good intentions evidenced above, values of model-builders cannot be completely eliminated from the information specification and collection and model building process. Value issues enter this process in several ways. First, models are representations of some relevant reality and the information used by those models represents what the model-builder feels is the best pertinent and available subset of the information available. Choosing what to keep and what to omit is a decision based on a perception of what the issues are and the values at work in the underlying problem. However, the model-builder may ignore or misinterpret these underlying values. This error, though made innocently, may lead to models at odds with the decision-maker's values. For example, a bank loan officer may indicate that she wants to maximize loan interest revenue while keeping default rates within acceptable levels. A model-builder may take this guidance and build a decision model whose application results in discriminating against minorities. The end result may be antithetical to one of the loan officers core values. While some advocates implicitly assume if the model-builder is good enough and works hard enough, the methodology ensures a model which incorporates all of the relevant values for the decision equation, there is no guarantee that following good practices yield models that represent all relevant underlying values. Worse, by following a process that has the appearance of thorough rationality and objectivity, the model user may be lulled into thinking results are based on one value set when, in fact, they may be based on another.

Information is the second way for the model-builder's values to enter the equation. Though the normative procedure is to first elicit the information needs of the decision-maker then structure the model, in fact, the information collected is a combination of what the decision-makers say they want, what is available and what the model-builders feel is needed. Moreover, information even when identified by type, still may differ by attributes such as level of detail, timeliness, format, accessibility, and completeness. To resolve questions concerning the myriad of details that occur when building an information system, the builder may introduce his or her own values into the analysis.

The above issues are magnified when the model-builder has an agenda concerning the decision and deliberately introduces his/her values in ways which supersede those of the decision-maker. These values may result in modifying the "correct" model, in redefining the "correct" information or in presenting the results in a way to bias the decision. Even though the decision-maker is ostensibly in control, s/he is constrained by the structure in which s/he works and the information which is available. Going beyond the model and information systems boundaries, while possible, is difficult and requires heroic efforts. Biases built into the system may result in biased decisions. The ultimate risk lies in computer mediation presenting the aura of impartiality when, in fact, the process may reflect the hidden biases and values of the builders.

8. Values and Completely Automated Decision-Making

Many of the value issues relevant for computer mediated environments are also applicable for completely automated environments. Examples of completely automated decision making environments include expert systems and artificial intelligence. Perhaps the most important is the innocent or overt incorporation of the model-builder's values into the decision model. A significant difference in the completely automated environment is now there is no decision-maker interacting with the model to serve as a check on those values. A related issue is values obsolescence, which occurs when the values of the decision-makers and stakeholders used in developing the decision system change, without the system itself changing. The result is that the decision system will be making decisions in conflict with the new values of the decision-maker. A hypothetical example of this would be a medical diagnosis system where a new medical advance has changed the assumption behind the existing diagnosis. The result would be recommended treatments that would be inappropriate, given the changed values regarding proper treatment.

Automated decision systems are likely to prosper in structured environments where decisions are too complex to be made in timely fashion by a human decision-maker. Often these are characterized by large amounts of information that must be analyzed and/or a exceedingly short time-frame in which the analysis must be done. We see these today in computerized systems used in airplanes, automobiles. temperature control devices and telephone networks. Many of these applications are value neutral. For example, the value issues in a system that regulates the fuel intake in an automobile engine or chooses the route for a telephone call are relatively minor. However, value issues may arise in the future as automated systems move more in the mainstream of our every day lives. Two examples of this are in the areas of medical diagnosis (Schwartz, Patil, and Szolovitis 1987) and corporate strategy (Light, Welles, Woolley, and Nathans 1992). In each case artificial intelligence models currently support human decision makers. However, as the models evolve and become independent of human interfaces, the model values will become predominant.

Perhaps the most intriguing situation of values and completely automated decision-making is the prospect of the system itself having values which evolve over time. The most striking example of this was the computer HAL in the film *2001: A Space Odyssey*. One scenario of decision systems developing values begins with an artificial intelligence system that is developed for a problem too complex for a human decision-maker. Initially, values are incorporated into the application. Given the capability of artificial intelligence systems to learn from the environment, these values may be modified by the system itself. One example is a system for selecting investment strategies. Given the plethora of available information, computer systems are supporting traders and, in the case of programmed trading, even supplanting them for certain decisions. It is a small step from this current environment to one where computer systems replace traders for more decisions, and in making those decisions develop their own set of evolving values regarding investment strategies.

In many situations, the presence of a decision-maker can be viewed as a moderating factor, ameliorating the rigid rules and regulations of an impersonal system, but it can also lead to incorporating biases resulting in less equity. Automated systems, conversely, can be also be viewed as either more equitable or more rigid. Given human nature for control, it is doubtful that completely automated decision making will supplant computer mediated environments in unstructured environments.

9. Conclusions

Business organizations use information technology as a key to competitive advantage. To achieve its strategic end, a company must manage its information system as a productive part of the organization. Efforts to improve modeling and supporting information systems are very promising. In our opinion, the most significant value-related issues that will affect computer mediated and completely automated decision systems involve *value clarification, value gaps, indeterminate responsibility, value obsolescence, modeler bias, domain misalignment, and system evolution.*

Value Clarification. Though computer decision models will continue to evolve, our feeling is they will supplement rather than supplant human decision makers in unstructured situations. As such, increasingly sophisticated computer mediated environments will be the norm. This creates the opportunity for decision-makers to access and experiment with larger amounts of information, faster and in ways more visually appealing. The result is the opportunity for the decision-maker to experiment with the logical implications of his or her underlying value structure. In this process, values may be reexamined and clarified. The result may be better decisions that also are more representative of the values of the decision-maker and the affected stakeholders in the organization.

Value Gaps. These consist of situations where the values of the decision-maker are hidden and are thus not incorporated into the decision model and situations where the values are known but not amenable to incorporation. In computer-mediated environments the decision-maker is still present and can help close the gap; this opportunity disappears in completely automated environments. One solution to this problem is to limit the scope of the automated decision systems to only those problems where value issues are well defined and amenable to computerization. Generally, these include situations where values can be operationalized and are measurable. Because many real world problems concern values not in this class, either the scope of computer-based decisions will remain limited or the resulting decisions may be undesirable.

Indeterminate Responsibility. The manager is responsible for his/her decisions, while the model-builder's responsibility is in assembling the necessary capabilities with which the manager interacts. The model-builder must be adept in communicating in the business-problem area and must have the analytical skills to formulate the mathematical representation and the computer-technical skills to execute a solution. These different skills are very demanding. If a model suggests a decision contrary to the value structure of the organization, is identifying and correcting it the responsibility of the decision-maker or of the model-builder? Organizations depend upon accountability to continuously adjust their structure and approach. A serious problem arises when a decision contrary to the current value system is implemented and the responsible party cannot be determined. This situation is particularly possible in group decision systems which provide for anonymity of responses.

Value Obsolescence. Here, values that were once relevant, change. If the computer-based decision model does not change, the resulting decisions are incorrect, given the decision-maker's revised value structure. Two approaches to combatting value obsolescence are monitoring and selective avoidance. Monitoring intrinsic values can be formalized and should be linked to values that are implicit or explicit in the decision-making system. The avoidance option would be to restrict decision systems' scope to only those areas with stable values. Littlewood and Strigini (1991) discuss how software errors can be costly and even deadly in computer systems and suggest limiting their role. Similar solutions could result in situations where values obsolescence is perceived as a significant risk.

Modeler Bias. When decisions are made by automated systems, the builders and maintainers of those systems can incorporate their value biases into the decision process, and thereby distort the results. Regardless of whether the motivation was intentional or unintentional, as the decision-maker recedes into background, the model-builder and maintainer becomes a central, often invisible, presence. A counterweight to this trend is the increasing accessibility and ease of use of software used in decision support systems and expert systems. Increasingly user-friendly software creates the possibility for decision systems to be constructed directly by the decision-maker. Though databases and user knowledge may restrict the final product, this prospect ameliorates the possibility of handing off responsibility for the systems to third parties.

Domain Misalignment. Models are developed to solve particular problems or a type of problem. Sophisticated model management systems allow the decision-maker to gain access to a multitude of models without going through a structured modeling phase aided by a professional model-builder. This poses the problem that the decision-maker's inexperience in modeling may allow him/her to select and use a model inappropriately. Since values are implicitly and explicitly resident in models such misapplication can have serious consequences which may not surface immediately.

System Evolution. As decision systems evolve and become more sophisticated, the opportunity arises for the system itself to develop values apart from the decision-maker. Through the *2001* example mentioned above, we can visualize less exotic situations where a decision model, through the process of its own learning and evolution, in effect develops its own values. The challenge for the model-builders and users is to recognize and identify these risks and to ensure the proper controls are in place to guarantee congruence between model values and decision-maker's values, particularly in situations where all decision-making responsibility has been delegated to the model.

Numerous research opportunities exist in the area of values as applied to automated decision-making systems. Many of the issues discussed above can benefit from empirical study. Also, work should be done on the process of explicitly incorporating values as part of the model development methodology. As information technology evolves and the nature of work changes, values issues need to be clarified. Understanding how values affect decisions made with computer-based decision systems is essential.

References

Bettis, R., S. Bradley and G. Hamel (1992). "Outsourcing and Industrial Decline," *Academy of Management Executive,* 6:1, 7-22.

Bui, T, and M. Jarke (1986). "Communications Requirements for Decision Support Systems," *Journal of Management Information Systems,* 2:4, 8-20.

Edwards, W. and D. von Winterfeldt (1987). "Public Values in Risk Debates," *Risk Analysis,* 7:2, 141-158.

Engemann, K., and D. Moscato (1988). "Tapping the Potential of Modeling in Business Decision-Making," *Thought: A Review of Culture and Idea*, 63:248, 17-31.

Engemann, K., H. Miller, and R. Yager (1993). "A General Methodology for Decision-Making Under Uncertainty with a Risk Management Application," *Proceedings of the 2nd International Symposium on Uncertainty Modeling and Analysis*.

Garnto, C. and H. Watson (1985). "An Investigation of Data Base Requirements for Institutional and Ad Hoc DSS," *Database*, Summer.

Hogue, J. (1987). "A Framework for the Examination of Management Involvement in Decision Support Systems," *Journal of Management Information Systems,* 4:1, 96-110.

Howard, R. (1980). "An Assessment of Decision Analysis," *Operations Research*, 28, 4-27.

Kahneman, D. and A. Tversky (1979). "Prospect Theory: An Analysis of Decision-Making Under Risk," *Econometrica,* 47, 263-291.

Kahneman, D. and A. Tversky (1981). "The Framing of Decisions and the Psychology of Choice," *Science,* 211, 453-458.

Keeney, R. (1984). "Ethics, Decision Analysis, and Public Risk," *Risk Analysis*, 4:2, 117-129.

Keeney, R. (1992). *Value Focused Thinking*, Cambridge, Mass.: Harvard University Press.

Keeney, R. and T. McDaniels (1992). "Value-Focused Thinking About Strategic Decisions at BC Hydro," *Interfaces,* 22:6, 94-109.

Kroeber, D. and H. Watson (1987). *Computer-Based Information Systems: A Management Approach*, New York: Macmillan.

Levy, J. (1992). "An Introduction to Prospect Theory," *Political Psychology,* 13:2 171-186.

Light, L., C. Welles, S. Woolley, and L. Nathans 1992. "Software Even a CFO Could Love: 'Smart' Computers are Starting the Help Employees Plot Strategy," *Business Week,* 132-135.

Littlewood, B. and L. Strigini (1991). "The Risks of Software," *Scientific American,* 267:5, 62-67.

McNeil, B., S. Pauker, H. Sox, and A. Tversky (1982). "On the Elicitation of Preferences for Alternative Therapies," *New England Journal of Medicine,* 306, 1259-1262.

Miller, H., and K. Engemann 1992. "Decision-Making in a Crisis: Information, Process, and Values," *International Journal of Value-Based Management,* December.

Rockart, J. (1979). "Chief Executives Define Their Own Data Needs," *Harvard Business Review,* 57:2, 81-93.

Rockart, J. and A. Crescenzi (1984). "Engaging Top Management in Information Technology," *Sloan Management Review,* Summer, 3-16.

Schwartz, W., R. Patil, and P. Szolovits (1987). "Artificial Intelligence in Medicine: Where Do We Stand?", *New England Journal of Medicine,* 316, 685-688.

Shafir, E. 1992. "Prospect Theory and Political Analysis: A Psychological Perspective," *Political Psychology*, 13:2, 311-322.

Strategic Decisions Group 1992. *Decision Quality: Opportunity for Leadership in Total Quality Management,* Menlo Park, Cal.

Sprague, R. (1987). "DSS in Context," *Decision Support Systems*, 3, 197-202.

Sulek, J, and A. Marucheck 1992. "A Study of the Impact of an Integrated Information Technology on the Time Utilization of Information Workers," *Decision Sciences*, 23, 1174-1191.

Watson, H, and R. Sprague 1993. "The Components of an Architecture for DSS," *Decision Support Systems: Putting Theory into Practice*, 99-110.

Chapter Sixteen

PEIRCEAN PRAGMATISM AND THE SOCIAL VALUES OF AMERICAN BUSINESS

F. Byron Nahser

1. Introduction

Is business properly serving or filling its role in society? Alfred North Whitehead stated, "A great society is one in which their men of business think greatly of their function."[1] Today, in the late twentieth century, can business again be thought of as a vocation? Can business regain its heart? American business today knows that change is necessary but as yet does not see how profound this change must be.

I participate in this book as an American advertising executive and a doctoral student at DePaul University in Chicago specializing in the pragmatism of the nineteenth-century American philosopher Charles Sanders Peirce. One of the goals in my dissertation is to reclaim Peirce's concept of pragmatism for American business. This is an endeavor deeply permeated with values and social implications. It is also deeply fraught with potential for misunderstanding, thanks to the fact that what we conventionally mean by "pragmatism" is very different from what Peirce originally meant. In this chapter I want to clarify Peirce's "pragmatism," illustrate how we are applying it to our business, and offer some implications which such an application has for our society, as well as for business. My purpose is to foster the process of dialogue and being in relationship, as well as to help create the "learning organization" built on dialogue between business people. Peirce's philosophy can get us, as business people, deeper into solutions to the individual-collective tension that plagues our industries and society as a whole. The basic questions running through this chapter are: What is the story of this philosophy, and how does it come alive for business people to live it? Does it hold the key to rediscovering the great function business must perform for society?

2. Peircean Pragmatism

It may come as a surprise that the way out of many of our current business dilemmas lies in being more pragmatic. My project has been to reclaim pragmatism for the American business practitioner. When I studied Peirce and I came to recognize the true meaning of pragmatism, then I realized that I was like the Frenchman who found out at the age of 60 that he had been speaking prose all of his life. I found out at the age of 53 that I had been practicing pragmatism all of my life. My own view, as I studied philosophy, has been that of a pragmatist; not only in having conversations with experienced philosophers, but also in deciding on courses of action with my fellow practitioners in business.

This notion itself is Peircean. Peirce himself addressed this split, very much a feature of American philosophy, between theory and practice. Practitioners rarely think about wider issues as they decide on action. Business people have a narrow perspective because we focus mainly on our product categories and on competitive action. And theorists rarely get involved in mainstream American business practices that face the pressures and demands of the marketplace.

I realize that contemporary American business is lacking in sustained philosophical argument and likes to process information very quickly. When I heard the phrase "sustained philosophical argument," I thought, "That's what I haven't heard in 30 years in business!" Being a business person myself, I realize that business people are doers and prefer a philosophy based on action. Midst the swiftly changing business scene, we have short attention spans.

This is the story of rediscovering and reclaiming the pragmatism of Charles Sanders Peirce and seeing it in a new and useful way. Peirce's followers–Josiah Royce, William James, and John Dewey–also had ideas that have great relevance today. Peirce, Royce, James, and Dewey were American philosophers concerned with how Americans approached problems and, particularly, how the American emphasized individual action based on individual opinion. It was on the work of Peirce that the well-known philosophers James and Dewey, as they themselves acknowledged, built their methods of thought.

When we call ourselves "pragmatic," we usually mean that we are not hampered by an ideology but we do whatever it takes to get the job done. The "Machine Model" of business has dominated business thought: fix the problem by replacing people, jobs, slots, getting the machine to work, etc. This definition of "pragmatism" based on a Machine Model is too narrow and, in the opinion of many business observers, this "philosophy" has led us to the short-term-reactive business performance which characterizes much of American business today.

Pragmatism is the unofficial philosophy of business, and business people need to realize how gripped as a society we are by an assumption about pragmatism. This assumption, however, is an amputation of what Peirce really meant. Pragmatism is a method of inquiry; it is not a "fixed system of ultimate answers and great truths."[2] Peirce founded it; Royce saw religious aspects of it; James misunderstood it; and Dewey furthered the idea of pragmatism in his writings, namely, in *Logic: The Theory of Inquiry* and *A Common Faith.*

The story of the creation of pragmatism is a dramatic tale of misinterpretation and frustration, as a tradition was created that proved to be very far from what Peirce had intended. This misinterpretation of "pragmatism" traces back to William James's "kidnapping" of Peirce's original philosophy. James was a widely known, distinguished Harvard psychologist and philosopher and had an intellectual respectability far exceeding Peirce. Few beyond James, Royce, and Dewey recognized the importance of Peirce's ideas.

James first introduced pragmatism to the American public in a speech made at the University of California, Berkeley, on 26 August 1898. He stated: "This is the principle of Charles Sanders Peirce, the principle of pragmatism. I think myself it should be expressed more broadly than Mr. Peirce expresses it. The ultimate test for what a truth means is indeed the conduct it dictates or inspires."[3]

James felt that your beliefs didn't mean anything if you didn't act on them: beliefs are really rules for action, and you become what you habitually do. By bringing pragmatism to the attention of the nation, William James is responsible for pragmatism coming to be defined as "practicalism."[4] James asserted that holding beliefs must have consequences, or "cash-value,"[5] because beliefs are irrelevant if they don't make a difference in your actions. James's view of pragmatism as putting your beliefs into action overshadowed the richer and more powerful definition of Peirce and, ultimately, can be traced to the narrow focus and the reactiveness of contemporary business. James's interpretation missed the core idea of the communal nature of inquiry, leaving only the action of the individual based entirely on individual experience. Pragmatism then became a philosophical approach congenial to the American spirit and our cultural belief system, and was reduced to "doing what works."

Even 160 years ago the problems associated with this orientation were recognized, most notably by Alexis de Tocqueville. De Tocqueville maintained in Democracy in America that Americans are not given to philosophizing as a people; we are people of action. "Less attention, I suppose is paid to philosophy in the United States than in any other country in the civilized world."[6] He then went on to state what is, in my opinion, still the best description of our method of philosophical inquiry:

> To seek by themselves and in themselves for the only reason for things, looking at results without getting entangled in the means toward them and looking through forms to the basis of things–such are the principle characteristics of what I would call the American philosophical method. To carry the argument further and to select the chief among these various features, and the one which includes almost all of the others within itself, I should say that in most mental operations each American relies on individual effort and judgement.

The history of America has been built on "rugged individualism." Tocqueville defined individualism as a "calm and considered feeling which disposes each citizen to isolate himself from the mass of his fellows and withdraw into the circle of family and friends. With this little society formed to his taste, he gladly leaves the greater society to look after itself."[7] This sets us off on a trail leading to isolation, and eventually to egoism: "a passionate and exaggerated love of self which leads man to think of all things in terms of himself."[8] We cling to our dualism: me vs. you; "what's in it for me?"

So, what did Peirce really intend "pragmatism" to mean? It is ironic that Peirce, who so stressed the issue of interpretation, was misinterpreted for most of his life and had to bear the frustration of decades and decades of failuring to be understood for what he really meant. Pragmatism does have an action element, but now it is misconstrued to be reaction, as opposed to inquiry and learning. James's essays are collected in the volume *The Will to Believe*, which James dedicated to Peirce. While Peirce thanked James for this dedication, later Peirce said the following: "I thought your Will to Believe was a very exaggerated utterance such as injures a serious man very much."[9]

C.S. Peirce coined the term "pragmatism" from the Greek word for "deed" or "act." Peircean pragmatism makes three fundamental claims: (1) the scientific method is best; (2) the scientific quest provides further development of concrete reasonableness; (3) the scientific method is a social and self-correcting communal process promoted by smoothly functioning habits and beliefs that are upset by doubt.

Peirce took as his task applying the scientific method of inquiry to philosophy and logic, not just to the hard sciences. The collective, shared pursuit of the truth is central to Peirce: that we must be open one to the other. A key component is the constant interaction, interpretation, and awareness of a larger perspective. The pragmatic method of inquiry begins with a doubt or a surprising fact which leads to the formulation of an hypothesis. Then test the hypothesis by interpreting the signs, trends, facts, of what you see around you. This is a process closer to scientific reasoning: "If thus and so is true, then, of course, the result is this." Pragmatism, then, is a way of handling predictability by a scientific process. Pragmatism itself is not predictable; it is not action and reaction. It is a constant pursuit of the truth. Peirce stated: "Yet my attitude was always that of a dweller in a laboratory, eager only to learn what I did not yet know...."[10] He felt that passionate aspirations are devotion to the truth and that a sense of wonder should color all of our work.

Peirce was one of the first to realize what we are now coming to realize as a culture: that interpretation is the key to knowledge, and knowledge is based on relationships between people. Interpreting strikes at the roots of individualism, perception, community, and sharing of a connection between people. Peirce investigated how groups of people go about knowing or discovering something. He proposed the view that a person does not exist in isolation but in a social circle. He picked up Tocqueville's idea of Americans as shut up within their own view of things. Peirce felt that this limited creativity because it hindered the sustaining of two conflicting ideas. Creative insight, to Peirce, occurs when someone compares facts with ideas or theories, then finds a new third idea which mediates, illuminates and interprets their relationship. Peirce's scientific community is composed of different people looking at evidence and trying to determine what is going on. Peirce describes the scientific method as a cable, not a chain, for this makes it stronger and more powerful. The cable image also reflects the spiral nature of truth, in which all hangs together and also goes to deeper levels. Peirce's way out of individualism is through the idea of a community of inquirers, the scientific community. In his essay, "The Doctrine of Chance," Peirce came to the startling conclusion that "to be logical men should not be selfish."[11] Peirce uses the example of the soldier rushing the wall in battle even though he knows the odds are great that he might be killed. The soldier, however, has given his life to a larger cause. He sees himself as part of a larger effort or story, a central idea we will develop later in this chapter.

Josiah Royce, one of the three noted, yet least known, of the Peircean followers, referred to a community of interpreters as the "Beloved Community." Royce focused the greater part of his writings on the religious aspects of pragmatism and used the example of the Pauline community of Believers which came together to tell the story, as they had experienced it, of Jesus' life and works.

John Dewey brought pragmatism as a philosophy into twentieth- century American life. Dewey captured the pragmatic method in *A Common Faith*, where he stated:

> The mind of man is being habituated to a new method and ideal: there is but one sure road of access to truth, the road of patient, cooperative inquiry operating by means of observation, experiment, record and controlled reflection. It is constituted by a method of changing beliefs by means of tested inquiry as well as arriving at them.

3. Applications of Pragmatism in Contemporary American Business

"Patient, cooperative inquiry," like "sustained philosophical argument" noted earlier, are not words which characterize the short-term, reactive decision-making mode of American business today, and, as I have shown, Americans have deep cultural biases which keep us from embracing Peircean pragmatism. Our aim in reclaiming Peircean pragmatism for American business is to help move business away from this short-term, reactive mode which is proving increasingly inadequate. Business people are focused on quarterly profits, bottom lines, and a limited, narrow view of competition.

Today the leading American business schools are attempting to broaden the focus yet, on a recent visit to the Harvard Business School, where I was a guest in the class of my friend Professor Ken Goodpaster, I saw how deeply ingrained this notion is. I went to observe Ken's ethics class in Harvard's famous case method of instruction. Ken's students were conducting an analysis of the case of Wisconsin-based Warner Brake and Gear Company. The case dealt with union-management relations and the question of how management should handle a situation which could have long-range impact on the company. Should they take labor into their confidence and tell them all the facts, or should they not enter into discussions fully trusting the labor group? There was a lot of history of bad faith between the two.

The students quickly looked at the evidence from the point of view of maximizing return to shareholders and came up with a decision that would manipulate the workers and not enter into a full trusting relationship with them. Ken persisted in asking if there might be other decisions or other motives that management should look to. Despite his continued hammering away, none came forward in the next hour and a half.

After class, in talking with several students, we asked if they had thought of the action of management doing the right thing and just telling the union the full story. The three students stopped and one thought about it for a moment and finally said: "Why would they do that? No one in our society does something for that reason. We only do things to get something. Why, even our religious culture tells us that. We only do good things to get to heaven. Why should business be any different?" I was reminded then that the Puritan Work Ethic and the Exchange Model is alive and well. Perhaps the case method does, in the words of one professor, "breed a very narrow type of mind."[12]

This same concern has been echoed by Professor Piper at Harvard University:

> MBA Education seems to have failed in its most important responsibility: to generate excitement about careers and the opportunity for making a difference...the expansion of job opportunities and investment banking brought employer pressure for more extensive skills and analysis and we staffed up for teaching those. Without realizing it, we gradually reduced our attention to issues of responsibility and purpose.

A. Pragmatism and Advertising

Specifically in the advertising business, as a creative community, I witness how our individualism hampers getting the best ideas out as one person staunchly defends his or her own idea. The advertising business has not been known for collective thought, and we have many sayings to show our disdain for committee thought: "My idea was nibbled to death by ducks." Or, advertising patriarch David Ogilvy's poem: "Search the parks in all your cities, you'll find no statues to committees."

Clearly, our American individualism has hampered us in trying to run our businesses in new and more effective ways. Dr. Robert Bellah describes the "emotivist individualism" as follows: "The goal of living is to achieve some combination of occupation and 'life-style' that is economically possible and psychically tolerable, that 'works'."[13] Peirce's pragmatism is well suited to answer the questions raised by Bellah of how you live and act in the day-to-day world of business.

What is offered here is a way of thinking as old and as intuitive as our American culture, but is one that has been overlooked and too seldom, if ever, practiced in business. Pragmatism offers a method for corporate inquiry, discovery, interpretation, and, most importantly, action to help American business reclaim the minds and hearts of their employees. "In the workplace of the future, the fiercest competition between firms may not be for customers, but for the hearts and minds of employees."[14]

Being in the advertising business, this is our world and we deal with trends constantly. They keep coming at us. In my business we are always looking to interpret, and even predict, the consumer trends coming at us, *e.g.*:

> Downsizing, rightsizing, re-engineering, new rules, HMOs, HIV, LBO, MTV, Dr. Death, Pro-Life, the homeless, implants, transplants, two-tier societies, hoffices, the triple-squeeze generation, PUPPIES, SKIPPIES, MOBYs, DOBYs, Biocides, green teens, Zoo Doo, clothes chic, global cops, urban yoga, aromatherapy, cosmoseuticals, component life-styles.

What's Going On is a study we have just completed that looks at over 6,000 facts, books, articles, and conversations. The result is a 250-page study aimed at business practitioners. These statistics and facts are like the thousands of dots in an pointillist's canvas, or the dots which make up the four color picture in a magazine. Seen up close by themselves they mean nothing and offer no clues as to what is going on. You need to stand back and gain some perspective. These facts begin to form patterns into trends. We look at the bigger picture and, instead of asking: "What is our business doing in the micro-sense?", we ask: "What is our business doing in the macro-sense?"

This larger perspective gives business practitioners help in answering some of their pressing questions:

> How does a business person get out of the short-term, reactive rut that most are currently stuck in?
>
> How do you plan more accurately for the future when things are changing so fast?
>
> How do you spot the larger patterns and forces that are going to affect your business?
>
> How do you stimulate creativity and flexibility and innovation in a time when people are scared for their jobs?
>
> How do you evaluate the performance of your business in a way that goes beyond the quarterly profit and loss statements?

Companies are responding to the current business climate with a commitment to quality, values, and innovative ways of bringing people together. Our agency, Frank C. Nahser, Inc./Advertising, undertook this lengthy study as a result of the development of our Corporantes Pathfinder Notebook. The Pathfinder is actually a scientific notebook, and this method of corporate inquiry is based on the pragmatism of Peirce. We have used the Corporantes Pathfinder Notebook in 25 U.S. companies, including the Quaker Oats Company, Bang & Olufsen, and the Harris Bank & Trust Company.

B. Pragmatism and a Religious Foundation

One of the key elements of the pragmatic method of inquiry is continuity: to see how issues and ideas have developed throughout the history of the corporation. The corporation has its own story: its culture, history, philosophy, mission, and vision. Naturally, this goes beyond the machine model of business. Because interpretation is central to the process, we get away from the traps of "perception"–reacting to whatever we see–and "conception"–hanging on to ways of seeing reality.

The Pathfinder challenges business people to look at their own methods and beliefs, articulate an hypothesis, and then weigh their hypothesis against the evidence of what is going on in the world around us. The aim is to come then to a different point of view, a broader point of view, as to how the world might work. We see the movement in the life of the corporation and what are then possible next steps of the corporation. To put the life of a corporation in the form of a narrative or story, we gain an extremely important perspective. This perspective is one, in my belief, that can only be labeled as "religious." This finding has led us to what we believe has been a major breakthrough in the application of pragmatism for reclaiming a religious foundation for business and the meaning of work.

In developing a statement of mission and vision for business which grows out of the story of the corporation we are doing something that places us in the traditions going as far back as the Greeks. "Generally to adopt a stance on the virtues will be to adopt a stance on the narrative character of human life."[15] I take Alasdair MacIntyre's remarkable insight to mean that, since stories deal with the dangers and opportunities facing everyone, they help define the virtues which guide our behavior. Stories tell us where our lives have been, where we are now, and what we are becoming.

Through the sacredness of the narrative, we are led to interpretation, a reading of the signs of the evidence of the world around us. This narrative view reveals how the corporation is developing and responding to circumstances. Our aim is neither to react simply in a machine-like way, nor to hold to a conception of the world. In fact, the corporation can interact and interpret what's going on in a true Peircean pragmatic sense.

I share with the insightful observers M. Scott Peck, Peter Senge, Alasdair MacIntyre, and Robert Bellah the concern to break out of the traps of dualism and individualism that prevent us from coming together as a community. In *The Fifth Dimension*, Senge proposed the "learning organization" and "systems thinking," which foster real dialogue by suspending certainty in the presence of another. Peck recognizes the need for abandoning the "fixation of belief" as a precondition for community. I share with Bellah a need to develop language and techniques that would permit and sustain substantive moral discourse. And MacIntyre is sensitive to the moral state of business and the loss of virtue that plagues our society.

C. Pragmatism and Social Values

Luther McKinney, the corporate counsel for the Quaker Oats Company, once reminded me of the original purpose of incorporation for a business. States issued articles of incorporation only because a corporation was deemed to be providing a service to society. In other words, our major corporations got their start originally out of a mindset that was built on social value. They were permitted to exist because they provided a valuable service which promoted the general welfare.

During the 1980s, when the cry was "Greed is Good" and everyone was "Looking out for #1," we lost our tradition of social values in business. Peircean pragmatism is helping to restore social values to American business. Business ethics do not equal simply "what works." Peircean pragmatism gets us past this ethical expediency. From individualism we move to a collective method of inquiry. We move past the action/reaction, machine-model mode. Peircean pragmatism gets us out of the dualistic way of thinking by seeing beyond either-or thinking. Peircean pragmatism requires cooperative, joint effort to determine the truth.

4. Conclusion

According to many observers, we are at a hinge point of about a 300 year change, the "Post-Capitalist Society." Today we have an opportunity to again bring together spirituality, social values, and work.[16] The work of our agency, "*What's Going On*" and the Corporantes Pathfinder Notebook, is really a searching for a religious basis for business. I began this pursuit because I had a doubt: What is the role of business today? Can business have a spiritual foundation for action? Is business properly serving its role in society?

Business has an unprecedented opportunity to be a leader in this change because of its position at the center of power and change in our society. We see this in the fact that office buildings have replaced the churches and government offices as the most predominant buildings in our cities. Alfred North Whitehead understood this when he noted: "The business mind dominates our social thinking."[17] How is business suited to shoulder this great responsibility to help foster a better society that is fair and just for all?

Corporations are struggling with the search for a philosophy, a purpose, a meaning which can capture the hearts of their employees and also provide the foundation for their marketing strategies. By using Peircean pragmatism, American business people can come to see the points of view of others, which then leads them out of their individualism and helps them realize that their products and marketing have an impact on the mental, spiritual, and physical ecology of our culture.

For example, at Frank C. Nahser Advertising we see advertisers as the symbol-makers of society: we create symbols which represent goods and services. As such, we are in the role of helping people lead productive, fulfilling lives. In this powerful role advertising must no longer manipulate the consumer. The goal of our agency is to provide creative, productive work that serves the needs of society.

Frank C. Nahser, Inc./Advertising has benefitted from using Peircean pragmatism also in terms of developing ideas for our clients to see how their goods and services help their consumers to live, prosper and be successful in a changing world. In the internal agency structure our goal is for people to contribute to the fullest level of their talents in developing the work for our clients. As President and Chief Executive Officer, I have responded to the various pressures and trends of business by endeavoring to give our agency, and my career, a virtuous foundation and to make the best business decisions as we compete and work in a rapidly changing world.

On a deeper personal level, the Peircean perspective has helped me to take a long-term view of the continuity of my life, the agency, and the role that we in advertising play in society. I see that I am part of a longer story of people in advertising who have wrestled with the questions of integrity in creating sales messages. I see that I am part of a larger story: that business has become central to the future of our civilization.

Ultimately, we will make one modest change in that great Benedictine rule, "Labore et orare," with the addition of one letter: "Labore est orare." Thus, we can see that the work we do is holy work. It is a wonderful story, at the base of which is a religious reading of the signs of God's presence and our work as co-creators in the world.

The final answer will be the continued devotion to the truth we do not yet know. In the inspiring spirit of the Gospel: "Those who have eyes, let them see; those who have ears, let them hear."

Notes

1. Alfred North Whitehead, *Adventures of Ideas* (New York: Mentor Books, 1955), p. 104.

2. *The Encyclopedia of Philosophy*, (New York: Macmillan Publishing Co., 1967), Vol. 6, p. 435.

3. William James, "Philosophical Conceptions and Practical Results," *University Chronicle* (September 1898), p. 291.

4. *Ibid.*, p. 304.

5. *Ibid.*, p. 308.

6. Alexis de Tocqueville, *Democracy in America* (Garden City, N.Y.: Anchor Press, 1969), p. 429.

7. *Ibid.*, p. 506.

8. *Ibid.*

9. William James, *The Will to Believe* (Cambridge, Mass: Harvard University Press, 1979), p. xxii.

10. Charles Sanders Peirce, *Philosophical Writings of Peirce* (New York: Dover Publications, 1955), p. 1.

11. *Ibid.*, p. 162.

12. Jeffrey L. Cruikshank, *A Delicate Experiment* (Boston: Harvard Business School Press, 1987), p. 75.

13. Robert N. Bellah, *Habits of the Heart* (Berkeley: University of California Press, 1985), p. 47.

14. *The Economist* (17 July 1993), p. 16.

15. Alasdair MacIntyre, *After Virtue* (Notre Dame, Ind.: University of Notre Dame Press, 1981), p. 135.

16. In my view, the first time was with Benedict, bringing together work and prayer in the monastery. The second time was with Luther and vocation. The third time was with Weber and the Protestant Work Ethic.

17. Whitehead, *Adventures of Ideas*, p. 104.

CONTRIBUTORS

J. Wayne Brockbank is on the faculty of the School of Business Administration at the University of Michigan. Prior to his arrival at Michigan, he taught at Indiana University, UCLA, Loyola Marymount University. His teaching focuses on business strategy, strategic human resource management, and international business. His research and consulting address issues of strategy implementation, the linkages between human resource practices business strategy and culture creation in complex organizations. At the University of Michigan's Executive Education Center, Professor Brockbank is the Director of the Strategic Human Resource Planning Programs. His Ph.D. is from the Graduate School of Management at the University of California at Los Angeles.

Gene A. Burns, former Corporate Executive Vice President, Chief Financial Officer and Director of CPC International Inc.. took early retirement in 1988. He received a bachelor's degree in economics from the College of William and Mary and attended the master's program in finance and management at New York University Graduate School of Business. He is also a graduate of the advanced management program of Harvard University Graduate School of Business Administration.

Peter Davis, Ph.D. is a course leader for the Law and Employment Relations M.A. (University of Leicester). He has 20 years experience in Industrial Relations, Human Resource Mangement, and Managerial Development. He is a specialist in co-operative and mutual societies. He has published widely in the fields of Cooperative Studies, Employment and Business Ethics.

Kurt J. Engemann, Chairman and Professor in the Management Science and Systems Department of the Hagan School of Business at lona College, received his Ph.D. in Operations Research from New York University. Dr. Engemann's main areas of interests are computer based modeling and data analysis, systems simulation, optimization, decision support systems, and operations management. His consulting and research concentrates on the development of models and information systems to support executives within the functional areas of business.

Joel R. Gavriele-Gold, Ph.D. is a psychologist and psychoanalyst in private practice in New York City for the past 25 years. In addition to writing, he presents workshops and teaches. He is currently preparing a book on the relationship between emotions and psychosomatic dysfunction. Dr. Gavriele-Gold has served as a member of the Board of Directors of the American Psychological Association and of the Training Institute of the National Psychological Association for Psychoanalysis and was the Dean of Training for a number of years. He also is currently on the Board of Directors of the Institute for Expressive Analysis where he is Director of Programs.

Dr. William J. Heisler currently heads up Newport News Shipbuilding's organizational change efforts to make the company more competitive. The overall thrust of these initiatives is to enhance organizational leadership, communications, empowerment, and accountability. Prior to his present assignment, Dr. Heisler was Director, Human Resources Planning and Career Development. Before joining Newport News Shipbuilding in 1981 as Manager, Management Development, Dr. Heisler was a Professor of Management at the Babcock Graduate School of Management, Wake Forest University, and also served as Director of their Executive MBA Program. He came to Wake Forest in 1976 from the University of Notre Dame where he was a member of the business faculty. Dr. Heisler earned Ph.D. and MBA degrees in Business Administration from Syracuse University in 1972 and 1970, respectively.

Dr. Georgia M. Keightley is Assistant Professor of Theology at Trinity College, Washington, D.C. The focus of Dr. Keightley's research and writing is Christianity's dialogue with contemporary culture. She teaches and writes on social ethics, the feminist critique of religion and society, and lay Christian spirituality.Dr.

Dr. John E. Kelly studied in Canada, the United States, Germany, and Italy. He was graduated from the University of Toronto, and took his advanced degrees from the Catholic University of America in Washington, D.C. He has lectured and written in the fields of ancient philosophy, the philosophy of Hegel, Catholic social thought, and medical ethics. He has served on the New York State Medical Society Task Group on Ethics of Care in HIV infection, and on the Board of Trustees of the Buffalo General Hospital. He has also served on the Committee on Research and Education, and has been a member of the Ethics Committee at the Buffalo General Hospital since 1984. He is currently Chair, Department of Philosophy, Canisius College, Buffalo, New York.

Hugh McCabe is Associate Professor at Westchester Community College in New York where he is also the Chairperson of the International Business Curriculum. Professor McCabe holds a B.A. and M.B.A. from Iona College and teaches courses in Business Organization and Management and International Business. He is the recipient of the State University of New York Chancellor's Award for Excellence in Teaching and The National Institute for Staff and Organizational Development (University of Texas) Teaching Excellence Award.

Holmes E. Miller is Assistant Professor of business at Muhlenberg College. He holds a Ph.D. from Northwestern University. Prior to joining Muhlenberg he worked for several Fortune 500 companies in the chemical and financial services industries. His current research interests included decision making under risk, quality, and service sectors operations management. He has published articles in *Operations Research, Socio-economic Planning Sciences,* and *Interfaces.*

F. Byron Nahser is President and CEO of Frank C. Nahser, Inc./Advertising. He holds a B.A. degree from Notre Dame University, and an M.B.A. from Northwestern University, and an M.A. in Religious Studies from Mundelein College. Currently he is Executive-in-Residence at De Paul University Graduate School of Business, and is pursuing a Doctorate in Philosophy at De Paul concentrating on American business philosophy.

Samuel M. Natale, D.Phil. is Research Director (USA) of the Oxford Center for the Study of Values in Education and Business (OXSVEB) and concurrently Professor, Studies in Corporate Values, Hagan School of Business, Iona College, New Rochelle, New York.

Michael J. Naughton is Assistant Professor at the University of St. Thomas where he holds a joint appointment in the theology and management departments. He is the author of *The Good Stewards: Practical Applications of the Papal Vision of Work* which examines the relationship between organizational issues ad the papal social tradition. He has published articles in the *Journal of Business Ethics*, *The Thomist*, *Review of Social Economy*, and *Social Justice Review*. Dr. Naughton is the associate director of the University of St. Thomas' Center for Christian Social Thought and the Management Professions which explores the relevance of the Christian social tradition to the management disciplines.

William O'Neill is member of the Philosophy Department, Iona College, and Director of Institutional Planning. A Woodrow Wilson Fellow, he held a Carnegie Fellowship and also study grants to Third World countries in Asia and Africa. He teaches business and health-care ethics, and philosophy of knowledge. Other interests: philosophy of science and philosophical analysis of practical virtue and conscience.

Janine Prete graduated from Iona College with Honors in August 1993, receiving a Master Degree in Human Resource Management. Currently, she is working in an Organizational Development consulting firm dealing with the complex issues of employee motivation, training, and job satisfaction. Ms. Prete is socially conscious and supports many worthwhile efforts.

Carole A. Rayburn, Ph.D., M. Div., is a clinical, consulting, and research psychologist in Silver Spring, Maryland. A past president of the Maryland Psychological Association and of the APA Division of Clinical Psychology's Section on the Clinical Psychology of Women, she is a fellow of the American Psychological Association (a fellow of APA Divisions of the Psychology of Religion, Clinical Psychology, Consulting Psychology, and Psychotherapy), of the American Orthopsychiatric Association, of the American Association of Applied and Preventive Psychology, and of the Maryland Psychological Association. Dr. Rayburn has a private practice of psychology in Silver Spring. She is a graduate of American, George Washington, Catholic, and Andrews Universities.

Brian M. Rothschild received his MBA from Iona College in 1992 and is currently an adjunct lecturer at Iona College and Westchester Community College. He has published articles in the fields of Business Ethics and Human Resource Management.

Joseph W. Sora is currently a Doctor of Arts Candidate at St. John's University, Jamaica, New York. He is an assistant editor at the H. W. Wilson Company. He has published several articles in Business Ethics.

Sebastian A. Sora received his doctorate in Management and Information Systems from Pace University, New York. He obtained an MBA, PMC in Operations Research and Management Information Systems from Iona College, New Rochelle. He has written and published in the areas of Quality, Technology, and Information Ethics. He currently is consultant for IBM and is Associate Professor of Management and Information Systems at Montclair State College in New Jersey

Robert Strittmatter is Associate Professor of Accounting in the Hagan School of Business, Iona College. He received a B.S. degree from Mount Saint Mary's College in Maryland and an M.B.A. from New York University. He is a Certified Public Accountant in New York. Publications include *Computer-Based Educational Software for Advanced Accounting* in 1989 and co-authorship of *Accounting in the Soviet Union* in 1992.

J. Milburn Thompson is Chair and Associate Professor of Religious Studies at Saint Joseph College, in West Hartford, Connecticut. He received his doctorate in Theology from Fordham University in 1981. He is the author of *Martin Luther King, Jr. and the Dream of a Just Community*. (Pax Christi USA, 1986) and has published articles in *New Theology Review*, the *Annual* of the College Theology Society, *Choice*, and *Emmanuel*.

Frank D. Tinari, Ph.D. is Professor of Economics at Seton Hall University. He received his doctorate from Fordham University in 1976. In addition to teaching at Seton Hall University, he has taught at Fordham University,

Pace University, Purdue University, Drew University, and Felician College. He served as a Captain in the United States Army, from which he received the Army Commendation Medal upon discharge. In 1983 and 1985, he was an invited lecturer at the University of International Business and Economics, Beijing, People's Republic of China.

Ailsa M. Watkinson received her Ph.D. in educational administration from the University of Saskatchewan in 1992. Prior to returning to the University in 1989, she worked for 12 years with the Saskatchewan Human Rights Commission. She held a number of different jobs during the twelve year period including Director of Education and Manager of Public and Special Programs. Dr. Watkinson is currently working as a private consultant/researcher.

INDEX

VALUE INQUIRY BOOK SERIES

VIBS

1. Noel Balzer, **The Human Being as a Logical Thinker**.

2. Archie J. Bahm, **Axiology: The Science of Values.**

3. H. P. P. (Hennie) Lötter, **Justice for an Unjust Society.**

4. H. G. Callaway, **Context for Meaning and Analysis: A Critical Study in the Philosophy of Language.**

5. Benjamin S. Llamzon, **A Humane Case for Moral Intuition.**

6. James R. Watson, **Between Auschwitz and Tradition: Postmodern Reflections on the Task of Thinking.** A volume in **Holocaust and Genocide Studies.**

7. Robert S. Hartman, **Freedom to Live: The Robert Hartman Story,** edited by Arthur R. Ellis. A volume in **Hartman Institute Axiology Studies.**

8. Archie J. Bahm, **Ethics: The Science of Oughtness.**

9. George David Miller: **An Idiosyncratic Ethics; Or, the Lauramachean Ethics.**

10. Joseph P. DeMarco, **A Coherence Theory in Ethics.**

11. Frank G. Forrest, **Valuemetrics[ℵ]: The Science of Personal and Professional Ethics.** A volume in **Hartman Institute Axiology Studies.**

12. William Gerber, **The Meaning of Life: Insights of the World's Great Thinkers.**

13. Richard T. Hull, Editor, **A Quarter Century of Value Inquiry: Presidential Addresses of the American Society for Value Inquiry.** A volume in **Histories and Addresses of Philosophical Societies.**

14. William Gerber, **Nuggets of Wisdom from Great Jewish Thinkers: From Biblical Times to the Present.**

15. Sidney Axinn, **The Logic of Hope: Extensions of Kant's View of Religion.**

16. Messay Kebede, **Meaning and Development.**

17. Amihud Gilead, **The Platonic Odyssey: A Philosophical-Literary Inquiry into the *Phaedo.***

18. Necip Fikri Alican, **Mill's Principle of Utility: A Defense of John Stuart Mill's Notorious Proof.** A volume in **Universal Justice.**

19. Michael H. Mitias, Editor, **Philosophy and Architecture.**

20. Roger T. Simonds, **Rational Individualism: The Perennial Philosophy of Legal Interpretation.** A volume in **Natural Law Studies.**

21. William Pencak, **The Conflict of Law and Justice in the Icelandic Sagas.**

22. Samuel M. Natale and Brian M. Rothschild, Editors, **Values, Work, Education: The Meanings of Work.**